Working with Alienated and Families

This edited volume is written by and for mental health professionals who work directly with alienated children and their parents. The chapters are written by leaders in the field, all of whom know how vexing parental alienation can be for mental health professionals. No matter how the professional intersects with families affected by alienation, be it through individual treatment, reunification therapy, a school setting, or support groups, he or she needs to consider how to make proper assessments, how to guard against bias, and when and how to involve the court system, among other challenges. The cutting-edge clinical interventions presented in this book will help professionals answer these questions and help them to help their clients. The authors present a range of clinical options such as parent education, psycho-educational programs for children, and reunification programs for children and parents that make this volume a useful reference and practical guide.

Amy J. L. Baker, Ph.D., is the author of *Adult Children of Parental Alienation Syndrome: Breaking the Ties That Bind,* as well as over 65 peer-reviewed publications on the topic of parental alienation, psychological maltreatment, child welfare, and parent-child relationships. She conducts research at the Vincent J. Fontana Center for Child Protection.

S. Richard Sauber, Ph.D., has been in practice for 30 years as a forensic family and clinical psychologist. He is certified in Family and Clinical Psychology by the American Board of Professional Psychology and licensed by the Ordre des Psychologues du Québec, Canada. He has also been the editor-in-chief of the *American Journal of Family Therapy* since 1976.

Working with Alienated Children and Families

A Clinical Guidebook

Edited by
Amy J. L. Baker and S. Richard Sauber

NEW YORK AND LONDON

First published 2013
by Routledge
711 Third Avenue, New York, NY 10017

Simultaneously published in the UK
by Routledge
27 Church Road, Hove, East Sussex BN3 2FA

Routledge is an imprint of the Taylor & Francis Group, an informa business

Library of Congress Cataloging in Publication Data

Working with Alienated Children and Families: A Clinical Guidebook / edited by Amy J. L. Baker & S. Richard Sauber. — 1st ed.
p. cm.
Includes bibliographical references and index.
ISBN 978–0–415–51802–4 (hardback : alk. paper) — ISBN 978–0–415–51803–1 (pbk. : alk. paper)
1. Alienation (Social psychology) 2. Parental alienation syndrome—Handbooks, manuals, etc. 3. Children of divorced parents—Counseling of—Handbooks, manuals, etc. 4. Family psychotherapy—Handbooks, manuals, etc. I. Baker, Amy J. L. II. Sauber, S. Richard.
HM1131.W67 2012
362.82'86—dc23
2012024782

ISBN: 978–0–415–51802–4 (hbk)
ISBN: 978–0–415–51803–1 (pbk)
ISBN: 978–0–203–12357–7 (ebk)

Typeset in Minion
by Swales & Willis Ltd, Exeter, Devon

Printed and bound in the United States of America
by Edwards Brothers, Inc.

Contents

Foreword

I am very interested in the topic of parental alienation (PA). I talk about it a lot in conversations with professional colleagues, friends, and relatives, and sometimes total strangers. Most people do not recognize the phrase, "parental alienation," so I usually say something like:

> It's when there's a lot of fighting between parents. It's usually when they're divorced, but not always. Sometimes the children side with one parent and refuse to have anything to do with the other parent, even though they previously had a good relationship with the parent they are now rejecting.

After hearing that brief explanation of PA, the person usually says they know all about it already. They tell me PA happened to himself in his first marriage or to herself when she was a child. They tell me PA happened to their brother-in-law or their best friend at work. They almost always mention how painful it was to experience or hear about PA.

I have had this conversation many times. A professor of psychiatry told me that her mother alienated her from her father; later in life, she re-established a good relationship with her father and then her mother rejected her. A friend told me her son was getting divorced and PA had become a problem between her son and grandson. When I told the Fed-Ex man that he had just delivered copies of a book I had edited, *Parental Alienation, DSM-5, and ICD-11,* he said his brother was struggling with PA. I discussed the diagnosis of PA with a clinical psychologist; a month later she told me she had identified PA in a family she had just evaluated.

In the last few years, I have learned that PA affects children and families in every part of the United States and also in many other countries. Psychologists, psychiatrists, attorneys, and judges—from locations and cultures as disparate as Argentina, Lithuania, Israel, India, and Japan, for example—have published articles regarding PA in professional journals. In some countries (Brazil for instance) legislators have passed laws that define PA and provide for sanctions against individuals who cause children to become alienated from their parents. An important supranational agency—the European Court of Human Rights—has identified PA in some cases and ordered national governments to pay damages to affected individuals. It is remarkable to observe the similarities in the scenarios of parental conflict and the pattern of emotional and behavioral symptoms in the children in reports from different parts of the world.

Although the problem of PA is widespread and the concept is easy to understand, there is a lack of knowledge about PA among the people who matter the most, i.e., the front-line therapists who work with children, teenagers, and families. I believe it is common for mental health practitioners of all types—social workers, nurse practitioners, family therapists, psychologists, and psychiatrists—to identify troubled children of high-conflict divorces, but not know what to do about it. When faced with major battles clouding the family landscape, many practitioners are not sure how to evaluate the children and their families. Some become convinced of the compelling stories told by the alienated children. They are at a loss as to how to intervene on behalf of the children. That is the reason for developing this book, *Working with Alienated Children and Families.* For both novices and experienced mental health professionals, this book provides general guidance and specific practical advice in addressing PA. The editors, Drs Baker and Sauber, have gathered together many leaders in the field who are experienced in identifying and treating PA.

Psychological theories and the treatment of psychiatric disorders have consistently generated controversy among mental health professionals as well as the general public. There is unending discussion, for instance, regarding the relative importance of heredity and life experience in the etiology of mental illness. There are perennial debates regarding the causes, diagnosis, and treatment of common conditions such as autism and attention deficit hyperactivity disorder. In the 1980s there was a period of intense, colorful clash of opinions regarding the reality of satanic ritual abuse and what to do about it. In the 1990s there was debate among clinical psychologists and research psychologists over recovered memories. Those topics were dissected in professional discussions and also in legal settings—both criminal courts and civil trials.

For the last 20 years, controversies regarding PA have played out primarily in family courts and in the professional literature of psychologists and psychiatrists. The disagreements have taken many forms: whether PA actually exists; whether PA is caused by both mothers and fathers; whether PA is simply a transitory phenomenon that goes away as children grow up; whether PA was "invented" as a way to protect pedophiles or batterers from detection; the appropriate treatment for PA; whether PA should become an official diagnosis as a mental disorder or a relational problem; and so on. At times, the debate regarding PA has taken on a life of its own, and the intensity of affect in the scholarly discussions regarding PA seemed to echo the intensity of anger and suspicion manifested by parents in high-conflict divorces.

At the same time, many of the core tenets of PA theory are nearly universally accepted, such as the fact that some children can become aligned with one parent against the other parent with whom the child once shared a close and loving relationship. Most mental health professionals who evaluate and treat children of divorce feel it is time to move beyond the debate. We need to find ways to help the thousands of children and teenagers who have been damaged by PA. We need to find ways to prevent PA from occurring in the first place and to identify cases in which the symptoms of PA are mild and more easily treated. We also need to learn how to intervene in the more severe cases of PA. Further complicating matters is that much of what we now know about diagnosing, treating, and intervening in PA cases can be counterintuitive to the novice or untrained clinician. That is the purpose of this book. *Working with Alienated Children and Families* will help current practitioners and the next generation of trainees learn innovative ways to prevent and treat PA. If you are an experienced psychotherapist, this book will expand your repertoire of treatments. If you are a student, I hope the book helps you understand a serious mental condition that you will encounter in your future clients. If you are an attorney or judge, the message of *Working with Alienated Children and Families* is that PA can be reliably identified and successfully treated. If you happen to be a parent experiencing PA, this book should give you hope that improvement is possible.

William Bernet, M.D.
Professor Emeritus
Vanderbilt University School of Medicine
Nashville, TN

Author Biographies

Jane Albertson-Kelly, Ph.D.
Dr. Albertson-Kelly has worked with individuals and families in crisis for over 20 years. Dr. Albertson-Kelly has a doctorate in clinical psychology as well as a master's degree in education. She has been affiliated with the Adolescent Psychiatric Unit at Mather Hospital, Port Jefferson, NY; the North Suffolk Center Child Treatment Program, Smithtown, NY; and the Northport Veterans Association, Northport, VA. A former teacher, Dr. Albertson-Kelly has particular interests in working with families adjusting to separation and divorce, and with adolescents. She is recognized as an expert witness in the areas of parenting, custody, and sexual abuse and has presented on topics related to these areas.

Katherine Andre, Ph.D.
Dr. Andre is a licensed psychologist with a clinical practice in northern California for nearly 20 years. She has been a family law mediator for 10 years. She earned her doctorate from the University of Georgia, where she received specialized training in child neuropsychology. She is recognized as an expert in parental alienation. She has published in peer-reviewed journals and has appeared on the Internet and radio shows. Her therapeutic work with children and their parents is derived from evidence-based practice.

Amy J. L. Baker, Ph.D.
Dr. Amy J. L. Baker is a researcher, author, and nationally recognized expert in parent–child relationships. She earned her doctorate in developmental psychology from Teachers College of Columbia University. In addition to *Adult Children of Parental Alienation Syndrome*, Dr. Baker is the first author of *Child Welfare Research Methods* and is the author or co-author of over 70 academic articles. She is also the co-author, along with Katherine Andre, of *I Don't Want to Choose: How Middle School Children Can Avoid Choosing One Parent Over the Other.*

J. Michael Bone, Ph.D.
Dr. Bone has spent over 25 years dealing with high-conflict divorce as a therapist, expert witness, mediator, evaluator, and consultant, both nationally and internationally. Dr. Bone worked extensively with the late Dr Richard

Gardner, who first described parental alienation syndrome in 1985. Dr Bone served on the Scientific and Professional Advisory Board of the Parental Alienation Research Foundation in Washington, DC. In 2006 Dr. Bone closed his clinical practice and began a full-time consultative practice devoted entirely to the development of remedies for and education about parental alienation.

Barbara Burkhard, Ph.D.
Dr. Burkhard has provided psychological services to young children and their families for over 35 years. She holds a doctorate in clinical psychology from Stony Brook University and has specialized training in the area of child abuse assessment. She has served as program director for several Suffolk County programs serving children and families, including the Child Treatment Program of North Suffolk Mental Health Center, Smithtown, NY.

Paul R. Fine, LCSW
Paul Fine is a licensed clinical social worker and psychotherapist in practice at a community mental health center in northern New Jersey. He is the co-author of *Beyond the High Road: Responding to 17 Parental Alienation Strategies Without Compromising Your Morals or Harming Your Child.* He has extensive experience of working with adults, children, and families.

Benjamin D. Garber, Ph.D.
Ben Garber is a New Hampshire-licensed psychologist, state-certified guardian *ad litem*, and parenting coordinator. He provides child-centered family (custody) evaluations and expert witness services in the best interests of the child. Dr. Garber is a frequent contributor to popular press and professional publications and is the author of *Keeping Kids Out of the Middle* and *Developmental Psychology for Family Law Professionals.* He is an internationally received speaker on topics in family law and child and family development.

Lorna Goldberg, LCSW
Lorna Goldberg is Dean of Faculty at the Institute for Psychoanalytic Studies and the President of the International Cultic Studies Association. She earned her master's degree in social work from New York University and was certified as a psychoanalyst by the New Jersey Institute for Training in Psychoanalysis, where she was director of the Child and Adolescent Training Program. She is the author or co-author of numerous articles published in professional journals and books. Ms. Goldberg has a private practice working with children, adolescents, and adults in Englewood, NJ.

William Goldberg, LCSW
William Goldberg retired from the Rockland County (NY) Department of Mental Health in 2008 after working there for 33 years. He received his master's degree in social work from New York University, and was certified as a psychoanalyst by the Institute for Psychoanalytic Studies. He has authored or

co-authored eight articles that have been published in professional journals and books. He is presently an adjunct instructor in the Social Work and Social Sciences Divisions of Dominican College, Orangeburg, NY. He is also a member of the faculty and a supervisor for the Institute for Psychoanalytic Studies. Mr. Goldberg has a private practice working with adults, adolescents, and children in Englewood, NJ.

Linda J. Gottlieb, LMFT, LCSW

Linda Gottlieb received her master's degree in clinical social work with a specialization in family therapy from Adelphi University School of Social Work, Garden City, NY in 1980. She studied for 9 years at the Minuchin Center for Family Therapy, New York, NY and was personally trained for a year in the techniques of structural family therapy by Salvador Minuchin, M.D. She then served on the faculty of the Minuchin Center from 2003 to 2007. She is the author of a recently published book entitled *The Parental Alienation Syndrome: A Family Therapy and Collaborative Systems Approach to Ameliorati*on. Ms. Gottlieb is currently in private practice and specializes in the diagnosis and treatment of PAS families.

Karen Lebow, LCSW

Karen Lebow received her master's degree in social work from the University of Southern California, and her master's in Jewish communal service and an honorary doctorate from Hebrew Union College, Los Angeles, CA. She is a community organizer and a psychotherapist. She is founder of the International Support Network for Alienated Families, Inc. She was the first director to head up the Los Angeles Bureau of Jewish Education's Department of Parent and Family Life Education for their 150 schools. She was the first woman to be appointed executive director of a Jewish community center when she became executive director for the Orange County Jewish Community Center. She has launched myriad support groups for cancer patients and their families at Kaiser Permanente Woodland Hills Medical Center, Woodland Hills, CA, at the same time establishing the Cancer Patient Family Care Fund there. Karen Lebow believes in the power of the group—the healing of people through taking part in a community.

Steven G. Miller, M.D.

Steven Miller has degrees in psychology and medicine from Brown University and completed his residency training at Brown and Harvard. For the past 30 years he has been on the staff of Harvard Medical School. Board certified in internal medicine, he has a special interest in the medicine–psychiatry interface. A popular speaker, he has directed many courses and given over one thousand lectures on clinical reasoning and medical decision-making. He has also been involved in developing national guidelines and decision-tree algorithms for a variety of clinical conditions. He currently does research on the cognitive science of clinical problem-solving.

Joe Rabiega, MA, LPC

Joe Rabiega is a licensed professional counselor in private practice in Raleigh, NC. He earned a master's degree in psychology from Marywood University, Scranton, PA. He has also completed additional post-master's education and training in a clinical psychology doctoral program. In addition to having more than 7 years of diverse mental health counseling experience, Mr. Rabiega frequently participates in community education workshops on various wellness topics. Mr. Rabiega is passionate about helping individuals understand the impact of divorce and negative parent relationships, and how these issues impact a child's well-being and development.

S. Richard Sauber, Ph.D.

S. Richard Sauber, Ph.D., is a Board-Certified Diplomate in Clinical and Family Psychology by the American Board of Professional Psychology. He conducts a national family forensic practice from his local office in Boca Raton, Florida, and holds a license in psychology to practice in Canada. Formerly, he was Professor of Psychology in the Departments of Psychiatry in the Medical Schools of Brown, Columbia and the University of Pennsylvania. He has been the Editor of *The American Journal of Family Therapy* since 1976. He has authored or edited 16 professional books including the first edition of *The International Handbook of PAS: Conceptual, Clinical and Legal Considerations* with Richard Gardner, M.D. and Demosthenes Lorandos, Ph.D., J.D. He also has edited the second edition in press entitled *Parental Alienation: The Handbook for Mental Health and Legal Professionals* with Demosthenes Lorandos, Ph.D., J.D. and William Bernet, M.D.

Jack Weitzman, LCSW

Jack Weitzman is a psychiatric social worker in San Jose, CA. He graduated from the University of Michigan. He works in the Child and Adolescent Program at Kaiser Permanente in San Jose and also has a private practice. He has worked for 28 years with children and families, and has published articles on child maltreatment, adolescent depression, domestic violence, and related areas.

Abe Worenklein, M.Sc., Ph.D.

Abe Worenklein is a clinical and forensic psychologist in private practice in Montreal, Québec, Canada, where he is also a professor at Dawson College and a lecturer at Concordia University. In addition to his practice in clinical and forensic evaluation and psychotherapy, he is certified as a family mediator. Dr. Worenklein has been declared an expert witness in Superior Court and in Youth Court several hundred times, primarily in Canada but also in the United States and the Caribbean, and has presented on this topic at numerous professional conferences in Canada, the United States, and Europe. He has been quoted in significant judgments dealing with parental alienation and high-conflict divorces. He is a member of the Canadian Register of Health Service Providers in Psychology and has been certified by the Association of State and Provincial Psychology Boards.

1 Introduction

Amy J. L. Baker

Parental alienation—defined generally as the problem of children's unjustified rejection of a parent in response to inter-parental conflict and loyalty issues—is not a new problem. It has been around as long as there have been two parents to compete for the love of a child. In the 1980s Richard Gardner (1998) coined the term parental alienation syndrome (PAS) to describe eight behaviors that children exhibit when they have been manipulated by one parent to unjustifiably reject the other parent. Since then, there has been intense interest in this problem and a growing consumer demand for information and solutions.

Despite the overwhelming documentation that some children can be subjected to parental pressure that results in their vehement and unwarranted rejection of the other parent, there are voices of dissent in the field. While most endorse the basic tenet that children can be manipulated to reject a parent with whom the child has had a positive relationship up until that point and has done nothing to deserve such treatment, some take issue with the classification of PAS as a disorder believing it will result in stigmatizing children and not holding parents accountable for their behavior. Others object because the concept can be misused by zealous attorneys who want to deflect blame from battering husbands. Still others argue that targeted parents—while not necessarily physically abusive—typically lack parenting skills, which accounts for the rejection by their children.

It is beyond the scope of this book to systematically identify and address each of the criticisms but suffice it to say that the editors believe none of these considerations are supported by the facts or, if true, would invalidate the concept. Nonetheless, the detractors have made it difficult to disseminate research findings to a broad audience because some journals have formed opposing camps of those that will and those that will not publish parental alienation research. They have discouraged the kind of dialogue and knowledge-generation activities that are necessary for improved prevention and intervention.

As this book demonstrates, it is time for the field to move beyond these distracting and side-tracking issues and focus systematically and thoughtfully on gathering information and knowledge and making wisdom garnered from clinical experience available to those on the front line. Despite the controversy, professionals in the trenches know what they are dealing with and want tools for addressing the real and complex problems posed by parental alienation. This book represents the first collected volume of writings by and for clinicians identifying and treating parental alienation. Below, eight themes that are echoed throughout the book are briefly introduced.

Importance of Differentiating Alienation From Estrangement

As Kelley and Johnston (2001) rightly argued—and Gardner himself made this point as well—not all children who refuse visitation have been manipulated to do so. Some cases of visitation refusal represent rational responses to abusive parenting or reflect developmentally influenced responses to parental divorce that are outside the scope of manipulation of the favored parent. Thus, it is critical that clinicians in decision-making positions are familiar with the differential diagnosis between estrangement and alienation and are sufficiently competent and courageous to identify alienation when it is present. It appears likely that many clinicians (parenting coordinators, child and family counselors, mediators, custody evaluators, reunification specialists) fall back on the position that "most cases are hybrid cases." This is problematic for two reasons. First, no nationally representative data exist to support this claim. Second, even if it were true, each case must be evaluated and treated on its own terms with the clinician open to the possibility that it might be alienation, it might be estrangement, or it might be a combination of the two. If the clinician starts from the premise that alienation is rare, he or she may prematurely and falsely conclude that a particular case is one of estrangement rather than alienation. Miller (this volume) demonstrates the faulty logic and poor clinical practice that such thinking reflects and how it can result in disastrous outcomes for children and families.

Seeing Beyond "He Said/She Said"

Alienation is likely present in high-conflict divorce cases, characterized by ongoing litigation regarding access and abuse. A custody evaluation is likely to occur at some point during the litigation and the evaluator will be appointed by the court to conduct personality, parenting, and child and family assessments. Each parent will have an opportunity to present to the evaluator his or her version of the family's history, the parenting capacities of the other parent, and the functioning of the children; a version likely to be diametrically at odds with the other parent's presentation. Sauber and Worenklein (this volume) suggest that in all cases, especially those in which alienation is a potential issue, the evaluator must take a PA-informed approach, paying careful attention to false allegations, discrepancies between the words and actions of the favored parent, the validity of the child's stated reasons for rejecting one parent, and a thorough consideration of collateral contacts. There are no short cuts in such an evaluation. Further, concluding that alienation is present—that the blame is not evenly distributed between the warring parents—is likely to anger the favored parent and his or her attorney as well as create discomfort for the judge, who will be placed in a position of having to go beyond a "middle of the road" decision. Approval seeking and non-threatening recommendations will not be helpful to the best interest of the children. For these reasons, alienation places some professionals outside their comfort zone of "he said/she said" and is, therefore, not for the faint of heart.

Targeted Parents Need to be Strategic

Dealing with alienation is in many respects counterintuitive for both the clinician and the parent. Usual strategies for responding to one's rageful and spiteful ex-spouse and disaffected and entitled children do not work and can actually exacerbate the situation. Targeted parents need help in developing strategic responses to the many frustrations and challenges they face. As a result, some parents are choosing to work with a mental health consultant, a new role in this burgeoning field. As described by Bone and Sauber (this volume), the mental health consultant can help targeted parents navigate the many landmines of the legal and mental health systems in order to achieve the right to preserve or repair relationships with their children. Other targeted parents, however, will go it alone. Regardless, there is practice wisdom available for targeted parents that can be offered by and explored with therapists, by family attorneys, and potential mental health consultants to their case. For example, while it may be natural to respond to a child's false accusation by vehemently providing proof of the child's mistake, this may backfire and entrench the alienation, as well as increase the level of conflict between the already embattled targeted parent and the angry and disaffected child. Baker and Fine (this volume) propose a PA-informed approach entailing starting from a place of empathy and mutual problem-solving with the child (without apologizing for something that did not happen). By remaining calm, loving, and empathically attuned to the child, the parent can show him- or herself to be a safe, loving, and available parent, which can be an effective antidote to the lies and misinformation of the alienating parent.

Working with Targeted Parents Can be Stressful and Frustrating

Providing individual therapy to targeted parents can be a complicated and difficult endeavor because of the level of intense emotion likely to be expressed and felt by the client. Short of the death of a child, being a targeted parent is one of the most painful experiences a parent can face and unlike a death there is no closure and often an absence of sympathy or understanding from previously supportive friends and family. Clinicians working with targeted parents must ensure that they are well read on the subject and able to tolerate the intense grief and pain their clients are facing. As William and Lorna Goldberg (this volume) highlight, therapists of targeted parents must contend with the client's profound frustration—if not anger—that the therapist cannot directly fix the problem; rage at the injustice inflicted by a seemingly incompetent and uncaring family court system; as well as the paralyzing shame of being rejected by one's children. Therapists must be immensely empathic while exquisitely clear that they hold no magic wand to bring the child around and no crystal ball to know which actions will work to end the pain. Some of the emotional issues experienced by targeted parents are also present for the therapist, in a parallel process. For example, therapists of targeted parents may also become demoralized by the shame of not being powerful enough to fix the targeted parent's problem. They too may become guilt ridden when experiencing pleasure in the face of such pain. They too may need to take a break from dealing with alienation in order to recharge and regain their energy and focus for tackling such a complex problem. Awareness of these parallel process issues can help clinicians working with targeted parents maintain their balance and hone their clinical skills so that they can provide a much-needed source of support to these embattled and fragile parents.

The Healing Power of Support for Parents and Children

Being a targeted parent is a shame-inducing, frustrating, painful, and demoralizing process. A common experience for targeted parents is to feel like they are the only one going through this and that no one can possibly understand the level of pain and the degree of frustration involved. Thus, unlike dealing with cancer, divorce, or even the death of a child, being a targeted parent involves the double experience of facing a significant trauma while being denied the natural base of support to cope with the pain and suffering. Unfortunately, many people in the existing network of a targeted parent are likely to misunderstand the experience and either minimize the problem (i.e., say that the children will figure it out and come running back in no time) or encourage the targeted parent to take actions that could be quite unhelpful (i.e., taking a "wait and see" attitude).

In response to these common experiences of targeted parents, parental alienation support groups have sprung up on the Internet as well as in communities around the country. The International Support Network for Alienated Families (ISNAF) may be the largest such group. Lebow (this volume) identifies several issues that are likely to be particularly salient for PAS social support groups, including conflict between those with a mothers' rights perspective and those with a fathers' right perspective, tension between those who want to engage in advocacy and those who want to focus on social support, and the feelings that can arise when members of the group are at different stages of alienation. While there are no hard and fast rules for dealing with any of these complexities, a seasoned mental health professional familiar with parental alienation can address each of these considerations in a sensitive manner that enhances the community of the group and the healing of the individuals.

Children whose parents are divorced or engaging in behaviors that evoke feelings of divided loyalty also need social support. Many schools already offer a support group for children of divorce but none of the existing groups appear to focus on loyalty conflicts/parental alienation per se. Schools represent ideal locations for such groups because they are neutral locations (i.e., not specifically affiliated with either parent) and have a vested interest in helping children effectively cope with their emotional issues in order to prevent them from interfering with academic and behavioral functioning. The I Don't Want To Choose (IDWTC) program (Baker & Andre, this volume) is based on the premise that children generally benefit from having a relationship with both parents and that what they need are tools for removing themselves from the conflict which do not involve aligning with one parent against the other. Four such tools are presented throughout the IDWTC book and workbook, and form the basis of the activities in the school-based program (e.g., critical thinking skills, considering options, listening to one's heart, and asking for support). The IDWTC program holds promise for helping prevent alienation and its long-term negative outcomes for children and families.

The Child's Therapist as a "Port in the Storm"

When co-parents become intractably conflicted, when they separate or divorce, their children typically struggle with a great breadth of powerful and disruptive emotions. In response, parents commonly seek out mental health supports for their children. Unfortunately, in the absence of proper precautions, the mental health professional who accepts this child in psychotherapy is at very high risk not only of doing harm to the child but compromising his or her own professional ethics and legal responsibilities.

Garber (this volume) discusses how the destructive dynamics that characterize many high-conflict divorcing families can triangulate the child therapy and the child's therapist. He describes the steps that the conscientious child-centered mental health professional must take to screen every child referral from the first contact so as to minimize the risk of therapist alienation. The key, he writes, is the therapist's willingness and ability to establish proper roles and boundaries, and to incorporate both parents within the limits of the law while always respecting the child's confidentiality, so as to provide the child a port in the storm.

Alienated Children Can be Reunified

Some targeted parents are able to prevail upon the courts to order an intensive residential reunification for the rejected parent and the alienated child, such as family bridges (Warshak & Otis, 2010). Obviously, this is not the norm as few such programs exist, are costly, and too few judges have the courage and foresight to order that kind of intervention. Thus, a common solution in such cases is outpatient therapeutic reunification. It appears that many clinicians claim to conduct reunification therapy when in fact they do nothing more than routine individual or dyadic therapy—and there is no evidence that either of these modalities alone can reverse severe alienation. In fact they may cause great harm (Sauber, 2010). By contrast, three promising parental alienation-informed outpatient approaches are offered in this volume (by Weitzman, Kelly & Burkhard, and Gottlieb).

The common thread among each of these approaches is the importance of working with the courts to create a clear and compelling incentive for the alienating parent to participate in the effort. In the absence of the threat of sanctions it is highly unlikely that any outpatient treatment can reverse alienation because as soon as the alienating parent senses the child moving towards a more balanced relationship with both parents, he or she will refuse to deliver the child to treatment and/or actively turn the child against the therapist. Only a highly skilled clinician who can balance empathy with a willingness to use threats of the "strong arm of the law" can make headway with cases of entrenched alienation. Needless to say, the courts must have the courage of their convictions to impose these sanctions or else, like most court orders, they will be nothing more than paper tigers.

It is Never Too Late to Recover and Reunite

Ideally, the courts, the mental health community, and the parents will work together to allow children to make and maintain the healthiest relationships possible with both parents before alienation takes hold in their hearts and minds. Next best is swift and effective interventions, such as those described in this book, while the affected children are still young and can repair the damage due to the alienation and loss of the rejected parent. Unfortunately, for all of the reasons outlined in this book (faulty diagnosis of the problem, ineffective approaches, poor or no planning for the solution by clinicians and evaluators, sabotage of treatment by alienating parents, improper therapeutic interventions, and so forth), many children reach adulthood still alienated from one parent by the other.

Some enter psychotherapy for the first time as adults who come to therapy on their own—outside the reach of the courts. For many, this is the first opportunity to receive mental health counseling and supportive assistance in taking a second look at their childhood. Often these individuals enroll in therapy for reasons related to alienation (poor interpersonal relationships, depression/anxiety, difficulty trusting others, low self-esteem) while not being aware of alienation per se or its impact on their life. Like any sub-population of clients, there are unique issues that are likely to arise over the course of treatment, such as shame at having participated in the alienation, grieving for the "lost years," deciding whether and how to confront the alienating parent, and working through reunification with the targeted parent. Rabiega and Baker (this volume) provide concrete guidance to clinicians as well as an inspirational first-hand account of living with and recovering from parental alienation syndrome.

Each chapter in this book provides the latest and very best thinking from a team of dedicated and experienced clinicians. Each chapter calls for the very best information and guidance from mental health professionals, including consultants who choose to work with families affected by parental alienation. The impetus for this effort is the prevention of the likely long-term negative consequences of unfettered alienation on the well-being and functioning of children over the course of their life (Baker, 2007). Understanding these long-term effects should embolden the courts and the clinicians to go above and beyond routine care to apply a parental alienation-informed perspective to diagnosis, custody evaluations, social support groups for children and parents, individual therapy and education for parents and children, and efforts to achieve family reunification. Anything less is too little, too late.

References

Baker, A. J. L. (2007). *Adult children of parental alienation syndrome: Breaking the ties that bind.* New York: W. W. Norton.

Gardner, R. A. (1998). *The parental alienation syndrome: A guide for mental health and legal professionals.* Cresskill, NJ: Creative Therapeutics.

Kelly, J. B., & Johnston, J. R. (2001). The alienated child: A reformulation of parental alienation syndrome. *Family Court Review, 39(3),* 249–266.

Sauber, S. R. (2010). *Why forensic evaluations are more effective than traditional psychotherapy in helping alienated children.* Presented at the Canadian Symposium for Parental Alienation Syndrome, Mt. Sinai School of Medicine, New York, U.S.A.

Warshak, R., & Otis, M. (2010). Helping alienated children with family bridges: Practice, research, and the pursuit of "humbition." *Family Court Review, 48(1),* 91–97.

2 Clinical Reasoning and Decision-Making in Cases of Child Alignment

Diagnostic and Therapeutic Issues

Steven G. Miller

A Lost Opportunity

The Jones family is referred by a family court to a psychotherapist for "reunification therapy" following a contentious divorce and custody dispute. The therapist, a clinical psychologist, has been in practice for 20 years. The parents have been divorced for 7 years. The mother, Anne, has physical custody of the 13-year-old daughter, Dawn, but shares legal custody with the father, Bruce. After the divorce the father had "liberal visitation," including overnights. Dawn spent one-third of her time with him. Three years ago the mother told the father that Dawn was afraid of him and no longer wished to see him. Subsequently, Dawn and the father did not see each other and the father went to court to seek physical custody.

After a 2-day trial, the judge found the mother guilty of contempt for violating the court-ordered parenting plan, writing, "The mother frequently disparaged the father in front of the child, blocked the child's access to the father, blocked the father's access to the child, and made false allegations of threats, abuse, and neglect. The mother falsely told the child the father wanted to kill them." Nonetheless, citing Dawn's low opinion of the father and their lack of recent contact, the judge declined to reverse custody and, instead, ordered "reunification therapy."

The therapist begins by conducting individual 45-minute interviews. The mother is poised and calm. She tearfully reports "verbal abuse" by her former husband. Asked why Dawn does not wish to see her father, she replies, "Because he's abusive. Now that she's older, she can finally stand up to him." The mother says she encourages Dawn to visit her father but Dawn declines. The father presents as anxious and intense. He reports that before seeking custody he tried to see Dawn but was "thwarted at every turn." He emphatically denies having been abusive.

He states that his former wife has a personality disorder. He claims she is "unstable" and "a master manipulator." Citing the judge's findings, he relates that she told Dawn he had threatened to kill them. Of this, he says, "She made it up out of thin air." He offers to provide eyewitnesses to establish this but the therapist says that is not necessary. The father asks whether the therapist might wish to review Dawn's psychotherapy records to verify his account—including his previously good relationship with Dawn—but the therapist declines, explaining it might compromise her objectivity.

The father asserts that if Dawn remains with her mother the situation will become worse. "The main problem is not that Dawn doesn't see me," he says. "That's a big problem but it's not the main problem. The main problem is that Dawn is being abused by her mother. That's why I tried to get custody."

Dawn arrives holding her mother's hand. She says she wants her mother present for the interview. The therapist agrees. Asked why she is there, she replies, "So you can tell the court I don't want to see my father." Dawn describes her father as "not a good man." Asked to be more specific, she says he is "mean," gave her "time-outs," and "yelled a lot." Her mother confirms this. Dawn describes her mother as "an excellent parent," adding, "She always makes me do my homework."

The therapist's assessment is mixed alienation and estrangement (i.e., that the case is a hybrid). She bases that on three observations. First, the court found the mother had disparaged the father and blocked access, suggesting alienation. Second, she notes the father's intensity during the interview and his criticisms of the mother, suggesting estrangement. Third, she believes the father's desire for custody suggests a need for power and control, another negative. She concludes that, except for her relationship with her father, Dawn is generally doing well as evidenced by her cheerful demeanor, strong bonds with her mother, and good grades in school.

The therapist's treatment plan consists of weekly 45-minute sessions with Dawn and her father. She also plans occasional joint sessions with Dawn and her mother. The goals are to facilitate communication, improve the parenting skills of both parents, and create cognitive dissonance in Dawn so she will see that the mother's harsh portrayal of the father is not entirely accurate. To achieve these goals, she plans to use a combination of family therapy and psycho-education.

During the first 6 months, the therapist strives to form a therapeutic alliance with each person. She refrains from taking sides, tries to mediate disputes, and teaches communication techniques such as mirroring, validating, and empathizing with each other's statements. "So it upsets you when I ..." "That makes sense to me because ..." "I can imagine how you must feel." Dawn refuses to use those techniques and rejects the psycho-education, saying, "I know what happened!" The therapist urges the father to "apologize for something" so Dawn will see he can admit his faults. The father does that but wonders if he has sent the wrong message.

After 12 months, Dawn still refuses to see her father except in the therapist's office. Those sessions do not go well. Dawn is focused on the father's alleged abuse of the mother. Turning to the therapist, she says, "He abused my mother! I don't want to see anyone who abused my mother!" The father asks the therapist how to handle this. At the therapist's suggestion, he tells Dawn he is sorry she feels that way. Dawn becomes enraged. Later, privately, the father expresses frustration over the lack of progress. The therapist counters that there *has* been progress, as the father now sees Dawn once a week whereas before he didn't see her at all. The father contends that the mother has continued to undermine his relationship with Dawn. The therapist points out that the father has not witnessed that first hand but concedes he "may be right." Since the therapist is no longer optimistic about changing the mother's behavior, she proposes to work with the father on his parenting skills.

Meanwhile, both Dawn and the mother accuse the therapist of not believing them when they relate negative things about the father. In subsequent sessions, Dawn refuses to speak. The therapist admits to a "treatment failure" and suspends treatment entirely. The father, disappointed with this outcome, wonders whether a different approach might have been more effective.

Introduction

Few mental health problems are more difficult to sort out or more resistant to treatment than the triad of a severely alienated child, a severely determined alienating parent, and a severely rejected targeted parent. Many treatment recommendations entail modest modifications of conventional psychotherapy techniques. That is not surprising since most therapists are trained to treat relationship problems and thus view parental alienation (PA) as a relationship problem.

While PA certainly *is* a relationship problem (or set of problems), severe cases are often associated with serious co-morbid psychopathology, particularly on the part of the alienating parent. Therefore, treatment of the relationship problems per se, while necessary, is seldom—if ever—sufficient. Effective intervention invariably requires treatment of both the alienation and any co-morbid condition (such as mental illness or a personality disorder). Moreover, one must develop a treatment plan for each individual client: the child (who is locked in a delusion); the alienating parent (who is likely to have one or more co-morbid conditions); and the targeted parent (who probably requires coaching and emotional support).

Thus, severe cases tend to be clinical in a *medical* sense of the word—the underlying psychopathology is often associated with severe cognitive distortions (including shared delusions and/or other psychotic or quasi-psychotic thinking), profound emotional dysregulation, and extreme or bizarre behavior. If clinicians fail to consider the total clinical picture—including any underlying psychopathology—they may fail to appreciate the severity and complexity of the situation. That, in turn, has major implications for diagnosis, treatment, prognosis, and outcome.

Such cases are not for the novice. Cases of severe alienation often exceed the expertise of highly skilled practitioners unless their special expertise includes treatment of severe child alignment, treatment of severe mental illness, and treatment of severe personality disorders. Treatment of all three may be necessary to achieve a good outcome or even to prevent catastrophic deterioration.

To further complicate matters, clinicians who treat PA do not yet have the benefit of large, well-designed clinical trials to guide them. Thus, clinicians who practice in this area cannot always base their treatments on hard scientific data—they are often not there.

What *should* clinicians do? One alternative is to rely on experience and intuition. While that is common practice it is not a good solution unless the clinician has extensive experience, outstanding intuition, and sophisticated clinical skills (including a thorough understanding of certain advanced clinical principles). Otherwise, cases of severe alienation are likely to be highly counterintuitive. Clinicians who attempt to manage them without adequate skills are likely to find themselves presiding over a cascade of clinical and psychosocial disasters.

But how can clinicians base their practices on sound scientific principles if there are few clinical trials and a paucity of outcome data? The answer is that clinicians may need to use first principles—fundamental clinical rules and concepts that can be applied to almost any clinical problem. To apply first principles, however, one must be thoroughly familiar with them. In addition, one must have a sophisticated understanding of clinical reasoning (with the possible exception of compassion, there is no more important quality in a clinician) yet studies show that many mental health practitioners lack adequate training to properly apply scientific principles (Baker, McFall, & Shoham, 2009; Begley, 2009; Mischel, 2009; Tavris, 2003).

The purpose of this chapter, then, is to review some of those principles and to provide both a conceptual framework and conceptual tools for mental health professions who work with severely alienated children and their families.

General Approach to the Client or Patient

During the past six decades, a large body of research has shed new light on the cognitive processes that underlie clinical reasoning and medical decision-making (Croskerry, 2009b; Elstein, 1976; Eva, 2005; Graber, 2008; Hall, 1967; Kahneman, 2011; Kassirer, Wong, & Kopelman, 2010; Kassirer, 1989; Mark, 2012; Meehl, 1954; Norman, 2005; Norman & Eva, 2010; Nurcombe, 2012). Clinical problem-solving is now conceptualized as a series of distinct but integrated phases. Through a process of logical elimination, competing hypotheses are mentally tested then either discarded or retained.

Perhaps surprisingly, research shows that both expert and novice clinicians approach problems in remarkably similar ways (Elstein, 2009). Almost immediately, they begin to gather information. Simultaneously, they generate hypotheses in an attempt to explain the problem. This usually begins within seconds of a clinical encounter. Despite the often-repeated advice (given especially to students) to gather copious amounts of data and consider a wide variety of possibilities, that is not necessarily what experts do. Typically, experts engage in a mental pruning process that quickly discards unlikely hypotheses and focuses on the most promising ones (Elstein & Bordage, 1988). Such streamlining is necessary owing to the limits of short-term memory, which can only deal with 5 to 10 items at a time (Kassirer et al., 2010; Mark, 2012; Miller, 1994). As data gathering continues, clinicians determine the differential diagnosis, which is a list of diagnostic possibilities. Ideally, competing hypotheses are ranked both in order of likelihood and order of importance, so that the remote possibility of a life-threatening problem might warrant greater consideration than the high probability of a minor one.

Along the way, clinicians employ a variety of cognitive strategies—some conscious, some unconscious—to make sense of the data. Their approaches fall on a cognitive continuum with intuitive reasoning at one end and analytical reasoning at the other (Hamm, 1988). They draw upon associative memory in an attempt to match presenting signs and symptoms with cases they have seen, heard, or read about in the past. Ideally, they also employ two types of logical inference: deductive logic (i.e., if the premises are true the conclusion must be true) and inductive logic (i.e., based on findings or observations there is a certain probability that the conclusion is true) (Fiedler, Walther, Freytag, & Nickel, 2003). At some point they arrive at a working diagnosis and, eventually, a final diagnosis.

Unfortunately, the above process is error prone. The good news is that the errors tend to be predictable and, at least in theory, preventable. The bad news is that some of the most serious and common errors arise from fundamental flaws in human thinking that are deeply ingrained. These are "hard-wired" as a result of natural selection and are notoriously difficult to eradicate or even modify. Since one can seldom correct a problem one does not recognize, it is important for clinicians to be aware of these limitations and pitfalls. Clinicians who deal with PA may be particularly susceptible to such errors because of the emotional and complex nature of the subject.

Such errors can be divided into two groups: cognitive errors and clinical errors. Cognitive errors are thinking errors. They often reflect deep-rooted tendencies for humans to reason in erroneous ways. Clinical errors are deviations from good clinical practice. Many clinical errors arise because of cognitive errors, others because of insufficient information, others because of inadequate understanding of scientific principles. Strategies to reduce clinical errors have recently received much attention (Croskerry & Nimmo, 2011; Norman & Eva, 2010).

Perhaps surprisingly, lack of knowledge is one of the least common clinical errors, except among novices (Graber, Franklin, & Gordon, 2005; Norman & Eva, 2010). Most clinical errors arise from inadequate data collection, faulty interpretation of the data, flawed reasoning, or lack of understanding of scientific principles (Graber, Gordon, & Franklin, 2002).

An expert's primary advantage is in having a large number of previous cases in memory. This leads to better pattern recognition, which in turn permits the expert to match the current case with a mental template. In general, that is an asset but it can also be a liability because it can lead to misdiagnosis by stereotyping. This is particularly relevant to the diagnosis and management of severely aligned children since many alienating parents have learned to manipulate professionals by mimicking a self-serving stereotype.

When experts place too much emphasis on intuition and not enough on logical analysis their judgments may be no better than those of novices. Similarly, expert judgment is often surpassed by simple algorithms or decision rules (Dawes, Faust, & Meehl, 2002; Grove & Lloyd, 2006; Grove & Meehl, 1996). For that reason it might be helpful to review the essential elements of a proper, systematic clinical evaluation.

Data Gathering

Clinical History

Medical textbooks invariably stress the need to obtain an adequate history. That is particularly true for clients with mental health problems since, in most cases there are no diagnostic tests to supplement the history.

History taking can be problem-focused, comprehensive, or in between. The history must include pertinent positives and negatives. If the patient is a poor or unreliable historian, one may need to use special techniques to elicit and clarify key points (e.g., to refocus the patient's attention, explain terminology, or clarify questions). While a review of interviewing techniques is beyond the scope of this chapter, a sophisticated understanding of those techniques—including forensic techniques—is essential when dealing with PA because the provided history is likely to include intentional misrepresentations. Wise practitioners will address this by cross-checking the provided history with collateral source information. Indeed, it is a fundamental principle of forensic psychiatry and forensic psychology that evaluators must obtain adequate collateral source information (American Academy of Child & Adolescent Psychiatry, 2011). Likewise, one must seek and clarify any discrepancies or inconsistencies. These forensic points are critical because a wrong diagnosis (e.g., misdiagnosing alienation as estrangement) can have devastating effects on outcome.

Physical Examination

Except for psychiatrists, many mental health practitioners believe they are neither qualified nor expected to perform a physical examination as part of their assessments. That is not quite correct. While those who practice in non-physical domains are not expected to "lay on hands," much can be learned from educated observation. Indeed, simple observation is a key component of any physical examination. What is the client's general appearance? What about speech, demeanor, and body language? Is there psychomotor agitation or psychomotor retardation? Is there evidence of emotional distress? Are there abnormalities on mental status examination? Such observations amount to a de facto physical examination. They can be just as relevant to a psychotherapist as to an internist or surgeon.

Diagnostic Testing

To be useful, a diagnostic test must have good validity. Unfortunately, some commonly used tests do not meet that standard. For example, many therapists use projective drawings in their practice. While such techniques can be useful for eliciting information, identifying issues and facilitating discussion, it is important to distinguish between using them as an adjunct to assessment and/or psychotherapy and using them for diagnostic testing. When used for testing, such techniques have strikingly poor validity. As one group of experts put it (Hunsley, 2003), "Until hypotheses based on projective drawings are formulated in a manner that can be subjected to scientific scrutiny and are supported in rigorous studies, there can be no basis to the claims for the validity of these approaches." Nevertheless, despite the lack of scientific support, projective tests (such as the Draw-a-Person test and the Rorschach inkblot test) remain in widespread use. This raises troubling questions because tests with poor validity can be exceedingly misleading.

Treatment

After making a working diagnosis, even if only a symptom (e.g., "emotional distress"), clinicians address treatment. If urgent treatment is indicated (e.g., crisis intervention) that must be provided. If there are multiple problems, clinicians must address each of them. Therapeutic considerations include the type, dose, and frequency of treatment. For psychotherapists, that means the type, length, and frequency of sessions. One must also consider whether ancillary services are required, such as a parenting coordinator or accompanied visits.

The treatment plan must also take into account the severity of each problem. The treatment of severe alienation is very different from that of mild alienation. A 45-minute weekly outpatient session with the alienated child and the rejected parent is grossly inadequate for severe cases, particularly if the child continues to live with the alienating parent (in which case the prognosis is poor regardless of the duration and frequency of office-based sessions—indeed, reversal of custody, limiting contact with the alienating parent, and/or other interventions are generally required to achieve a good outcome). Some children may require treatment in a non-office setting such as a retreat (Warshak & Otis, 2010). Some may need to be moved to neutral ground such as a boarding school (Sullivan & Kelly, 2001). Some are trapped in a cult-like situation and may require treatment similar to the "deprogramming" of cult victims (Baker, 2007; Clawar & Rivlin, 1991; Warshak, 2001).

Another consideration is that in severe cases conventional psychotherapy is typically ineffective and can make things worse (Warshak, 2001). The abysmal failure of conventional therapy in this setting is related to at least four factors:

1. At least initially, the therapist is likely to have an adversarial relationship with some family members, including the alienating parent and the alienated child (or children).
2. It is likely that the alienating parent and child (or children) are there reluctantly, either by court order or other outside pressure. They are likely to be poorly motivated and deeply determined to undermine both the therapy and the therapist.
3. There is usually co-morbid psychopathology, particularly in the alienating parent. Several authors have observed an increased prevalence of personality disorders, such as antisocial and borderline personality disorders, among severely alienating parents (Baker, 2007; Neff & Cooper, 2004). Antisocial personality disorder is notoriously resistant to treatment. Borderline personality disorder, though treatable, requires highly specialized treatment such as dialectical behavioral therapy; conventional therapy often makes things worse (Klosko & Young, 2004; Linehan, 1993; Paris, 2010). It is therefore not surprising that alienating parents who have antisocial, borderline, or related personality disorders are resistant to treatment for PA, particularly if one understands that such individuals may not react well to "looking in the mirror."

4. If the psychotherapy is focused on improving the relationship between the child and the targeted parent it may fail to address the primary underlying problem, which in severe PA is the alienating parent's problematic thinking, emotional instability, and harmful behavior. In severe cases, the alienating parent is too determined, too disturbed, and too delusional to respond to treatment—conventional or otherwise. Therapists who insist on a trial of conventional therapy (e.g., to "see for myself") are exceedingly unlikely to succeed.

But, some might say, "Why not give it a try?" While there is certainly a place for therapeutic trials in clinical practice, this is not one of them. Such trials are only appropriate when the potential benefits outweigh the potential risks. They are not appropriate when the treatment will almost certainly be futile, the upside potential is negligible, and a delay might be devastating. Such an approach is worse than worthless because while the therapist provides futile treatment, the child, already injured, is deprived of effective intervention—including protection.

Why, then, do some clinicians provide predictably futile treatment? For one thing, many practitioners—including some putative experts—lack the clinical expertise to manage severe, complicated cases. For another thing, many clinicians are overconfident (Berner & Graber, 2008; Croskerry & Norman, 2008; Dawson, Connors, Speroff, Kemka, Shaw, & Arkes, 1993; Friedman et al., 2005). Additionally, some clinicians believe (with little scientific justification; see note 4) that most cases are hybrids (i.e., a combination of alienation and estrangement) and therefore (borrowing a principle from marriage counseling) focus on the parent who is most able to change, which is usually the targeted parent. That leaves the harmful effects of the alienating parent unopposed. Finally, when swift, bold, decisive action is indicated—such as removal of a severely alienated child from a toxic home environment—many clinicians lack the temperament to support such action. By nature, they are timid clinicians. When they encounter severe or complex problems timid clinicians tend to do little or nothing. This can lead to a paradox in which higher-risk patients are less likely to receive essential treatment than lower-risk patients (Ko, Mamdani, & Alter, 2004).

On the positive side, many practitioners *do* have both the clinical sophistication and the temperament to manage such cases effectively. But one must match the practitioner with the problem. To assist with that, a variety of potentially effective strategies and techniques are presented elsewhere in this book.

Regardless of which treatments are selected, providers have their work cut out for them. Along the way, they will need to rely on a number of fundamental clinical principles, or axioms. Presented in three groups—general, diagnostic, and treatment—12 of the most important are discussed in the following section.

Clinical Axioms

An axiom is a rule or principle that is self-evident—so obviously true it requires no proof. Clinical practice is governed by several such axioms. Based on centuries of experience, they reflect well-established principles and practices that transcend all clinical disciplines and all clinical situations. The purpose of this section is to review some of the most important, with special reference to severe alignment. These are illustrated in Table 2.1. Note that there is much overlap between axioms.

General Axioms

Axiom 1: Consider the Total Clinical Picture

Clinical findings must be viewed in context. Incomplete information can be misleading. Snap judgments can be catastrophic. In dealing with severe alignment, clinicians must consider the total clinical picture. One common error is to fail to distinguish between the *fact* that a child has rejected a parent and the *reason* the child has rejected that parent. Those who make this error tend to focus on the *strength* rather than the *cause* of the rejection. If the reason for the rejection is that the alienating parent has taught the child to believe things that are untrue—or worse, has caused the child to become delusional—those are critical findings, particularly if the child's prior relationship with the rejected parent was good. A co-morbid psychiatric disorder, previous psychotherapy records, and other collateral source information can provide essential data. All of these things are part of the total clinical picture. Failure to consider the total clinical picture is a very serious clinical error, which is why it is listed first.

Axiom 2: Gather Adequate Evidence

This axiom pertains to both diagnosis and treatment. It requires clinicians to obtain adequate diagnostic data and to understand the scientific data upon which they base their treatments. For either purpose, clinicians must carefully consider both the amount and quality of any evidence. In assessing child alignment, for example, a second-hand report ("Jane said her husband hit her") should generally be given less weight than a first-hand report ("I saw him hit her"). Because some parties may not be reliable historians, collateral source information can be critical. Likewise, circumstantial evidence can be critical (and powerful).

As for treatment, evidence-based practice (EBP) does *not* mean one must have research or a clinical study upon which to base decisions. EBP merely means that clinicians should use the best available evidence (Evidence-Based Medicine Working Group, 1992). Sometimes that means expert consensus, rational extrapolation, or use of first principles. With respect to PA, EBP does *not* mean that therapists should withhold potentially helpful treatment simply because there are no randomized clinical trials (RCTs) on point. For instance, a

Table 2.1 Application of the 12 axioms to clinical problem-solving

	Axiom	*Comments*	*Examples of questions that clinicians should ask*
1	Consider the total clinical picture	Consider all aspects of a problem.	What was the prior relationship between the child and the rejected parent? Is the favored parent manipulating the child? Is there credible evidence that the rejected parent is abusive or neglectful? How cooperative is each parent with respect to both therapy and co-parenting? How credible are their stories? Are there discrepancies or inconsistencies? Does either parent breach court orders? Is there psychopathology?
2	Gather adequate evidence	Obtain sufficient high-quality evidence.	Do I have an in-depth understanding of this family? Do I have enough high-quality evidence? Do I need additional collateral source information? Have I overlooked disconfirmatory evidence? Have I overlooked circumstantial evidence?
3	Use proper reasoning	Always employ metacognition (thinking about thinking).	Have I used both System 1 and System 2 (intuition and analytic reasoning)? Have I displayed any biases? Have I followed the laws of logic and probability? Have I found a plausible explanation rather than the correct explanation?
4	Consider the natural history of the disease, disorder, or condition	Consider the clinical course with and without treatment.	What is the prognosis with and without intervention? What will happen if I do little or nothing? If either parent has psychopathology, is that likely to improve or get worse? Is the alienating parent likely to follow court orders?
5	Have a high index of suspicion	Consider atypical presentations, uncommon conditions, and/or intentional misrepresentation.	Could this be an atypical presentation? Is there evidence of intentional misrepresentation? Has the child been programmed? Am I being unduly influenced by the force and conviction of the child's statements? Could this parent be a high-functioning borderline?

6	Develop an adequate differential diagnosis	Rank competing diagnoses for both probability and importance.	What are the possibilities? I need to rank them.
7	Consider severity	Grade severity using a sliding scale and consider whether problems are getting better or worse.	Is the child's alienation mild, moderate, or severe? Is the parent's behavior mild, moderate, or severe? Is the behavior pathological, e.g., delusional, bizarre, or extreme? Am I guilty of severity neglect?
8	Analyze the evidence	Analyze the evidence with respect to amount, quality, strength, and weight. Seek confirmatory and disconfirmatory evidence. Seek direct and circumstantial evidence. Explain any discrepancies and inconsistencies. Obtain additional evidence if necessary.	What is the evidence for alienation? What is the evidence for estrangement? If both are present what are their relative contributions? Are the parents' behaviors causally connected to the child's alignment? Have I confused the strength of evidence with the weight of evidence?
9	Determine treatment priorities	Consider whether urgent treatment is required Determine the timing of various treatments.	What is the highest priority: to stop any ongoing abuse/alienation of the child or to restore the child's relationship with the targeted parent? How likely is the alienating parent to change his/her behavior? Do I need to protect this child? Do I need to inform the court?
10	Conduct a risks/ benefits analysis	Consider the risks and benefits of each treatment option, including the pros and cons of doing little or nothing.	What are the risks and benefits of: reversing custody; permitting the alienating parent to continue to alienate/abuse the child; failing to act promptly; failing to treat the parent's psychopathology; relying on office-based therapy?
11	Provide timely, appropriate treatment	Provide urgent treatment when indicated.	Is this a child in crisis? Is this a family in crisis?

Table 2.1 Continued

Axiom	*Comments*	*Examples of questions that clinicians should ask*
	Use scientific treatments.	How effective is weekly psychotherapy in a case this severe? If ineffective, what else is required?
12 Treat the underlying condition	Treat the root cause(s) of any problem(s) if feasible.	What is the primary problem? Is there more than one? Does either parent require treatment for a mental illness and/or personality disorder? Does the child have any psychopathology that requires treatment, such as pathological splitting or shared delusions? Does the child believe any false allegations? If so, what should be done about that? Can the child be deprogrammed if he/she continues to live with the alienating parent?

clinician might be reluctant to use psycho-education because there are no RCTs to establish its effectiveness, yet there is strong theoretical support and promising empirical data (Fidler & Bala, 2010; Warshak & Otis, 2010). Given what Kelly has called the "bleak prospects for the children's own future psychosocial well-being" in markedly alienated children (Kelly, 2010), clinicians are not only permitted but encouraged to consider new approaches to therapy—provided they are firmly rooted in science.

Axiom 3: Use Proper Reasoning

Clinicians have a variety of reasoning tools. These include: deductive logic (i.e., if the premises are true the conclusion must be true); inductive logic (i.e., inferring conclusions from observations based on probabilities); multivalent logic (i.e., placing variables on a continuum and assigning degrees of truth or "grading the gray"); approximate reasoning; probabilistic reasoning; rational extrapolations; and others. Through metacognition—thinking about thinking—clinicians should select the most appropriate cognitive tools.

Axiom 4: Consider the Natural History of the Condition

Clinicians must understand the usual clinical course of the condition(s) in question, both with and without treatment. As an illustration, consider the natural history of a severely alienated child whose custodial parent is an active alienator with borderline personality disorder (BPD). Some people, ignoring both the increased risk for BPD in children of borderline parents (Paris, Nowlis, & Brown, 1988) and the increased risk of suicide among those with BPD (Linehan et al., 2006), claim children are "resilient," a platitude that is true of some but certainly not all children. Moreover, children of borderline parents are at significant risk of developing BPD and/or other serious psychiatric disorders (Macfie, 2009; Stepp, 2012; Stepp, Whalen, Pilkonis, Hipwell, & Levine, 2012). Individuals with BPD have a lifetime risk of *completed* suicide of up to 10% (and the risk of *attempted* suicide is much higher) (Soloff & Chiappetta, 2012). Since the risk in the general population is about 1% (Minino, Murphy, Xu, & Kochanek, 2011), the risk with BPD is about 10 times higher. If a patient is at risk of developing a condition that can increase suicide risk by 1,000%, most people (even laypeople) would understand that those who deal with PA should take vigorous measures to prevent that from happening. Why would any clinician fail to do that? The most likely reason is failure to recognize the risk owing to failure to consider the natural history of PA in a child whose alienating parent has BPD.

Diagnostic Axioms

Axiom 5: Have a High Index of Suspicion

For serious problems, it is not enough to make the correct diagnosis *most* of the time; clinicians need to make the correct diagnosis *almost all* of the time. To do that, clinicians must have a high index of suspicion with respect to uncommon conditions, atypical presentations, and intentional misrepresentations. Regarding the latter, professionals must identify and clarify any inconsistencies or discrepancies. When clinicians *do* make diagnostic errors, they should be "no fault" or unavoidable errors—not errors due to inadequate data gathering or faulty thinking.

Axiom 6: Develop an Adequate Differential Diagnosis

One of the most common causes of diagnostic errors is failure to *think* of the diagnosis. With respect to child alignment, any competent therapist knows to consider alienation versus estrangement; what distinguishes superior clinicians is their ability to recognize atypical presentations and identify co-morbid conditions.

Axiom 7: Consider Severity

All clinical problems should be classified by severity. This should be done in two ways. First, one must ask whether the condition is *inherently* severe (e.g., a heart attack or anorexia nervosa). Second, one must assess severity *compared with others* who have the condition. While that might seem obvious, failure to do so is a common problem. That is particularly unfortunate with respect to PA because techniques that are often helpful in mild alienation can be harmful in severe cases (e.g., Imago relationship therapy (Hendrix, 2008), in which mirroring, validating, and empathizing can reinforce a child's delusions and encourage a targeted parent to "validate" them).

Axiom 8: Analyze the Evidence

Clinicians must carefully analyze each piece of evidence. The single most common cause of clinical errors—for both novice and experienced clinicians—is failure to interpret the evidence correctly. Here are four caveats. First, clinicians must distinguish between the *strength* of the evidence and the *weight* of the evidence. Though the two terms are often used interchangeably, as used here the strength of evidence is defined only by how dramatic it is—regardless of its truth. For instance, an allegation that a parent has sexually abused a child is very strong but, in itself, conveys nothing about its truth. In fact, according to the laws of logic, the stronger the statement, the less likely it is to be true (since extraordinary claims require extraordinary evidence). By contrast, the weight of evidence refers to how true and valid it is. Unfortunately, humans are hard-wired to pay more attention to strength than to weight. Clinicians must compensate for this by carefully weighting each piece of evidence. Second, clinicians must consider both confirmatory evidence and disconfirmatory evidence. That is critical because, in general, disconfirmatory evidence is more powerful (Nurcombe, 2012). Third, unless they see it with their own eyes, some therapists are reluctant to conclude that an alienating parent is continuing to alienate. That is unfortunate because circumstantial evidence can be extremely powerful. Fourth, clinicians must distinguish between a plausible diagnosis and a correct diagnosis. One of the hallmarks of a weak clinician is to accept a plausible diagnosis—one that is coherent and "explains things"—without verifying that it is, in fact, the right diagnosis. Indeed, studies show that many clinicians have great confidence in their incorrect conclusions (Berner & Graber, 2008; Croskerry & Norman, 2008).

Treatment Axioms

Axiom 9: Determine Treatment Priorities

Clinicians should give explicit thought to treatment priorities. Consider, for example, a family in which the child is severely alienated, the alienating parent is incorrigible, and the targeted parent has not seen the child in a year. What is the top priority—to stop the ongoing alienation or to "reunite" the child with the targeted parent? Since PA is a form of child abuse—specifically, psychological and emotional abuse (Baker, 2007; Kelly & Johnston, 2001; Warshak, 2010)—there is expert consensus that, at least in severe cases, preventing further abuse is an even higher priority than getting the child to spend more time with the targeted parent. As Warshak (2010) observed, "Our society's standard of care regarding abused children is to prioritize protecting them from further abuse." And yet, those who treat such families often focus more on restoring the child's relationship with the targeted parent than on stopping the ongoing abuse. That is a major error. The priority is to prevent further child abuse.

Axiom 10: Do a Risks/Benefits Analysis

Clinicians must carefully weigh risks versus benefits. One of the most common mistakes is to fail to consider the risk of doing nothing. In fact, doing nothing is doing something. Summarizing the research on this, Hallinan (2009) wrote:

> As a general principle, people feel more responsible for their *actions* than they do for their *inactions*. If we are going to err at something, we would rather err by failing to act. That's because we tend to view inaction as a passive event—we didn't *do* anything. And since we didn't do anything, we feel less responsible for the outcome that follows.

With respect to alienation, such thinking may explain why some clinicians fail to intervene despite obvious reasons to do so. If they are uncertain about risks versus benefits, they are likely to opt to do nothing. If that decision is based on a proper risk/benefit analysis it may be reasonable. If it is based on vague intuition rather than rational analysis it may be a serious error.

Axiom 11: Provide Timely, Appropriate Treatment

When treating progressive conditions, timing can be critical. Unfortunately, with respect to severe PA—which tends to be progressive—prompt intervention is not always provided. All too often, months and years pass with little effective treatment—even for children in crisis. In some cases, the clinicians may lack the training or experience to provide urgent intervention. Even if knowledgeable, timid clinicians may lack the temperament to provide swift, bold intervention (e.g., to confront a persistent alienator or recommend a change of custody). Since psychological and emotional abuse of a child can cause lifelong problems, permitting months or years to pass without effective intervention can be a tragic mistake.

Axiom 12: Treat the Underlying Condition

Sometimes it is not feasible to treat the underlying condition. That said, this is one of the most important principles in medicine. Consider, for instance, a patient with a long-standing cough. If the cause is a curable cancer, it can be a fatal mistake to simply prescribe cough medicine. Similar principles apply to PA. Consider a 10-year-old boy whose mother has convinced him (falsely) that his father wants to physically hurt him. Under such circumstances it would be normal behavior for the boy to reject the father and align with the mother. For therapy to have any chance of success, one must treat the underlying condition (i.e., disabuse the boy of his mother's false allegations). Nonetheless, many therapists violate this fundamental axiom. Rather than recognizing that it is mandatory to treat the underlying condition—or at least to arrange for it to be treated—they either ignore it or make token gestures, with predictably poor results. Meanwhile, they attempt to work with the targeted parent to improve his or her parenting skills. Strong parenting skills on the part of a targeted parent, however, are exceedingly unlikely to neutralize the toxic effects of a determined alienator.

While some would say there's an exception to every rule, only rarely would there be a legitimate reason for a clinician to violate any of the above axioms. And yet some clinicians do violate them—frequently. What accounts for that? One possibility is that such clinicians rely on intuition, which can be misleading. A second possibility is that they are susceptible to cognitive biases that can compromise rational thinking. A third possibility is that they rely on clinical aphorisms that lack scientific rigor. These and related problems are discussed in the following section.

Heuristics and Biases

All clinical disciplines rely on mental shortcuts known as heuristics. Typical heuristics include rules of thumb, clinical aphorisms, and conventional wisdom. They also include certain intuitive judgments. Used properly, heuristics can be useful. They permit experts to make quick, efficient judgments that are usually accurate. They work well under most, but not all, circumstances. By definition, however, a heuristic is a rule of thumb, not a true rule. There are exceptions to every heuristic. When heuristics fail, they can lead to serious clinical errors (McDonald, 1996). Thus, heuristics are always associated with biases (Tversky & Kahneman, 1974).

As in other clinical disciplines, the mental health professions have a substantial heuristic-based component. That is not necessarily bad—again, heuristics can be useful—but it can be problematic if clinicians attempt to solve complex clinical problems with simplistic heuristic thinking. It is one thing to employ heuristics as an aid to decision-making; it is another thing to rely on them in place of sound scientific reasoning.

With respect to clinical issues there are two types of heuristics: cognitive and clinical. Cognitive heuristics, also called judgment heuristics, are hard-wired, deep-rooted, inherent patterns of human thinking. They are largely unconscious and account for intuitive reasoning. Clinical heuristics are essentially aphorisms. They are rules of thumb that serve as touchstones for problem-solving. In addition to heuristic-related biases, there are other cognitive biases that are unrelated to heuristics. Several of the most important heuristics and biases are presented in the following section. They are illustrated in Table 2.2.

Table 2.2 Heuristics, biases, and metacognition

Heuristic	*Definition and comments*	*Sample applications*
The availability heuristic	Making a judgment based on how readily information can be recalled from memory.	Have I seen or heard about a recent case that is unduly influencing my judgment in this matter?
The representativeness heuristic	Making a judgment based on similarity, i.e., on a stereotype.	Am I stereotyping? How well does this case fit the typical pattern? Are there aspects that don't fit?
The affect heuristic	Making a judgment based on an emotion or feeling—can lead to "emotional reasoning."	Does it make me feel better to think this is estrangement, not alienation? Do I find the rejected parent off-putting because she is anxious and/or assertive? If I feel uncomfortable, is that rational or irrational? Am I engaging in emotional reasoning? What do the facts say?
Anchoring effect	A phenomenon by which judgment is unduly influenced by initial information; often accompanied by inadequate adjustment when new information becomes available.	After reading the guardian *ad litem* report I believed the rejected father was a victim of alienation engineered by the mother, but four credible sources say that is not true. My evidence now supports the mother but I'm having trouble believing it. Am I anchored to the GAL report? Have I failed to make adequate adjustments?

Table 2.2 Continued

Heuristic	*Definition and comments*	*Sample applications*
Confirmation bias	A tendency to focus on evidence that might *confirm* a hypothesis while neglecting evidence that might *refute* it.	Have I been paying too much attention to information that supports my initial impressions? Am I neglecting evidence that might refute those impressions?
Premature closure	Making a diagnosis or other decision before obtaining and/or considering sufficient information.	Do I have enough high-quality information to provide a proper opinion? What else could be going on? Don't jump to conclusions!
Framing errors	Presenting identical information in a way that will lead to a different conclusion, depending on how it is presented.	The court framed this as a problem between the child and the rejected mother. It ordered "reunification therapy." Maybe that's a framing error. Maybe I should re-frame the problem as child abuse by the father. Maybe it's more important to protect the child from the father than to reunite the child with the mother.
The fundamental attribution error	Concluding that a behavior is dispositional when in fact it is situational.	The mother is angry. Is she an angry person in general or is she angry because of the situation?
Base rate neglect	Failure to adequately consider the pre-test or prior probability that a hypothesis is correct when considering new evidence. Giving too much weight to clinical findings and not enough weight to prior probability.	The mother presented well but often denigrated the father in front of the child. The father had a good prior relationship with the child. Thus, the prior probability of alienation is high. That information will be critical when interviewing the child.
The ecological fallacy	As used clinically, giving too much weight to group/epidemiological data and not enough weight to an individual patient's clinical findings.	Some people claim most cases of child alignment are hybrids. Even if that is true, I should not assume this case is a hybrid. Group data should only be used for hypothesis generation, not hypothesis confirmation.

Cognitive Heuristics

Human thought is not always analytical. For the most part, people do not make decisions by carefully weighing (or weighting) evidence and processing it in accordance with the laws of logic, probability, and statistics. The human brain is not well wired for that. Rather, they draw conclusions based on intuitive judgments. Such judgments rely on cognitive templates that permit humans to make quick, efficient, reasonably accurate decisions. As previously noted, these templates are known as cognitive heuristics.

To qualify as a cognitive heuristic, the mental shortcut must involve attribute substitution, an unconscious process by which a difficult question is simplified by substituting an easier one (Kahneman & Frederick, 2002). For instance, if asked to determine whether an individual is a fit parent, an evaluator might substitute an easier question such as: "How did that parent act in an interview?" or "Do I like that parent?" Although attribute substitutions make questions easier to answer, they introduce substantial error. Interviewing skills might not reflect parenting skills. Consequently, all heuristics entail a trade-off between simplicity and accuracy. Here are 10 cognitive biases, including three cognitive heuristics:

The Availability Heuristic

The availability heuristic holds that many judgments are based on the ease with which information comes to mind (Tversky & Kahneman, 1973). For example, a clinician who once saw a rare disease might be predisposed to diagnose that disease in the future. Availability can be a good thing—it is an important part of expert reasoning—but it can also cause errors (Mamede et al., 2010). Like other heuristics, this one is more appropriate for hypothesis generation than hypothesis refinement.

The Representativeness Heuristic

The representativeness heuristic maintains that people commonly base judgments on superficial similarity (Kahneman & Tversky, 1972). It is occasionally called the similarity heuristic. Clinicians make extensive use of this heuristic. In most cases that is a plus because it permits them to match findings in a new case with exemplars stored in memory. However, because it relies on stereotyping, it is more likely to be accurate in simple cases than complex ones (Elstein & Schwarz, 2002). If relevant differences are not appreciated then reasoning by representativeness can fail. When that happens, expert decisions are often no better—and can be worse—than decisions by lay people (Borak & Veilleux, 1982).

The Affect Heuristic

The word "affect" means emotion or feeling. The affect heuristic states that emotions can affect judgment (Slovic, Finucane, Peters, & MacGregor, 2002), which can lead to emotional reasoning. If one has a "warm and fuzzy" feeling about something, one is likely to have a lower perception of risk and a higher perception of benefit. The affect heuristic can undermine rational decision making: a custody evaluator might be influenced by a vague feeling that one parent is more appealing than the other; a therapist might side with the favored parent and alienated child because it "feels better" to please two people than one; a therapist may elect to do nothing because that produces less anxiety than being proactive.

Anchoring Effect

Anchoring occurs when thinking is unduly influenced by initial information and there is inadequate adjustment when new information becomes available. In theory, one should be able to correct for an anchor by overriding it with logical thought. In reality, most people are unable to override a strong anchor (Epley & Gilovich, 2006). This has tremendous implications for clinical practice.

Anchoring, while no longer considered a heuristic per se because it does not involve attribute substitution, can lead to both diagnostic and treatment errors. With respect to diagnosis, subjects who skillfully manage first impressions can create powerful anchoring effects that are highly resistant to new evidence. With respect to treatment, consider a therapist whose goal is to restore 50/50 parenting time for a targeted parent who has joint physical custody. The therapist recommends a "phase-in period" starting with a single, weekly, 3-hour visit. While that might seem reasonable the downside is that the children and the alienating parent can become anchored to the brief weekly visits and become even more resistant to longer, more frequent visits. This is an example of how treating severe PA as a typical relationship problem can do more harm than good.

Confirmation Bias

Confirmation bias is a tendency to focus on evidence that would help *confirm* an existing belief while neglecting evidence that might *refute* it. A type of "tunnel vision," it is difficult to avoid even if one is aware of it. If one is focused on confirmatory evidence, one is less likely to seek contradictory or disconfirmatory evidence. This is a tremendous problem because, as mentioned earlier, disconfirmatory evidence tends to be more powerful than confirmatory evidence. A study involving psychiatrists found that the tendency for less-experienced clinicians to seek confirmatory over disconfirmatory evidence was associated with "poor diagnostic accuracy"; indeed, psychiatrists who focused on confirmatory evidence made a wrong diagnosis 70% of the time (Mendel et al., 2011). This bias can be extreme—it is not uncommon for clinicians to ignore multiple pieces of disconfirmatory evidence while focusing on a single piece of confirmatory evidence. Clinicians who initially suspect estrangement are likely to show confirmation bias in favor of estrangement; those who initially suspect alienation are likely to show confirmation bias in favor of alienation. All clinicians must consciously compensate for that.

Premature Closure

Premature closure refers to finalizing a diagnosis before gathering and considering sufficient evidence (jumping to conclusions). Premature closure is related to both anchoring and confirmation bias. These biases tend to reinforce each other and, in concert, can lead all but the most careful clinicians astray. Paradoxically, perhaps due to overconfidence, experienced clinicians may be more susceptible to this error than less-experienced clinicians (Eva & Cunnington, 2006).

Framing Errors

Framing errors occur when people draw different conclusions from identical information, depending on how that information is presented (Tversky & Kahneman, 1981). One example is the leading question. "When your dad gave you that gift, did you consider it a bribe?" Other examples abound. Assume, for instance, that a 10-year-old boy has barely seen his mother in 2 years and a court has concluded the problem is PA. Further assume that the alienating parent is an obsessed alienator (Darnall, 1998). If the court refers the boy for "reunification therapy," the mere fact that the court used that term can radically alter the therapist's approach—both consciously and unconsciously. Consider, for instance, how that wording might influence the therapist's priority setting. What is the first priority? Is it to restore contact between the boy and the rejected parent or is it to stop the alienating parent's destructive and abusive behavior? Common sense mandates that the first priority should be to prevent further child abuse. If that was the judge's intention he did not convey it—quite the opposite—in which case the term "reunification therapy" represents a framing error.

Additionally, the phrase "reunification therapy" entails a second framing error because it focuses on the child's relationship with the targeted parent (a laudable goal) but fails to address the need to deprogram the child (which is essential). Without all three directives from the court—to prevent further child abuse, deprogram the child, and restore the child's relationship with the targeted parent—one or more of these goals may be overlooked.

The Fundamental Attribution Error

The fundamental attribution error refers to a situation in which an observer incorrectly assigns a dispositional, characterological, or internal cause rather than a situational or external cause to a behavior (Ross, 1977; Ross & Anderson, 1982). For instance, just because a person is angry about a specific situation does not mean he or she is an angry person in general. Unfortunately, and to an extreme degree, the human brain is hard-wired to give too much weight to dispositional factors and not enough to situational factors. Therefore, because they can feel perfectly natural, incorrect judgments about people's disposition and character can be made with great confidence (Forgas, 1998).

Base Rate Neglect

When considering new evidence about a hypothesis, clinicians must know or estimate the prior probability of that hypothesis before they can determine the updated or posterior probability. That is required by the laws of probability. Failure to properly consider prior probability is known as base rate neglect (Tversky & Kahneman, 1982). Humans have a striking hard-wired tendency to neglect prior probability. For that reason, base rate neglect runs rampant in every field, even forensic practice (Mossman, 2000). Clinicians who make this mistake give too much weight to clinical findings and too little weight to prior probabilities.

Suppose, for example, one needs to distinguish whether a child is alienated or has been abused. The child is a 12-year-old girl who has rejected her father, claiming he mistreated her at a party. A psychologist is asked to investigate. Before interviewing the girl, he speaks with four adult witnesses who report the father did *not* mistreat the girl. Unless the psychologist doubts the credibility of those witnesses, the prior probability of mistreatment (at least on that date) would be low. If, during an interview, the girl describes the alleged mistreatment—vividly and tearfully—the psychologist, being human, might be inclined to believe her. To do so, however, he would have to discount four credible eyewitness reports, which would represent egregious base rate neglect. He would also have to confuse the strength of the evidence with the weight of the evidence, as previously discussed.

The Ecological Fallacy

Another cognitive error is the ecological fallacy (Piantadosi, Byar, & Green, 1988). That involves the use of group data to draw conclusions about individual people. Originally, the term was applied to the interpretation of data in research studies in which some epidemiologists assumed, incorrectly, that certain characteristics of groups were true of individuals in those groups (Robinson, 1950). An analogous mistake can be made in clinical reasoning whereby clinicians assume that characteristics of a group (e.g., in a published study) necessarily apply to their own individual patients. Clinicians who make this fallacy give too much weight to epidemiological data and too little weight to case-specific clinical findings. In that sense, it is roughly the opposite of base rate neglect.

It is important to recognize this fallacy when reading the literature. For example, one author has stated that rejected parents, "appear to be the more influential architect of their own alienation" (Johnston, 2003).[1] Others have claimed that, in their experience, most cases of child alignment are hybrids (i.e., a combination of alienation and estrangement [Friedlander & Walters, 2010]). Even if these statements are true—and that has certainly not been established except, perhaps, in certain subgroups—one cannot use such information to make a diagnosis in any individual case, except in accordance with Bayes' rule (discussed later), which places strict constraints on how such data can be used.

Clinical Heuristics

In contrast to cognitive heuristics, clinical heuristics are task- or domain-specific rules of thumb. In effect, they are clinical aphorisms. Some are reasonably reliable; others are deeply flawed. One useful heuristic is Occam's razor which is used in every scientific field. It holds that the simplest solution to a problem is usually correct. Some useful heuristics describe the characteristics of alienated children (Gardner, 1999; Kelly & Johnston, 2001). Other useful heuristics address the characteristics of alienating parents, such as Darnall's description of obsessed alienators—parents who wish to destroy the child's relationship with the other parent—and, tellingly, may repeatedly violate court orders to do so (Darnall, 1998). Another useful heuristic is Baker's finding that severe alienators tend to have personality disorders (Baker, 2007). Other heuristics provide valuable advice regarding the treatment of PA (Kelly, 2010; Warshak, 2010; Warshak & Otis, 2010). On the other hand, flawed heuristics are also common. Because their use can cause great harm, the remainder of this section will discuss 10 flawed heuristics that should *not* be used.

A 10 doesn't marry a 1 Although there is a grain of truth to this quip, most people understand that it should not be used for serious decision-making. Astonishingly, that understanding is not universal and this pseudo-heuristic is used by some professionals. "He married her; there must be something wrong with him!" To apply this to a case of severe alienation is to assume that the targeted parent must have done something to deserve the child's rejection simply because, in the past, he or she married a spouse who later became an alienating parent. To believe that shows a poor understanding of psychopathology, as many people with serious mental disorders, including sociopaths and borderlines, can convincingly mimic normal behavior and, particularly when courting or being courted, can be deceptively charming.

He says this; she says that. The truth is probably in the middle This is the famous "He says/She says." If used as a heuristic, it is not only unreliable, it is unconscionable. Such thinking makes it impossible for a victim of false allegations to receive a fair assessment since the victim's true account is likely to be given as much weight as the victimizer's false account (possibly less weight if other biases are at work, which they often are). Those who make false allegations know this and can easily manipulate professionals who are naïve enough to employ this type of fallacious reasoning. "If I sling enough mud something will stick."

If we turn this over to an expert, he or she will figure it out This may or may not be true. Even among experts, the errors reviewed in this chapter are common. Blind faith in this dictum by those in the legal arena can be catastrophic, especially if a court "punts" and the putative expert is given too much authority with too little oversight.

How parents behave in a clinical evaluation is diagnostic Despite much research to the contrary, there is a widespread misconception that a clinical interview has high validity. In fact, research has shown striking limitations regarding information obtained through interviewing (Griffin & Tversky,

2002). Some claim, for example, that if a parent is anxious and intense in an interview, he or she is probably like that when parenting. Such thinking entails the fundamental attribution error. The key question is not whether the parent is acting that way, but rather, why. If the parent is anxious and intense owing to rejection by his or her own child, the observed affect may not be diagnostic. From a psychological perspective, that parent is having a normal fight or flight reaction. Failure to recognize that—to view the behavior as dispositional rather than situational—is a serious but very common error (see Sauber & Worenklein in this volume).

A parent who criticizes the other parent when speaking with a therapist or custody evaluator probably criticizes the other parent in front of the children This, too, entails the fundamental attribution error. Consider a targeted parent who is seeking physical custody of an alienated child. In court, that parent has the burden of proof to show that the custodial/alienating parent is unfit. There is no way to do that without criticizing the other parent. If the targeted parent does explain the reasons for seeking custody (e.g., that the child is being abused by the other parent), a professional who employs this misleading heuristic would hold that against the targeted parent—as if the criticisms were mere name-calling. That puts the targeted parent in a no-win double-bind.

Both parties always contribute This faulty heuristic implies that all cases of alignment are due to a combination of alienation and estrangement (i.e., are hybrids). It also assumes that a targeted parent must have done something to deserve or warrant rejection. This is an example of how alignment issues can be counterintuitive to those who lack adequate clinical understanding. Obviously, it is possible for both parents to be deficient (although if the targeted parent has done something to warrant rejection the term "alienation" should not be used). That does not mean that most cases are hybrid. Furthermore, even if it were true, it would be inappropriate to assume that any individual case is a hybrid. Imagine the firestorm if such a heuristic—that both parties always contribute—were still applied to victims of domestic violence or rape (which, in many parts of the world, it is).

If a child is adamant about a memory, there must be some truth to it This baseless belief flies in the face of massive research on false memories (Bruck & Ceci, 1999; Lilienfeld, Lynn, Ruscio, & Beyerstein, 2010; Loftus, 1997; Loftus & Pickrell, 1995; Schacter, 2001; Tavris & Aronson, 2007). False memories are remarkably easy to implant. They can feel every bit as real as true memories so children who have been programmed are often adamant that they "remember" events that did not happen. To quote Loftus and Pickrell (1995):

> [Research] on memory distortion leaves no doubt that memory can be altered via suggestion. People can be led to remember their past in different ways, and they can even be led to remember entire events that never actually happened to them. When these sorts of distortions occur, people are sometimes confident in their distorted or false memories, and often go on to describe the pseudo-memories in substantial detail.

Note that this excerpt refers to adults. Children, of course, are even more susceptible.

Performance in school usually indicates how a child is doing in general There is no credible evidence to support this premise. In fact, the opposite can be true because some children who live in a toxic home find a safe haven in school. There is certainly no evidence that academic or social success protects the victims of PA from lifelong dysfunction due to trust issues, intimacy issues, esteem issues, anger issues, impulse issues, boundary issues, and the like.

Children are resilient; time heals all wounds This implies that most children suffer no long-term harm from PA. That is dangerously incorrect. For one thing, as illustrated by the literature on post-traumatic stress disorder, time does not heal all wounds—even in adults. In addition, it fails to account for severity. Naturally, children who sustain only mild alienation may experience only mild long-term effects. By contrast, it is well documented that those who suffer from severe alienation can suffer severe long-term effects (Baker, 2007). It also represents a striking example of the ecological fallacy. At most, the statement is true of some children in the general population. One cannot use such group data to conclude that any individual child is resilient. Anyone who doubts this need only recall that suicide is a leading cause of death among adolescents (Nock et al., 2008). Furthermore, many alienating parents have BPD, and the children of borderline parents have a significantly increased risk of developing BPD themselves (Stepp, Whalen, Pilkonis, Hipwell, & Levine, 2012). Since BPD is associated with up to a 10% lifetime risk of suicide, it should be clear that this flawed heuristic entails a potentially life-threatening clinical error.

When a man seeks full custody, it is because he wants power and control This is Paleolithic logic. While it is reasonable to question whether anyone who seeks custody might be doing it for the wrong reasons it is neither fair nor ethical nor accurate to assume that, especially based on gender.

Clinicians are sometimes told: "Trust your gut." That, of course, means to trust one's intuition. While there are times when that is good advice, it can lead to bad judgments when intuition is not coupled with proper analytical reasoning. That is particularly important for clinicians who manage pathological alignment because, as discussed earlier, such cases can be highly counterintuitive. For that reason, the next section will further explore the respective roles of intuition and analytical reasoning in clinical practice.

The Dual Process Theory of Reasoning

Human thought falls on a continuum from intuitive to analytical (Hamm, 1988). This understanding is now codified as dual process theory, which has recently emerged as the dominant theory of human cognition (Croskerry, 2009a, 2009b; Croskerry & Norman, 2011; Evans, 2008, 2010; Pelaccia, Tardif, Triby, & Charlin, 2011). It provides a powerful new tool for understanding clinical problem-solving and, at least in theory, preventing clinical errors.

The theory posits that, in effect, the human brain has two distinct "processors"—one intuitive, one analytical. Each has a different "personality," with different strengths and weaknesses. Each interacts with and influences the other. And each is essential to competent clinical practice.

The purpose of this section is threefold: (1) to present an overview of this influential new theory, (2) to explain its relevance to clinicians who deal with child alignment issues, and (3) to illustrate how it can be used to improve metacognition.

System 1 and System 2

Current terminology refers to the two systems as System 1 and System 2. System 1 operates at an unconscious level. Relying on cognitive heuristics, it is responsible for intuition. It is fast but unreliable. It relies on pattern recognition and stereotyping—not logic. It is impulsive and prone to emotional reasoning. It has an inborn component and a learned component. The learned component handles certain aspects of expert reasoning, namely those that, through repetition, are learned so well they become automatic.

System 2 operates at a conscious level. Almost entirely learned, it is responsible for analytical thought. It is rule-based and logical. It is relatively resistant to emotional influences, makes few errors, and is quite reliable (though its performance can be impaired by stress or fatigue). System 2 has two roles: one is to handle analytical tasks, the other is to monitor System 1 and correct any errors (i.e., to perform a rational override). System 2 is lazy, however, and may not bother to correct System 1 unless it is employed consciously and deliberately. It might seem that System 2 is superior to System 1 but that is not the case. Each is skilled at different things. Both are necessary for optimal reasoning.

Relevance to Child Alignment Issues

Consider a case of child alignment that has been referred to a custody evaluator. First—unconsciously—the evaluator would begin by deploying System 1 for preliminary data gathering, initial hypothesis generation, and pattern recognition. Next—consciously—the evaluator would deploy System 2 for additional data gathering, data analysis, hypothesis testing, logical inference, probability assessments, and other analytical tasks. If there is conflicting evidence, for instance, if each parent is telling a different story (which is usually the case), System 2 would be required for logical analysis. Note that System 1 is most appropriate for hypothesis generation; System 2 is generally required for hypothesis confirmation (Elstein & Schwarz, 2002). Simple cases can often, but not always, be diagnosed by System 1 pattern recognition. Complex cases require System 2 as well.

Bayes' Rule

Bayes' rule, also known as Bayes' theorem, is a simple mathematical equation that defines the relationship between a hypothesis and the evidence for that hypothesis. It governs conditional probability—the probability of one thing given another thing—and dictates how to combine and integrate new evidence to update one's belief in a hypothesis. Clinically, the hypothesis is often a possible diagnosis and the evidence is often a clinical finding. Each piece of clinical information should be combined in accordance with Bayes' rule. Because it is a mathematical equation, Bayes' rule implies that clinicians who have the same information should reach the same conclusions (Elstein & Schwarz, 2002).

Suppose one needs to determine whether a child is alienated. The usual approach would be to interview the parties, note various findings, and use intuition to make a diagnosis. The problem with that approach is that intuition can be unreliable, and most people (including clinicians) are poor statistical thinkers and do not assess probabilities well (Kahneman, 2011; Tversky & Kahneman, 1971). A better approach is to use Bayes' rule to determine the probabilities. This requires clinicians to understand that each clinical finding is, in effect, a diagnostic "test" much like a blood test or an X-ray. It also requires clinicians to assess the accuracy of each finding. That is done by estimating the sensitivity and specificity of each piece of evidence.[2] Fortunately, great precision is not required. Few physicians know the precise sensitivity or specificity of most tests but they do know the general range (e.g., very poor, poor, fair, good, or excellent). For clinical purposes, that is usually sufficient.

Additionally, and critically, Bayes' rule requires clinicians to estimate the prior probability of the condition. As previously noted, failure to do so is known as base rate neglect, a serious clinical error. Prior probability is determined or estimated by taking into account everything that is already known before considering any new evidence. Without all three parameters—sensitivity, specificity, and prior probability—it is impossible to make proper use of *any* clinical finding. With those parameters, one can calculate what is known as the post-test or posterior probability. Although the calculations are simple they are beyond the scope of this chapter but have been published elsewhere (Miller, in press).

Case Presentation

You have been asked to evaluate a 14-year-old boy who is strongly aligned with his father and overtly hostile toward his mother. There are no allegations of abuse or neglect. According to the father, the boy simply wants no contact with his mother.

You have already interviewed both parents. The father seemed credible. He was poised and articulate. The mother had some negatives. She was anxious and defensive. She accused the father of "brainwashing" the boy. Your intuition tells you the mother has weak parenting skills and you believe that is why the boy rejected her. Indeed, you believe the probability of estrangement is about 95% and the probability of alienation is only 5%.

However, in a 2-hour interview, you find that the boy meets all five of the criteria for PA that appear in Table 2.3 (for C4, the child meets C4-A, not

Table 2.3 Alienation criteria for the evaluation of a strongly aligned child

Criterion		*Description*
C1		The child manifests unreasonable negative beliefs, feelings, and/or behaviors about the rejected parent, such as anger, hostility, hatred and/or fear, that are significantly disproportionate to the child's actual experience with that parent *and* there is a consistent pattern of denigration for which the child provides only weak, trivial, frivolous, and/or absurd reasons.
C2		The child expresses views about the parents that suggest pathological splitting, such as a marked lack of ambivalence and/or reflexive support for the favored parent in almost any conflict or discussion.
C3		The child engages in cruel or unkind treatment of the rejected parent *and* there is little or no expression of guilt or remorse regarding that mistreatment.
C4		The child's use of language suggests that the child's opinions have been unduly influenced by the favored parent, as evidenced by the choice of words, syntax, or other parameters.
	Either	
	C4-A	The child expresses opinions, relates incidents, or otherwise criticizes the unfavored parent in a way that is either age-inappropriate or implausible and that closely resembles the beliefs and attitudes of the favored parent.
	Or	
	C4-B	*In addition to meeting C4-A,* the child, without prompting by the evaluator or anyone else, volunteers or spontaneously claims that he or she is expressing his or her own negative views or feelings about the rejected parent and has not been influenced by anyone else.
C5		Through actions or language, the child expresses either animosity toward, or rejection of, the friends and/or extended family of the unfavored parent *and* the child had a good prior relationship with those individuals.

C4-B). These criteria have been modified from those described by Gardner, Kelly & Johnston, and others (Gardner, 1999; Kelly & Johnston, 2001).

Before interviewing the boy, you believed the probability of PA was only 5%. Now that he meets these five criteria what is your updated belief?

Case Discussion

To use Bayes' rule, one must assess the accuracy of each criterion. In practice, the most common way to express accuracy is through sensitivity and specificity. For the sake of discussion, assume the sensitivities and specificities in Table 2.4.

It is important to note that since C1 contains some essential features of PA (it is a *sine qua non*) one cannot use this model unless the child meets C1. It also serves to screen out so-called hybrid cases.[4]

Table 2.5 presents the results using Bayes' theorem. It provides the probability of PA for a child who sequentially meets all five criteria (using C4-A, which is less powerful than C4-B).[5] The posterior probabilities do not have to be

Table 2.4 Estimated sensitivities and specificities of the criteria for children

Criterion	*Sensitivity (%)*	*Specificity (%)*
C1	94	94
C2	80	85
C3	80	85
C4-A	80	85
C4-B	40	95
C5	60	75

These assumptions are based on expert input and are intended to be conservative (i.e., they are considerately lower than the mean estimates by a group of more than 20 experts and are thus weighted against PA [Miller, in press]).[3]

Table 2.5 Posterior probabilities of child alienation using conservative assumptions and sequential calculations

Criterion	*Posterior probabilities of child alienation for each criterion for various prior probabilities (%)*				
	Prior probability 5%	*Prior probability 10%*	*Prior probability 25%*	*Prior probability 50%*	*Prior probability 75%*
C1	45.19	63.51	83.93	94.00	97.92
C2	81.47	90.27	96.53	98.82	99.60
C3	95.91	98.02	99.33	99.78	99.92
C4-A	99.21	99.62	99.87	99.96	99.98
C5	99.67	99.84	99.95	99.98	99.99

The decimal places are helpful only for higher prior probabilities. For instance, it is useful to distinguish between 99.98% and 99.99% because rounding the latter to 100% would be misleading. The use of decimal places does not imply clinical precision to those decimal places.

calculated sequentially (they can be done in any order) but are presented sequentially to simplify the illustration. To provide perspective, the table includes calculations for prior probabilities of 5%, 10%, 25%, 50%, and 75%. As mentioned previously, the calculations have been published elsewhere.

As these figures illustrate, even with a prior probability of only 5%—an extremely skeptical prior probability (meaning heavily weighted against the hypothesis)—if a child meets all five criteria the posterior probability of PA is greater than 99%. The other columns are equally informative.

For most people, including most experts, these results are extremely counterintuitive and may be difficult to accept. Mathematically, however, they are irrefutable. If one accepts the assumptions regarding accuracy then one *must* accept the conclusions regarding probability. A similar approach should be taken when interviewing the parents, evaluating collateral source information, and so on. When considering the total clinical picture, clinicians should estimate the accuracy of each piece of evidence and combine that evidence using Bayes' rule.

That is not controversial. The failure by many clinicians to apply proper Bayesian methods to clinical problems has been noted by some of the most prominent psychologists of modern times, including Paul Meehl (Meehl & Rosen, 1955), Arthur Elstein (Balla, Iansek, & Elstein, 1985), Scott Lilienfeld (Lilienfeld, 2011), Daniel Kahneman (Kahneman, 2011), and Amos Tversky (Tversky & Kahneman, 1982). It runs rampant through every clinical discipline and is a major problem in the diagnosis and treatment of child alignment.

Analysis of the Clinical Vignette

Obviously, the therapy did not go well. That should not be surprising because the therapist, however well-intentioned, made a multitude of mistakes. While space does not permit a detailed discussion, here are some examples.

Biases The therapist displayed all 10 cognitive biases described in this chapter. Five of the most egregious were: representativeness errors (stereotyping); anchoring errors; confirmation bias; framing errors; and fundamental attribution errors.

Violations of clinical axioms The therapist violated each and every clinical axiom in this chapter. Five of the most serious violations were: failure to consider the total clinical picture; failure to consider the natural history of the condition; failure to properly consider severity; failure to set proper treatment priorities; and failure to treat the underlying condition(s).

The last example is particularly instructive. The mother did not merely badmouth the father; she told the child the father threatened to kill them. Common sense dictates that no amount of competent parenting by the father would reverse that type of malignant programming—particularly since the child lived with the mother. And yet, rather than focusing on the mother's behavior, the therapist proposed to work on the father's parenting skills. Meanwhile, the child continued to believe the father had abused the mother. Seen in that light, the treatment plan was not only inadequate, it was dangerous.

Errors in reasoning There were errors in logic, probability, and general reasoning including:

1. Failure to properly employ deductive logic. For instance, the mother falsely told the child the father threatened to kill them. That was severe emotional abuse. Severe emotional abuse is severe child abuse. Therefore, the mother had engaged in severe child abuse. And yet, the therapist focused on the child's relationship with the father.
2. Failure to properly use inductive logic. For instance, since the mother had abused the child in the past, and since the mother continued to abuse the child in the present, there was a high probability that, without effective intervention, the mother would continue to abuse the child in the future.

3. Failure to make appropriate use of circumstantial evidence.
4. Overreliance on intuitive/emotional reasoning.
5. Underuse of analytical/rational reasoning.

Other errors Other instructive errors include:

1. Inadequate assessment of the child's psychological and emotional state. Based on only two pieces of information—the child's cheerful demeanor and grades in school—the therapist concluded that, except for her relationship with the father, the child was "doing well." That assessment should not have been based on such meager information. Children who live in a toxic home often find a "safe haven" in school.
2. Enabling the alienating parent. The treatment plan was a tremendous "victory" for the mother. It assured that the child would have minimal contact with the father; that contact would be confined to the therapist's office; and that the mother could continue to alienate the child. The net result was to empower and embolden both the mother and the child to act out against the father. The proper approach would have been for the therapist to engage in non-punitive limit-setting.
3. Use of inappropriate techniques. The therapist's use of "mirroring, validating, and empathizing" was ill-advised. It is not appropriate to ask a parent who has been the victim of false allegations to mirror and validate a child's delusions regarding those allegations. This is an example of how a technique that is helpful in one setting (couples counseling) can be harmful in another setting (severe PA).
4. Ineffective use of cognitive dissonance. The therapist expected the child to have positive experiences with the father that would be dissonant with her previous low opinion of him. That can be a useful technique but it can also backfire. For one thing, it assumes that future experiences will be positive. In this case, the experiences were not positive. For another thing, there are several ways to reduce dissonance. One is to change one's beliefs. That is what the therapist hoped for. Another is to reject the information and defend those beliefs. That is what actually happened. Therapists who use cognitive dissonance must do so with great care and skill.
5. Inadequate treatment. To provide only one example, weekly 45-minute sessions were grossly inadequate.

The above comments are not comprehensive. Astute readers will recognize numerous other errors.

Conclusion

This chapter has presented some concepts, principles, and techniques that may be useful to clinicians who deal with severe child alignment. To briefly summarize:

- In recent years there has been a revolution in the field of clinical reasoning and decision-making. One advance has been a better understanding of heuristics and biases. This is reflected in dual process theory, which focuses on the relative roles of intuitive and analytical thinking.
- There has been a shift toward evidence-based practice. It is unacceptable for clinicians to employ unscientific methods that produce suboptimal outcomes.
- There is greater awareness of the need to employ Bayesian principles. Clinicians who violate Bayes' rule often make inaccurate judgments.
- Clinicians must engage in metacognition—they must think about thinking.

In expert hands, the methods in this chapter can be powerful tools for dealing with alienation, estrangement, and related problems. They can also be applied to other clinical situations.

Notes

1 This, incidentally, represents a misuse of the word "alienation." By definition, if the rejected parent played the more influential role then the primary problem is estrangement, not alienation.

2 Sensitivity refers to how accurate a test (or finding) is at detecting patients who actually have a condition. It is the true positive rate. Specificity refers to how accurate a test is at detecting patients who do not have the condition. It is the true negative rate. (Specificity is the inverse of the false positive rate which equals 100 minus specificity.)

3 These estimates were derived from a review of the clinical literature, a survey of over 20 mental health professionals with extensive experience in the area of child alienation and estrangement, and other expert input. For each criterion, the estimates are considerably lower than the mean and close to or lower than the lowest estimates from any expert. For C1, the mean sensitivity and specificity were 96% and 95%, respectively. However, though considered plausible, they have not been validated in a clinical trial and must therefore be considered provisional. A clinical trial to further validate them is in progress. For now, they are offered only as an illustration of how to apply Bayesian reasoning to clinical problem solving.

4 Through its stringent requirements, C1 eliminates the vast majority of cases in which estrangement is playing a clinically significant or causative role. For a hybrid to slip through the C1 filter the estrangement component would have to be both mild and minor. Otherwise, the rejected parent's conduct would have to be severe enough to warrant strong rejection yet mild enough that the child cannot provide a plausible explanation for the rejection. In the absence of undue influence from the favored parent, that combination is neither likely nor common.

Since all parents have flaws, one can always find something wrong with a rejected parent. Advocates of the hybrid hypothesis tend to neglect the relative contribution of each component (thus violating axioms 1, 7, 8, and possibly 12). They tend to call the case a "hybrid" even if the rejected parent has played only a minor role (which is a form of severity neglect). Also, they sometimes misuse the word "alienation" which, by definition, cannot be used if there is clinically significant abuse or neglect. That said, this model provides for a degree of mild estrangement in that each of the criteria has a significant false positive rate (equal to 100 minus specificity). Similarly, it provides for the possibility that a rejected parent might have suboptimal parenting skills or that a child might be biologically vulnerable.

This model is not intended to take the place of clinical judgment. Rather, it is intended to inform clinical judgment. When considering the possibility of a true hybrid, clinicians must consider the total clinical picture.

5 Mathematically, the combined sensitivity and specificity of C4-A is only two-thirds as powerful as that of C4-B. For those familiar with Bayesian methodology, the former has a positive likelihood ratio (true positives/false positives) of 5.3, the latter of 8.0.

References

American Academy of Child & Adolescent Psychiatry. (2011). Practice parameter for child and adolescent forensic evaluations. *Journal of the American Academy of Child and Adolescent Psychiatry, 50(12)*, 1299–1312.

Baker, A. J. L. (2007). *Adult children of parental alienation syndrome: Breaking the ties that bind.* New York: W. W. Norton.

Baker, T. B., McFall, R. M., & Shoham, V. (2009). Current status and future prospects of clinical psychology: Toward a scientifically principled approach to mental and behavioral health care. *Psychological Science in the Public Interest, 9(2)*, 67–103.

Balla, J., Iansek, R., & Elstein, A. S. (1985). Bayesian diagnosis in presence of pre-existing disease. *Lancet, 325(8424)*, 326–329.

Begley, S. (2009). Ignoring the evidence: Why do psychologists reject science? *Newsweek* (October 2, 2009).

Berner, E. S., & Graber, M. L. (2008). Overconfidence as a cause of diagnostic error in medicine. *American Journal of Medicine, 121(5 Suppl.)*, S2–S23.

Borak, J., & Veilleux, S. (1982). Errors of intuitive logic among physicians. *Social Science and Medicine, 16(22)*, 1939–1943.

Bruck, M., & Ceci, S. J. (1999). The suggestibility of children's memory. *Annual Review of Psychology, 50(1)*, 419.

Clawar, S. S., & Rivlin, B. V. (1991). *Children held hostage: Dealing with programmed and brainwashed children.* Chicago: American Bar Association.

Croskerry, P. (2009a). Clinical cognition and diagnostic error: Applications of a dual process model of reasoning. *Advances in Health Sciences Education: Theory and Practice, 14(Suppl. 1)*, 27–35.

Croskerry, P. (2009b). A universal model of diagnostic reasoning. *Academic Medicine, 84(8)*, 1022–1028.

Croskerry, P., & Nimmo, G. R. (2011). Better clinical decision making and reducing diagnostic error. *Journal of the Royal College of Physicians of Edinburgh, 41(2)*, 155–162.

Croskerry, P., & Norman, G. (2008). Overconfidence in clinical decision making. *American Journal of Medicine, 121(5 Suppl.)*, S24–S29.

Darnall, D. (1998). *Divorce casualties: Protecting your children from parental alienation.* Dallas, TX: Taylor.

Dawes, R. M., Faust, D., & Meehl, P. E. (2002). Clinical versus actuarial judgment. In T. Gilovich, D. Griffin, & D. Kahneman (Eds.), *Heuristics and Biases: The Psychology of Intuitive Judgment* (pp. 716–729). Cambridge, UK: Cambridge University Press.

Dawson, N. V., Connors, A. F., Speroff, T., Kemka, A., Shaw, P., & Arkes, H. R. (1993). Hemodynamic assessment in managing the critically ill. *Medical Decision Making, 13(3)*, 258–266.

Elstein, A. S. (1976). Clinical judgment: Psychological research and medical practice. *Science, 194(4266)*, 696–700.

Elstein, A. S. (2009). Thinking about diagnostic thinking: A 30-year perspective. *Advances in Health Sciences Education: Theory and Practice, 14(Suppl. 1)*, 7–18.

Elstein, A. S., & Bordage, G. (1988). Psychology of clinical reasoning. In J. Dowie, & A. Elstein (Eds.), *Professional judgment: A reader in clinical decision making* (pp. 109–129). New York: Cambridge University Press.

Elstein, A. S., & Schwarz, A. (2002). Clinical problem solving and diagnostic decision making: Selective review of the cognitive literature. *BMJ, 324(7339)*, 729–732.

Epley, N., & Gilovich, T. (2006). The anchoring-and-adjustment heuristic: Why the adjustments are insufficient. *Psychological Science, 17(4)*, 311–318.

Eva, K. W. (2005). What every teacher needs to know about clinical reasoning. *Medical Education, 39(1)*, 98–106.

Eva, K. W., & Cunnington, J. P. W. (2006). The difficulty with experience: Does practice increase susceptibility to premature closure? *Journal of Continuing Education in the Health Professions, 26(3)*, 192–198.

Evans, J. S. B. T. (2008). Dual-processing accounts of reasoning, judgment, and social cognition. *Annual Review of Psychology, 59(1)*, 255–278.

Evans, J. S. B. T. (2010). Intuition and reasoning: A dual-process perspective. *Psychological Inquiry, 21(4)*, 313–326.

Evidence-Based Medicine Working Group. (1992). Evidence-based medicine. *Journal of the American Medical Association, 268(17)*, 2420–2425.

Fidler, B. J., & Bala, N. (2010). Children resisting postseparation contact with a parent: Concepts, controversies, and conundrums. *Family Court Review, 48(1)*, 10–47.

Fiedler, K., Walther, E., Freytag, P., & Nickel, S. (2003). Inductive reasoning and judgment interference: Experiments on Simpson's paradox. *Personality and Social Psychology Bulletin, 29(1)*, 14–27.

Forgas, J. P. (1998). On being happy and mistaken: Mood effects on the fundamental attribution error. *Journal of Personality and Social Psychology, 75(2)*, 318–331.

Friedlander, S., & Walters, M. G. (2010). When a child rejects a parent: Tailoring the intervention to fit the problem. *Family Court Review, 48(1)*, 98–111.

Friedman, C. P., Gatti, G. G., Franz, T. M., Murphy, G. C., Wolf, F. M., Heckerling, P. S., Fine. P. L., Miller, T. M., & Elstein, A. S. (2005). Do physicians know when their diagnoses are correct? *Journal of General Internal Medicine, 20(4)*, 334–339.

Gardner, R. A. (1999). Differentiating between parental alienation syndrome and bona fide abuse-neglect. *American Journal of Family Therapy, 27(2)*, 97–107.

Graber, M., Franklin, N., & Gordon, R. (2005). Diagnostic error in internal medicine. *Arch Intern Med, 165(13)*, 1493–1499.

Graber, M., Gordon, R., & Franklin, N. (2002). Reducing diagnostic errors in medicine: What's the goal? *Academic Medicine, 77(10)*, 981–992.

Graber, M. L. (2008). Taking steps towards a safer future: Measures to promote timely and accurate medical diagnosis. *American Journal of Medicine, 121(5 Suppl.)*, S43–S46.

Griffin, D., & Tversky, A. (2002). The weighing of evidence in the determinants of confidence. In T. Gilovich, D. Griffin, & D. Kahneman (Eds.), *Heuristics and biases: The psychology of intuitive judgment* (pp. 230–249). Cambridge, UK: Cambridge University Press.

Grove, W. M., & Lloyd, M. (2006). Meehl's contribution to clinical versus statistical prediction. *Journal of Abnormal Psychology, 115(2)*, 192–194.

Grove, W. M., & Meehl, P. E. (1996). Comparative efficiency of informal (subjective, impressionistic) and formal (mechanical, algorithmic) prediction procedures: The clinical–statistical controversy. *Psychology, Public Policy, and Law, 2(2)*, 293–323.

Hall, G. H. (1967). The clinical application of Bayes' theorem. *Lancet, 290(7515)*, 555–557.

Hallinan, J. T. (2009). *Why we make mistakes.* New York: Broadway Books/Random House.

Hamm, R. M. (1988). Clinical intuition and clinical analysis: Expertise and the cognitive continuum. In J. Dowie, & A.Elstein, (Eds.), *Professional judgment: A reader in clinical decision making* (pp. 78–105). New York: Cambridge University Press.

Hendrix, H. (2008). *Getting the love you want: A guide for couples.* New York: Henry Holt and Company.

Hunsley, J., Lee, C.M., & Wood, J.M. (2003). Controversial and questionable assessment techniques. In S. O. Lilienfeld, S. J. Lynn, & J. M. Lohr (Eds.), *Science and Pseudoscience in Clinical Psychology* (pp. 39–76). New York: Guilford Press.

Johnston, J. R. (2003). Parental alignments and rejection: An empirical study of alienation in children of divorce. *Journal of the American Academy of Psychiatry and the Law Online, 31(2)*, 158–170.

Kahneman, D. (2011). *Thinking fast and slow.* New York: Farrar, Straus and Giroux.

Kahneman, D., & Frederick, S. (2002). Representativeness revisited: Attribute substitution in intuitive judgment. In T. Gilovich, D. Griffin, & D.Kahneman, (Eds.), *Heuristics and biases: The psychology of intuitive judgment* (pp. 49–81). Cambridge, UK: Cambridge University Press.

Kahneman, D., & Tversky, A. (1972). Subjective probability: A judgment of representativeness. *Cognitive Psychology, 3(3)*, 430–454.

Kassirer, J., Wong, J., & Kopelman, R. (2010). *Learning clinical reasoning* (2nd ed.). Baltimore: Lippincott, Williams & Wilkins.

Kassirer, J. P. (1989). Diagnostic reasoning. *Annals of Internal Medicine, 110(11)*, 893–900.

Kelly, J. B. (2010). Commentary on "Family bridges: Using insights from social science to reconnect parents and alienated children (Warshak, 2010)." *Family Court Review, 48(1)*, 81–90.

Kelly, J. B., & Johnston, J. R. (2001). The alienated child: A reformulation of parental alienation syndrome. *Family Court Review, 39(3)*, 249–266.

Klosko, J., & Young, J. (2004). Cognitive therapy of borderline personality disorder. In R. L. Leahy (Ed.), *Contemporary cognitive therapy: Theory, research, and practice* (pp. 269–298). New York: Guilford Press.

Ko, D. T., Mamdani, M., & Alter, D. A. (2004). Lipid-lowering therapy with statins in high-risk elderly patients: The treatment-risk paradox. *JAMA: The Journal of the American Medical Association, 291(15)*, 1864–1870.

Lilienfeld, S. O. (2011). Distinguishing scientific from pseudoscientific psychotherapies: Evaluating the role of theoretical plausibility, with a little help from Reverend Bayes. *Clinical Psychology: Science and Practice, 18(2)*, 105–112.

Lilienfeld, S. O., Lynn, S. J., Ruscio, J., & Beyerstein, B. L. (2010). A remembrance of things past: Myths about memory. In S. O. Lilienfeld, S. J. Lynn, J. Ruscio, & B.L. Beyerstein (Eds.), *50 great myths of popular psychology: Shattering widespread misconceptions about human behavior.* UK: Wiley-Blackwell.

Linehan, M. M. (1993). *Cognitive-behavioral treatment of borderline personality disorder.* New York: Guilford Press.

Linehan, M. M., Comtois, K. A., Murray, A. M., Brown, M. Z., Gallop, R. J., Heard, H. L., & Lindenboim, N. (2006). Two-year randomized controlled trial and follow-up of dialectical behavior therapy vs therapy by experts for suicidal behaviors and borderline personality disorder. *Archives of General Psychiatry, 63(7),* 757–766.

Loftus, E. (1997). Creating false memories. *Scientific American, 277(3),* 70.

Loftus, E., & Pickrell, J. (1995). The formation of false memories. *Psychiatric Annals, 25(12),* 720–725.

Macfie, J. (2009). Development in children and adolescents whose mothers have borderline personality disorder. *Child Development Perspectives, 3(1),* 66–71.

Mamede, S., van Gog, T., van den Berge, K., Rikers, R. M. J. P., van Saase, J. L. C. M., van Guldener, C., & Schmidt, H. G. (2010). Effect of availability bias and reflective reasoning on diagnostic accuracy among internal medicine residents. *JAMA: The Journal of the American Medical Association, 304(11),* 1198–1203.

Mark, D. B., & Wong, J.B. (2012). Decision-making in clinical medicine. In D. L. Longo, A. S. Fauci, D. L. Kasper, S. L. Hauser, J. L. Jameson, & J. Loscalzo (Eds.), *Harrison's Principles of Internal Medicine* (18th ed.). New York: McGraw-Hill.

McDonald, C. J. (1996). Medical heuristics: The silent adjudicators of clinical practice. *Annals of Internal Medicine, 124,* 56–62.

Meehl, P. E. (1954). *Clinical versus statistical prediction: A theoretical analysis and review of the evidence.* Minneapolis, MN, US: University of Minnesota Press.

Meehl, P. E., & Rosen, A. (1955). Antecedent probability and the efficiency of psychometric signs, patterns, or cutting scores. *Psychological Bulletin, 52(3),* 194–216.

Mendel, R., Traut-Mattausch, E., Jonas, E., Leucht, S., Kane, J. M., Maino, K., Kissling, W., & Hamann, J. (2011). Confirmation bias: Why psychiatrists stick to wrong preliminary diagnoses. *Psychological Medicine, 41(12),* 2651–2659.

Miller, G. A. (1994). The magical number seven, plus or minus two: Some limits on our capacity for processing information. *Psychological Review, 101(2),* 343–352.

Miller, S. G. (in press). *Clinical use of Bayes' theorem for the diagnosis of parental alienation.*

Minino, A., Murphy, S., Xu, J., & Kochanek, K. (2011). Deaths: Final Data for 2008. *National Vital Statistics Reports.* 59*(10),* 5.

Mischel, W. (2009). Connecting clinical practice to scientific progress. *Psychological Science in the Public Interest, 9(2),* i–ii.

Mossman, D. (2000). The meaning of malingering data: Further applications of Bayes' theorem. *Behavioral Sciences and the Law, 18,* 761–779.

Neff, R., & Cooper, K. (2004). Parental conflict resolution. *Family Court Review, 42(1),* 99–114.

Nock, M. K., Borges, G., Bromet, E. J., Cha, C. B., Kessler, R. C., & Lee, S. (2008). Suicide and suicidal behavior. *Epidemiologic Reviews, 30(1),* 133–154.

Norman, G. (2005). Research in clinical reasoning: Past history and current trends. *Medical Education, 39(4),* 418–427.

Norman, G. R., & Eva, K. W. (2010). Diagnostic error and clinical reasoning. *Medical Education, 44(1),* 94–100.

Nurcombe, B. (2012). Clinician decision making in psychiatry. In M. H. Ebert, P. T. Loosen, B. Nurcombe, & J.F. Leckman (Eds.), *Current Diagnosis and Treatment: Psychiatry* (2nd Ed.). New York: McGraw-Hill.

Paris, J. (2010). Effectiveness of different psychotherapy approaches in the treatment of borderline personality disorder. *Current Psychiatry Reports, 12(1),* 56–60.

Paris, J., Nowlis, D., & Brown, R. (1988). Developmental factors in the outcome of borderline personality disorder. *Comprehensive Psychiatry, 29(2)*, 147–150.

Pelaccia, T., Tardif, J., Triby, E., & Charlin, B. (2011). An analysis of clinical reasoning through a recent and comprehensive approach: The dual-process theory. *Medical Education Online, 16*, doi: 10.3402/meo.v16i0.5890.

Piantadosi, S., Byar, D. P., Green, S. B. (1988). The ecological fallacy. *American Journal of Epidemiology, 127(5)*, 893–904.

Robinson, W. S. (1950). Ecological correlations and the behavior of individuals. *American Sociological Review, 15(3)*, 351–357.

Ross, L. (1977). The intuitive psychologist and his shortcoming: Distortions in the attribution process. In L. Berkowitz (Ed.), *Advances in experimental social psychology* (pp. 173–220). New York: Academic Press.

Ross, L., & Anderson, C. A. (1982). Shortcomings in the attribution process: On the origins and maintenance of erroneous social assessments. In D. Kahneman, P. Slovic & A. Tversky (Eds.), *Judgment under uncertainty: Heuristics and biases* (pp. 129–152). Cambridge, UK: Cambridge University Press.

Schacter, D. L. (2001). *The seven sins of memory: How the mind forgets and remembers.* Boston: Houghton Mifflin.

Slovic, P., Finucane, M., Peters, E., & MacGregor, D. G. (2002). The affect heuristic. In T. Gilovich, D. Griffin, & D. Kahneman (Eds.), *Heuristics and biases: The psychology of intuitive judgment* (pp. 397–420). Cambridge, UK: Cambridge University Press.

Soloff, P., & Chiappetta, L. (2012). Subtyping borderline personality disorder by suicidal behavior. *Journal of Personality Disorders, 26(3)*, 468–480.

Stepp, S. (2012). Development of borderline personality disorder in adolescence and young adulthood: Introduction to the special section. *Journal of Abnormal Child Psychology, 40(1)*, 1–5.

Stepp, S., Whalen, D., Pilkonis, P., Hipwell, A., & Levine, M. (2012). Children of mothers with borderline personality disorder: Identifying parenting behaviors as potential targets for intervention. *Personality Disorders: Theory, Research, and Treatment, 3(1)*, 76–91.

Sullivan, M. J., & Kelly, J. B. (2001). Legal and psychological management of cases with an alienated child. *Family Court Review, 39(3)*, 299–315.

Tavris, C. (2003). The widening scientist-practitioner gap. In S. O. Lilienfeld, S. J. Lynn, & J. M. Lohr (Eds.), *Science and pseudoscience in clinical psychology* (pp. ix–xviii). New York: Guilford Press.

Tavris, C., & Aronson, E. (2007). *Mistakes were made (but not by me): Why we justify foolish beliefs, bad decisions, and hurtful acts.* Orlando, FL: Houghton Mifflin Harcourt.

Tversky, A., & Kahneman, D. (1971). Belief in the law of small numbers. *Psychological Bulletin, 76(2)*, 105–110.

Tversky, A., & Kahneman, D. (1973). Availability: A heuristic for judging frequency and probability. *Cognitive Psychology, 5(2)*, 207–232.

Tversky, A., & Kahneman, D. (1974). Judgment under uncertainty: Heuristics and biases. *Science, 185(4157)*, 1124–1131.

Tversky, A., & Kahneman, D. (1981). The framing of decisions and the psychology of choice. *Science, 211*, 453–458.

Tversky, A., & Kahneman, D. (1982). Evidential impact of base rates. In D. Kahneman, P. Slovic & A. Tversky (Eds.), *Judgment under uncertainty: Heuristics and biases* (pp. 153–160). Cambridege, UK: Cambridge University Press.

Warshak, R. A. (2001). Current controversies regarding parental alienation syndrome. *American Journal of Forensic Psychology, 19(3)*, 29–59.
Warshak, R. A. (2010). Family bridges: using insights from social science to reconnect parents and alienated children. *Family Court Review, 48(1)*, 48–80.
Warshak, R. A., & Otis, M. R. (2010). Helping alienated children with family bridges: practice, research, and the pursuit of "humbition". *Family Court Review, 48(1)*, 91–97.

3 Custody Evaluations in Alienation Cases

S. Richard Sauber and Abe Worenklein

Finding the Truth: "He Said/She Said"

The parents had been married for 11 years and had two sons, aged 8 and 11 years. The father was a senior salesman for a Fortune 500 company and was a very intelligent, successful, and persuasive man. He alleged among other things that the mother was neglectful as well alcohol-dependent and alienating. The mother was employed full-time in a successful Internet marketing career. She had her own set of complaints against the father, including that he had been manipulative and verbally abusive to her and their sons during their marriage and that he had continued to be so since their separation.

It was clear that a custody evaluation was required in order to resolve the disputes regarding time-sharing and childcare responsibilities. Both parties retained high-powered lawyers who each presented three names to the judge. The judge had his own favorite mental health professional who he typically appointed; but in this case, the judge decided to appoint the psychologist on the list with the most impressive credentials for specializing in alienation. The argument of parental alienation syndrome (PAS) versus abuse was presented in court, with each side accusing the other of making false allegations and attempting to alienate the boys.

The PA expert/forensic custody evaluator (CE) was brought in to conduct interviews, administer psychological tests, observe the children with each parent, review documents, interview collateral contacts, and finally submit a report to the court with recommendations. Throughout the process, the children appeared confused, apparently feeling the strain of their divided loyalties. When in the presence of each parent, the children echoed that parent's party line. Through hypothesis testing, the CE was able to rule out substance abuse of the mother, and he found the father to be abusive in his efforts to alienate the children from their mother. The evaluator determined that the children were "mildly" alienated. The CE admitted that, for some time, he himself had felt confused as to which parent to believe as each of them was so convincing in their presentations and complaints about the other. The final report was thorough and provided extensive evidence to support the findings and conclusions in order to ensure that there was no bias in the process. The results of the father–son interviews and observations were especially helpful "data," providing the most credible evidence of the father's attempts to indoctrinate the children. The CE testified at the custody hearing as to his findings, which resulted in a change from equal time sharing to the mother's assignment as primary residential custodian, with the father having standing visitation every other weekend and one afternoon a week. The father was admonished by the judge to stop alienating and abusing the children, although he did not impose sanctions, so that there were no restrictions to the father's behavior other than a non-enforceable "warning."

Introduction

Custody assessments that include allegations of abuse and alienation are very stressful, not only for the parents but also for the CE who is presented with two convincing but conflicting stories. Often, it is difficult to differentiate whether the allegations are genuine or contrived. It is imperative that the CE resist the temptation and pressure to uncritically accept the child's position, knowing that it is possible for children to be manipulated into having false ideas and holding manufactured feelings about a parent. Further, the CE needs to recognize that the targeted parent can be in a state of extreme distress and volatility as a result of the alienation and the fear of losing the children, which may be exacerbated by false accusations and from having his or her expressed concerns continually ignored. As a result, the behavior of the targeted parent should not be taken as a diagnostic indicator of the overall functioning and personality of this parent. Frequently, targeted parents have become educated consumers of the research and written resources on alienation and present to the CE conclusions regarding the alienating parent's personality style/disorder. These negative statements need to be considered in the appropriate context and not necessarily indicative of badmouthing the other parent.

The custody evaluation in cases in which PA is a potential causal factor should include an assortment of assessment instruments in order to develop an accurate and complete understanding of the functioning of the parties and their inter-relationship and family dynamics, including interviews, standardized as well as non-standardized instruments, observation, collateral contact sources for investigation, and a review of the documents offered and those not offered but requested. Clearly, each case should be carefully considered and analyzed when determining which tools to use. Generally, constructing a customized package of assessment instruments may require hours of thought and planning. Alienation cases are different than standard custody evaluations. Each allegation must be addressed and resolved, with evidence, to determine parent and child credibility to the court in order to hope to stop the alienation. Often these false allegations receive honorable mention without them being addressed as core issues and examples of the more subtle attempts of child indoctrination and programming by the alienating parent. Assessment instruments can assist the evaluator in providing some of the evidence needed.

Although there are ethical guidelines governing all custody evaluations, those involving potential alienation need to be specially crafted to ascertain whether alienation exists; and if so, to explain the dynamics and causes as part of the empirically based evaluation. The evaluator must consider all of the issues relevant to the criteria set forth in the relevant state statutes pertaining to shared parenting responsibility and the best interests of the child. In every case, it is important that the CE be court appointed, as opposed to retained by one side, in order to ensure impartiality and credibility.

Disputes sometimes erupt in court regarding the appointment of a custody examiner, with the favored parent objecting to a CE with experience in PA. This issue can become sidetracked with arguments about whether alienation exists and whether it should be classified as a syndrome. This debate is beyond the scope of this chapter and the reader is referred to *Parental Alienation, DSM 5, ICD-II* (Bernet, 2010). Like Gardner (1998) as well as Kelly and Johnston (2001) and Johnston and Roseby (1997), the position taken herein is that some children can be manipulated by a parent to unjustifiably reject the other parent whereas other children have valid reasons for their rejection. Differentiating the former (alienation) from the latter (estrangement) is a major focus of the work of a CE where children have become aligned with one parent against the other. In doing so, the evaluator must consider each factor that could explain a child's expressing dislike for and resistance to contact with a parent. In other words, the evaluator must ascertain whether alienation or realistic estrangement or bona fide abuse is the underlying cause of the family dynamic (Sauber, 2010).

In making this differential diagnosis it is important to bear in mind the pressure (internal as well as external) that may impinge upon a CE's ability to make a valid and impartial diagnosis. In particular, five factors may be present to compel a CE to conclude that the case is a hybrid (i.e., a mix of alienation and estrangement):

1. The CE may have been exposed to professional opinions that "most cases are hybrids." While this may or may not be true in general, it certainly should have no bearing on the CE's work in an individual case.

2. The favored parent may be particularly charming and persuasive about his/her victimization at the hands of the other parent and at the same time may pay lip service to wanting the children to have a good relationship with the other parent.
3. The aligned child may be very compelling, forceful, and emotional in his or her conviction about the inadequacy of one parent and the numerous excellent qualities of the other.
4. There is always some flaw in the rejected parent (who is cast as too weak/too strong, too messy/too tidy, and so forth) such that the rejection of the child might appear to be a plausible and rational response to that imperfection.
5. Concluding that a case is a hybrid may be more comfortable for the CE who is equally casting blame among the parties.
6. Concluding that a case is a hybrid may also be more comfortable with the judge, whom the CE wants to please in order to be the recipient of future referrals. In this sense, the hybrid solution is an easy way out for the CE, for whom concluding alienation is present may represent an inconvenient truth.

If the CE determines that a child has been alienated from one parent by the other, the CE must recognize that alienation is a serious form of psychological and emotional abuse having a significant impact on the alienated child throughout his or her life (Baker, 2007).

This kind of work is not for everyone. Mental health professionals wishing to enter family forensic work should consider obtaining supervised training or beginning as an assistant evaluator in these cases. Individuals lacking sufficient experience in such evaluations should have a mentor or supervisor to work with in order to avoid the "landmines" and traps set up by the alienator and attorney to compromise and undermine the evaluation. The transition from classroom to the courtroom is a complex, tension-producing, and difficult path in alienation cases and to think of these evaluations as being no more difficult than other evaluations is a mistake. One's license may be challenged through the alienator's complaints to the state regulating boards and each parent and their advocating attorney are prepared to use every legal tactic to assert the advantage to their position. Nonetheless, it is the mission of the evaluator to be the *just* presenter of the facts, offering an experienced and substantiated opinion rather than being concerned with potential complaints and defending his or her work-product from public critique and state regulators.

Components of a Custody Assessment

Document Review

A review of the documents is essential in order to learn what has happened, what is happening, and what is expected to happen. The attorneys and/or their clients select documents they believe to be essential for the evaluator's review.

This usually includes recent motions and cross-motions, transcripts from prior hearings, the original marital separation agreement (if one exists), and prior evaluations and affidavits from collateral sources, as well as video tapes and copies of correspondence between the parties. Once the evaluator has an initial understanding of the case, documents not originally submitted in the original package may be requested. It should be expected that as the evaluation proceeds, the clients and attorneys will send additional documents that were intentionally or accidentally omitted in the initial packet, such as police reports, school attendance records, pediatric information, and/or domestic violence court information forms, as well as e-mail correspondence between the parties.

The evaluator can also make a list of other information to request. Reviewing the basic documents takes place as part of the process of becoming acquainted with the case and the parties whereas the final review of the documents may not occur until late in the evaluation. For example, it may be that several police investigations and findings with child protection services were "unsubstantiated" and, therefore, they were not submitted, but reading the actual report, nonetheless, may be quite revealing and it could be requested if not originally submitted. Toward the end of the evaluation the CE may obtain this additional information, which takes on a different relevance and significance with respect to the intentional distortion of facts, who filed or called the authorities to investigate, whether there was sufficient valid information to make a determination, the cooperation level of the parties, whether the recommendations offered by the Department of Children and Families were followed or ignored, and so forth.

Parent Interviews and Assessments

Individual interviews with each parent form an important part of any custody evaluation. It should be expected that the parents have given much thought about what they want to say and how they want to express and present themselves. However, it is probably true that no matter how much planning for "impression management" the parent has engaged in, once in the examining room, the parent's emotional energy is likely to take over and can be very revealing. Conducting a psychosocial history will be useful for forming competing hypotheses. In addition, asking parents about how they provide guidance, affection, limits, and discipline to the children is a good place to start these discussions. The evaluator is cautioned not to interrupt and only to offer empathetic patience. Listening and note-taking is the role of the evaluator in this first meeting with the parents after having explained the purpose of the evaluation, the limits of the CE role, and the procedures to be followed. As time goes on, the evaluator may ask a parent pointed questions based on apparent discrepancies or gaps in his or her story. Knowing that custody evaluations in general are oriented towards parent's efforts at presenting positive impressions and covering up deficiencies, alienation examinations will be replete with deceptions, distortions, and corrupt manipulations intended to mislead even the most experienced CE.

In conducting parent interviews, some evaluators work from a prepared list of questions while others spontaneously ask questions that follow from the client's responses and the flow of the conversation based upon their training and experience. Either approach or a combination of both is acceptable, as long as the evaluator is aware of the process taking place and is flexible enough to pursue new directions that may be uncovered as part of the process. Rigid procedures that demand completion of the interview in a fixed time format can be counter-productive in alienation cases. Specific to alienation cases, as opposed to general custody evaluations, the use of standardized questionnaires such as the Ackerman variety (e.g., ASPECT or the Quickview Social History published by Pearson/PsychCorp) is ill-advised or cautioned against. While they are useful short cuts and efficient methods in obtaining information from the clients completing the questionnaires, they obscure the spontaneous value of the skillful interviewer in discerning discrepancies, listening to the way in which allegations are described, and carefully noting the confabulations of past history taking and present storytelling. There is no substitute for the observation of the "here and now" in encountering the alienating or targeted parent that cannot be derived from reading questionnaires answered by clients controlling the pencil while they contemplate how to best respond to each item presented in the booklet.

While engaged in the interview process, there are a number of themes or factors that the CE can bear in mind as potential "red flags" that alienation has occurred. Some of these have been compiled by Rohrbaugh (2008) based on research in the field (Clawar & Rivlin, 1991; Johnston & Roseby, 1997; Kelly & Johnston, 2001; Stoltz & Ney, 2002). These factors include an authoritarian or overly permissive parenting style, prior unresolved experiences of loss and separation, ineffective coping strategies (especially around loss), fear of abandonment, impaired ability to be empathic with the child and tolerate the child's separate and unique experiences and needs, and whether either parent has a new partner who is viewed as a replacement parent for the children.

The potential motivation for a parent to want the children to reject the other parent must also be noted (Baker, 2007; Clawar & Rivlin, 1991; Gardner, 1998), including the desire for revenge, self-righteousness, fear of losing the child, jealousy, and financial incentives. The CE should bear these in mind as the personality and behavior of each parent becomes revealed through the interviews and observations. While these elements may reflect a natural human response to the challenge of divorce and custody conflict, many people are able to keep them in check. People with narcissistic or sociopathic personality disorders, however, are more likely to act on these emotions, leading them to sacrifice the child's well-being and deny themselves the benefit of periodic breaks from childcare duties and the benefit of having a co-parent. They tend to believe the other parent is not only useless but actually a detriment to the children, who would be better served by no longer having that parent in their lives. Thus, an inability to contemplate the value of the other parent to the child is an alarm sounding for alienation, as that attitude sets the stage for tactics in the removal of that parent.

Although parents in a high-conflict divorce may have difficulty in identifying strengths in the other parent's contributions to the children, alienating parents in particular often will begin with a litany of complaints about the other parent's weaknesses and express great difficulty in asserting any positive traits or characteristics that they would like their child to emulate, or to justify the need for that parent to play a meaningful role in the child's life. By contrast, the targeted parent will speak in more moderated tones of their disappointment in the alienating parent's anger and malicious tactics of revenge in disproportionate magnitude to the stated source of their rage. Some targeted parents express hope for the other parent to move beyond anger and begin to co-parent in a constructive manner so that both parents can contribute to the lives of their children.

Discussion about enforcement of visitation will also be very instructive. It is relatively easy to recognize the targeted parent's plight and agony of only wanting to love and be with the children while the children are vocalizing terrible things about that parent, whom they say they hate and despise, and whom they profess to never want to see again. At the same time, the alienating parent typically has a long list of punishments and restrictions that they would like to see imposed on that parent, which would most likely result in the crippling of the rejected parent's ability to maintain or re-establish any meaningful relationship with the children. Other alienation clues include a parent claiming to be unable to enforce visitation (while managing to elicit cooperation from the children for every other aspect of their lives, including completing homework, attending school, doing chores, and so forth) and a parent claiming to support the child's decision regarding visitation (when the parent does not allow the child to make other equally important choices, such as which school to attend, whether to have vaccinations, and so forth).

It is also useful to ask a parent about their views of the other parent's parenting capacities. Although there are a variety of parenting assessment tools (e.g., the Parent–Child Relationship Inventory and the Parenting Stress Index), none of these measurement instruments specifically address the issues of alienation. Utilizing open-ended questions about parenting behavior and perceptions of the other parent can be quite helpful in obtaining insight into how each parent perceives the other parent's abilities and related personality traits. Asking about the other parent's contribution to child rearing will produce contrasting viewpoints, with the favored parent being hard-pressed to admit that the other parent actually participated in any aspect of the children's upbringing. Targeted parents, on the other hand, often describe a more mixed picture, being able to appreciate the good that the favored parent has done for the children.

Likewise, each parent should be asked about his/her strengths and weaknesses and those of the other parent. Alienating parents will be unable to identify a single strength of the other parent, while targeted parents will usually concede that the other parent loves the children while being misguided in his or her expression of that love. Asking how they would like their child to grow up, similar to and different from the other parent, can be revealing as to whether they hold rigid black/white views of the other parent or whether they can retain perspective and appreciation for that parent's positive contributions to the child. Parents who present a picture of the other parent as "all bad" and completely lacking any positive attributes are likely to present this view to the child and contribute to the alienation. A Scale for Parental Competency of the Other Parent has been developed (Sauber, 2010), which may prove useful. The parents are given the option to discuss or exchange their ratings with one another, hoping to provoke discussion, confrontation, and clarification. In one case, the favored parent was "forced" to admit on the scale that the rejected parent was "a competent parent" despite her extensive criticism of him to their children and the court.

Family History

The initial interviews with each parent should include a detailed gathering of family history. The history of the parent as an individual and as a child growing up is relevant and necessary to understand the personality, attitudes, emotional problems, priorities, and life position of that parent. A complete and detailed history of each parent sheds light onto his or her beliefs about parent–child relationships and can suggest possible mental disorders and/or agendas of the parent which need to be addressed in the evaluation process. For example, a history of abandonment may suggest the likelihood of a borderline personality disorder, leading the evaluator to administer the Inventory of Altered Self-Capacities. Perhaps a mother was sexually abused as a child and worries that her former husband may do the same to their daughter although there are no indicators that this would be the case. By considering the family history, the CE can determine if there is a foundation for boundary violations which may explain parentification (viewing the child as an extension of oneself). Obtaining a personal and family history will include inquiring about substance abuse as well as about sibling relationships, dating history, conduct and performance in school, and parent involvement and discipline, plus childhood activities and interests. All of this information will enrich the CE's understanding and appreciation of the motives and behavior of the parent, and be useful for hypothesis testing and elimination of alternative explanations.

Personality Assessments

Personality inventories provide one way of obtaining information and determining consistency in findings. Use of these instruments is recommended by both the American Psychological Association (1994) and the Association of Family and Conciliation Courts (AFCC, 2006). The evaluator needs to be aware of the psychometric properties of any instrument that is administered, including its strengths and weaknesses and the appropriate sample of individuals for whom the test is intended. Frequently, psychopathology of the alienating parent can be identified in the use of personality inventories such as the Minnesota Multiphasic Personality Inventory-2 or MMPI-2 Restructured Form, the Personality Assessment Inventory, and/or the Millon Clinical Multiaxial Inventory-III. These tests also provide an index of validity and lying, or truth and honesty, versus intentional distortion of items and presenting socially desirable responses to certain items, all of which are highlighted in the validity scales.

Cases of alienation often challenge the evaluator to be aware of "impression management," with both parents diligently presenting their side of the story in which their faults are minimized in comparison to those of the other parent. Some targeted parents are able to concede that they are not perfect parents and admit they may have to some degree caused conflicts with their children. While personality tests are not expected to directly detect or lead to conclusions related to alienation, these scales often provide useful information towards a better understanding of the parents. For example, a parent who scores high in terms of sensitivity to perceived or actual abandonment by significant others, and may rely on his or her identity as emanating from their role as a parent, may be more prone toward alienation than a parent who does not demonstrate these characteristics. However, it is imperative to ensure that the test data are not "overinterpreted" and undue reliance is not placed upon them. Ideally they are used to generate hypotheses, which then require corroboration from other sources.

Projective Tests

Projective techniques such as the Thematic Apperception Test (TAT) for storytelling, drawings, and completing sentence blanks can be useful for gaining insight into the world and family view of parents and children. However, projective assessment offers opportunity for the opposing attorney to criticize because of their lack of objective scoring and established validity. Nevertheless, their use has survived the test of time and this form of assessment can provide extremely valuable information because the "right" answer is not always easy to detect by the person being evaluated. The evaluator should devote as many hours as is necessary to carefully selecting which projective measure to use and how best to administer it, knowing that events that occur just before the administration of the test can impact the results, such as which parent is in the waiting room, who brought the child, whose house the child was residing at prior to the testing. Unique to custody evaluations are TAT-like pictures of family conflicts and courtroom settings that provide the opportunity for the parties involved to project their stories of what is happening, what led up to the situation depicted in the picture, and what will happen. Selection of different items from different sets is acceptable as long as the evaluator can defend the choices. Often these instruments offer face validity, as one child described a courtroom picture in which he said his mother was telling the judge that his father was abusive to the children. Upon inquiry, the child admitted he did not know what "abusive" meant.

Parent Feedback

The evaluator may choose to administer a consumer satisfaction scale for parents "to evaluate the evaluator" (Sauber, 2009). This should be accomplished in person on the last session prior to any reports being released, although some collateral interviews may still take place. The form may already exist or can be constructed by the evaluator. The measure should include items about the evaluator's observational and interview skills as well as rapport building with children. Should the ratings be favorable, once the report is issued and one side begins to object to the findings, the scale can be useful to indicate that the evaluation and its various components were acceptable to both parties prior to their reading the final report and its recommendations.

Interviewing Collateral Sources

A collateral contact is any person outside the immediate family who can contribute information about the family to the CE. Collaterals can be professionals involved in the case (e.g., the child's therapist, a school guidance counselor, the pediatrician) or can be friends and extended family members of the parents. It is not assumed that these sources are impartial or neutral. The AFCC (2006), in its Model Standards of Practice for Child Custody Evaluations points out that:

> Valid collateral source information is critical to a thorough evaluation … In utilizing collateral sources, evaluators shall seek information that will facilitate the confirmation or disconfirmation of hypotheses under consideration.

Gould and Martindale (2007) assert that:

> The acquisition of reliable and relevant collateral information is arguably the most important component of a child custody evaluation. Information from people who have direct observational knowledge of the parent and child in different situations may be among the most important data obtained in a child custody evaluation. (p. 106)

In cases unique to alienation, the evaluator can never second-guess the provided list of collateral contacts. Some contacts will provide reflexive and automatic support for the parent with whom they are aligned. However, others may actually reveal a surprising amount of independence of thought and opinion and offer useful insight into the family dynamic. For example, in one case an alienating mother listed her sister as a reference. When contacted by phone, she described the father as the primary parent with respect to the children's extra-curricular activities for many of the years preceding the marital separation. The sister's report was counter to the impression given by the mother and daughters, who claimed that the father had never shown any interest nor was he ever involved with his children in their after-school and community activities. The mother and daughters explained that it was his lack of interest that resulted in an absence of bond between the children and their father, justifying their refusal to ever see him again.

Ideally, every recommended collateral should be contacted. In order to make this manageable, it may be helpful to limit the time devoted to each interview. The interviews can be conducted in person or by phone. Careful questioning can bring out a benefit of almost every discussion. For example, in one case the evaluator asked the maternal grandmother why her alienating daughter called the police and filed a missing persons report and kidnapping charge against the father during his parenting time, as opposed to simply calling her former husband at his home or his office to inquire about the whereabouts of or speak to their children. The grandmother responded by asking, "Whose side are you on?" revealing the kind of tribal warfare that is consistent with alienation (Warshak, 2010). Sometimes, children can be encouraged to bring a friend with them to an interview, which can result in helpful information being revealed by someone who has close contact with the child and their family but is outside the reach of the alienating parent's programming effort. Of course, permission is required from the child's parent.

Observations of Parents and Children

It is imperative to conduct observations of the parent–child interactions, including siblings in various combinations. These can take place in the parent's home or in the CE's office. Special attention should be paid to the child's degree of comfort with each parent as well as the child's reactions, emotions, and spontaneity, all of which are extremely important for recognizing discrepancies between the child's statements during interviews and the child's actual behavior. Comparing the child's behavior when in the presence of that parent with the child's ratings about each parent can be extremely informative (e.g., by using the Scale for Children of Divorce: Parental Preferences[1]). Some alienated children claim to be terrified of the rejected parent but in that parent's presence they are provocative, rude, arrogant, and disrespectful, hardly the behavior of a frightened child. Likewise, some children who proclaim to hate a parent may actually express feelings of love, security, and playful enjoyment when alone with that parent. Without direct observation, it is easy to be misled. Particular attention should be paid to whether the child is equally compliant and respectful to each parent. If the child is pleasant and cooperative with the favored parent and rude and disrespectful with the targeted parent, the CE is able to observe what is situational (depending upon the parent in the room) and what is characteristic of the child regardless of which parent is present. Because some siblings function as "assistant alienators" (reporting to the preferred parent if a child demonstrates any affection to the rejected parent), each child should be seen alone with each parent in order to eliminate any potential undue influence of a surrogate alienator.

Child Interviews

At some point during the custody evaluation, each child over the age of 3 years should be interviewed alone. Child interviews occur after the process has been explained to the child, often in the context of a brief family orientation session. The timing of the interview, what questions to ask, and who brings the child to the office should all be given careful consideration. Being sensitive to the themes of alienation, asking opened-ended questions, and not challenging inconsistencies prematurely is essential. Asking the child to elaborate and further embellish his/her stories, sometimes to the point of absurdity, and asking the child about his or her understanding of each parent's position is a useful strategy and will assist in the diagnosis of alienation and its severity.

Children's Exposure to Parent's Alienation Behaviors

Baker and Fine (2008, and this volume) have identified 17 parental behaviors associated with alienation because they induce children to unjustifiably reject the other parent. They include: badmouthing, limiting contact, withdrawal of love/ getting angry when the child is positive towards the other parent, telling the child that the targeted parent does not love the child, forcing the child to choose/express loyalty, telling the child that the other parent is dangerous, confiding in the child about adult relationships, limiting photographs of the other parent, forcing the child to reject the other parent, cultivating dependency on the alienating parent, asking the child to spy on the other parent, telling the other parent that the child does not love him or her, referring to the other parent by his or her first name, referring to someone else as "Mom" or "Dad," having the child keep secrets from the other parent, and changing the child's name. The evaluator should keep these behaviors in mind when talking with the children about the parents.

Children's Exposure to Programming

In speaking with children, the evaluator should ascertain whether or not they have been exposed to parental programming efforts (Worenklein, 2010) by considering Rohrbaugh's suggested questions based on Clawar and Rivlin's (1991) detection factors. Some of these questions are closed-ended and may be considered too leading, and are offered for illustrative purposes in Table 3.1 as to the type of question with which to engage the children in conversation rather than as the actual question.

Children's Manifestation of the Eight Symptoms of Alienation

As noted throughout this chapter, alienation refers to cases in which a child has been manipulated by one parent to unjustifiably reject the other parent. Not all children who reject a parent, however, do so because of alienation. When a child has a valid reason to reject a parent, such as abuse, neglect, or abandonment, the term "realistic estrangement" is appropriate. As the opening vignette demonstrates, sometimes it is difficult for non-professionals and some mental health professionals to recognize whether the child's refusal to spend time

Table 3.1 Indicators of alienation that may be detected through child interviews

Indicator	*Question*	*Child's answer that reflects alienation*
Forbidden to love both parents	"Do you feel free in your heart to love both of your parents?" "Is there anything that you are really afraid of that could happen because of the divorce?"	"Dad said that if I go to live with Mom I'll never see him again."
Inappropriate and unnecessary information	"Is Mom/Dad upset about anything special that you know of?"	"My Dad was having an affair while my Mom was having me in the hospital."
	"You seemed very angry when you mentioned Mom. Do you know why you feel angry at her?"	"Mom never wanted me to be born. Dad said she wanted an abortion, but he wouldn't let her do it."
One parent seen as martyr	"Is there something that you think could happen that would make the family situation better now?"	"Mom destroyed our family with this divorce. Dad always says that he still loves her and that she can come back."
Contradictory statements	"How do you feel about your dad?"	"Daddy's a bad man. I never want to see him again. But I really love him. I miss him a lot."
Use of indirect statements quoting brainwashing parent	"How did this weekend go? Does Mom have an opinion about the time you spend at Dad's?"	"When I get home Mom says things like, 'Too bad you had to go with your dad this weekend—you missed a great ski trip. I bet you only watched TV.' As usual, Mom's right, Dad is boring."
Character assault on target parent	"What do you like about being at Mom's?"	"Mommy has lots of boyfriends who sleep over. Daddy says she's a whore because the Bible says so."
Anxiety arousal	"Are there things that are upsetting to you now?"	"Mom and Dad [the stepfather is called 'Dad'] have to listen when Steve [biological father] telephones us because if he finds out where we live, he might kidnap us."
Good parent versus bad parent	"How do you feel about Mom at this point?"	"I know Mom is bad because Daddy says so, and I believe everything he says. My dad never lies to me."
Collusion or one-sided alliance	"Sometimes children think things may be unfair. Is there anything that you think is unfair?"	"Dad just bought a new car but Mom's poor—he should have given us the money."
Scripted views	"You said you were confused about the fight and what really happened. What does Dad think happened?"	"I really thought I saw Dad's girlfriend hit Mom first but Dad says he saw Mom start it. I'm confused now."

Table 3.1 Continued

Indicator	*Question*	*Child's answer that reflects alienation*
Changed and dysfunctional behavior outside family	"I heard you've become a really good student—even better than before. Why do you think this has happened?"	"My grades have really improved since Mom and Dad decided to split. I figured out it's because school is the only place where I can escape."
Guilt about own role in family or custody dispute	"Is there anything that you feel guilty about since this whole family change started?"	"I testified against my mom in court, and I lied to the judge."
Nonverbal messages	"People can send messages with words and with gestures. Does Mom/Dad use gestures? How?"	"I know Dad doesn't want to hear anything about Mom. If we did something special with her, and we're still excited when we see him, he acts [looks away as if to imitate Dad] like he doesn't care."
Child as spy or conduit of information	"Is there anything that you've done during your parents' separation that makes you feel not as good as you'd like about yourself?	"I brought Mom some of Dad's business receipts to help her in court because he says he has no money."
Age-inappropriate statements	"When you talk about your father, you use the word 'father' but when you talk about your stepfather, you use the word 'Dad'. Could you tell me why you use different names?	"Anyone can be a father but it takes someone special to be a dad."
Colludes in secret-keeping	"Are there secrets that are bothering you about this whole custody problem?	"Dad told me to keep this a secret, but we're running away if he loses in court."
Coaching behavior	"How do you know that?"	"My mommy told me to tell you he did."
Confusion about birth parent	"Could you explain how your stepfather became your 'real' father?"	"My mom and dad got married, had me, and then divorced. They [mother and stepfather] told me that now I have a 'real' father. Can you tell me how I got born again?"
Fear of contact with target parent	"You say you pray every night. Are Mom and Dad in your prayers?"	"We read the Bible every night and pray for Dad to get better. I don't know what's wrong with Dad but I hope he'll be okay. Maybe he's even dangerous because we're not allowed to give him our telephone number or address."

Child statements mirror those of brainwashing parent	"Why do you think your father is trying so hard to make sure he has more time with you?"	"Dad doesn't really love me or want me to live with him—he just wants custody to hurt Mommy."
Unmanageability for no apparent reason	"Are there things that you'd like to be able to tell Mom/Dad, but find it difficult?"	"Yeah. I miss Dad, but I can't tell Mom. It's because of her that I don't see him and we moved so far away. I was always really bad when I was with him. I think Mom liked it when I gave him trouble. I wish so much that I could tell her that I want to see him."
Brain-twirling confusion, anxiety alliance, and hostility	"On the one hand, you say that the joint custody was good in a lot of ways. On the other hand, you say you don't want it any more. How come?"	"I always thought I wanted joint custody [equal time in this case], and it was working in the beginning. But then my dad started so much trouble with Mom, it just isn't worth it anymore."
Child as parent's confidant	"You have some criticisms of how your dad treats you. Are there things that your dad could do to improve the relationship between the two of you?"	"Dad treats me like a baby. He won't tell me anything or even let me do the things Mom lets me do. My mom and I are more like best friends than mother and daughter."
Fear for own physical survival	"Is there anything scaring you at this time?"	"Sometimes I'm afraid of my mom. She loses it a lot lately. I've been slapped around. She's really a lot rougher on my sister, especially when she tells Mom that she wants to live with Dad. I'm too smart to get her that mad—as long as I keep my mouth closed, I'm safe."
Child threatens parent	"I heard that you said you wanted to tell the judge certain things about your mom. What's the story?"	"Yeah, I told my mom she better do what I want because my dad told me I should tell him whenever Mom does something wrong, because the judge will punish her."

with one parent is the result of alienation or estrangement. Gardner (1998) identified eight behaviors that he found (and that have now been supported by research and clinical observations [Evans & Bone, 2011]) to differentiate alienation from realistic estrangement, as shown in Table 3.2.

Table 3.2 The eight behavioral manifestations of parental alienation syndrome and their detection in child statements

Manifestation	*Description*	*Example of child's statement*
Campaign of denigration	Utter rejection of one parent, willingness to tell others, erasing past positive aspects of relationship and memories.	"I never loved my mother." "I can't wait to tell the judge how despicable 'Frank' is."
Weak, frivolous, absurd reasons for the rejection	When pressed to explain the rejection will give reasons that do not make sense or explain the level of animosity, are false memories (proclaiming to remember something from a very young age), or are patently untrue.	"Dad slurps his soup and made us go to Disney World." "My mother wears cowboy boots and skirts. How ridiculous!"
Lack of ambivalence	One parent is seen as all good while the other is viewed as all bad.	"I love my father to death!" "There is not one good thing about my father that I can think of. Everything he does is stupid and bad."
"Independent thinker" phenomenon	The child strongly emphasizes that the favored parent played no role in the child's rejection of the other parent.	"I have free will, Mom, and have decided all on my own to never see you again." "Dad, Mom had nothing to do with my decision. I figured it all out for myself."
Reflexive support of the alienating parent in the parental conflict	Always taking the favored parent's side in all disagreements.	"I don't have to see the bank statements. I know that Mary stole my college money." "My father lied to me and there is nothing he can say to make it up to me."
Absence of guilt	Appearing to have no qualms about cruel and harsh treatment of the rejected parent.	"Mom only gave me that money to look good for the judge. I don't have to thank her." "Dad doesn't deserve to see me."
The presence of borrowed scenarios	Use of words and phrases that mimic or parrot those of the favored parent.	"Dad is a womanizer." "I only want good childhood memories."
Rejection of extended family of rejected parent	Refusal to spend time with or acknowledge formerly beloved family members.	"I never see Grandma. I don't need to go to her funeral." "I cannot attend the family gathering in Hawaii; Dad and I made plans already."

Assessing the Veracity of Allegations

An important function of the data collection efforts on the part of the CE is to understand and then evaluate the validity of each parent's allegations against the other. For example, if the favored parent is correct that the rejected parent is abusive/coercive or uninvolved/neglectful, then the children's resistance to visitation would be considered an indication of estrangement. On the other hand, if the rejected parent's accusations are accurate that the favored parent has manipulated the children, poisoned them against him/her, and there was no justified reason for the rejection, then the resistance of the children would be considered a reflection of alienation. No custody evaluation is complete without a thorough understanding of the truthfulness of the accusations made by and against each parent. The first step in this process is to ask the parents to make a list of each of their allegations. The next step is to ask them to repeat this assignment at another time in order to ascertain the consistency of the complaints. The third task is individually to discuss and question each and every item with the clients. In this way, the evaluator will have a *complete* accounting of each of their objections, complaints, accusations, and possible confabulations.

The follow-up during the process of the evaluation consists of examining *every* allegation. The confirmation or refutation requires sufficient evidence to justify the initial (working) and final hypothesis. There should be consistency in the parents' complaints; and if not, questions should immediately be expressed and then the client gently confronted by the examiner. For example, a mother had stated on one of her lists that she suspected the father had molested their 12-year-old daughter, who refused to visit her father. Upon inquiry, the mother admitted that she did not really believe the father inappropriately touched their daughter but she could not offer any other reason for her daughter's behavior. The actual reason for this refusal was later determined to be the result of her daughter suffering from maternal separation anxiety, which had nothing to do with the father and everything to do with the mother's psychopathology. Thus, as the mother discussed her list of allegations with the evaluator, she chose to withdraw the sexual abuse claim realizing that this was such a remote possibility and she had no justifiable reason to believe her own suspicion. Unfortunately, allegations take on a life of their own, become reified as if they were true, and as time continues they become more difficult for the child to believe that they originally were fabricated (Sauber, 2010). Nonetheless, the CE remains outside the influence of the family myths and objectively examines the allegations with a fresh and impartial stance.

Generally, most or at least part of the accusations made in the context of a custody evaluation are false. Unfortunately, if the allegation proves to be false there are often few, if any, consequences for the fabricator. Too often, no one seems to care if a false allegation is made; and at most, the parent who made the claim is reprimanded by the presiding judge for wasting the time of the county's child protection services and possibly the police force, and unnecessarily requiring the court's attention. For the CE, however, veracity of the allegations is essential because it is relevant for ascertaining the cause of the child's visitation refusal/rejection of the other parent and the credibility of the parent making the claim. If false allegations have been made, it behooves the CE to explore the details with the favored parent in the context of the deliberate intention of that parent to obstruct visitation in order to enjoy unilateral decision-making. The alienator is likely to justify exclusion of the other parent based upon spurious claims, trying to draw attention to the fictitious allegations. Rather than seeming relieved to discover the allegations are unfounded, most alienating parents will maintain a firm belief in the abusiveness of the other parent regardless of the report by the authorities. In this way, the fabrication of the allegation calls into question the credibility of the fabricator. It is essential that the CE pursue this matter of credibility and begin to list other false allegations so that in the CE report and testimony it becomes incontrovertible evidence that the alienating parent has repeatedly lied, misrepresented the "facts," and brought in third parties intentionally to mislead the court. Most insidious is the negative impact on the child, who either has to experience a child protection investigation or partake in parental collusion to support or to be the focal point of the false allegation against the other parent.

If the evaluator determines that one parent's accusations about the other parent are true, the CE may need to bring this finding to the attention of the court, which is likely to take action under these circumstances. The CE must be well versed in child abuse reporting laws and should understand that there can be no error on the part of the evaluator. If there is doubt or the evaluator feels that the issue to be examined escalates beyond the examiner's expertise, this information needs to be immediately communicated to the court. The evaluator may request in writing that an expert in the identified specialty area be appointed to assist with the evaluation. Another option to consider is for the evaluator to seek a supervisor to review the evaluation process, methods, and findings, payment for which would be the responsibility of the evaluator, not the client(s).

Making a Determination of Alienation

The determination of alienation as the cause of the children's visitation refusal/rejection of the other parent is based on the culmination of the evidence collected during the course of the evaluation. It is vital for the CE to hold an open mind as to the ultimate question until all of the data have been collected in order to avoid confirmatory bias (i.e., paying more attention to the evidence that supports the hypothesis/conclusion than to evidence that does not support it). While there is no single formula that can be applied to each case, it is helpful to consider the following four steps presented by Baker, Burkhard, and Kelly (2012):

1. Presence of a positive relationship prior to the current visitation refusal/rejection.
2. Absence of abuse/neglect on the part of the now rejected parent.

3. Use of PA strategies on the part of the favored parent.
4. Exhibition of many of the eight behavioral manifestations of alienation in the children.

If all four points are in the affirmative, then it is most likely that alienation is the cause of the children's current rejection of the targeted parent. Where it becomes more complicated, obviously, are cases in which some but not all four points are affirmative, such as a case in which there has been a positive relationship with the targeted parent but that parent has shown a major lapse in parenting judgment which hurt the children. In response, the now favored parent has engaged in alienation strategies and the children show some but not all signs of alienation. In cases such as these, the clinical skills and judgment of the CE will be extremely important for arriving at clinically sound conclusions about the family dynamics underlying the children's rejection of a parent.

If it has been determined that the issue is one of alienation, then the focus becomes one of differentiating the classification as mild, moderate, or severe. Although each level affects the child in different ways and in varying intensities, the moderate and severe forms of alienation offer greater challenge because of their often chronic state of indoctrination. Moderately or severely alienated children express consistent negative feelings regarding the targeted parent, whether or not in the mother's or father's company, in the examiner's office, in their school setting or on the playground with their friends, or in any other environment when the topic of parenting arises (Worenklein, in press). These symptoms appear with more complex, problematic short- and long-term consequences.

Custody Evaluation Conclusions and Recommendations

Some evaluators find that conclusions and recommendations are the most difficult to formulate and write and others have stated it is the easiest component to complete. This section of the report should always include any PA findings and these results should be intertwined with the state regulations and guidelines for shared parental responsibility and the best interests of the child, such as co-parenting, joint decision-making, and sharing medical and activity information.

Conclusions and recommendations according to Warshak (2010) should include the following elements:

1. A detailed discussion of why there was or was not alienation or estrangement, focusing on each of the parent's assessment results and statements as well as factual material, collateral sources, reactions, etc.
2. Detailed and clear recommendations with a focus not so much on labeling or blaming but on constructive interventions to reduce the conflict and normalize the relationship between the children and the targeted parent. Such recommendations should ensure the continuity of mental health

professionals working with the family as well as one judge who remains with the case, and one CE who can be asked to provide the court with updates.

3. Discussion of whether the alienation, if present, is mild, moderate, or severe, and detailed reasons, if possible, using quotations from the parents or children.
4. Discussion of the effects of conflict on the children in light of child development.
5. Discussion of the present and future effects of alienation, if present.
6. Consideration of whether there needs to be a change of custody and whether there should be no contact for a period of time between the children and the parent with whom they are aligned. Generally, a change of custody should be considered only after taking into account the parental capacity, including strengths and weaknesses of the parent receiving custody, as well as the child's circumstances. This is necessary in view of the significant behavioral and emotional challenges often found in the child who is severely alienated, and only with mental health interventions and support in place.
7. Recommendations for therapeutic intervention, and the nature of such intervention, by a professional who is qualified to deal with alienation issues.
8. Consideration of a parenting coordinator who is well versed and experienced in PA.
9. Recommendations for the parents in terms of how to protect the children from badmouthing, and other alienation strategies, and how to possibly use more effective communication strategies.

Too often, evaluators of contentious, high-conflict cases will want to offer "middle of the road" suggestions to appease each parent (i.e., concluding that every case is a hybrid case in which the favored parent has engaged in alienation but the targeted parent has exhibited flaws which equally contributed to his/her rejection). While it is certainly true that some cases are hybrid, there is no reason to believe that all cases are. In some cases, one parent is more to blame than the other for the child's rejection of a parent and the CE must be able to state that truth, supported by evidence. Thus, it is vital that the evaluator be an experienced, thick-skinned, tough-minded professional who has and will exhibit the courage of his/her convictions. This stance contrasts with the tender-minded, sensitive, and gentle therapist whose aim is to develop rapport in order to build and maintain a relationship. What evaluators discover and believe will need to be disclosed with clarity and precision, without sugar coating.

Evaluators must not assume that they have to find something positive and negative about everyone to balance the evidence. In most divorces there will be both strengths and weaknesses of each of the parties. However, with PA cases being so vicious, replete with deception, false allegations, manipulations, exploitation, and impression management, it may be more difficult to find complimentary words to describe the alienator. It is the ethical duty of the evaluator to present, without bias, the true findings and not disguise or mitigate the findings for the purpose of self-protection or to protect the feelings of the parent.

Formulation of the actual conclusions and what recommendations make logical sense should be based on documented evidence in the report. Opinions can be used to supplement the objective evidence but they must have a rational and evidentiary foundation. The conclusions should bring to the fore the solution recommended and why and how to implement the justified change of circumstances. Recommendations should always include the statement that the judge will make the final decision beyond what is contained in the report through examination of all of the circumstances presented to the court and the history of evidence presented in the case. The evaluator should not mislead the clients since, at most, evaluators can only offer findings and recommendations but do not, cannot, and should not make decisions involving the case outcome. Ideally, the evaluation report may facilitate mediated settlements in the shadow of using the report findings in court.

Once the report is submitted—directly to the court and not to either party—no contact should follow with either party until approached by one or both of the attorneys. In one example, an attorney wrote a letter containing the client's objections and errors in the report's conclusions and recommendations and requested the evaluator to respond. The evaluator wrote back with a c.c. to the other attorney that no correspondence or verbal questions would be addressed other than in the format of a scheduled deposition.

Evaluators should expect that the attorney representing the client with the favorable outcome will wish to exploit the expert to support and extend the recommendations on behalf of his or her client. The attorney representing the client who receives an unfavorable recommendation is ready and willing to retain an expert to find flaws, shortcomings, and ethical violations in the methodology and procedure, and attack the findings in the report as well as the evaluator. Not surprisingly, the validity of the concept of PA is an area attorneys often focus upon because the criticisms are readily available. It is vital the CE know these criticisms and how to rebut them in order to avoid the recommendations being discounted as stemming from a spurious argument of an invalid theoretical basis.

The Written Report

In order to conduct a thorough and valid custody evaluation, the CE must be knowledgeable about psychological assessment, child development, and family dynamics, including alienation. Another skill set necessary is involved in the art of writing a technical, evidence-based report in a scholarly style designed to meet the standards of Frye or Daubert. The report must be clear and succinct, and outlined in such a way that the attorneys and judge easily can follow and make sense of the findings and understand the basis of the results and the facts that serve as the basis for the conclusions and recommendations, which flow from the consistent and substantiated procedure and methodology. The report must present the recommendations with full disclosure and acknowledgment that it is the judge who makes the decision after reviewing all of the reported evidence beyond what the report envisions as the solution.

Testimony

Testimony may or may not follow the report, depending upon the findings and other variables of the case, which may lead to settlement rather than litigation. However, in cases of alienation, winning at all costs often becomes paramount, such that the case often but not always proceeds to trial. When this happens, the evaluator becomes involved in the process: a deposition may occur to try to discover areas of weakness in the report and one side may retain an expert to review the report with the intended purpose of finding fault, arguing for dismissal of certain findings, and perhaps alleging ethical violations. It is vital to maintain impartiality; the evaluator ceases having contact with either of the parties until the trial date.

An obvious advantage is for the CE to be skilled in appropriate courtroom tactics and demeanor in preparation for cross-examination that is designed to discredit the CE and his/her findings. The evaluator must be prepared to explain his/her methods and defend the report and its conclusions. The CE must also be able to speak knowledgably and authoritatively about the theory and research on PA and to address the issues likely to be raised by opposing counsel, such as why PAS was not included in the *Diagnostic and Statistical Manual of Mental Disorders* and whether that indicates that PAS is not generally accepted by the scientific community. If these issues are not properly explained the entire report, including the conclusions and recommendations, can be "thrown out." The evaluator must be educated and trained in clinical, family, and forensic psychology to do this type of work and should have a background beyond a continuing education course to understand the interface between the law and psychology and how to act as a guest in the court of law.

Finally, experts conducting forensic evaluations should require the parent(s) to sign an informed consent form, a release of information form to obtain records from the school, pediatrician, mental health professionals and others, as well as a fee schedule/retainer agreement during the initial meeting while the client completes a general intake information sheet. Court-ordered evaluations do not need informed consent because the court order states that the information is to be provided to the court in the form of a report and/or testimony, thus waiving confidentiality and privilege. The initial retainer needs to be replenished prior to the continuation of further work as there cannot be any balance due prior to the release of the report to the court and to the attorneys representing each client. Otherwise, the issue of a contingency fee will be raised and questioned as compromising the evaluator's recommendation as impartial; further, the party receiving an unfavorable finding will likely refuse to pay any balance to support a finding that is contrary to his/her desires.

Unless the report takes a middle of the road, "everyone is a little bit to blame" approach (which may be true in some but not all cases) the CE is likely to disappoint and anger some parents and some attorneys. This work is not for the novice or approval-seeking mental health professional. The evaluator must be very familiar with alienation theory and practices, be able to recognize it when it is present, and have the courage of his/her convictions to describe it as it is, even when it is inconvenient and uncomfortable to one of the parties in the case.

The CE must be able to explain, describe, and defend each of the methods, procedures, and conclusions offered in the report. While these cases are extremely challenging, complicated, and often stressful, alienated children and targeted parents deserve high-caliber evaluations to bring to the fore the truth of the matter. Often, the cast of characters (e.g., the child's therapist, the guardian *ad litem* and the children's rights attorney, the parent coordinator and probably the judge as well) already have been persuaded, by the compelling stories of the children and the well-articulated complaints of the alienating parent, to shift the weight of emotions, not evidence, against the targeted parent in favor of the alienating parent. By the time that the CE is appointed to conduct an evaluation involving an alienation assertion, the opinions and attitudes have been formulated and the children are protesting contact with the rejected parent. The professionals sympathize with the children and often support their excuses for avoiding the previously agreed-upon visitation schedule now that they "know" and have been told how egregious the targeted parent has been. Enter the evaluator as the impartial expert, ordered under protest who must attempt to expose the truth in order to provide the judge with the evidence needed to make a fair and just ruling on behalf of alienated children and families. Welcome to the role of the evaluator in alienation cases!

Note

1 In progress, a study of standardization of a measurement instrument to differentiate alienation, realistic estrangement, and bona fide abuse (S. R. Sauber & A. Worenklein).

References

American Psychological Association. (1994). Committee on Professional Practice and Standards. Guidelines for child custody evaluations and divorce proceedings. *American Psychologist, 49*, 677–680.

Association of Family and Conciliation Courts. (2006). Model standards of practice for child custody evaluation. *Family Court Review, 45(1)*, 70–91.

Baker, A. J. L. (2007). *Adult children of parental alienation syndrome.* New York: W. W. Norton.

Baker, A. J. L., Burkhard, B., & Kelly, J. (2012). Differentiating alienated from not alienated children: A pilot study. *Journal of Divorce and Remarriage* 53(3), 178–193.

Bernet, W. (2010). *Parental alienation, the DSM, and the ICD-11.* Chicago: Charles C. Thomas.

Clawar, S. S. & Rivlin, B. V. (1991). *Children held hostage: Dealing with programs and brainwashed children.* Chicago, IL: American Bar Association Family Law Section.

Evans, R. A., & Bone, J. M. (2011). *Essentials of parental alienation syndrome.* Palm Harbor, FL: Center for Human Potential of America.

Gardner, R. A. (1998). *The parental alienation syndrome: A guide for mental health and legal professionals.* Cresskill, NJ: Creative Therapeutics.

Gould, J. W., & Martindale, D. A. (2007). *The art and science of child custody evaluations.* NY: Guilford Press.

Johnston, J. R., & Roseby, V. (1997). *In the name of the child: A developmental approach to understanding and helping children of conflicted and violent divorce.* New York: The Free Press.

Kelly, J. B., & Johnston, J. R. (2001). The alienated child: A reformulation of parental alienation syndrome. *Family Court Review, 39(30),* 249–266.

Rohrbaugh, J. B. (2008). *A comprehensive guide to child custody evaluations: Mental health and legal perspectives.* New York: Springer.

Sauber, S. R. (2009). *Parental alienation syndrome and conducting forensic evaluations.* Presented at the Canadian Symposium for Parental Alienation Syndrome, Toronto, Ontario.

Sauber, S. R. (2010). *Why forensic evaluations are more effective than traditional psychotherapy in helping alienated children.* Presented at the Canadian Symposium for Parental Alienation Syndrome, Mt. Sinai School of Medicine, New York, U.S.A.

Stoltz, J. M., & Ney, T. (2002). Resistance to visitation: Rethinking parental child alienation. *Family Court Review, 40(2),* 220–231.

Warshak, R. A. (2010). *Divorce poison: How to protect your family from bad-mouthing and brainwashing* (revised ed.). New York: HarperCollins.

Worenklein, A. (2010). *Using the themes energizing parental alienation to identify and diagnose it.* Presented at the Canadian Symposium for Parental Alienation Syndrome, Mt. Sinai School of Medicine, New York, U.S.A.

Worenklein, A. (in press). Moderate parental alienation. In D. Lorandos, W. Bernet, & S. R. Sauber (Eds.), *Parental alienation: The handbook for mental health and legal professionals.* Chicago, IL: Charles C. Thomas.

4 The Essential Role of the Mental Health Consultant in Parental Alienation Cases

J. Michael Bone and S. Richard Sauber[1]

One Story: Two Different Outcomes

Scenario 1: Naïve and Uninformed Client

Bob works as a computer systems analyst in a mid-size company, and Liz works part-time in an antique store. The early years of the marriage were good, and their first child, Bob Jr., was born 4 years after their wedding. Their daughter, Lexi, was born 2 years later. It was during this period of early childrearing that the problems began to emerge. The couple began to drift, argue, and become resentful towards each other. Liz became routinely angry and accusatory to Bob, which made him only withdraw more. Bob eventually moved out of the marital home and petitioned the court for a divorce. He was agreeable to the children primarily living with their mother as long as he had liberal access to visit with them and share in the role of parenting. Before he moved out, they agreed verbally to his ongoing involvement and access to their children, as well as a liberal visitation schedule.

However, once Bob left the marital residence, Liz began to go back on their verbal agreement. She hired an attorney and her friends influenced her to see Bob as more of a villain than he ever was. Liz was frightened of her new life as a single parent and a single woman. Her self-confidence was lacking and her new role was poorly defined. She admitted to being in a perpetual state of anxiety compounded by her uncertain future. She began to see Bob more through her insecure lens and she began to retrace her marital arguments, seeing them as evidence of his abusiveness towards her. She also began to view his parenting style as harsh and ill-tempered. She interfered with Bob's access to the children, saying that the children were "uncomfortable" being with him and began to speak critically about him to the other parents at the children's school. Bob felt like the world he had known before never existed according to Liz's new portrayal of their life together and he became extremely suspicious of every move Liz made. After a few weeks of her campaign against him, he was served with a summons notifying him that Liz was seeking an injunction for protection against him.

After the shock wore off, he was advised by his lawyer to agree to anger management classes in order to "make the problem go away" even though he never had any such problem nor demonstrated any impulse control difficulties. He had never been in a fight as a youth and he certainly never raised a hand to Liz or the children. Trusting the judicial system, he took his lawyer's advice and enrolled in a class, now being labeled as "angry and dangerous." When he saw his children, rare as it was, the visitation took place for an hour a week in a supervised visitation center. The children became more distant and inexplicably angry towards him. As the divorce progressed, Liz's lawyer asked the court to appoint a guardian *ad litem* (GAL) for the stated purpose of ensuring the best interests of the children. Bob's attorney saw this as beneficial and he did not want Bob to look unreasonable or oppositional to the judge. He persuaded Bob to accept this agreement.

The court-appointed GAL conducted an investigation, which included speaking with the parents and children in their respective homes as well as the supervisor at the visitation center. He filed a report with the court recommending that Liz be given primary residential custody and that Bob continue seeing the children in a supervised setting. He also recommended that Bob be psychologically evaluated to determine his level of dangerousness and to see if the prognosis for treatment could be provided in the hope that he could eventually, through psychotherapy, learn to modify his objectionable, undesirable behavior as described by Liz. Bob's lawyer, not wanting to rock the boat or challenge the court-appointed GAL, advised Bob to agree to these terms since the process would obviously reveal that Bob had no anger problem nor presented a danger to his children. Again, Bob trusted his attorney's advice and accepted the GAL's recommendations.

Bob met with the court-appointed psychologist, who stated that he could not guarantee that Bob did not have some anger issues because of his anger expressed at the situation in which he now found himself entrenched. With an abundance of caution, the psychologist recommended the continuation of the status quo and the court, taking a cautious approach, agreed. The judge stated that the truth or falsity of any such risk factors would eventually be disclosed over time. Several months passed and the children began to refuse to see their father at the visitation center, becoming hysterical and tearful at the prospect. The supervisor at the visitation center did not want to further traumatize the children after the stories she had heard from the mother and wrote a letter to the court advising that she no longer wished to continue working on the case. She documented the children's growing resistance to seeing their father as evidence that he likely had abused them earlier in their lives. The judge certainly did not wish to place the children in a situation that would trigger trauma reactions so the court ordered Liz to have sole custody, leaving open the question of future contact between the children and their father. Shortly thereafter, the judge was rotated from the family court to the criminal court, which was more consistent with his prior experience.

The newly appointed judge reviewed the file, and ruled in favor of maintaining the status quo. He stated that if the father wished to have any contact with his children, he would have to pursue this matter in court. Bob's lawyer, by now frustrated and professionally embarrassed, told Bob that mounting a legal campaign to reverse the current plan would cost between $50,000 and $100,000. He explained that expert witnesses would have to be hired and a comprehensive evaluation would have to be requested and conducted, which would take months and result in an uncertain but costly outcome. The attorney accepted no responsibility for these unfolding consequences and blamed the system and the client's bad luck in the appointments of the particular GAL, supervisor, and psychological evaluator. He himself questioned Bob's innocence during this succession of events.

Scenario 2: Educated and Informed Client

When Bob and Liz separated, Bob became concerned about Liz's accusatory attitude towards him. He began to feel very vulnerable. Liz had begun to accuse him of actions that he never made and she seemed to be deliberately interfering with his time with his children, telling him that the children were "uncomfortable" and they complained about being with him. He never noticed any change in the children's affection or attitude while spending time together. Liz would schedule activities such as play dates and shopping excursions during his parenting times. At first, Bob thought it was a coincidence and then he began to wonder whether it was intentional on Liz's part. Being a computer systems analyst, he researched the situation in which he now found himself. In his own due diligence, he learned that the family court is very unpredictable and that it can be manipulated by the adversarial process. He began to read horror stories of outrageous outcomes.

Alarmed, he sought advice from several well-known family lawyers. In each meeting, the attorneys informed him that his case was in no way unusual. Each attorney reassured him that they could easily present his position of shared parenting and his need to be involved with his children's lives to the judge in a straightforward manner. His concern about Liz's apparent mission to minimize his involvement with their children's lives did not seem to alarm them. Bob left each meeting unsettled and still concerned about Liz's motives and apparent disregard for his being with his children. Could no one see what was happening?

Since the apparent lack of concern did not jibe with Bob's now extensive research and his feelings of vulnerability, he thanked each attorney and said that he would call them back. However, instead, he decided to seek advice from a mental health consultant (MHC) who had years of clinical and forensic experience as a psychologist as well as familiarity with the family court process. He found the name of a particular consultant on the Internet through his authorship of several journal articles and a book on parental alienation. Bob reasoned, based on what he had gleaned from his Internet research, that the family court system respected input from experts who were routinely appointed to assist in providing input as to the "best interest of the child," a psychological concept used within a legal context. He remembered from his college psychology courses that psychological matters could be arbitrary and subject to interpretation. It made increasing sense that he needed someone on his team with this kind of mental health and forensic experience to advise not only him but his lawyer as well. He interviewed several MHCs who had the expertise needed and hired one to assist him in charting the unpredictable environment he was about to enter.

The consultant's first task was to help Bob find the most appropriate lawyer and he set to work interviewing several he had identified through his experience and network. A lawyer was selected and telephonic conference calls began between the consultant, Bob, and his lawyer. Early on, the consultant noted signs that Liz was posturing to vilify Bob, perhaps to secure her advantage with respect to custody. The consultant advised Bob how to manage his behavior with his children and Liz. He reviewed e-mail and text messages and alerted Bob to any potential dangers. When Liz went to court to ask for an injunction for protection, alleging that Bob was abusive, Bob and his team were ready to respond robustly at the hearing for the temporary injunction. It was argued that not only were the allegations untrue, Liz was attempting to exploit the family court system and eliminate Bob from his children's lives. As evidence, Bob came armed with text and e-mail messages of false allegations and visitation obstruction attempts. An expert witness had been selected and prepared by the consultant to respond to hypothetical questions about this dynamic, and several collateral fact witnesses testified about Bob's relationship with his children. Prior to the hearing, the MHC arranged for a psychological evaluation of Bob, which showed that he was well adjusted, with an absence of psychopathology and uncontrollable impulses of anger and explosiveness. The evaluation also showed that Bob lacked risk factors for child abuse, in order to counter the complaints by his former spouse. The MHC also interviewed several collateral contacts that Bob, with the help of his consultant, had identified, in order to identify those appropriate for court. Obviously, the MHC, by the very nature of this task, must be a qualified mental health professional (MHP) with years of clinical and forensic experience, and not be a junior member of the profession nor a lay person trying to create a niche in the divorce industry.

Since such an abundance of evidence in this kind of hearing was so uncommon, the judge set an evidentiary hearing for the case. The overwhelming weight and volume of the evidence, along with the well-organized presentation prepared by the team assembled by Bob and the consultant, was sufficiently convincing to the judge that he no longer was concerned about Bob but rather Liz, her malicious behavior, and her lack of credibility with the court. In the end, Bob prevailed and was able to maintain his relationship with his children and it was now Liz who found herself under a cloud of suspicion.

Points of Slippage in the Family Court System: The Need for a MHC

It is indisputable that the family court system is highly unpredictable in its rulings, and that family court judges have tremendous discretion. It is also well accepted that the family court system is appropriately oriented towards the protection and welfare of children. Any allegation of danger or imminent danger to a child automatically receives the court's attention on an emergency basis and this allegation is heavily weighted in the direction of preservation of the children's safety and well-being. The family court, therefore, is reliant upon objective psychological data and input because the nature of the allegations and the complaints are directly related to children's psychological well-being. Unfortunately, the level of sophistication, professional experience, and qualifications of some mental health providers is lacking, and decisions are made about protecting children based on faulty data or faulty interpretations of the data. State child protection agencies tend to be underfunded, leading to a reliance on workers who have limited psychological training or insight. For example, child protection workers may not be skilled at diferentiating parental coaching of children from authentic concerns a child might have.

Further complicating matters is the fact that despite psychological issues having prime importance to the tryer of fact within the family court system, the judge (obviously an attorney by training) lacks psychological expertise and thus may be ill-equipped to properly evaluate the veracity of the allegations and posturing taking place and being argued.

Yet another point of slippage is that each attorney represents and serves as an advocate for his or her client. The aim of the attorney is to present a one-sided view to the court, against the other parent, regardless of the truth of the claims. Attorneys often have a list of MHPs who are available to support a legal position, despite the fact that being a "hired gun" runs counter to MHP guidelines. Becoming an advocate for the paying client, as opposed to being an independent and neutral voice of scientific expertise, constitutes a violation of the discipline's code of ethics whether the MHP is serving in the role of the therapist, evaluator, consultant, or any other capacity. Nonetheless, these violations are common and problematic.

When an MHC is hired to aid in a case or as an expert witness, he or she may feel pressure to advocate the client's position, regardless of the facts, rather than being a voice of objective scientific presentation. When the experts finds themselves yielding towards pleasing the attorney and client by making the most favorable opinion to support them at the expense of objective scientific evidence, they are crossing the boundary into unethical territory. They are compromising their professional integrity with their role, discipline, and standing with the court under oath. Sometimes these "advocacy" roles are deliberate and other times they are unintentional as the expert becomes convinced by his or her own confirmatory bias and having been manipulated by the skillful sociopathic alienator and brainwashed children.

Taken together, these systemic issues in family law create what we refer to as "points of slippage" wherein the judge is vulnerable to being misled, including: (1) the court's bias towards the protection of children, (2) the unmatched discretion and latitude of the family trial judge, and (3) the fact of psychological matters being decided upon by someone unlikely to be trained in psychology. These are the places where error and distortion can overcome the truth, leading the court to issue orders based on flawed foundations. Because of these points of slippage, it is possible for judges to be misled to make rulings based on distortion rather than fact, distortions created by one parent purposefully vilifying the other parent by any means, malicious or otherwise. Once a court order takes place, it is difficult to change because that involves convincing the court of errors in the facts that initially compelled the order to be set into force. Thus, it is essential to present the best case possible from the first point of contact with the presiding judge.

The hypothetical case scenarios presented at the opening of the chapter depict the enormous variation in outcomes that are commonplace in family court cases where parental alienation is present. The purpose of this chapter is to define the unique role and value of the MHC in these complicated and often confusing battles that take place inside and outside the courtroom. Each party aims to reframe every episode to their advantage and line up their resources to support their position and cause damage to the other side. The "other parent" has become the "enemy" of the alienating parent and every tactic is considered acceptable and defendable, without discretion to boundaries or concerns for credibility.

The MHC can play a unique and valuable role in a custody case in which parental alienation may be a factor. Through awareness of the points of slippage, the MHC can help the client present an effective defense against false allegations and maintain his/her parenting role. The consultative role is different from and unique to other roles. It is neither supervisory nor psychotherapeutic. It is educational and advisory. The most applicable definition can be found in Gerald Caplan's *The Theory and Practice of Mental Health Consultation* (1970, p. 19), in which he writes of this specialty role as:

> A process of interaction between two professional persons—the consultant, who is a specialist, and the consultee, who invokes the consultant's help in regard to a current work problem with which he is having some difficulty and which he has decided is within the other's area of specialized competence.

The expertise of a MHC is especially warranted in alienation cases, which are heavily weighted with psychological matters and which must be effectively addressed to avoid distortion to the court. False allegations of abuse must be revealed as being false. The personality characteristics of the alienating parent must be revealed as being consistent with the tendency to vilify the other parent while accepting no responsibility for his or her deliberate actions. The errors that populate adverse psychological evaluations in cases with parental alienation must be exposed as lies and deliberate distortions and the facts must be explained to the court.

The Unique Benefits of a MHC

Unfortunately, for too many families, the phenomenon of parental alienation causes widespread, immediate, and long-term damage to children and many members of the child's immediate and extended family, as well as among friends (Baker, 2007; Sauber, 2006). Information and advice to parents is now widely accessible through the Internet via a number of well-intentioned organizations that provide information and guidance to families currently experiencing alienation. The shortcoming, from the perspective of the MHC, is that these parents may feel that they have the answers and confidently know how to proceed. Often, because of the complexity of these cases and the subliminal forces operating, they may make unfortunate choices that cause irreparable harm or require costly repairs. While mutual support groups can be quite beneficial (Lebow, this volume), restraint is needed to avoid the pitfalls of the patient trying to do the work for his own case, thinking it is simple but making errors, much like it is said that a surgeon should never operate on his or her own family member. Loss of objectivity is likely and the MHC can add a fresh and experienced perspective to help the stressed and confused parent consider all of the factors necessary when developing an effective strategy.

Not only can the MHC be objective in helping the team develop an effective strategy, but the MHC can draw upon professional case experience and the latest knowledge in the literature by regularly reviewing recently published studies, clinical approaches, and case laws. In order to maintain credentials, the MHC should contribute to the knowledge base through lectures at professional conferences and papers submitted to professional journals.

The MHC additionally can offer the legal team a rare perspective because of his or her own prior professional experiences, such as a psychotherapist for children and families, court-appointed evaluator in family forensic matters, rebuttal witness challenging other professionals' work, evaluator for substance abuse or mental illness, child abuse investigator, provider of court-involved therapy, reunification specialist, supervisor, mediator, and so on. Having served in some or all of these roles the MHC can be aware of and sensitive to the performance and role/functions, as they are involved in a parental alienation case, in a way that no other seasoned professional who has a vast array of experience in many different roles can. The MHC can also provide insight to the client about the procedures and interface between law and psychology, and courtroom tactics, obtained from his or her own experience undergoing depositions and offering testimony.

Although there is an additional up-front cost associated with the additional member of the legal team, this cost may be offset by reducing the overall cost of lengthy contentious motions and arguments in court hearings and proceedings, depositions, and other time-consuming, expensive litigation-related work that may well be unnecessary, as illustrated in the presented scenarios. In the first scenario, the client is blindsided by the sequence of events and passively follows the advice of his attorney, resulting in a terrible dilemma for the father and the eventual loss of his parental rights. He becomes trapped in a system and finds himself unable to regain his relationship and time sharing with his children without incurring even greater attorney fees. The second scenario represents an obvious cost benefit by altering the process and outcome of the father's journey, allowing him to assume a powerful position in the court, thereby eliminating the need for additional legal expenses. The attempts of the mother to exploit the system resulted in her loss of credibility with the court and cessation of her vicious attempts to obstruct the father's visitation and involvement with his children, both now and in the future.

Another important variable in the mix for a client to consider when hiring a MHC is the attorney's receptiveness to having such a person join the legal team. Many attorneys welcome forensic accountants but when it comes to a mental health specialist, some are wary of the kind of advice that may be imposed upon them and their client. A common concern for all involved is that the MHC and attorney may suggest opposing approaches to the case, which could be stressful to all parties. The MHC can remind the client and attorney from the outset that, by definition, the MHC is a "consultant" not a "collaborator," and will thus make suggestions and recommendations but will not share decision-making responsibility. The MHC needs to clarify for both the client and the attorney that the attorney has been retained to "represent" the interests of the client and has direct responsibility for making the final decisions as to the client's best interest. It is the attorney who chooses which direction to pursue, not the client, nor the MHC. Thus, the client can choose to take advantage of the opportunity of having the expertise of a MHC to contribute to understanding the problem and identifying potential solutions, within the restrictions of this consultative role. In some cases the MHC will be primarily involved with consulting with the client, in others the primary contact may be with the attorney.

Further, the MHC must adhere to the specific rules and ethical guidelines as required by his or professional affiliation (i.e., social work, psychology, etc.) and it is up to the MHC to be aware of and follow the ethical principals set forth.

The MHC should be able to articulate to prospective clients and attorneys what is the basis for his or her specialization in the area of parental alienation, as consultants in areas such as autism, adolescent conduct disorders, and alcoholism would do. The consumer, that is, the targeted parent, should not assume that a specialist in one area will have competency in another area. Thus, it is essential that the prospective client becomes familiar with the professional's training, education, experience, and expertise established in the field of parental alienation prior to inviting the MHC to join the team in one fashion or another.

Upon retention of the MHC, should the client and/or attorney discover that the consultant either lacks expertise in parental alienation or offers poor advice, it is always the client's prerogative to terminate these services and find another more competent MHC, much like clients frequently do in changing attorneys and therapists. The MHC, based upon expertise in parental alienation, should be able to assess the motions before the court, the psychological dynamics operating with the children, and the family circumstances generating conflicts between the parents, and make suggestions based on a reasonable sequence of planning strategies. A client and attorney should expect the MHC to make ongoing requests for information and not view these as a nuisance but rather as steps toward accumulating necessary evidence for an understanding of the case and the development of strategic thinking. Experience has shown that the MHC may be able to identify neglected areas of the case that represent serious shortcomings in the strategy developed. The MHC can play an important role in identifying and addressing these areas.

The MHC Accepting or Declining a Case

Prior to accepting a case, the MHC will want to determine whether the client is truly a targeted parent or whether the child's rejection is a result of realistic estrangement or due to bona fide abuse or neglect. This involves an initial screening based upon the information provided by the client and a review of the documents. Ideally the client is honest with the MHC, who explains that he or she can only be helpful if the client is straight, direct, and truthful in his/her descriptions of the current family dynamic. Additionally, the consultant must screen those clients who may be mistaken but honestly think that their children have been alienated when in fact this is not the case. Otherwise, any planning on the case will backfire and cause serious and often irreparable damage to the case and the cause of the client. A helpful list of considerations for the MHC to discuss with the client are provided below and further described elsewhere by Sauber (2011).

While the term "parental alienation" is not emphasized in the scenarios at the beginning of this chapter, the vignettes depict the early stages of children becoming alienated from a parent within the context of marital separation and divorce proceedings (Gardner, 1992). The four basic characteristics typically seen in parental alienation cases are: (1) false allegations of abuse to justify the visitation blocking, (2) access and interference with time sharing, (3) deterioration in the relationship between the child and the "targeted parent," and (4) the feared response on the part of the child to displeasing the alienating parent (Bone & Walsh, 1999). In assessing whether alienation is present in a particular case the MHC should consider the following criteria:

Step 1 Examine whether the children are exhibiting the eight behavioral manifestations of parental alienation as originally identified by Dr. Richard Gardner as early as 1987 and then clarified in his follow-up book in 1992: (1) the campaign of denigration; (2) weak, frivolous, or absurd rationalizations for the deprecation; (3) lack of ambivalence towards the parents; (4) the "independent-thinker" phenomenon; (5) reflexive support of the alienating parent in the parental conflict; (6) absence of guilt over cruelty to and/or exploitation of the alienated parent; (7) the presence of borrowed scenarios; and (8) spread of the animosity to the friends and/or extended family of the rejected parent.

Step 2 Determine whether the parents are engaging in parental alienation strategies described elsewhere in this volume (Baker & Fine).

Step 3 Consider the presence of other factors in the rejected parent that might account for a child's alignment with the other parent, other than that parent's use of alienation strategies: (1) abuse or neglect (due to substance abuse, harsh discipline, mental illness, or other reason); (2) ineffective parenting or failure to bond with the child; (3) parental experience of the child as particularly difficult to care for (due to illness, personality, etc.); (4) physical or mental illness of parent that compromises his or her ability and resources to care for child; (5) catastrophic accident or injury causing life-changing events or disruptive circumstances; (6) relocation due to job or family matters that result in major life changes and or challenges to contact (cost of transportation, time differences); (7) prolonged absence (e.g., military deployment, prison, illness, work schedules); (8) financial strain, (e.g., two jobs necessary and/or transportation problems) such that there is no real time for meaningful child time sharing; (9) introduction of new partner, with or without children and stepsiblings and/or half-siblings, into the family that may result in feelings of displacement and resentment.

Also as part of Step 3, consider the presence of factors within the child that might cause the child to align with one parent, other than the favored parent's use of parental alienation strategies such as:

1. Normal adolescent rebellion for the purpose of individuation and separation, e.g., a teenager playing one parent against the other in trying to escape the discipline and boundaries in one home by leaving to go live or spend time in the home of the other, more permissive and/or indulgent parent.
2. Developmentally expectable reactions that contribute to the child's negative attitudes and behavior, e.g., separation anxieties in infants/young children, primary attachment or gender identification with one parent, older sibling influences, adolescent negativity, and/or other childhood vulnerabilities.
3. Alignments due to high-conflict divorce causing negative attitudes and defiant behavior, e.g., divided loyalties and guilt, feeling or being placed in the middle of the conflict, worry and sympathy for the lonely divorced/rejected parent, and/or anger and hurt regarding the circumstances caused by the disruption of parental separation.

See Sauber (in press) for a more detailed discussion of these variables.

It will certainly be challenging for the MHC to obtain black and white evidence in alienation cases and offer absolute clarity because frequently the alienating parent is very clever in masking his or underlying malicious and destructive intent with a false sincerity. Further complicating matters is the vehemence and persuasiveness with which programmed children present the false rationale for their alignment. The key to unlocking these alienation cases rests with the consistency of evidence from multiple sources of data collection, which will ultimately converge on the truth as to the differentiating criteria described above.

While a thorough review of the case details using the above criteria is ideal, in many cases it is simply not possible owing to time limitations and available information. In these cases, the MHC must still satisfy him- or herself with respect to the case being presented by the client and/or the attorney. In all cases, the MHC must be able to confidently know that the client is, in fact, a targeted parent and not the alienating or abusive parent. The criteria listed above comprise the template for this determination, and the MHC is well advised to keep these criteria in the forefront of his or her mind and continually monitor the case evolution for countervailing evidence.

Should the MHC see signs that the initial conclusion was incorrect, the ethical duty is to act on that awareness and knowledge. This stands in contrast to the obligation of the attorney, who is responsible to advocate for the client, regardless of his or her actions. The MHC's ethical obligation is to submit to the ethical guidelines of his or her professional discipline and to the standards of the best interest of the child, regardless of the desires of the parent. Under some circumstances, the MHC may be placed in an oppositional position with respect to the client. The MHC must begin by attempting to encourage the client—who is now believed to be abusive or alienating—to modify his or her behavior. If the client is unable or unwilling to do so, the MHC is ethically bound to withdraw from the case. To do otherwise is ethically prohibited and morally unacceptable.

If it appears that the client is not a targeted parent but rather suffers from substance abuse problems and/or serious parenting deficiencies, it is the MHC's obligation and responsibility to encourage remedial and rehabilitative steps. It will be important to establish conditions of appropriate monitoring for the client over time, even if these recommendations appear detrimental to the client's immediate cause. The MHC has a moral and ethical obligation to not subterfuge, deceive, or manipulate the system to the benefit of the client. Clients often fail to understand the distinction between a MHC and an advocate at the outset, so it is important to have that discussion prior to the MHC accepting the case. It must be explained that the MHC, while being paid by the client, has a professional code of ethics that must be followed, even when that runs counter to the claims or desires of the client. It is possible that a displeased client will turn against the consultant who refuses to violate professional ethics, and the best way to prevent this is to provide clarity from the outset.

Functions of a MHC

The MHC often is the invisible force behind the case's planning and management. The opposing counsel is unaware of this team member unless at the time of trial preparation there is a request for disclosure of all experts relied upon for case preparation. Sometimes the MHC will observe the hearing or trial court proceedings, and the opposing counsel or the presiding judge may inquire as to whom this person is and request clarification as to the role he or she is serving. Other times, the retaining attorney will voluntarily disclose the expert and present the MHC's findings to the court based upon the analysis of the data reviewed. However, the MHC never functions as a rebuttal witness nor testifies. Similarly, a custody or psychological evaluator is prohibited from serving a dual role as a therapist on the same case.

Critiquing an Existing Custody Evaluation

The MHC may play an important role in critiquing the custody evaluation, which may be flawed in data collection, data interpretation, and/or in the conclusions drawn from the data. A common problem relevant specifically to parental alienation cases is that the custody evaluator will, despite the data, make recommendations that are unlikely to address the pernicious nature of alienation. It is well established in the literature that any forensic evaluation, of which a custody evaluation is one example, should be largely "fact finding." Properly executed evaluations should establish the truthfulness of all allegations (Gould & Martindale, 2007). Unfortunately, too many clinical and forensic evaluators are hesitant to take such a definitive position. This common shortcoming of such evaluations is to offer comfortable "middle of the road" findings that merely state the strengths and weaknesses of the parties rather than asserting what is likely to be an unpopular conclusion that defines one parent as the prime perpetrator of parental alienation. The MHC role in these instances is to bring the essential facts to the fore, clarify any ambiguities in the data, and point out ways in which the evaluator failed to draw an obvious conclusion based on the data he or she presented

Preparing the Client to Counter Claims of Abuse

Attempts to alienate a child may involve false allegations of abuse, alcoholism, neglect, and/or being unstable and uninvolved with the children. The targeted parent may be accused of being impatient or emotionally abusive to the former spouse and children, and having uncontrolled anger. These false allegations are generically referred to as "abuse" and are claimed as the justification for the children not wishing to have any contact with the targeted parent. Given the family court's obligation to protect children, such false allegations of abuse grossly exploit the family court system and its required protective stance towards children. The role of the MHC in these situations is to assist the team to present to the court that these claims are, in fact, false and deliberately fabricated with the intention of keeping the children away from the targeted parent.

Once the MHC is able to review the differentiating criteria with the client, he or she can formulate several hypotheses to serve as a basis to develop a plan. The MHC may need to educate the attorney about these considerations and the differentiating criteria in order to ensure that the team has an effective and coordinated approach.

Selecting Other MHPs, Experts, or Legal Professionals for the Case

An important role of the MHC is to assist the client and attorney in finding other professionals who will be involved in the case. Many high-conflict custody dispute cases are assigned to a court-appointed evaluator, who will then act as the court's expert. Often the judge will ask each side to proffer three names of potential evaluators and the MHC can play an active role in screening candidates. Sometimes the judge will ask for the names of professionals to conduct more limited evaluations. These may include a "time-sharing evaluation" to a "parental alienation evaluation," if alienation is brought to the fore in the court as a major complaint requiring clarification. Or the evaluation may be called a "social investigation" or a "simplified" psychological evaluation with one or both of the parties. The term "simplified" means that a psychological evaluation is ordered by the court. It should be noted that in cases of alienation there is never any facet of the case that should be considered "simple," because of intentional distortion of facts that may be difficult to uncover and document. These cases are not comparable with any other family law or clinical cases in that they are filled with conflict that may continue even when the court recognizes parental alienation (Baker, 2010).

The importance of having a qualified expert in parental alienation cannot be overstated. If the wrong evaluator is court appointed, then a host of errors may be set in motion. It is very difficult to challenge and overcome the findings of custody evaluators, even when in error. The effort and expense of retaining a rebuttal witness to attempt to dismiss and refute the court-appointed expert is another role for the MHC that should ideally be avoided in the first place through the careful selection process offered as a service by the MHC. The selection or recommendation of certain essential professionals is not limited to the role of evaluators but includes treating counselors, reunification therapists, collateral contacts, the GAL, the parenting coordinator, mediators, and even attorneys appointed to represent the child or children.

Organizing and Collecting Relevant Data

The MHC can also be helpful in preparing the client for participation in a custody or psychological evaluation. The MHC can work with the client to understand the purpose of the evaluation and how to best present his or her thoughts and feelings in a truthful and yet strategic manner to the evaluator. The MHC can assist the client in identifying collateral contacts for submission to the evaluator and can help the client prepare and organize documents to be of greatest utility to the evaluator.

The MHC can assist the client and attorney in preparing and submitting this information for the evaluation as well as preparation for court strategy. The consultant combs through whatever communications exist that reveal that the alienating parent clearly has an agenda to vilify the other parent. These indicators often are seen in text messages, e-mail correspondence, and voicemail messages. This material must be assembled, organized, and sorted to be presented in a consistent way so that the information can be communicated and used as evidence. Very often, the preparation of this type of evidence is inadequate, scattered, and poorly assembled. The goal is to compile the selected information as evidence in a coherent and succinct presentation for the evaluator, GAL, and/or trial strategy.

Selecting and Preparing Collateral Contacts

Another aspect of the role of the MHC is that of assisting the client and attorney in the choice and selection of particularly compelling collateral sources and witnesses, who are chosen based on the quality of their presentation, the credibility of their testimony, and how well they would resonate with the particular judge presiding over the case. For example, if the judge is a staunch family person with close relationships with his or her grandchildren, this information could and should be used in the selection process. If grandparents also have been targeted in the alienation, their testimony might be especially appropriate and compel the attention of the judge to their frustration and plight to maintain contact with their loved grandchildren. The consultant understands that certain emotional factors that should not nonetheless do impact the impartiality of the legal system. The judge has considerable latitude and discretion, which allows a variety of potential rulings based upon the best interest of the children.

Advocacy Roles

The MHC, the expert witness, and the therapist are roles often performed by psychologists of similar backgrounds. These roles require advanced degrees and substantive experience in the family forensic environment, but each uses this experience and education differently. The MHC operates in what might be considered a limited advocacy role. Since the family court is properly biased in favor of protecting children from real abuse (and cases with parental alienation are replete with false allegations of abuse which can tip the scale against the targeted parent), the limited advocacy role of the MHP can restore the balance. In most parental alienation cases, one parent is falsely accused of being abusive, negligent, or irresponsible as a parent. The court, in its first priority to protect children, is obligated to take allegations of abuse very seriously. Given that the process of evaluating and determining the accuracy of allegations can take months, the falsely targeted parent may be separated from his or her children as a result of caution by the court. This falsely targeted parent therefore enters the court environment with a defensive position, the balance of objective reality having become unbalanced and biased against him or her. The MHC can help identify and implement strategies to rectify this imbalance by, for example, "rebranding" the falsely accused and reversing the allegations in terms of the credibility of the alienator.

The targeted parent must be presented as a parent who has not been abusive but rather unfairly vilified for purposes of tactical advantage in the litigious custody dispute. The "limited" nature of this advocacy role is governed by a careful investigation that the falsely targeted parent is, in fact, falsely targeted. Of course, as previously noted, the MHC cannot and should not advocate for any parent who has been abusive to his/her children. If the children in question truly have been abused by that parent, then the MHC must withdraw from the case or accept a different role of assisting the client in seeking therapeutic and rehabilitative services. This limitation in the advocacy role is very different and distinct from the advocacy role of the attorney, who advocates on behalf of clients—even those who have been found to be abusive or alienating parents.

The expert forensic witness also is prohibited from any advocacy role. The expert witness is performing a role as the court-appointed evaluator, a behavioral scientist, having no agenda other than dispassionately evaluating what is best for the children in question. The expert witness has no loyalty or obligation to either parent, and has very limited and controlled interaction with both attorneys. In fact, it is very common practice for the expert witness to refuse any communication with one attorney without the other attorney also being present in person or in a three-way telephone conference. This type of insistence is what is required to best maintain objectivity and to best serve the court in determining what is best for the children.

The evaluator typically is given great latitude and control by the court in the performance of the evaluation: to set all of the appointments in a variety of configurations; direct the parties to bring whatever collateral information deemed to be necessary; and in all ways maintain neutrality. They give no advice to the parties, as this would taint their objectivity, and they reveal little in their thinking and data collection. There must be an avoidance of providing any premature feedback to the clients. Counselors and therapists are often referred to by the court as "advocates" for their clients. It is hoped that they obtain a correct diagnosis of the differentiating criteria and not advocate for the alienator, as sometimes occurs. The alienator and the alienated children are very convincing and it is the alienator who often pays for the child's therapy without the targeted parent's participation. This is the precise reason that it is helpful to have the court's order for the development of a reunification plan. Should the targeted parent be labeled and/or estranged from his children, he will need a carefully constructed blueprint to follow for successful reunification (Sauber, in press). The MHC can assist in the development of this plan.

Working with the Attorney

The MHC should be able to utilize his or her education and experience in a variety of capacities, including identifying goals and developing strategies with the client and attorney. The MHC can coach and prepare the witnesses with the attorney, and educate and prepare the parent who is undergoing an evaluation. The MHC can critique adverse psychological opinion, testimony, reports, and related materials, and aid the attorney in preparing for cross-examination of these witnesses. For example, if it is being alleged that the targeted parent is psychologically unstable, abusive, or addicted to some substance, these allegations are all within the realm of the MHC expertise. In each allegation, the consultant offers analysis and the data that support or refute the allegation.

Evaluating the Input and Work of Other Experts

Parental alienation cases often involve the expertise and involvement of other MHPs, including custody evaluators, psychological evaluators, therapists (individual, dyadic, family), parenting coordinators, and GALs. While each expert plays a unique role in a parental alienation case, each is susceptible to being misled by an alienating parent. It is well established that many qualified and competent MHPs, family attorneys, and GALs are familiar with and competent to opine on the problems presented by parental alienation. It is equally well established that alienating parents are adept at finding and choosing MHPs and attorneys whom they are able to convince and manipulate to adopt their point of view regarding the other parent's alleged danger to their children.

MHPs are subject to the same influences of confirmatory bias as are non-MHPs and are more vulnerable when they lack expertise with respect to the phenomenon of parental alienation and its powerful effects. If a therapist is approached by an alarmed parent who is seeking advice regarding an ongoing divorce, and that parent expresses fear that his or her child is in danger when exposed to the company of the other parent, the stage is set for the potential effects of confirmatory bias. That is, the therapist assumes that the other parent is in fact a threat and then seeks examples to support that hypothesis. If that therapist fails to get a detailed history and then insists on speaking with the other parent believing what they have been told, that same therapist may well find him- or herself responding to the protective impulses expressed by the initial parent who retains his or her services. Essentially, they join the chorus of unsuspecting promotion of alienation.

To counter this tendency, the MHP should consider all of the evidence in light of competing alternative hypotheses. As this unfortunate but common problem progresses, the parent continually feigning fear for the child provokes false and distorted information about that parent, whom the therapist fails to objectively assess. Thus, the bias develops against the other parent as the therapist becomes indoctrinated in much the same way as the child in a growing, expanded, and convinced negative impression of the other parent, with whom they either have never met or met briefly as the "enemy." Often, the alarmed parent meets with this naïve therapist and asks for a letter to the attorney or judge, expressing concern for the safety of the child in question. In the name of "child protection," a condemning letter is written as requested and the therapist officially becomes a part of the alienating parent's supportive team. The phenomenon of a therapist becoming unwittingly biased in parental alienation cases has become more recognized and understood; however, even the most competent attorney cannot be expected to be adequately attuned to this (Greenberg, Gould, Gould-Saltman, & Stahl, 2003; Sauber, 2010). The MHC can play a role in a parental alienation case by determining whether the other MHPs on the case have failed to consider alternative explanations for a child's purported fear and rejection of a parent.

Through a review of the extant materials, a strategy must be outlined and recommended to the lawyer to expose to the trier of fact the damaging bias of this otherwise well-intentioned therapist, and how such misinformation should be discarded. The lawyer may subpoena the office records of the therapist and/or conduct a deposition. The particular issues and pertinent questions would be identified and developed by the MHC. This process would include a focus on the ethical and administrative errors committed by this therapist and how these violations caused distorted and unreliable conclusions, such as meeting with one parent and excluding the other when permission/consent of both parents is required to see a minor child having separated or divorced parents unless one parent has sole custody (see Garber, this volume, for more information about this).

A Unique Role

A closing example is provided with respect to the various ways in which a MHC can pay a unique and vital role in PA cases. In this case, a court-appointed custody evaluator was a psycho-educational child psychologist who lacked forensic experience and training. In his custody report, he diagnosed the mother as paranoid based upon the psychological test result. However, the MHC was able to point out that the evaluator incorrectly administered the test, leading the mother to respond as if it were a marital questionnaire. Thus, the test results were based upon misinterpretations of the data. In addition, the custody evaluator relied on notes of the father's psychiatrists, which were nothing more than hearsay from the father about the mother. Again, the MHC provided a useful critique of the methods of the evaluator and was able to demonstrate that the wife, not generally suspicious in nature, was suspicious of the father and for good reason, as he was shown to be manipulative and maliciously undermining of the mother. A further problem on the case was the fact that the child's therapist believed the adolescent daughter instead of realizing that she was "bought off" by the father and was merely demonstrating typical teenage bids for freedom in her disrespectfulness and disobedience to the mother. The therapist viewed the daughter's rebellion against the mother's rules and appropriate restrictions and her demand to reside with the father as a developmental response to the divorce. The GAL absolutely refused to have an independent evaluation of the 14-year-old or even concede to a 1-hour interview by another MHP. Thus, the gatekeepers created obstacles to the mother's position that the child was being alienated.

The MHC was able to challenge the daughter's therapist in his court recommendation that the mother only have limited supervised contact. Further, the MHC exposed the deceptive tactics of her husband and thereby lent credibility to the mother's claims of alienation. With the assistance of the MHC, the attorney was able to enhance his cross-examination procedures in questioning each of the cast of characters who supported the alienating father and prove to the court the necessity for a reversal of custody based upon the malicious behavior of the father, the acting out adolescent daughter, and the father's unrelenting false allegations against the mother. The judge began to understand how the father had wasted valuable court and agency resources by exploiting the system and deliberately lying. The mother acknowledged the benefit of having a MHC to assist her attorney in restoring her parenting relationship with her daughter.

Note

1 The authors contributed equally to the chapter.

References

Baker, A. J. L. (2007). Knowledge and attitudes about parental alienation syndrome: A survey of custody evaluators. *American Journal of Family Therapy, 35(1)*, 1–19.

Baker, A. J. L. (2010). Even when you win, you lose: Targeted parent's perceptions of their attorneys. *American Journal of Family Therapy, 38(1)*, 292–309.

Bone, J. M. & Walsh, M. (1999). Parental alienation syndrome: How to detect it and what to do about it. *Florida Bar Journal, 73(8)*, 44–48.

Caplan, G. (1970). *The theory and practice of mental health consultation* (p. 19). New York: Basic Books.

Gardner, R. (1987). *The parental alienation syndrome and the differentiation between fabricated and genuine child sex abuse.* Cresskill, NJ: Creative Therapeutics.

Gardner, R. (1992). *The parental alienation syndrome* (2nd ed). Cresskill, NJ: Creative Therapeutics.

Gould, J. & Martindale, D. A. (2007). *The art and science of child custody evaluations.* New York: Guilford Press.

Greenberg, L. R., Gould, J. W., Gould-Saltman, D. J., & Stahl, P. M. (2003). Is the child's therapist part of the problem? What judges, attorneys and mental health professionals need to know about court-related treatment for children. *Family Law Quarterly, 35*, 241–271.

Sauber, S. R. (2006). PAS as a family tragedy: Roles of family members, professionals, and the justice system. In R. A. Gardner, S. R. Sauber & D. Lorandos (Eds.), *The international handbook of PAS: Conceptual, clinical and legal considerations* (pp. 12–32). Chicago: Charles C. Thomas.

Sauber, S. R. (2010). *Why forensic evaluations are more effective than traditional psychotherapy in helping alienated children.* Presented at the Canadian Symposium for Parental Alienation Syndrome, Mt. Sinai School of Medicine, New York, U.S.A.

Sauber, S. R. (2011). *Alienation, estrangement, and bona fide abuse: Differentiating criteria for the development of the reunification plan.* Presented at the Canadian Symposium for Parental Alienation Syndrome, Montreal, Québec.

Sauber, S. R. (in press). Reunification planning and therapy. In. D. Lorandos, W. Bernet, & S. R. Sauber (Eds.), *Parental alienation: The handbook for mental health and legal professionals.* Chicago: Charles C. Thomas.

5 Educating Divorcing Parents

Taking Them Beyond the High Road

Amy J. L. Baker and Paul R. Fine

"I Have Lost My Children"

A new client comes to a psychotherapist. She is a 42-year-old mother of two teenage girls. The mother is distraught and anxious. When she enters the room, she immediately launches into a lengthy explanation of how afraid she is that her daughters will want to move out of her home and live with their father full-time. She explains that she is recently divorced and does not understand what is happening to her family. She describes herself as a full-time stay-at-home mother who devoted herself to her children, taking care of them night and day while their father worked long hours and was generally unavailable to participate in childcare responsibilities. She was the class parent at school, the soccer mom after school, and the chaperone taking the girls to all of their lessons and activities. She relaxes noticeably when she speaks about her children and their accomplishments. Both girls, she explains, are talented young musicians who have joined the junior orchestra. In addition, they are popular girls who do well in school. As she describes their childhood, the mother smiles with obvious pride but then her face clouds over as she begins to share that there has been a lot of tension since the divorce and both girls seem upset with her and protective of their father. In fact, she is worried that her girls are no longer the same sweet, loving children that they have always been. They have started to rebuff her affection, telling their mother that they are too old to cuddle and that their father respects them as the mature young women that they have become. The girls have started to behave in a haughty and cold manner, refusing to spend time with her unless she takes them shopping. Even then, the girls do not actually spend time with her. They huddle together and tell secrets to each other and appear to be making fun of their mother while she scurries behind them carrying their shopping bags. Just last night, her eldest daughter called her a stupid cow as she left the house in a huff to spend extra "father–daughter bonding" time with her father. It was not his scheduled parenting time but because they all live in the same town the girls went there whenever they wanted. By way of explanation, the girls had said that it was only fair that they spend more time with their father since they had spent more time with her up until now. It appeared to this mother that her ex-husband was giving the girls too much freedom and encouraging them to spend more time with him than they were supposed to according to their agreement. She worried that their grades were slipping and that they were practicing their instruments less than they should. They had even missed a few rehearsals lately. When she raised her concerns with her ex-husband, he casually shrugged his shoulders, told her to "lighten up," and said that he could not help it that he was the better parent. At this point in the session, tears stream down the face of the mother as she expresses her worst fear that she has lost her children.

Introduction

In light of the high rate of divorce and marital conflict, clinicians of adult clients will probably work with several who are dealing with a parental alienation situation. It is vital that the clinician has an accurate understanding of what alienation is so that the client can be helped to determine whether she is dealing with it. The clinician may even have a sense before the client does that this is a relevant issue for her. The purpose of this chapter is to provide a clear and detailed understanding of the primary alienation tactics that parents use in an effort to turn the child against the other parent.[1] The behaviors of an alienated child are described elsewhere in this volume (Sauber & Worenklein and Bone & Sauber). These parental alienating behaviors are the presumed causal agent in the development in some children of an unjustified alignment with one parent against the other (i.e., the child strongly favors one parent and rejects the other parent in the absence of any realistic reason for doing so). This chapter will begin with a discussion of four issues to consider as part of the hypothesis formulation stage of clinical work. Next, the 17 major parental alienation strategies will be presented along with an explanation of how they work to create a psychological breach between the child and the other parent. This information will be useful for the clinician and can be shared with the client as well. Following that will be a set of issues to discuss with the client and principles to teach the client with respect to coping with being a targeted parent. More information about the decision-making process is presented in Chapter 2 in this volume and more information about ongoing psychotherapeutic work with targeted parents is presented in Chapter 6.

Four Therapeutic Issues

Share Information about Parental Alienation in the Context of an Ongoing Therapeutic Relationship and an Understanding of the Client

Having a working hypothesis about whether a client is dealing with parental alienation and sharing that information with the client are two entirely different things. Clinicians usually consider several working hypotheses as they come to know a new client and make meaning of the information shared by the client, and as they observe the characteristics of the client presented during therapy sessions. A clinician who begins to formulate a hypothesis regarding the presence of alienation may make a mental note of it but should only share it with the client in a way that would be appropriate in light of the therapeutic relationship.

There are two dimensions in particular that are worth attending to: the certainty that alienation is present in the family and the assessment of the client's readiness and ability to process that information. Specifically, some clients might be so suggestible that it would not be advisable to raise the issue of alienation unless the clinician is very certain it is present in the case. Some clients might be too depressed or too anxious to deal with alienation, which would need to temporarily take a backseat to concerns about helping the client regulate mood and affect. Further, the clinician must have some degree of trust that what is shared with the client will not be misunderstood or misused (i.e., repeated to others as if it were a diagnosis, used as a weapon against the other parent, shared inappropriately with the children, and so forth).

Propose Parental Alienation as a Hypothesis to be Explored Rather than as a Fact

In discussing the possibility that an alienation dynamic is present in the family, the clinician most likely will want to present it as a possibility rather than as a certainty. Unless he or she is an alienation expert, the clinician probably does not have sufficient background and training to determine with certainty that alienation is a factor in the client's life. Further, alienation is a family dynamic as opposed to an individual characteristic and thus unless the clinician has access to all of the parties or at least extensive objective documents and collateral contacts, he or she probably does not have enough information to conclude with certainty that alienation is present. Needless to say, most individual therapists only have access to one side of the equation (the information shared by the client) and must take that into account as well.

Another consideration is that there is no definitive diagnostic assessment protocol for determining presence of parental alienation. While the syndrome/disorder is not currently included in the American Psychiatric Association's *Diagnostic and Statistical Manual of Mental Disorders* (the DSM), even if it were included, that diagnosis would reflect the presence of alienation in the child and not the presence of alienating strategies in the other parent. For all of these reasons, what can at best be mentioned to the client is that some of the information she is sharing in session sounds consistent with parental alienation. It might be helpful for the clinician to begin by asking the client if she is familiar with that term and what she knows about it and proceed from there.

Be Aware that Some Parents May Latch onto Parental Alienation as a Way to Avoid Looking at Themselves

Some parents whose children reject them or are behaving in an oppositional defiant manner may be correct that the other parent is instigating the conflict and difficulties. Other parents may be experiencing conflict with their children for reasons entirely unrelated to the attitudes and actions of the other parent. Rejection by one's child is extremely painful, shaming, and frustrating and no parent wants to feel that she has done something that would warrant that kind of response from her own children. Indeed, there is considerable inducement for perceiving that the other parent has engineered the parent–child conflict. So again, caution must be exercised when raising the issue of alienation with the client.

If the assessment of the client's readiness allows, the clinician can suggest it as a possible influence in the family, something to be explored and considered. One suggestion is to ask the client to document the presence/absence of each of the 17 alienation strategies over the course of a few weeks in order to gather some objective "data." It is possible that the client is unrealistic about what is expected from a former spouse (i.e., an awkward greeting is probably par for the course and not an indication of alienation). While the "good divorce" is the goal of many (Ahrons, 1995), not achieving a genuinely warm and mutually respectful post-divorce relationship with one's former spouse is not equivalent to alienation.

It will be important for the client to explore the possibility that her own attitudes and behaviors may be contributing to the problem by either antagonizing the other parent and/or creating conflict and distance with her child. Raising these issues must be done carefully in order to avoid appearing as if the clinician is just one more person in a long line of people who does not understand what is really going on and is, therefore, "blaming the victim" rather than accepting that alienation is present.

Be Aware that Characteristics of the Client in the Therapy Session May Not be Diagnostic

Clinicians are trained to observe the behavior of the client in the therapy session, attending to whether there is, for example, pressured speech, lack of eye contact, and instability of mood and thoughts. All of this information is "diagnostic" and factors into the therapists' assessment of the client. Such information can be used by the clinician to imagine how the client behaves outside of the therapy session and can, thus, provide insight into the client's relationship patterns and modes of functioning. While this is often a helpful approach for gaining insight into the character and functioning of a client, it can sometimes be misleading in cases of alienation. It is likely that a client who is dealing with alienation may present in a manner that at first appears paranoid (believing that someone is obsessed with harming the client and her relationship with her children), hysterical (feeling that this is one of the worst things that could happen to a person), obsessive (ruminating over past interferences and frustrations and worrying about future run-ins), depressed/anxious, and so forth. It is possible for a targeted parent to be all of those things but it is also possible that speaking about the experience of being a targeted parent may create the appearance of having certain psychological issues that are not actually character based but rather are realistic and appropriate responses to this particular form of victimization. Sifting through what is a situational response to the alienation and what is characterological may take some time in order to avoid a misdiagnosis of the client.

Primary Parental Alienation Strategies

In Table 5.1 the primary parental alienation strategies are presented along with examples in order to provide the clinician and the client with a point of reference. When discussing the strategies the term alienating parent is used to refer to the parent engaging in these behaviors while the other parent is referred to as the targeted parent. These strategies have been identified in research with adults who, when they were children, were turned against the other parent (Baker, 2007) and by targeted parents (Baker & Darnall, 2006). Research has confirmed their validity as alienation strategies (Baker & Chambers, 2011; Baker & BenAmi, 2011; BenAmi & Baker, 2012).

Taken together, these 17 parental alienation strategies work to create psychological distance between the child and the targeted parent such that the relationship becomes conflict-ridden. Each of these strategies serves to: (1) further the child's cohesion and alignment with the alienating parent; (2) create psychological distance between the child and the targeted parent; (3) intensify the targeted parent's anger and hurt at the child's behavior; and (4) incite conflict between the child and the targeted parent should the targeted parent challenge or react to the child's behavior. It is important to note that not all 17 need to be present in order to determine that alienation is present in a family. In fact, there is no specific number required because what seems to be most important is how effective the other parent is at utilizing these strategies. Intensity, frequency, and duration may be as important as the absolute number.

Table 5.1 The 17 primary parental alienation strategies

Strategy	*Explanation and example*
Badmouthing	Alienating parent (AP) uses verbal and non-verbal communications that convey to the child that the targeted parent (TP) is unloving, unsafe, and unavailable. Existing flaws are exaggerated and non-existent flaws are manufactured. Statements are made frequently, intensely, with great sincerity, and unbalanced by anything positive.
Limiting contact	The AP violates parenting plans and/or takes advantage of ambiguities in the plan to maximize time with the child. The TP has fewer opportunities to counter the badmouthing message, leading to the attenuation of the parent–child attachment relationship. The child acclimates to spending less time with the TP and the court might even reward the AP by instituting the new "status quo" as the permanent schedule.
Interfering with communication	The AP demands constant access to the child when the child is with the TP but does not reciprocate when the child is with him/her. Phones are not answered, e-mail messages are blocked, and messages are not forwarded. The TP has fewer opportunities to be a part of the child's daily world and share with the child the small moments that make up a child's life.
Interfering with symbolic communication	Thinking about, talking about, and looking at pictures of a parent while away can help a child feel close and connected to an absent parent. The AP creates an environment in which the child does not feel free to engage in these activities with respect to the TP. Alienating parents, however, are able to make their presence felt to the child even when the child is with the TP. The child is preoccupied with thoughts of the AP, making frequent calls to check in, following rules imposed by the AP, worrying that the AP will be upset or angry. The child's mind and heart are preoccupied with the AP and there is no room left for the child's thoughts and feelings about the TP.
Withdrawal of love	APs make their approval of paramount importance to the child; so much so that the child would do anything to avoid the loss of love that is experienced when the child has disappointed or angered that parent. Typically what angers and hurts the AP most is the child's love and affection for the TP. Thus, in order to secure the love of one parent, the child must relinquish the love of the other. Although this is not something likely to be explicit to the child, it will be apparent to the TP that the child lives in fear of losing the AP's love and approval.
Telling the child that the TP is dangerous	A particular form of badmouthing, this involves creating the impression in the child that the TP is or has been dangerous. Stories might be told about ways in which the TP has tried to harm the child, about which the child has no memory but will believe to be true nonetheless, especially if the story is told often enough.
Forcing child to choose	The AP will exploit ambiguities in the parenting plan and create opportunities to seduce/compel the child away from the TP by scheduling competing activities and promising valued items and privileges. If both parents are present at the same event/location the child will favor the AP and ignore or be rude to the TP.

Table 5.1 Continued

Strategy	*Explanation and example*
Telling the child that the TP does not love him or her	Another specific form of badmouthing occurs when the AP allows or encourages the child to conclude that the TP does not love him or her. The AP might make statements that conflate the end of the marriage with the end of the parent's love of the child (i.e., Mommy left us, or Daddy doesn't love us anymore). The AP will foster the belief in the child that she is being rejected by the TP and distort every situation to make it appear as if that is the case.
Confiding in the child	The AP will involve the child in discussions about legal matters and share with the child personal and private information about the TP that the child has no need to know. The AP will portray him/herself as the victim of the TP, inducing the child to feel pity for and protective of the AP, and anger and hurt toward the TP. The confidences are shared in such a way as to flatter the child and appeal to his/her desire to be trusted and involved in adult matters.
Forcing child to reject the TP	APs create situations in which the child actively rejects the TP, such as calling the TP to cancel upcoming parenting time or request that the TP not attend an important school or athletic event. Not only is the TP being denied something that s/he truly desires but s/he is being delivered the news by the child, leading to feelings of hurt and frustration. The TP may respond by lashing out at the child, further damaging their already fragile relationship. Further, once children have hurt a parent, the alienation will become entrenched as the child justifies his/her behavior by devaluing the TP.
Asking the child to spy on the TP	TPs usually have information in their files, desk, or computer that is of interest to the AP, such as paystubs, receipts, legal documents, medical reports, and so forth. An AP might suggest directly to a child or hint that the TP has information that s/he is not sharing with the AP. The AP will likely create the impetus in the child by linking the information to the child's desires (i.e., if we knew whether Daddy got a raise we could ask for more money and buy a new dog for you). Once children betray a parent by spying on them, they will likely feel guilty and uncomfortable being around that parent, thus furthering the alienation.
Asking the child to keep secrets from the TP	The AP will ask or hint that certain information should be withheld from the TP in order to protect the child's interests. Such as, "If Mommy knew that we were planning on taking a trip she would take me to court and try to stop it. Let's not tell her until Saturday, when it will be too late for her to interfere." Like spying, keeping secrets creates psychological distance between the TP and the child, who may feel guilty and uncomfortable with the TP. Obviously, when the TP discovers that the child withheld the information, the parent will be hurt and/or angry at the child.
Referring to the TP by first name	Rather than saying "Mommy/Daddy" or "Your mommy/Your daddy" the AP will use the first name of the TP when talking about that parent to the child. This may result in the child referring to the TP by first name as well. The message to the child is that the TP is no longer someone whom the AP respects as an authority figure for the child and no longer someone who has a special bond with the child. By referring to the TP by first name, the AP is demoting that parent to the level of a peer or neighbor.

Referring to a step-parent as "Mom" or "Dad" and encouraging child to do the same	Once the AP is remarried, s/he will speak of the new partner as if that parent were the only mother/father of the child. This parent will be introduced to others (teachers, coaches, parents of friends) as the "mother/father" rather than as the step-parent. The AP will refer to that parent as the mother/father to the child and create the expectation that the child will do so as well. If the TP should find out that the child is doing this, she will be hurt and angry with the child.
Withholding medical, academic, and other important information from TP/keeping TP's name off medical, academic, and other relevant documents	All important forms from school, sports, religious education, and so forth ask for information about the child's mother and father. The AP will not provide information about the TP in the appropriate place on the form and may not include the information at all. In this way, the TP will be at a decided disadvantage in terms of accessing information, forging relationships, being contacted in emergencies, being invited to participate, being provided with changes in schedules/locations, and so forth. Further, the AP will not provide the TP with schedules, reading lists, notices, and the like from the school, coach, doctor, and so forth. Taken together, these twin strategies marginalize the TP in the eyes of the child and important adults in his/her life. They also make it considerably more difficult for the TP to be an active and involved parent.
Changing child's name to remove association with TP	If the AP is the mother, she may revert to using her maiden name after the divorce and will institute a practice of using that name for her children as well. If the AP is a mother and she remarries, she will assume the surname of her new husband and will institute a practice of using that new surname for her children as well. If the AP is the father, he may start referring to the child with a new nickname (convincing the child that s/he has always been called by this name) and in this way forge a new identity for the child in which the AP is the most important parent. The TP may feel distant and awkward with the child who now refers to him- or herself with a new name. The TP may feel that the name change represents a rejection of him/her and will experience hurt, sadness, and frustration because of that.
Cultivating dependency/ undermining the authority of the TP	Alienated children often speak of the AP as if that parent were perfect, exceptional, and in every way above reproach. They also behave as if they are dependent on that parent in a way that is not necessary or appropriate given their age and life experience. APs are able to develop dependency in their children rather than (as is typical of non-alienating parents) help their children develop self-sufficiency, critical thinking, autonomy, and independence. At the same time, they will undermine the authority of the TP in order to ensure that the child is loyal to only one parent. Examples include instituting rules that the child must follow even when with the TP, and mocking or overwriting the rules of the TP. The AP becomes elevated in the eyes of the child while the TP becomes less important and less meaningful.

Helping Targeted Parents Become Prepared and Educated

Keep a Diary of Notable Events to Ascertain Trends and Patterns

Targeted parents often find themselves caught off-guard and surprised at the ever-expanding and devious ways in which the alienating parent can interfere with their plans and relationship with their children. It often feels as if the alienating parent is always one step ahead. Clinicians can therefore encourage a client who is a targeted parent to think in a well-planned and strategic manner about how to respond to being a targeted parent.

One helpful technique for being more prepared (and hopefully more strategic) is to keep a record of every manifestation of alienation that is occurring in the family. This could be useful for possible future legal action but in the immediate time frame, the journal could prove useful in the therapeutic session because: (1) it could serve as a reality check in that perhaps what the client believes is alienation is actually not and (2) perhaps in reviewing the areas of difficulty, the client and clinician can identify possible patterns and trends regarding where the major problem areas lie.

For example, if transfer of the children from the alienating parent to the targeted parent is a major difficulty (the targeted parent perceives the alienating parent as hostile and confrontational and the children act out), perhaps the schedule could be modified such that the transfer occurs at the end of the school day, eliminating opportunities for both parents to be present at the same time. While many alienation strategies will not lend themselves to such quick fixes, especially if the alienating parent is determined to wreak havoc, it is advisable to explore whether some structural changes can reduce tension in the family. How the alienating parent responds to these suggestions can be instructive for ascertaining how committed that parent is to the alienation agenda.

Become Educated about Parental Alienation Syndrome and its Experts

Encourage the client to learn as much about parental alienation as possible. There is a burgeoning body of knowledge and information available on the Internet, including webinars, brochures, YouTube lectures, reading lists of articles and books, and so forth. Any parent concerned that alienation is a possible factor in her life could benefit from being an informed consumer of this knowledge base. It could also be helpful to the client to identify specialists in the field of alienation (attorneys, mediators, custody evaluators, psychologists) in the event that such experts are required. Should a crisis erupt (i.e., the child refuses visitation, the alienating parent threatens to move away with the children) the targeted parent will be prepared with names and numbers of respected and qualified professionals. That is preferable to trying to identify appropriate resources while feeling intense fear, panic, distraction, and anxiety that are likely to be activated by such a crisis.

Seek Legal Advice from a Parental Alienation-Informed Attorney

Too often, targeted parents make concessions to the alienating parent and allow infractions on their parenting time to go unchallenged. Unfortunately, these concessions can be exploited by the alienating parent to create a new, modified status quo in which the targeted parent has even fewer rights and less access time.

Precedence is a legal concept that might not be fully understood by the targeted parent. For example, if the parent fails to show up for a scheduled visit on one weekend, she could be opening the door to relinquishing her parenting time on other weekends. In the name of peace, the targeted parent might make certain choices that in the short run reduce tension but in the long run further empower the alienating parent to encroach on the targeted parent's time and relationship with the children. Every choice the targeted parent makes with respect to parenting time has to be considered from the lens of "how will this look to the courts" and in order to do that, the targeted parent should consult with an attorney who is familiar with family law in general and parental alienation in particular. This does not necessarily mean that the targeted parent plans to initiate legal action. It does mean that the actions taken by the targeted parent are informed by an understanding of her legal rights and by an awareness of the legal consequences of her choices.

Another avenue to explore is post-divorce mediation, a process whereby divorced parents can engage in structured facilitated sessions to resolve conflicts in a mutually agreed upon manner without going to court. Some of the advantages include being less expensive, possibly less stressful, and less adversarial than court. Parents who find themselves in constant conflict post divorce might want to consider mediation as a possible means for working through the areas of difficulty with the assistance of a trained facilitator. If issues of domestic violence are present in the family, however, mediation is typically not recommended as it may not be a safe place for the victim, and the mediation process may not be free from undue influence (bullying, threats, intimidation). Likewise, mediation is not ideal when one of the parties has considerably more power (money, influence, persuasion) than the other. This characterizes many alienation cases and therefore should be considered with caution.

Helping the Client go Beyond the High Road

As noted in Baker and Fine (2008), many targeted parents believe that the best and most ethical response to alienation is to "take the high road." This is interpreted as refraining from saying anything to the child in self-defense that could be construed as negative about the other parent. While the goal is a lofty one, the practice has some very real limits; chief among them is that as a model for action it only tells the parent what *not* to do (do not badmouth the other parent) and not *what* to do (how to protect the relationship that is being undermined). Further, some parents who "take the high road" become depressed or enraged, both of which are natural responses to the constant frustration and intrusion of the alienating parent in their lives. The problem is that being depressed and enraged interferes with optimal parenting and, in that sense, the targeted parent can unwittingly exacerbate the alienation.

"Beyond the high road" represents another way. Like the high road, it does not involve badmouthing the other parent or responding to the noxious influence of the alienating parent in a reciprocal fashion. But it goes beyond telling the targeted parent what not to do and offers concrete suggestions for what to do. However, before exploring with the parent how to go "beyond the high road" it will be important for the clinician to have a good sense from the client about her parenting style and attempts made so far to reduce the conflict with the other parent and maintain the parent–child relationship in the face of the alienation strategies. This should help the client feel understood and known by the clinician and will provide the clinician with important information about the strengths of the parent that can be built on and the weaknesses that can be shored up. It may be advised that the parent seeks parental education in order to develop and refine parenting skills as well as demonstrate to the courts her commitment to being the best possible parent, even though that parent may feel that she should not have to prove that she has adequate parenting skills.

A further consideration is that not every client will be immediately ready to focus on how to respond to the alienation. The client might need to process the experience of being a targeted parent and might need time to experience empathy and support from the clinician before feeling that she has the internal resources to think strategically about the alienation. It will help to clarify with the client that exploring these approaches does not imply that she is to blame for the alienation. In the absence of alienation, the targeted parent could be an imperfect parent (as all parents are) and it probably would not result in her children rejecting her. But in the face of alienation, the targeted parent must go above and beyond in her efforts to be the best parent possible and to strategically respond to the alienation. Being a targeted parent requires extraordinary effort and foresight as well as fortitude and a very thick skin. Make sure that the client understands that offering suggestions for how she can improve as a parent does not mean she is being blamed for the alienation.

Understand the Badmouthing Message that the Child is Receiving in Order to Counter it in Words, Deeds, and Relationship Style

The first strategy involves exploring with the client all of the aspects of the badmouthing message and other alienating strategies that the child is being exposed to in order to help the parent deeply understand the alienation from the child's perspective. Questions to address include what the details of the badmouthing messages are and which ones seem to have the most traction with the child. What is the "hook" that is keeping the alignment going from the child's perspective? For example, is the child afraid that the alienating parent will fall apart should the child love the targeted parent? Is the child being flattered and gaining ego gratification from being given excessive freedom and privileges? Seeing the alienation from the child's vantage point should help the client remember that the child—who may be behaving in a very rude, arrogant, and entitled manner—is a victim in this family drama.

Some parents may have difficulty remembering that their child is being subjected to intense emotional manipulation by the alienating parent because the child is hurting them so much and appears to be actively engaging in the alienation. Alienated children present as willing participants in the alienation who are choosing to reject the targeted parent of their own free will. Taking this presentation at face value can lead to a targeted parent making some tragic decisions, such as withdrawing from the relationship. But, if the targeted parent can understand the alienation from the child's perspective (the fear of losing the love of the alienating parent, the influence of the false idea that the targeted parent does not love him/her) then the targeted parent can maintain empathy for the child (see more on this below), can hang in there for the long run, and can hopefully identify some strategic ways of responding.

It is important to note that *how* the alienation is countered is of paramount importance. It is not merely a question of telling the child that she is being manipulated or that she is wrong or that she has become a puppet of the other parent. No child wants to be told that she has been tricked, lied to, or is acting as a stooge for someone else. Figuring out how to respond will take great care and can only be accomplished once the alienation dynamic is understood. Once the message is understood then the targeted parent can proceed to strategically determine how to respond.

Being strategic is critical. It is not enough to simply be safe, loving, and available, although that is essential. It is necessary to find ways to counter the badmouthing/alienation message in a way that will appeal to the child and have maximum impact. The parent can use her insight into the unique aspects of the child to think about possible ways to try to counteract the badmouthing message. Thus, for example, if the message is that the targeted parent is a pathetic social outcast then that parent can devise situations in which the child will have the opportunity to observe her being treated with respect by people whom the child admires. Situations that spark cognitive dissonance in the child (where two opposing beliefs collide, Festinger, 1957) can allow the child to reconsider some assumptions about the targeted parent without the parent having to state the obvious: "See, this person whom you admire respects me. Therefore, I cannot be as bad or as crazy as your other parent wants you to believe that I am."

Try to Spark Critical Thinking Skills in the Child by Asking Questions and Exploring the Child's Perceptions

Alienation is a process that involves the slow erosion of the child's critical thinking skills. Because alienation does not occur overnight, there is a window of opportunity to counter the badmouthing. One way to do this is by shoring up the child's critical thinking skills. Critical thinking is defined as the act of looking at one's thoughts and ascertaining if they are rational, based on best available evidence, and free from undue influence from outside sources (Halpern, 1998). Critical thinking involves considering whether there is bias in one's thoughts, undue pressure from an outside source to hold a certain belief, or countervailing evidence that could lead to a change in beliefs. The strategies of the alienating parent are likely to erode the child's critical thinking skills because they require the child to blindly accept ideas that are not consistent with the child's own experience, which the child does out of fear of losing the love and approval of the alienating parent. Thus, alienation involves the alienating parent overriding the child's own judgment, memories, and feelings and imposing a new reality and set of rules on the child in which the alienating parent is always right and good while the targeted parent is always wrong and bad. Thus, any opportunity to help the child develop/enhance her critical thinking, even if not directly related to parent–child relationships, might transfer to that relationship in a way that could counter the badmouthing/alienation messages (Halpern, 1998).

The parent might develop techniques for encouraging the child to think for herself and decide for herself what she believes about her parents rather than accept without reservation whatever other people say and think. The basic message to give the child is that the child might hear some bad and confusing things about the targeted parent but it is important that the child decides for herself what to believe. Gardner's *Boys and Girls Book About Divorce* (1985) provides parents with several examples of how to encourage children to think for themselves as does "*I Don't Want to Choose*" by Andre and Baker (2008) (see Baker and Andre in this volume for more about the "I Don't Want to Choose" program based on the book.)

Always be Empathic with the Child; Use Emotion Coaching

What some targeted parents fail to understand is that the most important aspect of responding to alienation is to be empathic with the child: "Wow, that must be sad for you to think that I stole your college money" and to show oneself to be safe, loving, and available. In general, what children remember is the feeling of an interaction (did they feel warm and safe and listened to) more than they remember the content of a specific conversation.

It may be particularly difficult for the targeted parent to navigate past the child's accusations because the parent feels understandably angry and desires to correct the misunderstanding in order to set the record straight. The targeted parent might feel angry at the child for making the accusation or being difficult with the parent. The parent might even feel hurt, frustrated, or helpless, all of which can make it difficult to remember that the child is actually the victim (how sad for a child to be told that her parent is stealing her college money, or broke up the family, or does not care enough to pay the bills). Thus, the targeted parent must as much as possible respond to what she experiences as the child's provocations with loving empathy. And while there may be time later to show the child the bank statement, the truth is that if the child does not feel emotionally attended to, seeing the bank statement will not make her feel better about the targeted parent.

It is vital for a targeted parent to remember that the intent of the alienating parent is to incite conflict between her and her child such that the targeted parent will be enraged/reactive/explosive or depressed/passive/helpless. Either way, the targeted parent becomes someone the child may want to avoid. If the manipulation is successful, the targeted parent participates in her own alienation. The targeted parent's response in the face of this intent must be to avoid that trap and remain calm, loving, appropriate, and empathic with the child. This is the true high road. Role modeling and practicing these types of responses with the targeted parent might be helpful so that the targeted parent can respond authentically to the child.

Another helpful resource is the work of John Gottman (1997), who coined the term "emotion coaching" to describe the healthy practices of parents who are aware of their child's emotions, recognize emotional expression as an opportunity for intimacy and teaching, listen empathetically, and validate their child's feelings. Gottman encourages parents to label emotions in words a child can understand, and help a child identify an appropriate way to solve a problem or deal with an upsetting issue or situation. Gottman's research has found that children of parents who employ these skills are more likely to have what Goleman (2005) refers to as "emotional intelligence." This means that the children are better able to regulate their emotional states and soothe themselves when they are upset, calm down faster after an upsetting incident, have fewer infectious illnesses, are better at focusing their attention, and relate better to other people. Emotion coaching will not only contribute to the child's long-term emotional health, it can add warmth and security to the parent–child relationship in the here and now because it allows for processing strong emotions that otherwise could contribute to the alienation.

Try to Spark Sense Memories and the Deep Attachment that is Underneath the Alienation

Inside the alienated child is a loving child who wants and needs the love of the targeted parent. That child is encased in a brittle shell of arrogance, entitlement, hostility, and rejection. As noted throughout the paper, the targeted parent must see through the hard exterior to the child inside. A useful metaphor is provided in the book *The Runaway Bunny* (Brown, 1942) in which the baby bunny (in the absence of alienation) explores the notion of separating from his mother. Rather than become angry or disappointed, the mother bunny joins the child's fantasy and assures her baby that no matter where he goes or who he becomes, she will always love and accept him. Thus, an important task for the targeted parent is to emotionally connect with that child trapped inside the alienation by evoking memories, thoughts, and feelings that remind the child that she does love the targeted parent. There are thoughts, feelings, and memories inside the child's mind that are deeper than the alienation (which can be pictured as a dark shroud covering the child's love of the targeted parent).

There are ways to get "under the cover" of the alienation and bypass the child's manipulated thinking and "speak to" the deeper part of the child's heart and mind. One way to do that is through evoking sense memories. As Marcel Proust reflected, "the smell and taste of things remain poised a long time … ready to remind us." (1982, p. 50–51). This phenomenon has now been borne out in empirical science: a single smell or sound has the power to conjure up entire scenes from the past (Gottfried, Smith, Rugg, & Dolan, 2004). Targeted parents can use this knowledge to their advantage by cooking certain foods or bringing the child into proximity to sights, smells, tastes, and sounds that trigger sense memories of the child's love for that parent.

Try to Have the Child Take Ownership of her Plan, Goals, and Dreams

Many a targeted parent feels as if she is in battle against the alienating parent and to make matters worse, the child joins in against her. Often it can seem as if the child will give up anything and everything to please the alienating parent. Thus, if the targeted parent suggests that the child study the flute, the alienating parent will object and the child will declare that the flute is certainly not a valuable or important instrument. If the targeted parent enjoys camping, predictably the alienating parent will find that objectionable (if not contemptible) and the child will readily concur. An approach for living within this constraint that can be explored with the client is for the targeted parent to openly and lovingly encourage her child to develop her own tastes, desires, and goals, within appropriate limits (Cline & Fay, 1990). One way to do this is to provide the child with choices whenever possible. The alienating parent may be less likely to object if the choice is the child's and not the targeted parent's and the child will be less likely to relinquish the goal, dream, or plan if the child came up with the idea herself rather than having it seemingly imposed on her by the targeted parent.

Involve the Child in Problem-Solving

When successful, parental alienation strategies incite conflict between the child and the targeted parent. The more conflict and tension there is, the less likely it is that the child will want to spend time with that parent. A suggestion for reducing conflict is for the targeted parent to engage the child in mutual problem-solving when disagreements arise. Thus, rather than impose a sanction on a child which the child will surely resent (providing the alienating parent with yet another opportunity to join with the child against the targeted parent), the targeted parent can ask the child what she thinks would be an acceptable solution to their problem. As much as possible the targeted parent should aim to present the problems from their joint perspective. For example, rather than saying, "I want you to clean your room before you go out with your friends" the targeted parent can say, "We have a disagreement about how the cleaning and playing will get done. What do you think we can do to resolve this?" This can be especially disarming when the conflict is incited by the alienating parent.

Thus, rather than the alienating parent and the child being on one side of the conflict and the targeted parent alone on the other, in opposition to the child, the targeted parent and the child can be together in trying to work out a solution.

Do Not Take in the Badmouthing/Alienating Message

For a targeted parent there is a constant and intense negative message about her very being, value, and worth that is delivered by both her former spouse/partner and her child. The badmouthing and alienating messages are very clearly directed toward the targeted parent's personhood, such as she is a lousy and incompetent parent, she is mentally unstable and dangerous, her family members are worthless, her career and avocations are contemptuous, her style and appearance are laughable, and so forth. Anything and everything about her can and will be criticized. Needless to say, it is extremely painful for a targeted parent to endure such personal attacks and a challenge to resist internalizing the message that is being projected onto her by the alienating parent and the child.

Typically, clinicians encourage and applaud self-examination and exploration of the validity of self-criticisms. In the case of alienation, however, it is important to help the targeted parent *not* take in the noxious messages being directed at her. The clinician and client can identify strategies for the client to remind herself that her child is being destructively influenced and is, therefore, at most only partially responsible for her alienation actions and attitudes. Of course, the targeted parent will not want to say to the child, "I know you are being brainwashed, so I am not really going to respond to that" because that is likely to offend the child. However, the targeted parent can keep this in mind because it can help her modulate her feelings and behavior. The clinician can help the targeted parent develop a powerful mental image that she can invoke that will help her (1) not take in the message and become defeated and self-hating and (2) not blame the child for being so hurtful. Any image that depicts the child's true self as a loving child can help prevent the targeted parent from hating herself and hating her child.

Summary

There are countless ways in which one parent can interfere with and undermine the child's relationship with the other parent. The primary strategies are listed in Table 5.1. All of these actions can create a psychological breach between the child and the targeted parent. They are designed (intentionally or otherwise) to invalidate the humanity and worth of the targeted parent and make the targeted parent irrelevant to the life, mind, and heart of the child. This could certainly lead to feelings of helplessness and hopelessness, as well as rage, and might result in a targeted parent giving up on the relationship or becoming consumed with frustration and anger.

There is only so much heartache a parent can take. Thus, it is vital for the clinician to help the targeted parent remember that she is still the parent of a child who needs her—regardless of the protestations of the child and regardless of the efforts of the alienating parent to invalidate her—and must therefore continue to try to be the best possible parent. The clinician can further the targeted parent's resistance to accepting the badmouthing message/projection of the child (and the alienating parent) and giving up on the relationship. The clinician promotes the targeted parent's realistic assessment of the alienation dynamic and supports the targeted parent's understanding about how to live under the many constraints and challenges of being a targeted parent.

Note

1 For ease of reading, the female pronoun will be used throughout but it is understood that alienation happens both to mothers and fathers, sons and daughters.

References

Ahrons, C. R. (1995). *The good divorce: Keeping your family together when your marriage comes apart.* New York: William Morrow.

Andre, K., & Baker, A. J. L. (2008). *I don't want to choose: How middle school kids can resist the pressure to choose one parent over the other.* New York: Kindred Spirits.

Baker, A. J. L. (2007). *Adult children of parental alienation syndrome: Breaking the ties that bind.* New York: W. W. Norton.

Baker, A. J. L., & BenAmi, N. (2011). To turn a child against a parent is to turn a child against himself. *Journal of Divorce and Remarriage, 52(7)*, 472–489.

Baker, A. J. L., & Chambers, J. (2011). Adult recall of childhood exposure to parental conflict: Unpacking the black box of parental alienation. *Journal of Divorce and Remarriage, 52(1)*, 55–76.

Baker, A. J. L., & Darnall, D. (2006). Behaviors and strategies of parental alienation: A survey of parental experiences. *Journal of Divorce and Remarriage, 45(1/2)*, 97–124.

Baker, A. J. L. ,& Fine, P. (2008). *Beyond the high road: Responding to 17 parental alienation strategies without compromising your morals or harming your child.* Available at: http://www.amyjlbaker.com.

BenAmi, N., & Baker, A. J. L. (2012). The long-term correlates of childhood exposure to parental alienation on adult self-sufficiency and well-being. *American Journal of Family Therapy, 40(2)*,169–183.

Brown, M. W. (1942). *The runaway bunny.* New York: HarperFestival.

Cline, F., & Fay, J. (1990). *Parenting with love and logic.* Colorado Springs, CO: NavPress.

Festinger, L. (1957). *A theory of cognitive dissonance.* Stanford, CA: Stanford University Press.

Gardner, R. A. (1985). *The boys and girls book of divorce.* New York: Bantam.

Goleman, D. (2005). *Emotional intelligence: Why it can matter more than IQ.* New York: Bantam.

Gottfried, J. A., Smith, A. P. R., Rugg, M. D. & Dolan, R. J. (2004). Remembrance of odors past: Human olfactory cortex in cross-modal recognition memory. *Neuron, 42(4)*, 687–695.

Gottman, J. (1997). *The heart of parenting: Raising an emotionally intelligent child.* New York: Simon and Schuster.

Halpern, D. F. (1998). Teaching critical thinking skills for transfer across domains. *American Psychologist, 53(4)*, 449–455.

Proust, M. (1982). *Remembrance of things past Part 1: Swan in love* (pp. 50–51). New York: Vintage.

6 Psychotherapy with Targeted Parents

William Goldberg and Lorna Goldberg

The Impact of Parental Alienation Syndrome on a Father of Three

Mr. R., a 37-year-old department store salesperson, walks into the therapist's office, sighs, and shakes his head. He says that he cannot understand the behavior of his three children, who had demonstrated so much love towards him in the past. He tells the therapist that the children, a 13-year-old girl, a 10-year-old boy, and a 6-year-old girl, are now rude and obnoxious to him. They deliberately misbehave when they are with him, call him names to his face and are disrespectful and unkind to his parents, with whom they had always had a loving relationship. He says that their behavior is baffling to him.

Mr. R. and his wife had divorced a year and a half before this initial interview. Although the court had granted his wife and him joint custody (his home and the children's mother's home are located a block and a half from each other), the children refuse to sleep at his house. They make such a loud public scene when he tries to get them to do so that he becomes embarrassed in front of his neighbors. He finally relented and agreed to have them stay with their mother, which was their professed desire. However, he wanted to see them two nights a week and on weekends.

Mr. R. says that when he knocks on his ex-wife's door to get the children to leave with him for the evening or weekend, the children will often hide or yell out the window, "We don't like you! Go away!" At other times they will come with him, albeit with faces that indicate that they are being forced to march off to a day of misery. Mr. R. relates that once they arrive at his house the two youngest, the 6-year-old daughter and the 10-year-old son, will, within a matter of minutes, be playing with him or doing their homework. The eldest, the 13-year-old daughter, will usually talk on her cell phone to her friends or her mother, and will have the most minimal interactions with him. Eventually, his eldest child joins in the activities despite herself, and Mr. R. knows that she is enjoying herself. Once she called her mother to ask if she and her siblings could extend their stay. She emphasized that her brother and sister were asking to stay longer and did not share her own desire to do so. The mother demanded that the children come home at the expected time.

Mr. R. reports that he and his children had attended family therapy sessions with a court-appointed psychologist, but that these sessions were a disaster. During the sessions the children would huddle together on a couch and yell at Mr. R., proclaiming that they were afraid of him. When the court-appointed psychologist asked them to explain to their father why they were so afraid, they would reply that he was "mean." Upon prodding, they could not be specific except for offering three oft-repeated stories. One story they told was about the day that the father had twisted the eldest girl's arm. The second was that the father did not want to pay for an operation for the son. The third was that he had once thrown his son on his bed in a fit of anger.

The court-appointed psychologist seems to have viewed his role as to accept the children's stories and accusations and help them to communicate their stated feelings to their father. According to Mr. R., the psychologist never challenged the authenticity of the children's alleged fear of their father—in the authors' experience, children who are genuinely frightened of their father do not usually sit in the room and yell at their father about how scared they are. The psychologist did not explore with the children why they refused to consider the father's explanation and the psychologist accepted as fact the children's declarations of fear of the father, despite the fact that the children's manifest behavior did not seem to indicate genuine fear.

Mr. R. offered the following explanations to the therapist for the three stories. The alleged twisting of his daughter's arm was the result of an incident when she had tried to jump out of the father's car onto a busy roadway. The father relates that he had grabbed his daughter's arm to save her from possible injury. The story of his not wanting to pay for an operation was a distortion of the fact that he had suggested that they solicit a second opinion before subjecting the child to a risky operation. Mr. R. expresses bewilderment as to the origin of the alleged bed-throwing incident except to recall that before the divorce he would sometimes play an "airplane" game with his children and would playfully throw the children onto their beds.

As the session with Mr. R. progresses, he discusses the context in which his children's behavior takes place. He reports that, although his 13-year-old daughter was usually defiant towards him, his 6-year-old daughter was often friendly, loving, and happy to see him. The only time she acts withdrawn and sullen around him is when her mother is present. The 10-year-old boy's behavior also is dependent on who is within earshot. If his mother or older sister is around, he will join with his sister in loudly denouncing his father, running away from him, or refusing to speak to him. If neither one of them is present he will be friendly and, on rare occasions, he will even act in a loving manner.

Over time, the therapist has the opportunity to assess that Mr. R's family is affected by parental alienation, which becomes a major focus of the therapist's psycho-educational approach to therapy. Mr. R.'s response to his children's rejection led to his adopting a depressed, withdrawn, and passive role (see below). His responses to his children's accusations were primarily to sigh, shake his head, and attempt to change the subject. At times, he would express bewilderment to his children as to how they could believe that he would act in such a selfish manner. At other times, he would try to reason with them, pointing out the inconsistencies in their accusations and telling them that their behavior was breaking his heart.

Mr. R. would sometimes try to reason with his ex-wife, telling her that she was distorting his position when she spoke to the children; but he was not as adept a fighter as she was. His ex-wife would respond to his pleadings with scorn and vitriol, and Mr. R. would back away from the confrontation. In therapy, Mr. R. was able to express anger at his ex-wife for her alienating behavior, but continued to find it difficult to confront her directly. He was able to express anger and frustration with his therapist about the fact that, while his responses to the situation could be modified, there was nothing that he or his therapist could do to change his ex-wife's destructive behavior.

Mr. R. found it helpful to keep an ongoing log of his encounters with his ex-wife and the children. Each week, he and his therapist would review this log and talk about the feelings that these encounters engendered in him and different ways that he could have responded. Over time, his responses became more strategic and productive. As of the date of writing this chapter, Mr. R.'s children continue to be alienated from him and initially to act in a hostile manner when they are with him. However, over time, Mr. R. has become less depressed as he has become more actively involved in attempting to change his situation and he continues to fight for his parental rights in court.

Introduction

The therapist working with targeted parents in parental alienation syndrome (PAS) situations needs to serve as both an educator and a clinician. In the beginning of therapy, it is crucial for the therapist to be involved in history taking. As part of the history, there needs to be specific focus paid to the genesis and the progression of the breach between the client and the children. This focus allows for the possibility of other explanations for the relationship problems (i.e., the therapist needs to keep in mind that an alienating parent is not the driving force behind every case of a child's rejection of a parent). For example, the rejected parent might have behaved in a manner that put off the child, or the rejection might be the result of feelings generated by the child because of new circumstances that affect the child's life, such as the birth of a new sibling, the impending marriage of the rejected parent or that parent's desire to relocate with the child to a distant place. At the same time, it is important to explore each of the parents' reactions to these events and how they presented and discussed these changes with the child. For example, sometimes, a new relationship or marriage will intensify the other parent's desire to alienate the child.

If, in fact, the rejection seems driven by an alienating parent, it is advisable initially to adopt a psycho-educational approach with the targeted parent by educating the client about PAS. This can help the targeted parent have a more realistic understanding of the genesis of the behaviors shown by the child. A psycho-educational approach also will give the targeted parent a better sense of control over a situation that might be experienced as overwhelming, frustrating, depressing, and/or bewildering.

Although throughout the therapy process the therapist will continue to inform the client about PAS dynamics, in this chapter the focus will be on those aspects of psychotherapy that are not primarily psycho-educational. This chapter intends to give the therapist a better understanding of how the various ways that the pain of being alienated from one's children may impact the targeted parent's personality. Although characterological reactions to stress can be intensified by the PAS situation, the emphasis will be on differentiating personality styles and characteristics that are typical responses to the alienation situation from those responses that might solely reflect the targeted parent's characterological reactions to difficult situations.

In the beginning of therapy, the therapist needs to consider that the client's initial behavior also might serve as a shield to protect against the children's continued rejection. In order to help the client move from responses that can be self-defeating to responses that might be effective, the therapist can utilize a variety of strategies, including focusing on more helpful coping mechanisms. As therapy continues, transference and countertransference feelings will emerge in the therapeutic situation. Transference feelings can range from idealization to denigration. As part of the parallel process, the clinician might experience a range of countertransferential feelings, including anger at the alienating parent and children, frustration at the court or mental health system, a sense of sadness for the targeted parent, as well as a sense of hopelessness or inadequacy.

Finally, the necessity of reminding the targeted parent to focus on the larger picture will be discussed. It is crucial for the therapist to aid the targeted parent to develop a long-term strategy. With this in mind, the therapist suggests that the client allows for a connection in the future, if not in the present, by reminding the alienated children, whenever possible, of the parent's continual love. However, this does not mean that the targeted parent should accept abusive behavior. In the face of long-standing alienation, it also helps for the therapist to encourage the targeted parent to focus on the need for support from others and the need to have as full a life as possible outside the stressful PAS situation. This will allow the targeted parent to be better equipped to deal with painful and frustrating situations as they arise. If the therapist is realistically hopeful, the client can be helped to feel this hopefulness as well.

The Presenting Issues

The therapist is likely to encounter several different predominant emotions and coping mechanisms utilized by the client in the initial sessions of therapy. Although, for some parents, these reactions are associated with a characteristic lifelong way of responding under stress, many of these emotions and coping strategies can be seen as typical reactions to the PAS situation. These are responses that may have become intensified by years of dealing with a frustrating conflictual marriage, even prior to the PAS situation. Reactions displayed also can serve as the targeted parents' protective defense against the pain of being rejected by the children. The therapist will need to consider that these initial presenting emotions may hide a range of other, often contradictory, feelings that will need to be explored as well.

When exploring emotional reactions with clients, it is crucial for therapists to be respectful and to allow for the space and time to deal with all these emotions as therapy unfolds. Therapists need to tolerate and reflect upon their own reactions to the painful circumstance of loss of a child's love. Sometimes, it is easier for therapists to defend against experiencing this pain and, instead, hold onto the attitude that there must be *something* that the client has done to cause this set of circumstances, thus blaming the victim. Although the client may have exacerbated the situation by handling the alienation ineffectively, the therapist's defensive use of this attitude can serve as a barrier that often mirrors the attitude of others in the targeted parent's life. Anna Freud (1966) labeled this defense as "identification with the aggressor." Typically, targeted parents will present therapists with a combination of the following reactions:

Depression, Withdrawal and Passivity

Often, targeted parents feel battered and their body language can convey this feeling. Some parents grimly enter the therapist's office, as Mr. R. did, with head bowed and shoulders slumped.

Sadness is a natural reaction to a sense of loss; and, as has been stated, these individuals are experiencing the loss of their children's affection. It is also painful to be called names by one's children, to have them misinterpret motives, to hear them profess hatred for the parent, or to fight against spending time with the parent. It is also painful to bear witness to the abuse and manipulation of one's child whose personality becomes warped by the PAS process. It takes an extraordinarily resilient person to be able to weather the alienation of one's children without feeling depressed.

Sadness and even some degree of depression also can be seen as a natural response to the constant warfare that some targeted parents endure, especially from their children. Depression can be seen, in part, as the emotional expression of the state of helplessness and powerlessness that targeted parents might feel and this also can be coupled with a general sense of inadequacy. Depression might also be connected to feelings of self-blame. For example, targeted parents can reflect on times in the past when they made mistakes with their children, feeling that perhaps the alienation would not have taken hold in the absence of these mistakes. Instead of acknowledging that all parents make mistakes, targeted parents might overemphasize their failings.

This state of depression and general loss of self-esteem and sense of effectiveness can lead to a withdrawn, passive reaction to the PAS situation. Although the tendency to withdraw and react with passivity may have been the characterological way that some targeted parents have responded to difficulties in the past, the therapist should keep in mind that this is a common reaction for those who have experienced PAS.

When working with depressed, withdrawn, and passive clients, the therapist first needs to focus on helping them to examine the dynamics of the PAS situation, as outlined in Baker and Fine (this volume) and then to develop a strategy for dealing with these tactics. When the therapist sees the PAS situation occurring, a reframing intervention can help to mobilize targeted parents to label the tactics used by the alienating parent. By generalizing targeted parents' experience and by showing that the tactics used are common and typical of a PAS situation, the therapist can help targeted parents to increase confidence in their cognitive abilities and general self-worth. The feeling of despair and helplessness that immobilizes many targeted parents can be overcome when they recognize that these ploys are not unique to their situation; that exaggerations, distortions, and misinterpretations are common to many targeted parents and that there are counter-strategies that targeted parents have employed in the past that can help the client to feel less isolated. For example, instead of feeling rebukes from the children as if they were a boxer's punches, clients can be helped to take a more active role and to develop a counter-response that will, in the long run, be useful. Instead of feeling each new challenge from the alienating parent as an insurmountable obstacle, clients can be helped to categorize each ploy with a label and to devise a counter-strategy. Of course, there are no perfect and completely effective means of dealing with every situation, but a plan of action developed with the help of the therapist can counteract the sense of helplessness and reactive passivity.

Finally, written logs of encounters with the children as well as with the alienating parent can help targeted parents recognize patterns and rehearse better responses. These logs can also be essential if the courts are involved in the dispute between the parents. In the case of Mr. R., chronicling his encounters with his children and ex-wife, then discussing the interchange with the therapist, helped him to devise better responses to provocations.

Anger

Sometimes the primary emotion displayed by the targeted parents is that of anger. This anger can be directed at the alienating parent, who is perceived (usually correctly) as being the driving force behind the rejection of the children. The targeted parent, feeling trapped and set up, can react with frustration and anger. Additionally, anger can be directed towards the children, who might be viewed as the carriers of the alienating parent's messages. Unfortunately, the children are often deliberately provocative, boldly and callously defying the targeted parent's authority. They might then use the targeted parent's reactions to these provocations as proof of parental "meanness."

In many cases, a pattern is established in which the alienating parent undermines the realistic rules for behavior established by the targeted parent by siding with the complaints of the children, thus intensifying the conflict between the children and the targeted parent. This results in the targeted parent becoming defined as the "bad parent" whose efforts to set appropriate limits and refusal to indulge the children are seen as abusive. For example, a targeted parent might impose fair consequences for misbehaviors, which the alienating parent will agree with the child are too harsh. In these circumstances, the targeted parent can explain to the child that, at the targeted parent's home (as well as school and other environments) certain ways of behaving are expected of children. The client is demonstrating that reasonable rules of behavior should be followed. Actually, since children might feel some underlying guilt for displaying provocative behaviors, by setting limits the targeted parent is helping the children deal with their conflicted feelings about this behavior more effectively and the client might be preventing the behavior from escalating. It also has been suggested that in cases of alienation, in which the targeted parent does not have the luxury of parenting as usual, it can be helpful to engage the child in mutual problem-solving instead of imposing a consequence on the child, which is likely to be exploited by the alienating parent (Baker, personal communication).

Client anger may also be directed towards others (judges, therapists, teachers, erstwhile friends, family of the alienating parents) who may side or be perceived as siding with the alienating parent. When the manipulation and alienating dynamics are so clear to the targeted parent, it can be infuriating that this is not apparent to these individuals. However, there are several possible reasons why others might side with the alienating parent, which can be explored with the client:

1. Sometimes, alienating parents (who can appear to be charming) induce others to sympathize with them by portraying themselves as a victim of the targeted parent by selectively revealing or distorting facts.
2. As mentioned previously, along with other cases of victimization, there might be an element of "blaming the victim," believing that the targeted parent must have done *something* to set the alienation in motion. This belief is bolstered by the need of others to protect themselves from the possibility that these unfortunate circumstances could happen to them.
3. Alienating parents might be intimidating, inducing others, even unconsciously, to keep on their "good side" to avoid the negative consequences of taking a different point of view or crossing them.

The therapist can accept and empathize with the anger while encouraging the development of a more modulated and effective style of expression. The therapist needs to be aware that anger also can also serve as a defense against sadness, despair, and a sense of impotence. Although the defensive use of anger is worth exploring, the therapist needs to be mindful that clients should be able to relinquish anger at their own pace. Ultimately, individuals can be helped to examine the following: whether the anger is "working" for them, how the anger impacts their general sense of well-being and other relationships, and what they imagine would happen if they gave up their anger.

The therapist needs to consider that an angry attitude might be the result of a frustrating PAS situation in which clients have experienced exploitation in the past. They bring into the therapy the expectation of exploitation. The therapist can focus on this experience and use the induced feeling of being treated with suspicion or "put off" to better help the client to understand what might be induced in others. Dealing with this countertransference reaction directly will lessen the possibility that the therapist will be seen as either judgmental or defensive.

The therapist might also explore with clients who express a lot of anger towards or about the child ways in which the child reminds the client of the alienating parent. For example, therapists might discover that target parents are quite upset when their child displays arrogant behavior and the flaunting of rules. In exploring this recognition, it might be considered that entitled or antisocial behavior reminds clients of the alienating parent. Therapists can help target parents express another point of view to the child without moralizing. This message will be most effective if targeted parents show the child their own desire to follow rules and treat others with respect. Targeted parents can review and reframe callous, arrogant, or antisocial behavior by sharing a viewpoint that expresses empathy and respect for others. Sometimes, targeted parents can reflect with the children on how the children's behavior might have undermined relationships with friends or teachers.

Impatience

Impatience is a natural response from targeted parents who feel that time is slipping away from them as their alienated children change and grow without their involvement and as they are left out of developmental milestones, day-to-day activities, and important ceremonies. There might be an expectation that once the manipulation has been named and described, the problem will shortly be solved. Targeted parents initially might believe that pointing out the unfairness of the situation will yield understanding from judges, friends, and other onlookers and, ultimately, a change in behavior from the alienating parent and the children. Of course, this rarely is the case.

Therapists can empathize with clients' frustration. However, if at the same time therapists help clients recognize and fully acknowledge partial victories and the importance of laying the groundwork for future successes, clients might feel less impatient than if they focus on more immediate indications of success. Sharing with clients the recognition that there is no magic wand with which to immediately effectuate change can be a moving and healing experience for targeted parents, as is sharing the sadness felt about the fact that there is no real way to control or impose change on anyone but themselves. This reality is part of the human condition and transcends parental alienation. If the therapist feels that it would be therapeutic to self-disclose some aspect of life that the therapist wishes were different, that might aid as a reminder that all humans suffer under the condition of having limited control over many aspects of their lives. At the same time, it is not inevitable to embrace a depressive or defeated stance about this fact, as it is always possible to have a sense of personal agency. There are other aspects of life that can be changed.

Bewilderment

As in the case of Mr. R., targeted parents might be perplexed that children who were once loving and responsive are now rejecting and cruel. The empathic connection appears to have been lost. The alienating parent's blatantly manipulative, self-centered, or insensitive behavior appears to be met with acceptance from the children, while the children consistently regard the targeted parent's behavior in the harshest light.

The therapeutic response to clients' bewilderment is to explain the dynamics of the PAS situation. By understanding the children's behavior, clients can see the children's reaction not as a condemnation of the targeted parent, but as the children's predictable reaction to the combination of pressure experienced from the alienating parent, the fear of angering the alienating parent, a heightened sense of importance, and an unsophisticated, simplistic worldview.

Shame, Guilt, and Self-Blame

Targeted parents might feel embarrassed when they consider that others (e.g., family members, courts, counselors, teachers, etc.) believe the distortions and accusations that are being leveled against them. They might even come to incorporate and accept as partially or entirely true some of the accusations expressed. All parents can think of times when they were not as sensitive, patient, loving, or responsive to their children as they would have liked to have been. Sometimes targeted parents will focus on those instances to the exclusion of other instances and, thus, distort their significance, replicating what their children are doing to them. Furthermore, in the face of tragedy, which surely PAS is, it is natural for people to believe that their behavior must have had some influence. Of course, there is always *something* that played into the PAS situation, but the therapist can remind the client that all parents are flawed and children rarely feel that they have license to be so freely insensitive to a parent without the other parent's permission or encouragement. As in all circumstances, children are acutely sensitive to parental cues.

Feelings of shame, guilt, and self-blame may lead targeted parents to attempt to appease the alienating parent and the children by making overly accommodating concessions to their demands, even when those demands are unreasonable. These accommodations, however, rarely stop the accusations and name-calling in a PAS situation.

The therapeutic response is to point out the distortions of reality that might be present in the perception of other people's reactions. Judges who are seen as being callous might merely be acting cautiously. School staff who are perceived as taking the alienating parent's side might be reacting out of a wish to not get involved in the dispute. In those instances when others uncritically accept lies and distortions presented by the alienating parent and the children, it is therapeutic to acknowledge the unfairness of the situation but, at the same time, to help the client not to be defeated by this unfairness. The therapist can point out that it can be realistic to acknowledge one's actual shortcomings as a parent, but only if those shortcomings are placed into perspective. When clients are overly self-critical, the therapist can point out this fact and explore the parental perception prior to the PAS situation. This usually allows the client to get in touch with a past loved and more confident self.

Assess the Client's Previous Coping Strategies

In addition to recognizing presenting reactions, it is beneficial for therapists to understand targeted parents' use of coping mechanisms to the PAS situation. A review of the client's coping history should include the following:

Dealing with previous disappointments and major losses and achievements What coping strategies have been used and have these been successful? For example, have clients been successful in delaying gratification when working towards a valued goal in other areas of life?

Education Have they found it helpful to read about PAS? To attend conferences and hear speakers? To hear the experiences of others who are dealing with similar circumstances? To receive support from a face-to-face group or an Internet group? To discuss reactions and strategies with a trusted ally?

The Support System Individuals who cope best with the PAS situation usually have a support network with at least one friend or family member who understands the situation and is sympathetic. This factor might be one of the single most important variables in terms of how well the targeted parent will be able to deal with the PAS situation.

Therapy Have clients sought out other therapists for aid in dealing with this situation? Have they utilized therapy prior to the PAS situation? What has been their experience?

The assessment of these coping aids will guide the therapist in recommending further remedial steps. Perhaps successful past coping strategies are not helpful now. At times, previous strategies can be modified. One client, for example, believed that reaching out to others was a sign of weakness. He was concerned that, if he displayed this weakness to others, they would lose respect for him. He coped with the PAS situation by isolating himself, bearing the indignities of his children's rejection in stoic silence. Although he was involved in a relationship, he could not bring himself to discuss his frustration and pain with his partner. Eventually, he was helped to see that sharing his feelings and acknowledging his frustrations and fears would not only improve his ability to strategize the PAS situation but also enhance his relationship with his partner. As he shared more and problem solved with his partner, this targeted father's despair lightened.

Transference and Countertransference

Clients bring their conscious and unconscious feelings about others from their life into the therapy and these reactions will become part of the therapeutic mix. Freud's original use of the term "transference" was limited to the displacement of feelings and attitudes that originated with important figures from early life (Freud, 1940). Wallerstein (1997) describes some of the transference responses of divorced clients in therapy as "crisis-driven" (i.e., they can stem from reactions to those within the divorce situation itself rather than from early life relationships). For example, a targeted mother who believed that her ability to parent was being questioned by assessing professionals began to constantly look to her therapist for signs of approval. Prior to her separation from her alienating husband, this client felt confident in her parenting ability and this was an extension of self-confidence and trust in herself that stemmed from experiences with parents in childhood. In fact, in her present situation, her parents were providing her emotional support.

Targeted parents are likely to have become involved with other systems (such as the legal system, the educational system, and the medical system) that may have been experienced as indifferent, callous, and/or not having a sound appreciation of PAS dynamics. All of these experiences will color the clients' expectation of and reaction to therapy and to the therapist. For example, some targeted parents initially might view the therapist as just another professional who will take their money without solving the problem, or perhaps as another onlooker who will blame them for the alienation.

For some, transferential reactions to the therapist initially take the form of idealization and the expectation that the therapist will somehow have the power to correct the situation. Johnston (2005) notes that the idealizing transference can be a response to the therapist's initial stance of empathic listening. This idealized transference can be exacerbated by the therapist's countertransferential need to rescue the targeted parent. These feelings will inevitably lead to disappointment when both the targeted parent and the therapist are faced with the therapist's limitations and the difficulties inherent in the PAS situation.

When working with targeted parents, therefore, it is crucial to discuss these reactions to the therapist and set realistic goals with clients, making it clear that it is unlikely that therapy will bring about a quick resolution of the PAS situation. However, therapy can help targeted parents to reflect on and more effectively respond to the situation at hand, to devise a planned strategy for intervening in future situations, to differentiate between issues that can and cannot be changed, and to lay some groundwork for future developments with the children.

Of course, the therapist's countertransferential response to the situation is also part of the dynamic with targeted parents. Although empathy can be defined as the "affect attunement" (Stern, 1985, p. 145) that therapists experience, countertransference occurs when therapists displace feelings from earlier situations in their lives onto the client (Moore & Fine, 1990). The therapist might be induced to join clients in feeling anger towards the alienating parent, anger towards the children, and frustration with the slow pace of the courts. Therapists also bring their own prior experiences and expectations to every therapeutic relationship, and the therapists' relationship with their own children, parents, or spouse can add to the feelings about the dynamic between the client and the therapist. For example, Wallerstein (1997) notes that therapists working in this area can experience guilt and anxiety for having too much (e.g., an intact family) in comparison to the parent involved with a divorce (p. 118). Countertransference reactions of guilt and anxiety might lead therapists to do too much and to take over the planning of strategy for their clients. Instead, therapists need to encourage clients to develop an approach that most comfortably fits the particular situation and the individual personalities of the targeted parent and the children.

Empathy can be beneficial for targeted parents who are constantly battered, but it is not helpful for therapists to become too emotionally involved in their clients' problems. However, therapists are human and may find themselves losing their objectivity and over-identifying with the targeted parent and beginning to feel helpless or incompetent. Good supervision and the therapist's own treatment can allow them to use these emotions to better understand the client and to eventually work through these feelings in a healthy way.

Therapists will need to avoid the temptation to become the client's savior and to overstep their role. For example, it may be tempting to engage in a dual role with the client but this is unwise and raises ethical concerns. This means that the therapist working with the targeted parent should not conduct evaluations, engage in reunification therapy, serve as a parent coordinator, or engage in any other services with the client or the family. Should the therapist be called to testify, forensic testimony should be limited to factual information about the therapy (Wulach & Shapiro, 2005).

Wallerstein points out that working with high-conflict families in a divorce situation can lead to "cumulative anxiety, irritability, and depression, intensified by physical fatigue and a sense of depletion." (p. 118). In general, when working with emotionally impacted clients such as targeted parents, it is beneficial for therapists to seek supervision and therapy, in order to mitigate the emotional toll of this work.

When clients are anxious about an impending evaluation or court appearance, although coaching is not advised, therapists can be helpful by encouraging them to express their expectations and fears. They can be helped to focus on information that they wish to provide to an evaluator or judge. In order to deal more effectively with the legal system, it also is recommended that the therapist suggests contact with a mental health consultant (Bone & Sauber, this volume).

Finally, it is wise for therapists to have a broad private practice if they choose to specialize in a phenomenon such as PAS. Not all rejecting children are victims of PAS, and therapists need to maintain their objectivity when assessing a situation in order to determine whether this is, indeed, a case of parental alienation. Having a practice that is too homogeneous can lead to erroneous assumptions about the etiology of symptoms and explanations for behavior. Furthermore, these cases are painful and move slowly. Clients often feel frustrated with therapists when planned strategies seem to have no effect. Therapists can feel discouraged, disheartened, and demoralized when problems sometimes do not appear to be fixable. Therapists might need to reduce their work in this area or take a break to maintain their sense of balance.

Preparing for Visitations with the Children

Again, it is stressed that therapists encourage targeted parents to keep in contact with alienated children, even if it is one-way contact. Caring e-mails, texts, and phone calls remind the children of the potentially available relationship.

Therapists should consider that targeted parents might be faced with the dilemma of needing to return to court to gain access to their children. It is likely that this action will be interpreted negatively by the alienating parent (and subsequently the children). However, this action allows the children to see that the targeted parent will fight for a continued relationship and to learn that the alienating parent is not the ultimate authority to establish the rules. Therapists will need to prepare targeted parents for the possibility that children, embroiled in situations with ongoing court involvement, will probably angrily indicate that they do not wish to spend time with the targeted parent.

Alienating parents might send a message, received by even a young child (either through feeling states or words), that it is not safe to leave "home base" and spend time with the targeted parent. In response to these messages, the child might have a fearful reaction (i.e., crying, becoming upset, or verbally expressing the wish not to leave), when separating from the alienating parent. Unfortunately, in this circumstance, some targeted parents become concerned about upsetting the child and they back off, deciding not to insist on visits. This can be the wrong strategy. With coaching and support, targeted parents can learn how to lovingly, but firmly, tell the children that although they are upset, this is their time to be together. Targeted parents can reassure the children that they will be returning to the other parent after a certain period of time. Once the children leave the home of the alienating parent they will probably calm down, particularly if the targeted parent is able to remain calm and soothing. If there are continued periods of upset, it helps to explore the child's concerns once away from the alienating parent. Targeted parents need to make their environment as comfortable for the children as possible. The children might have a room, special toys or hobbies, and a regular routine. It helps to have a support system in place, particularly a warm and experienced extended family.

It helps targeted parents to connect with the children when the parents acknowledge the difficult situation the children are going through and show an understanding of how some of the children's behavior might be a reflection of difficulties experienced. One targeted parent talked with his daughter about his own adolescence and some of his own struggles with pressures and then asked his daughter how they could better manage their time together. This resulted in somewhat lessening of tension between the father and his daughter.

The sharing of family experiences is a way to help the children see the value of relationships that have been lost. Children who are discouraged from seeing extended family members can hear stories about growing up with grandparents, uncles, and aunts. For all children, it helps to share memories of times together prior to the alienation. Family photographs as well as family stories can reignite positive feelings, even if the children do not outwardly express these emotions.

Redefining Expectations and Accomplishments

Therapists will need to help targeted parents reframe experiences in order to help to mitigate a feeling of powerlessness in the face of the PAS situation. If clients begin therapy filled with confusion or self-blame, the first task of the therapist will be to help them gain information about PAS dynamics, particularly focusing on explanations for how the children can be manipulated to attack and reject the targeted parent. Some of this education can take place within the therapeutic structure. However, other aspects of this reframing can be acquired from Internet resources, reading books, attending lectures, and joining a support group with other targeted parents. The purpose of the reframing is to help clients see the children's behavior as a predictable response to the situation. This understanding can help targeted parents to feel less isolated and helpless.

Therapists can aid the client in recognizing that children take cues from each parent about how to respond to the other parent as well as how to respond to others in their lives. Goldstein, Freud, and Solnit (1973) point out that children "will love both parents only if the parents feel positively towards one another. Failing this, children become prey to loyalty conflicts." (p. 12). Novick and Novick (2005) describe parents who are blind to the separate needs and experiences of their children and instead relate to their children as externalized parts of themselves. This can result in the children's inability to see themselves as separate from the needs of the alienating parent. Therapists can also help the client recognize that children are not really able to imagine the impact of their rejection on the targeted parent. For example, as Baker (2007) found, adults who were childhood victims of PAS recounted how surprised they were when their targeted parent, after being reviled, rejected, or ignored by them so many times, finally gave up and stopped showing up for their visits. As children, they just assumed that the parent would be there forever, despite the repeated rejections.

Therapists can educate clients that young children naturally tend to see the world in black and white terms, with "good guys" and "bad guys," and to believe that they have to side with one of the parents when they are in conflict. With normal maturity, in the absence of PAS, children develop the recognition of nuances and of ambivalence in relationships with others. Thus, viewing one parent as all good and the other as all bad in a divorce situation can be presented as a product of the immaturity of the child as well as the influence of the black and white world of the alienating parent.

Therapists should also remind clients that the children have most likely seen the alienating parent devalue and abandon anyone who has dared to question or criticize. Alienated children likely are afraid that rejection would ensue if the alienating parent thought that they were taking the targeted parent's side. It would be an unusual child who would be able to withstand rejection from the alienating parent. Simultaneously, children receive positive reinforcement for rejecting the targeted parent. Seeing alienation from the perspective of the children can help clients understand all of the forces that bind children to the alienating parent.

Taking all these factors into consideration, the therapist's task, then, is to help targeted parents focus on long-term gains rather than to seek the more immediate gratification of expecting the children to change their behavior. It may take a long period before the strategies outlined in this chapter yield results, and the targeted parent should expect the immediate response of the child to be negative or neutral at best, for the reasons outlined above. By helping clients to focus on the long-term goal, the therapist can help them deal more effectively with the disappointment, anger, frustration, and sadness that accompany the PAS situation.

Therapists can help targeted parents to redefine a victory as an instance in which they did not accept a distorted interpretation of their actions and were able to challenge that distortion. A victory can be seen as an instance when targeted parents remind the children that they are loved. A victory can be seen as a time when the targeted parent held fast to principles and a game plan, despite provocation and misinterpretation. At the same time, therapists can help clients to have hope that the situation will change in the future. In her book *Adult Children of Parental Alienation Syndrome,* Baker (2007) presents 11 catalysts that can lead victims of PAS to recognize that they were manipulated and deceived by the alienating parent. These catalysts include circumstances such as maturation, the turning against the adult child by the alienating parent, and experiencing PAS as a parent.

While it may be helpful to know that there are many ways to proceed from alienation to reconciliation, the reality is that there is no way to predict which catalyst will be relevant for a particular child and when it will take effect. There are so many variables and combinations of factors in life that such predictions are futile. However, it can be heartening to know that children who were victims of PAS come to recognize the manipulations through so many different means. It can be helpful to remind clients that most people have had the experience of re-evaluating many attitudes and stances that they adopted when they were children. It is that recognition and re-evaluation on the part of the older and more mature childhood victim of PAS that the targeted parent should be helped to visualize and address. In the future, when grown victimized children realize that they have been manipulated, they might experience remorse or guilt over the poor treatment of the targeted parent. These feelings, and their concern about how the targeted parent will respond to them, could inhibit the impulse to reach out to try to establish a relationship. It is at that moment that the adult child might recall the targeted parent's mantra, which was reported to be so annoying as a child, "I will always love you. I will always be your Dad (or Mom)." It is also important to note that some children find their way to having a relationship with both parents, despite the alienating parent's pressure to do otherwise. Of course, not all targeted parents have to wait until their children are grown to have a relationship with their child.

Strategies for Living with a PAS Situation

This section will focus upon and re-emphasize some of the helpful strategies for dealing with a PAS situation. Bearing in mind that there is no perfect response and that each case is unique, there are some general recommendations that the therapist should discuss with the client.

As Baker and Fine point out (this volume), targeted parents should not passively accept accusations, misinterpretations, and distortions of their motives and actions. Although they may feel that by refusing to respond they are being more mature, responsible, dignified, or fair, their passivity means that the accusations, misinterpretations, and distortions will be unanswered. From the intended audience, the children, it can almost be guaranteed that passivity will not result in a positive "verdict." Instead, the children will see the fact that the accusations are unanswered as indications of their validity.

However, it is not a good idea for targeted parents to answer these accusations with their own accusations and badmouthing. This approach will seldom convince the children that the targeted parent is correct, and can lead to a diversionary tactic in which the accusations and wording become the subject of a whole new set of accusations, misinterpretations, and distortions. Instead, it is recommend that targeted parents consider responding to an accusation by saying something like, "I understand that you feel I am putting my needs above yours and your other parent's; however, there's another way to view that situation. I would be glad to discuss this with you and to let you know why I acted the way I did." If the children's response is that they will not discuss the matter with the targeted parent, who is "a liar," it can help to discuss why they think that the parent is a liar and point out any distortions or misperceptions. If the children refuse to listen, the targeted parent can reiterate that the matter can be discussed whenever they are ready to do so. Again, the goal of this interchange is not to get children to change their minds, but to have them hear (and remember) that there is another explanation from the one they have been given. When they are mature enough to be ready to consider another side to the story, that statement may be remembered.

In most cases, targeted parents need to resist the temptation to blame the alienating parent for the distortion or to tell children that they are being manipulated or brainwashed. This strategy rarely is successful and is more likely to engender defensiveness on the part of the child. Exposing manipulation will not work with someone who is too young to understand the concept of manipulation or who is unable, at this time, to acknowledge the manipulation. Instead, depending on the age of the child, targeted parents can either state simply, "This is not an accurate picture of what took place" (for a younger child) or "I know that you want to find out what the truth is, and the way you relate this story is not accurate. Would you be willing to sit down with me and hear the truth as I see it?" (for an older child). Again, the goal is not to have the child immediately adopt the targeted parent's point of view but to remind the child that there is another side to the story. When the time is right, that side can be considered.

For a more comprehensive review of PAS strategies and responses, the therapist and client can consult *Beyond the High Road: Responding to 17 Parental Alienation Strategies without Compromising Your Morals or Harming Your Child* by Amy J. L. Baker and Paul R. Fine (2008).

Refusing to be Abused

Targeted parents should not be emotional punching bags for their children and should set reasonable limits on the amount of disparagement the children are allowed to display. By doing so, the parent models reasonable self-protective behavior and reminds the child of boundaries, a reminder that most children want and need. The underlying message to the child should be, "I'll always love you but I will not be abused by you."

In some cases, a parallel process of denigration and shame (a re-enactment of the PAS situation) can occur within the therapy when the targeted parent attacks the therapist because of frustration with the therapist's inability to change the situation (see "Transference and Countertransference" in this chapter). The therapist's countertransferential response of inadequacy or shame might be paralleling the client's underlying feelings.

Support from a Significant Other

After an encounter with the alienated children or the alienating parent, in which the targeted parent might have felt helpless in the face of unfair criticism, blame, and accusations, it is nurturing to process the painful situation with an ally so that the client can regain a sense of him- or herself as a person worthy of love.

Support Groups for Targeted Parents

There are support groups both online and in person that can offer comfort and encouragement for targeted parents. When a client feels so misunderstood, attacked, and isolated, it can be comforting to be in touch with others who are facing the same issues. Individuals who have been or are currently in similar situations can offer advice, suggestions, and experiences that no one else can offer. The therapist should encourage the targeted parent to join one of these groups. It should also be noted that it is important for the therapist to help the client process the support group experience, as not all advice given in a support group will be helpful or pertinent. See Lebows (this volume) for more on support groups for targeted parents.

Self-Acceptance for Mistakes

Therapists can remind targeted parents that it is inevitable that they will sometimes say the wrong thing or make mistakes. When clients encounter hostile, highly emotional, and disappointing situations that are common to PAS, it is understandable that they can react in a manner that is not productive. These errors are to be expected and are rarely irreparable. Sometimes "mistakes" such as a display of emotion can be exactly the response that is needed. There are no hard and fast/right or wrong answers. If a targeted parent has said something regrettable, sometimes an apology can help to remedy the situation. In any event, it is neither helpful nor realistic to expect oneself to be perfect. Sometimes a simple apology for "losing it" can stand in sharp contrast to the alienating parent's inability to accept any responsibility or criticism. This apology can be experienced as loving and sensitive by the child, even though the child's outward behavior might not reflect this recognition.

Do not Neglect Other Relationships

Therapists can remind targeted parents that they must not neglect other significant relationships because of the PAS situation. Relationships with non-alienated children as well as others can be nurturing and serve to remind targeted parents that they are worthy and capable of healthy relationships. Having a good relationship with other people in the targeted parent's life yields many benefits, including giving the targeted parent a respite from the ongoing conflicts and challenges inherent in PAS situation.

The Importance of Time Out

Sometimes a targeted parent may feel the need to take time out and step back from the situation in order to regroup or to focus on other aspects of life. If the targeted parent experiences guilt over the need to do so, the therapist can reframe this as a necessary component of the overall strategy rather than as an example of the client's weakness or selfishness. A temporary respite that allows for refueling can be a wise and self-protective action. If the client has difficulty moving away from feelings that this time out is weak or selfish, these undermining attitudes will need to be explored in therapy. Again, it also should be pointed out that a parallel process occurs with therapists, and it is advisable for therapists who have a number of PAS cases to also work with clients dealing with other issues.

Participate in and Enjoy Life

Some targeted parents react to PAS by obsessively ruminating about how unjust the situation is and, in general, making themselves feel miserable. This might be associated with some degree of magical thinking. The parents might unconsciously believe that if they suffer enough, that suffering will somehow induce the alienating parent to stop the vindictive or manipulative behavior and motivate the children to recognize the unfairness of the situation. Similarly, targeted parents might unconsciously believe that if they allow themselves pleasure, even though the relationship with the children remains problematic, this will have an adverse affect on the situation. The denial of pleasure by the targeted parent is counterproductive and leads to an exacerbation of depression, anger, and resentment. Some targeted parents might set an unrealistic standard of behavior for themselves and have difficulty in allowing themselves to focus on their own self-care, believing that giving themselves some pleasure is self-indulgent. All of this can be explored as part of the therapeutic process.

The therapeutic response to this obsession is to help the targeted parents bring this magical thinking to a conscious level, and to recognize that their pleasure will not damage the situation with the children. Actually, experiencing pleasure in his or her life will most likely help the targeted parent to better respond to the PAS situation. Furthermore, when the children are limiting their own pleasures by denying themselves a relationship with the targeted parent (and often with the targeted parent's extended family), as well as other valued experiences, it can be helpful for them to see that the targeted parent recognizes the value of a balanced life. The message that targeted parents want to convey is, "I wish that I could have enjoyed this experience with you." In this manner, targeted parents might want to remind their children of previous pleasurable experiences shared together.

Leading a more balanced life permits targeted parents to refresh and regroup. They can continue to respond to the immediate and long-range needs of the alienated child while being better equipped to deal with this painful and frustrating situation.

Conclusion

Dealing with the effects of the PAS situation is a formidable task for targeted parents. Central to this is the need of targeted parents to attempt to keep a tie with often rejecting and denigrating children. Therapists can empathize with those who seem to be unfairly attacked by their own children as well as by others in this situation. However, empathy can move to powerful countertransferential feelings for therapists. These feelings often parallel their client's emotional state. Therapists who can continue to understand and help clients to understand these powerful reactions can most effectively serve as guides through the difficult situations that emerge.

References

Baker, A. (2007). *Adult children of parental alienation syndrome: Breaking the ties that bind.* New York: W. W. Norton.

Baker, A. & Fine, P. (2008). *Beyond the high road: Responding to 17 parental alienation strategies without compromising your morals or harming your child.* Available at: www.amyjlbaker.com.

Freud, A. (1966). *The ego and the mechanisms of defense: The writings of Anna Freud* (Vol. 2). New York: International Universities Press.

Freud, S. (1940). *An outline of psycho-analysis* (Standard Edition). London: Hogarth.

Goldstein, J., Freud, A., & Solnit, A. J. (1973). *Beyond the best interest of the child* (p. 12). New York: Free Press.

Johnston, J. R. (2005). Clinical work with parents in entrenched custody disputes. In L. Gunsberg & P. Hymowitz (Eds.), *A handbook of divorce and custody* (pp. 343–363). Hillsdale, NJ: Analytic Press.

Moore, B. E., & Fine, B. D. (1990). *Psychoanalytic terms and concepts.* New Haven, CT and London, England: The American Psychoanalytic Association and Yale University Press.

Novick, J., & Novick, K. (2005). Soul blindness: A child must be seen to be heard. In L. Gunsberg & P. Hymowitz (Eds.), *A handbook of divorce and custody* (pp. 81–90). Hillsdale, NJ: Analytic Press.

Stern, D. N. (1985). *The interpersonal world of the infant: A view from psychoanalysis and developmental psychology* (p. 145). New York: Basic Books.

Wallerstein, J. (1997). Transference and countertransference in clinical interventions with divorcing families. In M. Solomon & J. Siegel (Eds.), *Countertransference in couples therapy* (pp. 113–124). New York: W. W. Norton.

Wulach, J. S., & Shapiro, D. (2005). Ethical and legal considerations in child custody evaluations. In L. Gunsberg & P. Hymowitz (Eds.), *A handbook of divorce and custody* (pp. 45–56). Hillsdale, NJ: Analytic Press.

7 Supporting Targeted Parents

The International Support Network for Alienated Families

Karen Lebow

I recall one shaman from the Bushman people who literally fell off the rock he was sitting on, laughing hysterically, when I told him how I work by listening to clients, helping them sort things out and talk about what is most bothersome. He was absolutely dumbfounded that I didn't bring together the whole community as witnesses to the healing. There was no dancing, shaking, chanting, or drumming in my description of psychotherapy. There was no calling to the spirits. There was no fire built for the healing ceremony. He asked if I had ever helped anyone with just talk.

Jeffrey Kottler (2010, p. 19)

A Mother Alone

The support group leader noticed that Joanna had been crying convulsively during group. She was being comforted and provided with hugs, sips of water, and Kleenex from group members all the while. This was Joanna's first support group meeting. In the intake interview Joanna revealed that she and her ex-husband had been involved in mean-spirited conflict around child custody and visitation arrangements that began just after their daughter's fourth birthday. That daughter is currently 9 years old. Joanna had remarried and given birth to a son now aged 7 years and another daughter now aged 5 years. Joanna was currently in the process of divorcing the father of the two younger children. The therapist noted that Joanna, a likable and accomplished 45-year-old African American Muslim woman, was showing severe somatic symptoms. She was suffering from colitis, headaches, and seemed to be unable to concentrate. She was continuously exhausted and was awakened by nightmares of her children lost, calling, and reaching out to her. She awoke most mornings with her chest pounding with fear and anxiety.

She shared with the group that she spent lunchtimes and breaks on her cell phone interviewing attorneys and trying to confirm the visitation schedule and activities with her ex-husband. Not surprisingly, she feared her job was in jeopardy. As it was, Joanna told the group her salary barely covered her living expenses and she was recently unable to purchase school supplies for her eldest daughter. Sinking ever deeper into debt, she had run up a tab of $50,000 with her current attorney.

Joanna explained that her ex-husband regularly complained to the children that their mother was stupid, selfish, crazy, and not fun. He encouraged the children to call their mother by her first name. He also failed to return the children in a timely way when they visited with him and he skipped visitation without explanation from time to time while the children waited for him. Later he would make a fuss in front of the children saying that Joanna was to blame for the missed visit. Joanna's former mother-in-law reinforced this disrespect and indicated to the children that Joanna was of a lower class, a different religion, and unworthy of the marriage.

Joanna reported that she knew no one else who was in a similar circumstance. Her friends, people with whom she worshiped at the mosque, her current therapist, and her loving family were ill-equipped to provide the support she needed. Joanna suffered from severe isolation. Her family and friends were fearful that whatever she was going through might be harmful to her physical and emotional well-being and they were putting pressure on her to give up her fight and turn the custody of her children over to her ex-spouse. Unintentionally, friends and family members were increasing the stress that might have contributed to Joanna feeling victimized, hopeless, and depleted.

Joanna continued to cry throughout her first support group meeting. At the end of the session she said her goodbyes and managed to leave the group with three new friends, who were in similar situations. The group leader called Joanna the next day, as is the custom with new support group members as well as any members who seemed particularly upset at a meeting. When she contacted Joanna the next morning she was surprised and delighted to be greeted by a voice full of optimism. Joanna said that she felt "normal and balanced" for the first time since her battles began. Through her contact with these new friends she realized that although she had been shut out, maligned, and bullied as a targeted parent, she had endured. When asked by the support group leader what made the difference, Joanna explained that she had not been fully aware of how very isolated she had been as a targeted parent. She felt enormous relief to realize that she was not the only person dealing with parental alienation because it meant that she could be understood. She said she now felt "focused, empowered, and connected" and ready to continue attending the support group.

She mentioned that the women she had met through the group felt the help they provided Joanna was mutually beneficial. Through giving to Joanna they had affirmed their own value as nurturing, kind, human beings who are worth something. Joanna and the other women from the group later reported that their sleep patterns had improved and that the depression and anxiety triggered by helplessness had decreased in intensity. In fact, in the months following this episode, they took each opportunity that emerged in the group and outside the group to be mutually compassionate and caring.

Introduction: So What Does the Shaman Have to do With it?

Shaman is an anthropological term meaning a guide who both teaches and heals. He is both the spiritual and physical leader of the community. By definition, members of the community look to him for he holds the memory of communal history, rituals, customs, and traditions (de Schweinitz, 2010). A shamanic intervention requires full attention and presence. It requires total absorption into the process of the others he is leading. He honors uniqueness even while putting the community first. Shamanic intervention goes far beyond just talk therapy: it has and creates its own magic, strength, and energy. The shamanic way means being aware of and practicing rituals, being publicly and privately accountable to the family, the village, the group, and to the individual in ways that are healing. The shaman values the community over the individual (Stoffel, 2010). She knows that shunning, marginalizing, and isolating physically or emotionally is in itself a most punishing consequence.

The shaman understands that to be human is to be interdependent and that interdependence evolved for survival of the early rigors of daily struggles in prehistoric times. Shunning kills the human spirit and destroys the ability to function as an individual. Being interconnected means survival. Support group leaders who facilitate healing among targeted parents use many of the same techniques and carry out roles similar to a shaman. The shaman contains the memory, history of the community, and like the group leader facilitates healing, comfort, and education among parents who are alienated from their children. Being a shaman or group leader means using the whole self in performing interventions. This means using what the mind knows, what the heart feels, and what the spirit helps us to transcend. A shamanic intervention means knowing how to apply knowledge to comfort and to teach. A shamanic intervention provides an opportunity to expose, exorcize, and limit hostile, evil, and destructive thoughts and actions so that the community members can turn their efforts and energy to celebrate and maximize the strengths that emerge with interdependence (Craffert, 2011). The case example that began this chapter demonstrates the healing power of the group as well as the healing dynamic of the interdependence of its individual members. The support of a group can be an important part of healing from and coping with alienation from one's children.

This chapter is about one such support group for targeted parents, the International Support Network for Alienated Families (ISNAF) and is organized into four sections. The first section provides the rationale for the support group, including a discussion of the power of support groups and person-in-environment theory. The second section describes the making of an ISNAF support group, and is followed by a guide for the group leader. The final section discusses some process and structural issues that the group has faced and are likely to be endemic to any support group for targeted parents.

Rationale for the International Support Network for Alienated Families

The Power of the Support Group

The power of a support group for targeted parents cannot be overstated. Humans are naturally meant to be interdependent and communal (Munn-Giddings & McVicar, 2006). Attachment, support, caring, compassion, and reciprocity reflect common behaviors and values that first occurred even in prehistoric times (Bowles, Smith, & Mulder, 2010). Hundreds of thousands of years ago human survival depended on belonging to a group, and it is deeply ingrained in us that there is comfort, protection, and safety in a communal setting. This is the thread that binds each of us to each other and to those who came before. Research shows that babies who lack human touch, warmth, and affection show developmental deficits (Harlow & Suomi, 1971). Adults need to feel that they are accepted and that they belong to a group as well; without human connection individuals may experience feelings of despair. A present-day example of this can be found in the many targeted, maligned, stigmatized, marginalized parents who live with the shame and guilt of having lost their children owing to parental alienation syndrome (PAS).

Cohorts are curative. A cohort is defined as a group of people who share similarities with one another. Similarities might include age, geography, professional training, personality, hobbies, age of the alienated children currently or when first alienated, marital or cultural status, and social class. It may also relate to pathology, such as addictions or prescription drug use. Ideally, for each member there should be at least two other group members with similar characteristics with whom he or she can bond. This element provides a source of interdependence that may be echoed in the group as a whole and upon which the larger community is based (Bekker, Arends-Toth, & Croon, 2011).

Person-in-Environment

Person-in-environment (PIE) is an all-encompassing interactive theory and practical approach to solving social problems that provides a foundation for ISNAF (Norton, 2009). It takes into account the effect of people on the environment and vice versa and what occurs in between. First conceptualized in the 1950s by Kurt Lewin (e.g., 1951), a noted social psychologist, PIE posits that the person and the environment co-create and shape each other. This is certainly true and demonstrable when studying and addressing the issues that impact targeted parents, as exemplified in the vignette. Joanna lives within a particular context. She is very profoundly affected by her situation. She makes a valiant attempt at maintaining her role as a "good enough mother" even while the bond between her and her children is being systematically and purposefully destroyed. Her somatic symptoms may indicate how deeply the stress, fear of loss, and the loss itself are affecting her very being. How she interacts with or makes use of psychosocial resources in her environment can determine how adequately she and her children maintain a healthy attachment to each other.

For Joanna, enduring the stress of PAS means paying a high price physiologically. At this juncture, an ISNAF support group can serve to support and strengthen her inner resources and maximize how she uses them. Examples of inner resources are self-image, esteem, critical thinking, and feelings of physical well-being. These are assets that she can then call on to help her persist in her efforts to parent her children and address new issues as they emerge. Potentially, the external psychosocial environment, mainly consisting of group participants, can enhance her resolve to do what she needs to do in order for her family system to survive the trauma resulting from PAS. An ISNAF group may be instrumental in preserving, healing, or repairing the parent–child bond. And, within this context, she is part of a cohort that acts as a social support.

PIE subscribes to the notion that we all live in a life space that is interactive and constantly evolving—never static. PIE emphasizes a positive or optimistic perception of life and of people's strengths. It does not deny pathology but it does not automatically assume that everything that needs to be addressed is caused by the pathological. PIE was heavily influenced by the gestaltist movement as a way to articulate the belief in the reality that humans naturally seek completeness, a dynamic which is viewed as motivating movement and growth over the course of the lifespan. PIE is holistic, paying attention to the entire gestalt or "whole," or the "totality." In the vignette, Joanna experiences her body's response to stress as well as her body's response to the healing presence of the group. She was able to find some solace and balance owing to participating in a support group, even after just one session.

Coming Together: The International Support Network for Alienated Families

The founding network of ISNAF is a non-profit charitable corporation located in southern Califonia, with participants throughout the state and even in other states. ISNAF has an organizational structure, including officers and a board of directors reflective of the general population of the network. There are currently more than 200 participants, defined as those who attend support group meetings and/or participate in ISNAF activities. ISNAF was founded by the author, who is the president and CEO and the person responsible for staffing the board and its committees and screening new members, running the monthly support group, and developing new programs.

Mission and Vision

The mission of the ISNAF group is to counter that sense of isolation and marginalization by providing a community, a place where social connection is nurtured and protected, where self-esteem is preserved and allowed to grow, where people can be interdependent, a part of something larger than themselves. There is a "hand to hold and others with whom to stand." It is a place where people can learn, teach, and grow; where professionals and lay people alike open their minds to new information about the scientific validity of parental alienation/PAS, and where people can find the strength and hope to persevere in the face of hopelessness. ISNAF is a place to come where people are encouraged to not give up their children just because they lack communal support. An aspect of the ISNAF vision is to form an ISNAF network of support groups and other services in each geographic area, with each new group beginning with an organizing team of at least three people.

ISNAF is designed as a support network for those suffering the pain and bewilderment of losing a child due to the dynamics of parental alienation or PAS. ISNAF's goal is to provide hope, comfort, and education for alienated families as well as for the public. But ISNAF is more than just a support group. ISNAF's mission is to function as a multipurpose organization dedicated to treating, preventing, and creating advocacy and awareness of the issue of parental alienation. In addition to the support group there are other activities, including all-day conferences with presentations by national and international leaders in the field, "salon sessions" in which a single presenter offers a workshop or discussion related to some aspect of parental alienation, and phone consultations with targeted parents and other support group leaders throughout the country. The ISNAF vision also includes the creation of an emergency fund so that parents do not have to make the choice between purchasing basic living necessities and paying for a qualified attorney or a counselor; no parent should have to choose between going hungry and paying for an attorney to fight a custody battle. The ISNAF dream is to provide training to parents and professionals, to research root causes, and to learn how best to reunify families.

The heart of the ISNAF network is the monthly support group meeting. The ISNAF support group draws on both traditional support groups and psychotherapy groups. In fact, it combines elements of support, therapy, and psycho-education, as well as psychosocial support. ISNAF uses catharsis, relational work, and an attachment focus from traditional psychotherapy. In addition, ISNAF also offers instruction on the latest approaches and methods as well as academic study and resource materials consistent with the psycho-educational model.

Selection and Orientation of Group Participants

Typically, a potential group participant (a targeted parent) becomes aware of the support group via the ISNAF website or from a professional or friend. The person is usually experiencing chronic grief or is in immediate crisis. There is an initial e-mail, phone call, or conversation with the referral source or the potential candidate and the process has begun.

Not every targeted parent, however, is a good candidate for the support group aspect of ISNAF. Before being invited into the group, prospective participants are met by the group leader and administered a brief but focused assessment. If the parent is experiencing too much anxiety to manage the feelings and shared experiences of others in a group setting, or if the parent is overcome with feelings of shame and guilt, he or she may not be ready to participate in a group process. These parents are offered individual counseling sessions until they are ready to join the group. Other individuals are excluded from the group owing to a history of violence, untreated psychopathology, or untreated addictions. Likewise, people with mental or physical disabilities that make communicating in a group context impossible are not invited to join the group. On ethical grounds people are excluded if they are viewed as likely to compromise participant privacy or impede another participant's group work for any reason. Those who are excluded are treated responsibly and sensitively. Referral for treatment, anger management, or for programs addressing addictions and referral to other agencies and resources may be appropriate.

Those candidates who are chosen are welcomed into the group by the group leader and the other participants. After someone is embraced and welcomed they are rarely eliminated from the network. In addition, if the targeted parent is amenable, their spouses and significant others are invited to also be full participants in the ISNAF group (after undergoing the assessment and orientation). They can provide valuable insights into the situation of the targeted parent. Others in the group provide support for these supporters and carers.

ISNAF participants are encouraged to socialize outside of the group, continuously deepening and extending supportive relationships. Being in the outside world facilitates normalization and interdependence. Other forms of social support are extremely important too. Group members are encouraged to participate in other social groups, such as attending gatherings of family and friends, and religious groups; going to the gym; participating in philanthropic or activist groups; or taking up hobbies or classes that enhance the person's feelings of making a contribution.

Some ISNAF support group participants are also simultaneously in individual therapy. It is vital that the therapist accepts the premise and reality of parental alienation and is knowledgeable about parental alienation dynamics in order to avoid common pitfalls of encouraging the targeted parent to "give the child space" or take a "wait and see" attitude rather than helping the parent stay in the game and work towards reunification. Too often, uninformed therapists do more harm than good by steering the targeted parent in the wrong direction. Those who are not in ongoing psychotherapy are encouraged to have the name and contact information of a mental health professional who is available in the event of a crisis. Again, it is critical that such a person knows about and understands parental alienation and parental alienation syndrome and is willing to be available for crises.

The Size of the Group

There is no maximum size of an ISNAF group. Matching participants to cohorts requires a group that is large enough to include the possibility of offering cohorts from a variety of settings, family configurations, ages, and stages of alienation. The ISNAF group can absorb a large number of participants by structuring activities or interactions where people can meet in both small and large configurations during the meeting.

The ISNAF Setting: Home is Where the Meeting is

Feeling welcome and as relaxed as possible is key for the group members and participation. Most participants feel at least some trepidation and anxiety about their status as a stigmatized and targeted parent. The author has found that group discussion flows more easily while sitting in an easy chair or an old overstuffed couch, a setting that is imperfect and appears "lived in." The home setting is by far the best context for facilitating discussion. The defenses and psychological walls disappear in this kind of setting people when people feel at ease. Usually the attendees bring "munchies" or even a potluck dish. Food brought by members brings comfort and is usually a safe topic with which to begin normal discussion and elicit genuine appreciation and compliments.

Structure of Each Meeting

During each meeting and other ISNAF events participants are assigned activities to serve the group. Examples include: greeting attendees, taking charge of the roster and sign in, bringing refreshments, and organizing a resource table. Appropriate tasks to consider also include offering one's home or another location as a meeting place, making reminder calls, organizing an after-meeting supper, posting flyers, and offering transportation. Involvement in these types of activities will be appreciated by others and may boost the self-esteem of group members. However, it is vital for the group leader to remember that these are clients and that the activity should be something that can be accomplished in the short term, allowing for the experience of success and completion.

Branching Out: New ISNAF Groups

It is the hope and expectation that other branches of ISNAF will emerge in other geographic areas. A new ISNAF group could start with as few as three people, although the ideal number of people is six very interested and motivated pre-assessed participants. The first meeting should include introductions, with each person having a chance to share his or her alienation story. The group leader reviews ground rules and the organizational mission, distributes and completes any paperwork, and initiates a plan to recruit additional participants. The group leader reviews the history of the organization and provides an understanding of the ISNAF mission. The agenda should also include a complete list of individuals, agencies, and other entities that might be a good source of new candidates, including connections with the media, local radio, TV, the press, the local bar association, and psychological associations. Receiving a commitment from the attendees to act as a temporary organizing/welcoming committee helps to normalize their situation, connect participants to each other, publicize the group, and bring in candidates. This secures their investment/ownership and pride in the group.

The Group Leader Guide

This section provides an overview of the role of the ISNAF group leader, including a discussion of qualifications, roles, and how to handle self-disclosure.

Role

The role of the group leader is to facilitate all aspects of the group process. She determines who can participate in the ISNAF group and who cannot, sets the meeting schedule, and ensures that participants adhere to the policies and practices of the group. The qualifications of the group leader include familiarity with and support of the theory and practice of the concept of parental alienation/PAS. The person must be trained and experienced in the family mental health field and be licensed or qualified by the particular state entity in charge of credentialing.

The role of leader is not always crystal clear in the ISNAF community. However, there are some constants that can be noted. The role of container and modulator is key. This happens successfully only when the group leader himself effectively reflects and sensitively feeds back to a participant an example of how verbalization might be modified or modulated so that listening participants can absorb the content and the feeling of what is being transmitted. The goal is for the participant to communicate a range of feelings without unnecessarily and destructively escalating or blocking the group discussion.

The Group Leader Empowers Participants

When the leader's main role is as a substitute nurturer and/or all-knowing parent who has the answers for everything, it is disempowering for the participants. So, in the style of Carl Rogers, during the most benign minor discussions, reminders and reinforcement of how powerful, competent, intelligent, and appealing a client is should be emphasized (Rogers, 1951; Schimmel, 2008). There is power with simply acknowledging each participant's presence. This is similar to the way parents may provide positive input to counter the programming of a severely alienated and brainwashed child.

Acknowledgement by the group leader that each participant carries his own reality with him is essential. The joy of a support group and a support network where participants exchange a range of information about resources, points of view, needs and feelings that the leader acknowledges and uses to keep the group flowing and rolling is what makes ISNAF successful (Goodman & Munoz, 2004). Systems theorists such as Virginia Satir subscribe to the notion that a hallmark of a healthy family is open communication, whereas an unhealthy family is closed and totalistic and acceptance comes from only one point of view (Haber, 2011). ISNAF, therefore, aims to mimic a healthy family in this respect, promoting and supporting open communication and the safe sharing of thoughts and feelings.

Furthermore, the leader's ability to acknowledge and connect members one to another during a group discussion is key. All participants are attempting to get their bearings while they are gaining mental and physical health (Gottlieb & Wachala, 2007). This is happening while they continue to live through serious loss and trauma. This complex process often proves a challenge to the leader as well as to the participants. Recognition of the complexity of these issues, which occur currently with the need for mutual support, is essential.

An effective group leader will also become part of the group from time to time and, over the course of any single session, may go in and out of the group. First and foremost she is the leader and must be able to function as an authority and as the one who takes charge of the group. She is responsible for creating a safe and healing environment. When participants feel comfortable and safe the leader's efficacy increases; she is then able to maximize the use of her clinical skills to manage and facilitate the group process.

Self-Disclosure

When the group leader judiciously uses appropriate self-disclosure, the participants are encouraged to also be self-disclosing. By accepting her flaws and imperfections the leader can model self-acceptance for the group, something that is vital for targeted parents to cope with their alienation experience. At all times the leader must be mindful that self-disclosure and sharing must be for the benefit of the group. It is not essential that the leader have experience with PAS per se, only that the leader is comfortable sharing something in her life that will allow her to be one with the group psychologically.

It may be a challenge to maintain leadership while at the same time being part of the group. Participating for her is an opportunity to model appropriately modulated feelings and behavior. The leader is more like the shaman who uses personal and community history as accepted tools for healing rather than distancing herself from the group members. She must look like the people she leads and appear as someone who is real, credible, knowledgeable, resourceful, respectful, and "matter of fact." By maintaining these values the group leader engenders the deep trust that is necessary to sustain authority and inspire group process.

Multiple Roles

At times the leader is the parent, at other times he is the friend, the peer, the moral support, the educator, the brother, the sister, or the wise grandparent. It is important that the leader understands this and feels comfortable in these multiple roles. The leader needs to understand that group members too have multiple roles, being witness to both crime and its victim.

The leader should understand and have first-hand experience with group dynamics and group cycles, and appreciate and acknowledge that insights do not emerge according to a schedule—they just occur, many times triggered after a group meeting or interaction. At those times the participant, depending on the type of insight emerging, should have the option of contacting the group leader or a cohort member to discuss this. Many times the insights are key and lead to other insights or revelations.

Staying Current

It is critical to stay on top of the latest information and research. For the group leader, consultation with other professionals in the alienation and group dynamics field, in terms of strategies addressing parental alienation/PAS, is important.

A Few Rules: ISNAF Standards, Ethics, and Boundaries

There are few rules, but an important one is that ISNAF participants are not permitted to harm each other physically, emotionally, or spiritually, whether this harm is actual or anticipated, or might be perpetrated or threatened. A second rule is that most of the discussions within the group and what is revealed at the assessment "stay in the group." They are private and confidential. This includes a policy that personal information may not be shared on the Internet. Along the same lines, the names and contact information of participants is not information that can be shared publicly. Every effort is made to respect privacy unless permission is given by the participant and the group leader to share or exchange information. A few exceptions of course exist, especially pertaining to Tarasoff's law. That is, the group leader must report a potentially harmful or life-threatening situation to a receiving agency (Ewing, 2012) or to a collaborating mental health professional association of the participant.

The Key to Being an Effective Group Leader: Self-Care

The full presence and attention of a group leader is essential. In addition to any job description, graduate degrees, responsibilities, personal qualities, and obligations, a group leader must be fully present and fully aware. She must be able to quickly grab opportunities for positive intervention, set limits, and be an excellent role model for participants. Through a range of appropriate feelings she fosters respect and nurtures hope in an inspirational manner.

However, the group leader is after all human. In order to facilitate and use all of her skills and knowledge to the maximum degree possible, self-care is absolutely essential. That may mean different things to each leader; but some universal principles apply: she should have healthy relationships with others in her personal life, have down-time, a wholesome diet, enjoyment of the arts and exercise, have a support system of peers with whom she can "let her hair down" and speak about absolutely anything, and pay ongoing attention to her spiritual needs and the health of her body. All of this is important and the ISNAF leader will need a guide to help her. She will also be a role model in accessing the support and help she needs in order to operate. Compassion, understanding, energy, respect, clear communication, solid judgment, and the ability to help and to lead derive at least in part from the ability to take care of oneself.

Group Process: Considerations Unique to Conducting a Support Group for Alienated Parents

Within the context of parental alienation, these are some of the unique characteristics and challenges of targeted parents and group leaders that affect group process.

People at Different Stages of Alienation

Alienated parents either have already or anticipate losing contact with their children. Many are experiencing deep grief over their loss or are anxious and fearful over an anticipated loss. When they come to the group they see others in the same predicament with a range of success or failure in maintaining or re-establishing their parental roles. Because every parent is at his or her own unique place on this continuum, it may be difficult for some members to deal with the reality of other members. For example, it may be threatening to realize that some members have been cut off from their children for years if not decades. Likewise, while it may be encouraging to hear about the success of other members, it also might evoke feelings of envy and anger. Recognizing that each person's story may trigger feelings in the other members of the group is an important part of the work of the group leader.

One way to address these concerns is to provide some basic information about parental alienation and the characteristics and phases of parental alienation in the orientation and assessment phases of each new participant's entry to the group. However, this information may temporarily increase anxiety and stimulate feelings of hopelessness and helplessness. Helping the new participant anticipate this will be important. During orientation it is important to paint a realistic picture by verbally preparing the prospective client for this type of support group, where everyone is at a different level. In this environment the stronger and more mature nurture, bring along, and encourage a person who is either newer at this or is just developing strategies. Thus, as stated in the previous sections, other cohort members are particularly important during the group process so that differences can be acknowledged and that real compassion and understanding of "where people are in the scheme of things" can take place. In doing this, participants gain a perspective and place for themselves in the group.

An ISNAF principle is that balance and diversity in the group are important (Hepworth, Larson, Rooney, Rooney, & Strom-Gottfried, 2009). Some argue for splitting the group based on stage of alienation, but an ISNAF group that links people together has room for every reality. Furthermore, divisions between stages are artificial and not reflective of real life. Some weeks a family situation may appear to be at one end of the spectrum while at other times it will be at another stage. Stages of alienation are not static or pure, but rather always in transition. Each stage carries with it features and degrees of other stages of alienation. In families with children at various stages of alienation the complexity grows.

Dealing with Uncertainty

Many targeted parents attend a group because they want to obtain specific advice about how to proceed in their situation. They wonder whether they should return to court to fight for their rights because that might backfire and increase the child's anger or the alienating parent's antagonism. They wonder whether they should relent to some of the child's unreasonable demands in order to keep the peace because that could create untenable precedents that they will regret later. Targeted parents may fear that any action will lead to further compromising their relationship with their children or cause harm to them or the child. Restraining orders, child welfare investigations based on false or misleading information, further rejections, and being demeaned has serious effects on a targeted parent and creates much confusion and uncertainty about how to respond.

While the group leader cannot provide legal advice or know for sure what is the best course of action (there simply is too little information about the course of alienation under different conditions), the premise of ISNAF is that the process of considering these issues in the group context is a helpful and important one. This constructive and positive activity, along with mental energy invested by targeted parents into developing strategies, taking action, and weighing risks and benefits of these actions, can be healing in and of itself, regardless of the outcome of any specific action. However, it is vital that the group leader clarifies that she cannot know with any certainty what the outcome of any specific action will be. Failure to do this can lead to great disappointment and anger later. Sometimes it is healing just to acknowledge the uncertainty and the shared wish to have a crystal ball to know the right course of action and a magic wand to impart immediate improvement.

Helping/Allowing the Targeted Parent to Feel Pleasure

Consumed with the day-to-day struggle of being a targeted parent and the ongoing feelings of loss and frustration with the impaired and damaged relationship with one's child, many targeted parents resist and express feelings of guilt around enjoyment of even simple pleasures. To enjoy a meal, a movie, or a night out with friends would be interpreted as meaning that they do not truly love their child. Thus, any engagement in the pleasures of life triggers a counterbalancing corrective response in order to avoid feeling like a bad parent. They would feel guilt and shame if they found themselves smiling or having their spirits lifted even for a few moments.

Part of what the support group can do is to help alleviate this shame and guilt by giving each other permission to enjoy some aspects of life while still despairing over the alienation. While a group member might not be ready to give him- or herself permission, that very same person can rationally explain to someone else why it is not a betrayal of the child to enjoy a movie. Needless to say, if they hear themselves say it to a friend they are also in a sense saying it to themselves. This is part of the magic of the group process—that each person is more generous, patient, and forgiving with others than they can be with themselves and by opening their hearts to each other they are also opening their hearts to themselves. Sometimes the leader can make this manifest and sometimes a group participant will comment when this is happening.

Other targeted parents have succumbed to melancholia, despair, and depression. It is not so much a conscious decision to be unhappy in order to avoid feeling like a bad parent as it is an uncontrollable pervasive sadness that permeates the person's experience of life. When someone is depressed and unable to find joy in life they have anhedonia, a serious symptom of depression that clouds judgment, actions, and thinking (Chentsova-Dutto & Hanley, 2010). For some, concentration and ability to focus can deteriorate whereas for others this condition results in hypervigilance. Suicidal thoughts and feelings of worthlessness are common (McKenzie, Clarke, Forbes, & Sim, 2010). It is important for the group leader to "take the pulse" of each person and keep an eye out for suicidal plans and intent among the group participants. Fortunately, while depressive episodes may be common, less common are actual suicidal plans.

Other Mental Health Concerns

Many targeted parents are very high-functioning, despite the unbearable pain and suffering inflicted on them. Others, however, do exhibit signs and symptoms of serious mental health issues. For example, some are so frightened of never seeing their beloved children again that they become paranoid. This can be triggered by knowing that some members of the group have had no contact with their children for extended periods, leading to avoidance of those people in the group. They struggle with understanding the normalcy of these feelings and thoughts and resist open catharsis. There is a tension between the intention of holding on and the shame or loss when letting go, releasing verbally their anger, disappointment, guilt, rage, and grief. They carry the sadness and embarrassment of having been maligned, marginalized, excluded, or shunned. These characteristics make the group facilitator's skill all the more important. As in the spirit of Carl Rogers (1951), honoring and encouraging the person to be herself, prizing her feelings as they manifest, and being non-judgmental is critical (O'Leary, 2012).

Advocacy Versus Support

Initially, many targeted parents state a preference for engaging in advocacy activities. That is understandable since that would take them away from their current gut-wrenching bewilderment and pain. It is the position of ISNAF that both advocacy and support are important and admirable. However, ISNAF encourages an emphasis on advocacy only after parents' own needs and care are reasonably attended to. It is believed that to be a successful advocate, group members must also move forward to meet their goals with their children. If there is a particular cause relating to PAS that resonates, members are encouraged to join but to bear in mind the ISNAF mission: to provide hope, education, information, and support. Our emphasis is on the individuals who attend the ISNAF support groups so they are ready to cope with and address the problems and the possibilities before them.

Gender Issues

Few issues are as heated for gender disputes as parental alienation. Fathers' rights groups, on the one hand, argue that the courts are systematically biased against competent fathers while, on the other hand, mothers' rights groups believe that parental alienation can be used as a ruse to shield abusive fathers from being held accountable for the realistic rejection of their children. ISNAF's position is that a support group leader must understand and educate participants in the consequence of disempowering and devaluing either parent. ISNAF honors the important and unique role each parent can play in the life and development of children.

Ideally, children will love and be loved by both mother and father and, at the least, no child should be manipulated to falsely reject a parent who otherwise could and would play a loving role in the child's life. Lack of attention from or abandonment by a parent can be traumatic for a developing child. When separating parents exert influence on the child to side with them and reject the other parent, it places the child in an untenable dilemma. The child might conclude that one or the other parent should be discounted, shunned, or is of little value. In a child's mind he may be omnipresent, having the power to make a parent disappear. The child also may feel minimized by having to reject the part of himself that loves and values the discarded parent. This can have a disabling effect on how the child will connect with others throughout his life (Yu, Petit, Lansford, Dodge, & Bates, 2010).

The ISNAF monthly support group meeting is attended by mothers and fathers. The program is gender neutral. In this case that means that the participants and the roles they occupy as both fathers and mothers are valued. Having the opportunity to have eye contact and develop a supportive relationship with a parent of the opposite sex from other participants in the group, as well as learn about their interior life and struggles, is a very important and valuable tool in terms of what happens within the ISNAF support system.

Socioeconomic Status and Court Involvement

A potential source of friction in a group of alienated families relates to social class and financial realities. Currently, ISNAF is populated by people from a range of socioeconomic strata but mostly upper middle and middle class parents. Perhaps this is because parents with monetary resources have the wherewithal to seek and obtain help from paid professionals (White, 2011). Instead of causing conflict and irritation among participants from differing socioeconomic backgrounds, ISNAF group participants find that the stress and shame of losing a child to parental alienation and the financial drain of ongoing litigation can "level the playing field."

Many targeted parents involved in the support group are simultaneously engaged in court battles. Involvement in protracted and costly court proceedings can dramatically increase stress levels and the need for support, explaining why they would be drawn to ISNAF. Employing a team of therapists, attorneys, and consultants can send anyone into bankruptcy or foreclosure. This is experienced as a profound loss. The impact is that once-wealthy families may lose their homes, lifestyle, and status in the community. Time with the children may be less flexible owing to work schedules and lack of ability to pay for childcare. Parents may become dependent on their own parents for the basics of food, school tuition, childcare, and housing. Those who have lost the most because of unsuccessful and protracted court battles are extremely stressed and in need of support. Stressors inherent in multiple court appearances include not fully understanding the ins and outs of the legal machinations and feeling helpless and frustrated when the attorney is unhelpful, ineffective, and unsympathetic. Some parents depend on the court process to protect parental rights and are as a result crushed when the outcome is unsatisfying. The support of the group can be a lifeline during these times.

A few ISNAF members represent themselves in court. The conventional wisdom is that this is risky at best. However, with some support and resources, increasing numbers are able to take some steps toward increased visitation time with the cooperation of a few judges. Group members confer with each other, share strategy, review attorneys and potential experts, and generally share the journey with each other.

Understanding the Impact of Stress on Cognitive Processing

It is also important for the group, from a cognitive standpoint, that people hear information accurately. When people are experiencing intense feelings it can be difficult to process information, which may lead to distortions and misunderstandings. When distortions occur it is important that the group leader involves the participants in a supportive way and uses this as an opportunity to examine how their perceptions of what is being discussed may be influenced by the distraction of emotional stressors that come with PAS and how misperceptions occur.

Cautionary Talk and Affirmation of Participants

Targeted parents are the experts on their own alienation story and so can also be the best judge in developing strategies. They should be encouraged to not automatically accept the conventional wisdom (i.e., "Things will get better, just wait a few years" or "Things are hopeless and nothing will help, so why bother?"). An adult's ability to use critical thinking in these instances is essential. When in crisis, some parents regress back to childhood—the time when thinking critically is not an expectation. Throughout the group discussions, participants should be encouraged to think critically. Perhaps using some cognitive behavioral therapy techniques as a resource would be useful. As an example, when the targeted parent is able to put the brakes on and switch direction with internal self-scripts (silently talking to ourselves) while an alienated child is trying to derail communication with a verbal attack of taunting and obscenities, a space is created where reality can exist and where parents might regain their role as respected, loved parent.

When a Participant Challenges the Group Leader

Sometimes members challenge the group leader owing to their despair and frustration with the lack of progress with their child. For example, a group participant can proclaim that every PAS situation is hopeless and ISNAF serves no viable function. Another way that this happens is when the group leader comes to represent an important person in the participant's life with whom there is unfinished business and conflicted feelings. The clue that this might be happening is when the expression of emotion and thoughts feels like the recitation of an old script and appears not to quite fit with either the content or the tone of the present discussion. This could be a sign that the member is not having his or her needs for understanding and compassion met (Dluhy & Rubenfeld, 2008).

The leader's task in such a situation is to carefully and in a supportive way guide the participants. The group leader might encourage the participant at the center and the other participants to explore some new ways to cope. It may be that the group leader takes this opportunity to schedule time outside of group session to explore this further. The participant at the center might want to discuss his feelings of inadequacy at failing to control the reactions of his child or ex-spouse or his inability to feel loved, respected, followed, and held dear. Often, conventional wisdom (that there are no options in terms of strategizing and taking action toward more contact with children) can be the expression of trying and failing at a variety of things, such as reaching out to a child, a former spouse, or the courts. Again, the group leader's skill to contain, reflect, or acknowledge without closing the doors to progress is key.

At times, just as targeted parents are blindsided by the alienation experience leading to disruptions in normal parental rights and access to one's child, leaders too can be surprised by negativity and undermining of the group by a member. When a participant is particularly angry, frustrated, and depressed, and they are demanding that the rest of the group agree with his viewpoint even when not in line with the realities of others' situations, this needs to be stopped and examined. The leader must not be afraid to examine and explore these darker emotions, otherwise they can fester and infect the group and undermine the leader's role.

Uneven Participation in Group Meetings

Targeted parents are in deep pain from ongoing loss and suffering. There can be some symptoms of post-traumatic stress disorder and deep grief involved with each participant. The symptoms may include flashbacks, lucid dreams, intense fear or anger, hypervigilance, and sleep problems (Hathaway, Bowles, & Ban 2010). There are times when a person may need to retreat, take a breather, or not come to group meetings, and work on fortifying himself so he can do the marathon required to move forward with the goal of reunification. During these periods it is important that he stays in touch with the group leader and has access to other appropriate resources. Taking leave is common and should not be a surprise to others. During these periods participants stay involved with assigned tasks or related projects. Acceptance, support, and understanding are essential from the other group participants as well as the group leaders. Badmouthing, put-downs, and diagnosing are taboo. By staying in touch with the absent member, the group leader can reassure the group that the person is working on healing, and if it is the case, is still connected.

Conclusions and Recommendations: A Look to the Future

Shunning, marginalizing, isolating, splitting, bullying, estranging, and alienating are all words created long ago to describe interactions that continue to this day. These are aspects of behavior which deeply hurt children and parents.

These words, when internalized, negatively color how we experience the community, family life, and self-worth. These words stop constructive acts to love, to learn, to contribute, to honor, and to bond. We know that once done, these actions require tremendous group effort and focus to undo. Armed with this information we must begin to address this terrible blight of hurting and sending each other away rather than coming together. Many who are victimized and rejected by their children owing to parental alienation indicate they feel like they are "hanging by a thread" and living without hope.

ISNAF emphasizes acceptance and compassion through support and education. So, in studying the impact of PAS, and the force it takes to address this problem, there are recommendations that come to mind. ISNAF is a network. This type of program by definition emphasizes the dynamics, values, and benefits reflected in interdependence. This is reflected in the ISNAF mission statement, "A hand to hold and others with whom to stand." ISNAF personifies the value of human connection. It exists within a community. The basic belief is that with enough support, understanding, and knowledge there may be motivation to develop more inclusive and less alienating options, approaches, and interventions requiring a new standard of behavior in our homes, communities, and public institutions.

In order to tackle this problem, humans must be able to identify and prevent those painful alienating dynamics to begin with. Information emerging from research into root causes and remedies for parental alienation/PAS is needed. This then could be used to create training programs from which research and positive adult role models evolve in our schools, from preschool through graduate school, in the corporate world, and in informal settings. Only after this is done can we hope to prevent behaviors that indicate a vulnerability to become either a victim or an alienator. Places to begin may include our homes, our communities, and public and private institutions. Like the shaman, while each of us has the capacity to intentionally hurt others, so too do we have the capacity and intention, if fully aware and present, to heal others.

References

Bekker, M., Arends-Toth, J. & Croon, M. (2011). Autonomy-connectedness, acculturation, and independence-interdependence among various cultural groups in a multicultural society. *International Journal of Intercultural Relations, 35(3)*, 368–370.

Bowles, S., Smith, E., & Mulder, M. (2010). The emergence and persistence of inequality in premodern societies. *Current Anthropology, 51(1)*, 7–71.

Chentsova-Dutto, Y., & Hanley. K. (2010). The effects of anhendonia and depression on hedonic responses. *Psychiatry Research, 179(2)*, 176–180.

Craffert, P. (2011). Shamanism and the shamanic complex. *Biblical Theological Bulletin, 41(3)*, 151–161.

De Schweinitz, P. (2010). Is there a Shaman in the house? *Journal of the American Board of Family Medicine, 23(6)*, 794–796.

Dluhy, M., & Rubenfeld, S. (2008). *Windows into today's group therapy.* New York: Routledge.

Ewing, C. P. (2012). *Tarasoff reconsidered.* Available at: http://www.apa.org/monitor/julaug05/jn.aspx [accessed March 13, 2012].

Gottlieb, B., & Wachala, E. (2007). Cancer support groups: A critical review of empirical studies. *Psycho-Oncology, 16(5)*, 379–400.

Goodman, H., & Munoz, M. (2004). Developing social group work skills for contemporary agency practice. *Social Work with Groups, 27(1)*, 17–33.

Haber, R. (2011). Virgina Satir's family camp experiment: An intentional growth community still in process. *Contemporary Family Therapy, 33(1)*, 71–84.

Harlow, H., & Suomi, S. (1971). Social recovery by isolation-reared monkeys. *Proceedings of the National Academy of Science, 68(7)*, 1534–1538.

Hathaway, L., Bowles, A., & Ban, J. (2010). PTSD symptoms and dominant emotional response to a traumatic event: An examination of DSM-IV Criterion A2. *Anxiety, Stress, and Coping, 23(1)*, 119–120.

Hepworth, D. H., Larson, J. A., Rooney, G. D., Rooney, R. H, & Strom-Gottfried, K. (2009). *Direct social work practice: Theory and skills.* Belmont, CA: Thomas Brooks/Cole.

Kottler, J. A. (2010). *On being a therapist.* San Francisco: Jossey Bass.

Lewin, K. (1951). *Field theory in social science: Selected theoretical papers.* D. Cartwright (Ed.). New York: Harper & Row.

McKenzie, D., Clarke, D., Forbes, A. & Sim, M. (2010). Pessimism, worthlessness, anhedonia, and thoughts of death identify DSM-IV major depression in hospitalized medically ill patients. *Psychosomatics, 51*, 302–305.

Munn-Giddings, C., & McVicar, A. (2006). Self-help groups as mutual support: What do carers value? *Health and Social Care in the Community, 15(1)*, 26–34.

Norton, C. (2009). Eco-psychology and social work: Creating interdisciplinary framework for redefining person-in-environment. *Ecopsychology, 1(3)*, 138–145.

O'Leary, C. (2012). Carl Rogers: Lessons for working at relational depth. *Person-Centered and Experiential Psychotherapies, 5(4)*, 229–239.

Rogers, C. (1951). *Client centered therapy.* Boston: Houghton Mifflin.

Schimmel, N. (2008). A humanistic approach to caring for street children: The importance of emotionally intimate and supportive relationships for the successful rehabilitation of street children. *Vulnerable Youth and Children Studies, 3(3)*, 214–220.

Stoffel, M. (2010). *The practical power of shamanism: Heal your life, loves, and losses.* Isanti, MN: Innovative Order.

White, K. (2011). A call for regulating third party divorce litigation funding. *Journal of Law and Family Studies, 13(2)*, 395–411.

Yu, T., Petit, G., Lansford, J., Dodge, K., & Bates, J. (2010). The interactive effects of marital conflict and divorce on parent-adult children's relationships. *Journal of Marriage and Family, 72(2)*, 282–292.

8 Psycho-Educational Work with Children in Loyalty Conflict

The "I Don't Want to Choose" Program

Amy J. L. Baker and Katherine Andre

Finding A New Program for an Age-Old Problem

A school psychologist has noticed that her group for divorced kids has started to lose enthusiasm and she wonders if there is another approach to working with children of divorce that could liven up the group as well as attract new members. She feels that the program she is currently running is not doing enough to help kids cope with the loyalty conflicts she thinks they are dealing with. She recently attended a professional conference and learned about a new program called "I Don't Want to Choose" (IDWTC), which aims to teach middle-school children critical thinking skills so that they can resist the pressure put on them by one parent to reject the other parent. This strikes her as an approach that could work with her group of 6th graders in the middle school in which she works. She becomes excited about the IDWTC approach because it might help the kids not only stay out of the middle of their parents' conflicts but could also help them resist peer pressure, always a topic of concern for middle-school staff and parents.

The school psychologist is familiar with some of the research literature that shows that parental conflict is a significant factor in post-divorce adjustment of children. She knows that it is not the divorce itself that is most often associated with long-term negative outcomes but rather post-divorce inter-parental conflict that has been found specifically to be a problem for children's adjustment in the years following the divorce (Emery, 1982), leading to both internalizing and externalizing behavior problems (Buehler et al., 1998), difficulties in interpersonal relationships (Bolgar, Zweig-Frank, & Paris, 1995), and poorer adjustment (Kline, Johnston, & Tschann, 1991). However, it is not simply the degree of parental conflict that seems to affect children detrimentally but rather the degree to which the children are drawn into the parental conflict (Buchanan, Maccoby, & Dornbusch, 1991). The school psychologist has read that children who are involved in their parents' conflict feel caught between their parents and experience stressful loyalty conflicts and cognitive dissonance (Amato & Afifi, 2006). The child loves both parents, who no longer love each other and may actually feel tremendous antagonism towards each other.

The school psychologist has actually seen some of this first hand as parents engage in tactics to draw the child closer to him/her and farther away from the other parent. She has seen parents erase the other parent's name from the contact information and emergency card, denigrate the other parent to the child, and exclude the other parent from school events and activities. Some of these parents are quite clever at making the other parent appear foolish or irrelevant in the eyes of the child. She is also aware that sometimes children succumb to these manipulations and pressure and take sides with one parent against the other. She understands that although such an alliance can resolve the child's immediate feeling of being caught in the middle, it entails its own set of problems for the child. These children seem to act in a haughty and cruel manner towards one parent while treating the other parent with an unquestioning hero worship that seems unnatural and unhealthy for children of their age. She knows that this behavioral scenario cannot be good for their moral development and character and is hopeful that the IDWTC program will help these children figure out that they can love and be loved by both parents.

Introduction to the Program

The IDWTC program is an outgrowth of research and clinical work with divorcing families dealing with loyalty conflicts. Research has established that most children experience immediate and predictable stress-related adjustments to their parents' divorce, but long-term negative outcomes are most likely to accrue to children whose parents are highly conflicted and pull them into their conflict. Most troubling are conflicts in which children are backed into an emotional corner and feel compelled to choose sides between opposing parents in order to cope. While other "children of divorce" programs exist and include loyalty conflict in their curricula, none focus extensively on this issue of loyalty conflicts (e.g., Pedro-Carroll, 1997, 2005; Margolin, 1996; Neuman, 1998; Spencer & Shapiro, 1993).

The program was developed to fill this important gap in the service delivery spectrum for children of divorce. The philosophical underpinnings of the program include that divorce represents a significant risk factor to children and that additional protective factors are required to prevent that risk from resulting in long-term poor outcomes. The importance of protective factors is consistent with work in the field of neurobiology (Siegel & Hartzell, 2003; Siegel, 1999; Siegel, 2007), which underscores the importance of healthy relationships for optimal brain formation and functioning as well as for immune system health. The way parents relate to children has far-reaching effects on children's development and psychological, social, and biological functioning.

The goal of the program is to teach children alternative ways to cope with loyalty conflicts that can protect them and strengthen vulnerable psychological areas in their life. The curriculum is built around four problem-solving approaches. These approaches provide critical thinking skills, problem-solving options, emotional and cognitive–behavioral problem-solving tools, and ways to find help and support. They are consistent with common factors that have been used in programs designed for building children's resilience in the face of stress (Grotberg, 1995).

Children forced to choose sides are not only placed in a stressful situation but also are at risk for numerous additional negative short-term and long-term outcomes. In the short term, there is the loss of the rejected parent and the excessive control wielded over them by the chosen parent. In the long term, there is the risk of numerous characterological, psychological, social, and interpersonal problems that are beyond the scope of this chapter but are discussed at length in Baker (2007). The goal of the IDWTC program is to intervene before these problems develop and to prevent alienation by strengthening children's ability to respond to the parental conflict without taking sides. The program is based on the premise that other than situations in which children reject a parent who is abusive or neglectful (which is referred to in the literature as realistic estrangement), children want to maintain relationships with both of their parents and fare better when they are able to do so.

Research has identified at least 17 common loyalty conflict situations that are likely to result in children feeling compelled to choose sides in parental loyalty conflicts (Baker, 2007; Baker & Darnall, 2006, Baker & Fine, this volume). In developing the IDWTC materials and program, we have identified four problem-solving skills that, when enhanced, could be used by children to resist the pressure to choose. It is important to note that the IDWTC program is not therapy per se and should not be seen as replacing any therapy in which a child or family is involved. The materials are psycho-educational in nature, meaning that the goal is to provide knowledge- and skill-building opportunities in a supportive peer group setting so that participants can learn and gain comfort from the shared experience with others. The materials are a coordinated book, workbook, and manual. The book and workbook can be given to individual children or worked on individually with them. For those professionals who want to use the IDWTC book and workbook with a group of children, the IDWTC facilitator's manual provides the curriculum for doing so.

The book is written for middle-school-aged children and includes an introductory note to caring adults and parents. The purpose of these notes is to explain to adults the importance of helping children resist the pressure to choose between parents and provides some guidance for how to discuss the issues in the book with children. There is also an introductory note to readers which sets the tone of the book. It addresses young readers in a warm and caring manner and lets them know that the book was written to help them love both parents. It explains that it is their right to *not* have to choose between parents and that the book contains tools to help them avoid doing so.

The workbook supplements the activities and suggestions in the book and contains additional structured exercises for increasing self-awareness and understanding of various loyalty conflict situations that could arise in the family. The workbook activities aim to appeal to children with different learning styles and interests. The activities include word games and puzzles, kinetic activities, and imaginative and fantasy play. Throughout, it is stressed that there is no right or wrong answer to any of the activities and that the purpose is to help the child find his or her own truth.

Children reading the book on their own and completing the workbook activities on their own may not want or need to explore all the family situations sequentially. Instead, they may prefer to focus on just the relevant exercises that apply to their family and they may elect to approach the situations in the book in a different order than from beginning to end. The materials are designed to be worked on in any order that feels right to the child. Each family situation stands on its own as a complete lesson. However, in the school-based program, children will be exposed to all of the loyalty conflicts (even those that do not necessarily apply to them) and will do so in the order in which they are presented in the materials and curriculum. It is hoped that they will gain insight into their own thoughts and feelings even when discussing a situation that happens not to apply to them at that moment. Further, the weeks in which the focus is on the topics that do not apply to them can provide them with opportunities to provide support to their peers who may be dealing with more intense experiences than they are. In this way, the children can gain confidence in themselves as people who care about others and are able to be helpful. These empathy-inducing experiences can help the children develop their own emotional intelligence by teaching them to identify, express, and regulate their emotions in a safe and accepting environment (Goleman, 2005; Greenberg, 2004).

The IDWTC manual provides a guide for the program facilitator. The manual includes tips for group process work; details regarding the logistics of running the program, including instructions for getting started, being prepared, recruiting participants, and obtaining parental permission; and week-by-week age-appropriate detailed scripts. Explanations for process issues are included, such as tailoring the material to the needs and interests of the group, dealing with loyalty conflict situations that are brought to the group out of order, developing ground rules, giving non-judgmental feedback, dealing with dominant or reticent participants, and working with parents. With the exception of the two introductory weeks and the final celebratory week, the remaining 17 weeks are used to explore each of the family situations described in the IDWTC book. Because it is not a therapy group program, and because age-appropriate scripts for introducing and processing each topic are provided, the facilitator can be a classroom teacher or any trained school staff member (school psychologist, school counselor, school social worker).

Rationale for a School-Based Program

Schools are Where the Children are

Teachers spend more time with children than most other adults except for parents or close relatives. They are often the first to see that something is different about a child, whether it is a significant lowering of grades, dampening of mood, sudden onset of agitation and aggression, or increase in social behavior problems. Children spend years in the same school and are known and observed on a routine basis by a host of educational and support staff, increasing the likelihood that someone will observe and make note of a significant shift in the child's social, emotional, or academic functioning and well-being.

Schools have easy access to children and routinely intervene in mental health issues as they arise by conducting assessments, providing counseling, and running psycho-educational groups when clusters of children appear to be dealing with the same issue. The routine of receiving services in a school does not carry the stigma associated with programs that are located off the school premises, such as in a therapist's office or at the courthouse. Schools can often offer educational resources and support to school children without having to obtain consent from parents who might try to sabotage a child's efforts to resist the pressure to choose between parents.

Further, schools bring together a team of educational and mental health professionals who are trained and mandated to promote the wellness of the youth in their care. These adults are highly trained professionals who are qualified to identify problems, make referrals, and, when appropriate, provide interventions in a neutral, safe environment. Further, these adults can function as enlightened witnesses who acknowledge the reality of children's loyalty conflicts and provide them with the resources for coping with their situations.

Schools Have a Vested Interest in Children Being Healthy

Healthy children are able to channel their existing internal resources (energy, attention, imagination, brain power) into academic and social learning and require fewer staff interventions than children distracted by family conflict and inner turmoil. If left untreated, the stress from a parental loyalty conflict could lead a child to exhibit externalized behavior problems that cause disruptions in the classroom and to engage in other types of misbehavior (bullying, vandalism, excessive absenteeism), all of which use up valuable staff time and resources. Additionally, the stress from loyalty conflict can lead to internalized problems such as social withdrawal, depression, and anxiety. These behaviors often impact grades, concentration, and ability to learn. Thus the stress from loyalty conflicts can disrupt the mental health trajectory of school children and can also interfere with their academic progress. For both these reasons, schools are highly motivated to address these issues before they take too great a toll on the children. Some of the effects of alienation have been studied by Baker (2007; Baker & BenAmi, 2011) and found to be profound, long-term, and sometimes life-altering. Thus, while the root of the problem might be an emotional conflict arising in the home, the impact of that problem can reverberate into the child's functioning in school and, hence, will fall upon the school to address.

Another reason for an intervention in schools is that schools help to shape moral and character development. When children are encouraged by one parent to reject the other parent—in the absence of a good reason to do so—the child's moral and character development becomes compromised. For example, when a child is encouraged to treat one parent badly or spy on that parent, to keep secrets from or ignore that parent, the child is learning how to be cruel and disrespectful and will no doubt end up lacking empathy and integrity. When a child is taught to walk away from a loving relationship rather than encouraged to resolve conflict in a peaceful and respectful manner, the child is not only denied the opportunity to have a relationship with a loving parent but also denied the opportunity to learn valuable relational problem-solving and interpersonal skills. When schools provide programs which help children resist the pressure of loyalty conflicts, they are helping to build character and to guide their moral development.

Another reason for an intervention program in schools is that schools have a vested interest in social functioning and appropriate social behaviors. By addressing loyalty conflict issues and providing children the opportunity to learn the skills they need to handle a loyalty conflict, they are also providing skills that could be transferable to other types of conflict, such as peer pressure to join gangs, use drugs, or drop out of school. Preventive interventions that teach protective skills in a supportive environment are effective and enhance resilience (Pedro-Carroll, 1997, 2005; Grotberg, 1995). Resilience that becomes internalized can then be applied in other areas of life, and hence indirectly benefit the school, home, or other environment in which these resilience skills are needed.

Schools Provide the Kind of Neutral Setting Required by the Principles of the Program

Alienation does not happen overnight. It is a process with a window of opportunity to intervene before it becomes entrenched in the child's personality structure. With proper intervention, alienation may be prevented along with the resulting long-term negative outcomes of alienation. Because children may need "permission" from a neutral third party who is not aligned with either parent, schools are an ideal setting for providing children with information and skills to manage the situation. The program is not aligned with either parent (the way a therapist or other caring adult might be, such as a relative or parent of a friend). Hence, children will not perceive themselves as favoring or betraying a parent by participating in the program and the content of the program will not be experienced by the child as part of one parent's agenda against the other parent. The facilitator makes it clear that parents are not a part of the program; they are not invited in and nothing specific the child says will be shared with either parent. The one exception is if the child indicates a plan to harm him- or herself or someone else. The program is designed to provide the children with a safe and neutral island of sanity and protection from the parental turmoil and conflict.

Structure of Each Session

Each of the 20 sessions of the IDWTC program is designed to follow the same general format in order to provide consistency and predictability for the participating children. Table 8.1 provides an overview of the structure and examples of each component.

Table 8.1 Components of the "I Don't Want to Choose" program

Program component	*Description*
Welcome	The room is set up and the facilitator waits for the children to arrive. The facilitator warmly greets each child and invites him or her to take a seat. When the starting time arrives, the facilitator welcomes everyone and asks who would like to read the ground rules. If no one volunteers, the facilitator reads them.
Review ground rules	The ground rules are developed by the group during the first session as statements regarding (1) privacy and confidentiality of the information shared during the group and (2) ways to respectfully behave during the group towards each other (such as speaking one at a time and being non-judgmental about what other children share).
Read a family situation	One of the 17 family situations, along with accompanying examples, is read out loud. For example, "One parent does not want you to have photographs of the other parent." The facilitator asks for a show of hands to see how many of the participants have had this experience. At this point there might be an activity to elaborate on what the situation is. For example, in the situation about one parent looking sad or angry when the child is leaving to be with the other parent, the facilitator might act out various emotions and have the group guess what the "parent" is trying to convey. The point is to show the participants that parents can subtly convey their objection to the child's relationship with the other parent without having to state it explicitly, and that parents might actually say that they want the child to go and have a good time with the other parent but convey to the child in other ways (with their facial expression and body language) that they really do not mean what they say.
Identify thoughts and feelings	The facilitator explores possible thoughts and feelings that a child might have in response to the family situation being discussed. The facilitator calls out various emotions, such as proud, scared, guilty, worried, and so forth, and asks the youth to stand (or sit or clap) if

Table 8.1 Continued

Program component	*Description*
	they have had that emotion. The facilitator ends with a reflection about how youth can have lots of different feelings and thoughts in response to the family situation being discussed and that there is no right or wrong feeling to have.
Problem-solving approach 1: Critical thinking	The facilitator engages the youth in an activity designed to activate their critical thinking skills. For example, in response to being asked to spy on a parent, the facilitator will ask the group to make a list of reasons why this would be a good idea and why this would not be a good idea. The facilitator will ask if there are different types of spying, and whether they are all equally bad, and will ask participants to make a list of why one parent might want to have a child spy on the other parent. The concept of creating a psychological wedge between the child and the other parent will be raised by the facilitator if no one brings it up.
Problem-solving approach 2: Considering options	In helping the children consider their options the point is consistently made that there is usually a way to respectfully decline to engage in a loyalty conflict. For example, with respect to the family situation of one parent saying mean and untrue things about the other parent, the facilitator hands out index cards and invites the participants to come up with a text message to tell the other parent that they do not want to hear mean and untrue things about the other parent. They are challenged to use as many symbols and abbreviations as possible (in order to make the exercise fun). At the end the facilitator also provides an example.
Problem-solving approach 3: Listening to one's heart	The facilitator engages the youth in an activity designed to activate their ability to listen to their heart. For example, when discussing the family situation in which one parent tells the child that the other parent is unsafe, the facilitator leads the participants in a guided imagery exercise, by saying, "Let's close our eyes and think about the parent that the other parent is saying is unsafe. Allow yourself to take a few deep breaths and relax. Picture that parent holding you and comforting you and taking care of you. How do you feel when you picture these things?"
Problem-solving Approach 4: Getting support	The facilitator engages the youth in an activity designed to activate their ability to seek support. For example, when discussing the family situation in which one parent refers to the other parent by first name, the facilitator asks the participants to conduct a survey of their peers to learn how they would handle this if they were dealing with the same situation. In addition, the facilitator leads a discussion about how sometimes talking about these situations can cause tension in our bodies and then guides the group in exercises (showing them how to stretch their backs and arms and legs even while sitting) in order to release tension.
Closing	Each weekly session concludes with a closing circle in which the participants go around and share (if they want) what they have learned from the group. The circle ends with the facilitator reminding them of the time and place for the next meeting, what the reading assignment is, and that s/he is available should any participants want to discuss something in private.

The Four Problem-Solving Approaches

The four problem-solving approaches, as presented in the IDWTC materials, are designed to realign children's reality and moral compass, which can become warped through exposure to loyalty conflicts. The program is designed to help them learn how to trust themselves and to make good choices, which can become difficult for children exposed to parental alienation strategies. In the IDWTC book, suggestions are made in response to each of the 17 family situations by working through the four approaches. In the IDWTC workbook, specific activities for the child to work on alone are provided to expand on these suggestions. In the IDWTC curriculum the children are engaged in interactive exercises that allow them to develop the skills they need to respond to parental alienation strategies without betraying a parent or themselves. Each level (book, workbook, curriculum) takes the concept one step deeper for the child and allows the child increased opportunities for applying the concepts to his/her own life. Each level presents the child with opportunities to engage in the four problem-solving approaches: (1) critical thinking skills, (2) considering options, (3) listening to one's heart, and (4) getting support. Each approach is described in greater detail below.

Critical Thinking

Critical thinking is the term used to describe mental/cognitive processes in which an individual is aware of and able to reflect on his or her beliefs and the sources of those beliefs (Halpern, 1998). The purpose of critical thinking is to ascertain whether one is functioning as a rational and free-thinking individual or whether one is thinking in a reflexive automatic fashion that is biased and closed to outside input and revision. A critical thinker is not necessarily critical in the sense of judging something harshly and focusing on the negative. In the IDWTC materials, the concept of "critical" is synonymous with "analytical" and "examined," and is the opposite of automatic and unexamined.

Critical thinking skills are likely to be eroded by exposure to parental alienation strategies because children are emotionally manipulated by one parent to hold certain beliefs about the other parent that are not based in reality. Such beliefs might be that the other parent is unsafe, unloving, and unavailable and are generated in order to secure the child's love for the parent perpetrating these false beliefs. When children are subjected to that kind of emotional pressure, where they feel that the love of a parent is "on the line," they may experience fear, anxiety, and panic, which can make rational appraisals even more difficult. Strong emotions are known to cloud judgment and often lead to a shutting down of critical thinking processes. Two examples are provided for illustrative purposes. If a parent asks a child to keep secrets from the other parent in an atmosphere of heightened emotional drama, the child will probably assume that: (1) the spied-on parent is withholding information that the other parent rightly deserves, (2) the spied-on parent must have done something wrong, and

(3) the other parent is a victim of the spied-on parent. This would be especially true if the parent doing the asking hints that or behaves as if the other parent is dangerous or unloving. Through this experience the child would be absorbing a message without being aware of it sufficiently to question it. By way of another example, if one parent acts afraid of the other parent, cringing and cowering when he or she is in proximity, the child will probably conclude that the other parent has done something to cause such fear and hence is dangerous. Again, the message bypasses the rational part of the child's brain and becomes incorporated into his/her belief system. In the absence of opportunities to reflect on these beliefs, the child will take them as truth and respond accordingly.

It is important to point out that there is reason to believe that children will act on these manipulations without fully endorsing the negative view of the other parent. In other words a child might side with one parent against another parent and even "buy into" some of the false beliefs while still loving and wanting to have a relationship with the other parent. The strength of the rejection has less to do with the extent to which the child really believes the lies, but more to do with the fear the child has of losing the love and favor of the parent who is creating the loyalty conflict and manipulating him or her. Through engagement in these behaviors, the parent is revealing to the child that his or her love for the child is contingent on the child rejecting the other parent and hence is conditional (as opposed to love for the child that is unconditional). Thus, the child complies with the alienation strategies and rejects the other parent as a response to fear of losing that parent as much if not more than as a true endorsement of the false belief that the other parent deserves to be rejected. The basis for this proposition is two-fold. The first is the in-depth research interviews with adults who were alienated from a parent as a child (Baker, 2007). These interviewees revealed that although they were behaving in an extreme position of alienation (rude, rejecting, cold, harsh) they still loved the parent whom they were treating so badly. The second source of this statement is the observation of the second author that many of these alienated children are found to warm up almost instantly with the rejected parent once the favored parent is not in the waiting room or is out of sight.

Thus, a child caught in loyalty conflict is experiencing pressure to adopt (endorse as opposed to actually fully believe) one parent's one-sided view of the world (that one parent is all good and the other is all bad). The child is being encouraged to bypass critical thinking to evaluate his or her beliefs. In the IDWTC book, workbook, and curriculum, the children are provided with numerous opportunities to make these false "beliefs" explicit and are encouraged to examine the basis for them in a safe and non-judgmental environment. A picture of a light bulb is used as an identifying icon in the IDWTC materials to symbolize shining light on a belief that was previously held in the dark. In the critical thinking exercises the children are encouraged to become aware of their beliefs and to ask themselves questions such as:

- What do I believe?
- Why do I believe what I believe?

- Is there evidence or facts to support my belief?
- Is my belief biased?
- Am I free to change my mind?
- If I don't change my mind, is there a consequence?

By working through these questions they can step outside the emotional manipulation and loyalty conflict behaviors in order to examine their beliefs and decide calmly and rationally for themselves what their truth is. The exercises in the IDWTC curriculum are designed to help children identify the hidden messages in parental actions and words in order to make explicit the messages that they are exposed to and might inadvertently be absorbing and assuming as truths.

Considering Options

Exposure to parental alienation strategies also involves pressure on the child to comply with parental demands for allegiance and loyalty. Some of the strategies result in children doing and saying things to please one parent that are likely to create a psychological wedge between the child and the other parent. Once children "go down that road" they are likely to feel guilty and ashamed and may want to avoid the other parent even more. They may demonize and devalue that parent in order to justify their misbehavior and one-sided loyalty. For all of these reasons, the second problem-solving approach involves helping children to slow down and consider their options when faced with a parental demand/command that is likely to entrench the alienation even further.

Gardner (1998) rightly recognized that alienated children will often add their own contribution to the campaign of denigration against the rejected parent, picking up the mantle of the favored parent and carrying the alienation to a new level. Thus, it is important to prevent children who are under pressure of alienation from making choices that will result in their feeling that they must justify their bad behavior by devaluing the other parent even more. Figuratively, they are painting themselves into a corner from which it is very hard to find their way out. When faced with a parental request, they are likely to feel that they must comply immediately. This is so for at least three reasons. First, many children are generally compliant with their parents and are taught to be so for their own safety and well-being. Second, they are likely being subjected to emotional manipulation designed to heighten the likelihood that they will comply. They may feel that the parent doing the asking will stop loving them unless they comply or they might feel as if they owe that parent their allegiance or they might feel that they would be selfish if they did not comply. Third, they might lack the skills to know how to respectfully not comply. They may not realize that they even have any options at all. Thus, the IDWTC materials include an examination of choices with respect to each of the 17 parental alienation situations presented in order to teach children that they might have more choices than they realize.

In the IDWTC materials, a picture of a road sign that has both left and right arrows on a road is used as an identifying icon to symbolize having choices. Children caught in loyalty conflict often feel as if they must comply with all parental requests, even when those requests go against their sense of self or against the other parent. An important part of the program teaches children to think about their choices and options without automatically being pulled into a loyalty conflict. When faced with a parental question that is likely to result in an alignment with one parent against the other, they are encouraged to ask:

- What are my choices?
- What am I being pressured to do?
- How can I appropriately and respectfully make a choice that allows me to maintain relationships with both of my parents?

These are some of the questions that children are taught to consider to help them resist the pressure to choose one parent over the other. The suggestions in the book, the activities in the workbook, and the interactive exercises in the curriculum are designed to help children brainstorm options and imagine how each would feel for them in light of their own values and their desire to maintain a relationship with both parents. The program materials do not dictate which option to choose, because that is viewed as inappropriate and undermining to their confidence in themselves and would be counter to the philosophy of the program that children know their own truth and will find ways to make choices that work for them. The exercises in the curriculum provide children with opportunities to take on different roles, try out various options, practice respectful ways to decline parental requests to betray the other parent, and figure out which one(s) feel right for them.

Listening to Your Heart

Another way to think about parental alienation is that it involves the child endorsing and/or adopting a truth that is not his or her own but rather a false truth imposed on him or her by a parent. When the alienation strategies are successful, the child adopts one parent's worldview as a replacement for his or her own independent beliefs, memories, and judgments. Parental alienation involves the child adopting beliefs that are not true, such as that one parent is dangerous and unsafe when the parent is actually loving and safe. It involves believing that is it acceptable to betray a parent. It involves believing that it is acceptable to be disrespectful to a parent (shunning them, referring to them by first name, resisting their authority, not sharing important information with them). These false beliefs become incorporated into the child's belief systems, at least partially (as noted above, it appears that alienated children also hold onto their own reality and truth underneath the surface), which in turn may shape their behavior and attitudes, especially when in the presence of the parent engaging in these behaviors.

The IDWTC materials are designed to teach children that: (1) they have their own truth and (2) it is important to honor that truth in order to feel good about themselves and to have integrity. By using their critical thinking skills and considering their options, they can find their way to making choices that allow them to sustain relationships with both parents. Emotional coaching (Gottman, 1997) and helping children to process their feelings is one part of the "Listening to Your Heart" component of the program. This part of the program teaches children to recognize and label their emotions and discern what those emotions are telling them. Are they feeling scared that one parent will not love them anymore unless they betray or reject the other parent? Are they angry at one parent but do not know what the sources of that anger are? Are they feeling overwhelmed with loving two people who hate each other and believe that it would be easier to chose one and get rid of the other? By talking about their emotions through the coaching experience, the children learn to examine and accept them, to regulate their emotional states, and to develop the ability to self-soothe and stay rational while faced with emotional pressure (Gottman, 1997; Siegel & Hartzell, 2003). When feelings are validated as opposed to minimized and are labeled in a supportive environment such as psychotherapy, individuals become empowered and strengthened (Greenberg, 2004). Although the IDWTC program is not a psychotherapy program, the children participating in IDWTC are in a supportive educational environment where their feelings are labeled and validated by a non-judgmental adult or peer. Thus, through a similar process, they can become empowered to gain strength and confidence to make choices that allow them to maintain relationships with both parents.

In the IDWTC materials, a picture of a stethoscope listening to a heart is used as an identifying icon to symbolize being true to oneself by being attuned to one's emotions and values. Activities included in the IDWTC curriculum to encourage the children to listen to their heart include identifying feelings, accessing one's inner truth, identifying core values, and affirming the importance of being true to oneself. In the curriculum there are several opportunities for children to use imagery and imagination to consider what it feels like to be with the parent who is the target of the alienation and to heed what their heart is telling them. They are encouraged to ask themselves questions such as:

- What do I know to be true about each of my parents?
- What am I feeling?
- What kind of person do I want to be?

These are some of the questions children are encouraged to explore in order to protect themselves from the undue influence of one parent trying to turn them against the other parent.

Getting Support

The fourth problem-solving approach has an internal and an external component. Inner support refers to (1) cognitive–behavioral processes that either support or detract from a child being able to cope with the stress and challenge of parental alienation and (2) physical processes that increase or decrease stress and tension in the body. From a cognitive–behavioral perspective, it is well understood that what people say to themselves in their thoughts and inner dialogue greatly impacts the choices they make and the way they feel (Seligman, 1994; Beck, 1976/1979; Ellis & Greiger, 1977). One very important internal process relates to attributions (why we think things happen). For example, when people infer that bad things happen to them because they are to blame and when they believe that everything is bad and everything will remain bad, they tend to experience depression. Likewise, if a child exposed to alienation strategies believes that nothing he does can make a difference, that he is powerless to resist, and that he does not deserve the love and support of both parents then that child is likely to succumb to the pressure to reject one parent.

Physical processes are also very important for the well-being of all children, especially children experiencing excessive stress in their family. Children exposed to alienation strategies are likely to feel a host of negative emotions such as anxiety, worry, guilt, shame, and anger, all of which can result in physical tension and illness.

External support is also an issue for children exposed to alienation strategies. External support refers to the people in the life of the child who could provide love, nurturance, guidance, and assistance to the child while he or she is facing parental alienation strategies. All of these people could be helpful to the child if she or he understood how to identify sources of support and how to use them. Peer support is particularly helpful to children dealing with emotional issues because simply knowing that other children are going through something similar can normalize the experience and eradicate some of the feelings of shame, isolation, and confusion that they may be feeling.

In the IDWTC materials a picture of hands that are meeting and shaking one another is used as an identifying icon to symbolize receiving support. When children feel tense and pressured by loyalty conflict, they need to know how to draw upon their own internal resources as well as how to receive extra help from others to help them to cope. Drawing on the principles of cognitive behavioral therapy (Beck, 1976/1979), activities are designed to teach children how to tune in to their inner self-talk and pay attention to the kinds of messages they are giving themselves. They are encouraged to examine whether their self-talk is positive or negative, helpful or detrimental. The self-talk may be creating a feeling of helplessness or hopelessness such as, "This situation will never change" or "There is nothing I can ever do to get out of this conflict." The program teaches participants how to manage their self-talk to avoid the negative kind that causes helplessness and depression. There is a particular emphasis on helping program participants perceive themselves as strong and courageous and able to face the challenges in front of them. The activities also teach children how to tune in to their bodies and identify whether and where they are experiencing tension. They are encouraged to pay attention to what their body is telling them and to take care of themselves as part of their overall strategy for staying healthy.

Table 8.2 Logistical considerations of the "I Don't Want to Choose" program

Logistic	*Explanation*
Number of children per group	About 10
Age of participants	Grades 5–8 (perhaps one group for 5–6 graders and one group for 7–8 graders).
Calendar	Twenty-week program with weeks 1 and 2 focused on group cohesion and the final week set as a concluding celebration. The program can start at any point in the school year as long as there is sufficient time to complete the program before the end of the year.
Location	A private room within the school which is free from intrusions, interruptions, and undue noise. The setting should be emotionally neutral (i.e., not a place where troubled children are taken).
Time	Should be during non-academic time such as lunch, free period, or before or after the school day.
Participants	Any children experiencing divorce of parents and/or parental loyalty conflicts.
Recruitment	A flyer is provided but the school can make its own.
Parental consent	The school decides whether parental consent will be necessary for participation.
Facilitator	Anyone with experience running groups and managing emotional issues. Ideally it will be someone the children trust and feel safe with.
Length of each session	Each meeting will take about 45 minutes.
Fees	The manual costs $50 and is reusable within the school. Each student will need a $9.95 book and a $12.95 workbook which, unless otherwise determined, will be provided to the youth by the school. Other costs include snacks for the meetings and incidental materials.

Program Logistics

There are also activities designed to help them find help from others by asking questions such as who are the trusted adults in their lives and how can they go about cultivating those external sources of support that every child needs. The participants are encouraged to view each other as a source of support as they take the journey through the program together. All of these sources, along with the other participants in the group, are sources of help that can be drawn upon to seek and create support when they feel drawn into their parents' loyalty conflict.

Conclusion

The school is a safe and neutral environment for the psycho-educational IDWTC program. When children are under pressure to choose between their parents they need to develop the skills necessary to resist the pressure to choose, so that they are able to love and be loved by both parents. Four problem-solving approaches are developed in the program in order to help children think for themselves, consider their options, be aware of what their heart is telling them, and obtain the support they need to cope with their family conflict. Seventeen family situations that create loyalty conflict provide the real-life context for participants to learn about and apply these processes so that they can resist the pressure to choose one parent over the other in their own families.

References

Amato, P., & Afifi, T. D. (2006). Feeling caught between parents: Adult children's relations with parents and subjective well-being. *Journal of Marriage and the Family, 68(1)*, 222–236.

Baker, A. J. L. (2007). *Adult children of parental alienation syndrome: Breaking the ties that bind.* New York: W. W. Norton.

Baker, A. J. L., & BenAmi, N. (2011). To turn a child against a parent is to turn a child against himself. *Journal of Divorce and Remarriage, 52(4)*, 203–219.

Baker, A. J. L., & Darnall, D. (2006). Behaviors and strategies of parental alienation: A survey of parental experiences. *Journal of Divorce and Remarriage, 45(1/2)*, 97–124.

Beck, A.T. (1976/1979). *Cognitive therapy and the emotional disorders.* New York: Penguin.

Bolgar, R., Zweig-Frank, H., & Paris, J. (1995). Childhood antecedents of interpersonal problems in young adult children of divorce. *Journal of the Academy of Child and Adolescent Psychiatry 34(2)*, 143–150.

Buchanan, C. M., Maccoby, E. E., & Dornbusch, S. M. (1991). Caught between parents: Adolescents' experience in divorced homes. *Child Development, 62(5)*, 1008–1029.

Buehler, C., Krishnakumar, A., Stone, G., Anthony, C., Pemberton, S., Gerard, J., & Barber, B. (1998). Interparental conflict styles and youth problem behaviors: A two-sample replication study. *Journal of Marriage and the Family, 60(1)*, 119–132.

Ellis, A., & Greiger, R. M. (1977). *Handbook of rational-emotive therapy* (Vol. 2). New York: Springer.

Emery, R.E. (1982). Interparental conflict and the children of discord and divorce. *Psychological Bulletin, 92(2)*, 310–330.

Gardner, R.A. (1998). *The parental alienation syndrome: A guide for mental health and legal professionals.* Cresskill, NJ: Creative Therapeutics.

Goleman, D. (2005). *Emotional intelligence: Why it can matter more than IQ.* New York: Bantam.

Gottman, J. (1997). *The heart of parenting: Raising an emotionally intelligent child.* New York: Simon and Schuster.

Greenberg, L. (2004). Emotion-focused therapy. *Clinical Psychology and Psychotherapy, 11(1)*, 3–16.

Grotberg, E. H. (1995). *A guide to promoting resilience in children: Strengthening the human spirit.* Netherlands: Bernard Van Leer Foundation. Available at: http://www.resilnet.uiuc.edu/library/grotb95b.html#appendix1 [accessed April 25, 2012].

Halpern, D. F. (1998). Teaching critical thinking skills for transfer across domains. *American Psychologist, 53(4)*, 449–455.

Kline, M., Johnston, J., & Tschann, J. (1991). The long shadow of marital conflict. *Journal of Marriage and the Family, 53(2)*, 297–309.

Margolin, S. (1996). *Complete group counseling program for children of divorce: Ready-to-use plans and materials for small and large groups, grades 1–6.* West Nyack, NY: Center for Applied Research in Education.

Neuman, M. G., & Romanowski, P. (1998). *Helping your kids cope with divorce.* New York: Times Books.

Pedro-Carroll, J. L. (1997). The Children of Divorce Intervention Program: Fostering resilient outcomes for school-aged children. In G. W. Albee & T. Gullotta (Eds.), *Primary prevention works* (pp. 213–238). Thousand Oaks, CA: Sage.

Pedro-Carroll, J. L. (2005). Fostering children's resilience in the aftermath of divorce: The role of evidence-based programs for children. *Family Court Review, 43(1),* 52–64.

Seligman, M. (1994). *What you can change and what you can't.* New York: Knopf.

Siegel, D. J. (1999). *The developing mind: Toward a neurobiology of interpersonal experience.* New York: Guilford Press.

Siegel, D. J. (2007). *The mindful brain: Reflection and attunement in the cultivation of well-being.* New York: W. W. Norton.

Siegel, D. J., & Hartzell, M. (2003). *Parenting from the inside out.* New York: Penguin.

Spencer, A. J., & Shapiro, R. B. (1993). *Helping students cope with divorce: a complete group education and counseling program for grades 7–12.* West Nyack, NY: Center for Applied Research in Education.

9 Providing Effective, Systemically Informed, Child-Centered Psychotherapies for Children of Divorce

Walking on Thin Ice

Benjamin D. Garber

I am privileged to work with Dr. Baker and many esteemed colleagues to bring this important book to press. Above and beyond the usual process of writing and editing necessary to complete a volume of this magnitude and significance, I believe that this effort has helped me (and perhaps others as well) to clarify and respect important theoretical differences. Chief among these issues is the syndrome question. Far from a punctilious grammarian's argument, the debate about if and how alienation constitutes a syndrome has far-reaching diagnostic, prognostic, treatment, and forensic implications. I offer this preface not in any effort to twist any arms or even to plead my case against identifying the family systems dynamic as a syndrome. I write, instead, to highlight that I believe that no matter where anyone stands on this and related issues, systemically informed child-centered interventions are critical to the future well-being of all involved, most particularly the children.

Benjamin D. Garber

When One Parent Speaks for Both

"I just wanted to help." It had all seemed so straightforward. Paul Robbins, LCSW, had been working for Downtown HealthCare Services Inc. for just over a year when intake booked Meaghan H. into his Thursday 1:00 p.m. slot. Midday was always hard to fill for a child therapist but this 9-year-old was home-schooled. The front office paperwork was pretty clear. Mom described Meaghan as the eldest of three girls. Mom reported that the child had been increasingly oppositional and defiant, with some nightmares and assorted fears. The parents were divorced. Dad was in sales and traveled a lot. Mom handled the transportation and co-pay. This was Robbins' cup of tea. He had seen a hundred of these oppositional defiant disorder kids before. Four to six sessions of cognitive behavioral intervention, a meeting or two to help Mom with behavior management, and the job would be done.

Or, should have been done. Meaghan came in for the first interview with rosy cheeks and a pony tail. Her arms were folded across her chest; her eyes were downcast, staring at the carpet. It had taken maybe 15 minutes to engage her while Mom sat in the waiting room. By the third session the child was eager to come see her "new friend," Paul. In fact, her drawings and then her words uncapped her previously bottled-up rage at her dad, whom she insisted on calling by his first name. "Fred" had "left them." Fred loved his new girlfriend more than he loved his family. Meaghan said she did not want to see Fred ever again. The idea of giving Meaghan a break from the pressures of seeing her dad made sense, so Robbins wrote a letter. He would arrange for a colleague to see the father and daughter together and recommended that once that work was on track, Meghan could resume seeing her dad.

Session number four: No Meaghan. No Mom. Instead, a process server with a restraining order and a subpoena. Paul Robbins, LCSW, was prohibited by the court from any contact with Meaghan H. pending a hearing scheduled for 6 weeks later, a hearing that Robbins was required to attend with file in hand.

Introduction

This fictitious therapist[1] is living one of our most common shared fears and very real threats: a well-intended, otherwise straightforward child therapy becomes caught in the midst of a larger legal conflict. A sound treatment plan provided by a seasoned and skilled professional not only fails to relieve the client's distress and resolve her dysfunction, it likely adds to her stress. In the process, the child's hard-won trust in her new therapist is shattered, reconfirming her belief that adults do not care. For his part, the therapist is now in crisis himself. In the near term he has to set aside the time to consult with his employers and legal counsel, to inform his malpractice carrier and his managed care panels, to review his clinical records, and to appear in court. At best, he will someday be able to look back on this incident the way a soldier recalls surviving a firefight. At worst, board complaints and malpractice suits, and the cost of attorneys and time spent out of the office, will ruin his career, cost him his license, and compromise his savings.

Psychotherapy may provide a "port in the storm" for children triangulated into their parents' conflicts, but can only do so to the extent that the psychotherapy itself avoids becoming similarly triangulated. The present chapter discusses the systemic, legal, developmental, practical, and therapeutic considerations relevant to conducting effective child therapy with this population.

Special emphasis is placed upon the need for the therapist to define roles and boundaries with both of the child–client's parents and among the many other professionals who commonly attempt to intrude upon and risk corrupting the child's therapy. This topic is particularly relevant for therapists working with alienated families and to the extent that alienation sets the stage for "if you're not with me, you're against me" thinking.

This chapter is intended to help the child clinician foresee and forestall these outcomes to the fullest extent possible. Nearly 30 years of providing mental health services to children and their families, working on behalf of children in the family courts, writing, consulting, and speaking on these subjects has proven that investing time, effort, and money up front to define boundaries and roles and procedures—even before the first phone call—is the best way to serve child–clients' needs and to preserve the therapist's own sanity.

Is this chapter about providing clinical services to children of divorce? On the face of it, the answer is yes. Slightly less than half of all first marriages and nearly three-quarters of all second marriages in the United States end in divorce. Approximately half of all children will live through the legal dissolution of their parents' relationship. While divorce need not harm children, as a practical matter it is true that the adversarial legal system can and often does harm children by exacerbating their parents' conflicts, draining family resources, laying very personal grief before the public, and prolonging the battles.

In fact, this chapter is not only about divorce. It is about providing effective clinical services to all children regardless of the legal relationship between their caregivers (Garber, 1994). The harsh reality is that intractable adult conflict harms kids, no matter the legal status of their parents' relationship. It does not matter whether the child–client resides in an "intact" conventional home with married, heterosexual parents; never married but cohabitating partners; nonconventional (lesbian, gay, intergenerational) co-parents; or migrates between parents who live apart, are divorcing, or divorced. So the answer is both yes and no. For ease of reference, this chapter talks about children and divorce, but the principles and procedures recommended herein constitute sound clinical practice for mental health professionals providing clinical services to children no matter the child's apparent family circumstance.[2]

On Diagnosis, Testing, and Individual Child Therapies

Because mental health practice has inherited the medical model, most therapists are trained to look at the individual child in order to determine both the nature of the problem and the best means of remedy. This works in medicine to the extent that an X-ray can identify a broken bone and a cast can help the break to heal. Unfortunately, trying to understand a child's social, emotional, and behavioral well-being in the same way risks doing more harm than good.

Consider 6-year-old Billy. His teacher reports that he is very active, distractible, and impulsive. Concerned, Dad takes Billy to his pediatrician, where a popular behavioral rating scale is completed, a physical exam rules out obvious illness, and the nurse reports that the child demolished the waiting room. Billy is diagnosed with attention deficit hyperactivity disorder (ADHD) and is started immediately on a popular stimulant medication. The pediatrician also refers Billy to a local therapist for cognitive behavioral intervention, recommending that the child needs help to understand his illness and to learn to better control his impulsive nature.[3]

The problem is that Billy does not have ADHD. True, he meets DSM-IV criteria, but if his brain chemistry could be examined it would be found that he is no different neurochemically than his same-age male peers. If only someone along the way had asked Billy's dad where Billy's mom is or had taken the time to understand Billy's day-to-day experience of the world, the child might never have had to cope with being inappropriately labeled, diagnosed, and medicated, a process that causes many more problems than it resolves.[4,5]

Looking closer, one can see that most children living in Billy's world would have difficulty concentrating and would be just as distractible, angry, and impulsive. That is because Billy's parents are at war. It does not matter that they are still married, living together, and maintain a very convincing public façade of normalcy. Mom is on the parent–teacher association. Dad is a successful businessman and community leader. The family attends church every Sunday with smiles on their faces. What no one knows is that Billy wakes up to screaming and name calling almost every morning. He often goes to sleep in the midst of one or both parents' drunken rages. He is rarely certain who will pick him up after school or if he needs to take the bus. The only thing that his parents seem to agree upon is that Billy is the prize that must be won at any cost. Mom whispers to him about Dad's indiscretions and how "he doesn't love us." Dad enlists Billy in making fun of Mom's "laziness." If the quality of a child's security is built upon the foundation of his parents' relationship (Sroufe, Egeland, Carlson, & Collins, 2005),[6] Billy's is undergoing tectonic upheaval.

Billy's situation is as common and tragic as it is instructive. A child's social and emotional (and resulting behavioral) difficulties cannot be adequately diagnosed or remedied in a vacuum. Diagnostic and treatment conclusions should never be based solely upon the child's presentation in a 45-minute office visit. The child's feelings, words, and behavior must be viewed as a function of his history and relationships. This means thinking about children systemically—as existing within and trying to adapt to a system of interlocking relationships—and, in so doing, conceptualizing the problem and structuring the corresponding intervention so as to carefully account for the systems in which child–clients live.

Attachment and the Child's Experience of Co-Parental Discord and Divorce

A great deal has been written about the varied and often profound social, emotional, behavioral, achievement, and long-term interpersonal costs that children pay for their parents' conflicts (e.g., Cummings & Davies, 2010;

Hetherington & Kelly, 2003; Wallerstein & Lewis, 1998). Rather than restate these voluminous findings and staggering statistics, consider instead a developmental framework within which the clinician might better understand and respond to the child's experience.

By birth (if not before),[7] healthy human beings begin to create an internal working model (IWM) of each of their caregivers (Bowlby, 1969, 1973). These models allow a child to anticipate how a particular caregiver will respond to her needs and thereby to shape her behavior accordingly. Evolution has done the fine-tuning here. The child who can successfully distinguish caregiver from not-caregiver and a responsive caregiver from an unresponsive caregiver has a survival advantage (Garber, 2012; Sroufe & MacIntosh, 2011). As a result, even though very few children in developed 21st-century societies are vulnerable to predators, our brains are hard-wired by evolutionary mandate to accumulate and distill precognitive–emotional models of our caregivers. By 12–18 months of age, the child's IWM can be witnessed in action and its behavioral correlates reliably measured (Ainsworth, Blehar, Waters, & Wall, 1978; Ainsworth & Wittig, 1969; Bowlby, 1969, 1973; Sroufe, 2005). Thus, if 14-month-old Sally has experienced Mom as sensitive and responsive to her needs (i.e., emotionally attuned, successfully reading her preverbal signals, comforting when comfort is needed, stimulating but not overwhelming) then Sally will respond to her presence with behaviors that are viewed as "secure." Most specifically, when Sally feels stress she will turn to Mom, reasonably expecting to be reassured and calmed. This is a secure attachment relationship. Mom has become Sally's secure base.

But imagine that Sally has had a very different experience of her other primary caregiver, her maternal grandmother. Grandma has always been less emotionally available and responsive (it does not matter to Sally that the older woman has a hearing deficit or that arthritis makes it difficult for her to bend over and pick up the squirming toddler). Direct experience has taught Sally that, when in a stressful situation, Grandma cannot be depended upon for safety and reassurance. Over time, Sally has built a model of Grandma which predicts that the older woman may not respond contingently to her needs. This relationship is "insecure." To an attachment researcher, Sally may look ambivalent or rejecting/indifferent to Grandma.

It is important to highlight that the quality of a child's attachments are not only a reflection of each unique relationship, they are also adaptive and dynamic over time. It is not the case that at some magic age the window of opportunity for attachment security slams shut and the child's (in)security is set in stone. Through the entire lifespan, experiences of the important people in an individual's life are constantly being revised in response to new information. By way of illustration: if Sally's grandmother gets a hearing aid and new arthritis medication, Sally may discover that Grandma has become a more sensitive and responsive caregiver. Over time, the child's model of Grandma will accommodate this change, affecting her expectations and thus her behavior in Grandma's care. In this way, Sally's relationship with Grandma may begin to look more secure. Conversely, if Sally's mother becomes depressed or her drinking starts to get out of control, Sally may find that the mother whom she had always known to be sensitive and responsive to her needs has become less so. Her IWM of Mom adapts to this information and Sally's behavior in Mom's presence may begin to look less secure.

The child clinician's job might be easier if the story stopped there. Insecure parent–child relationships could be repaired through some combination of interventions with the parent, the child, and/or otherwise within the dyad (e.g., Powell, Cooper, Hoffman, & Marvin, 2009).[8,9] Unfortunately, like the clinician who diagnoses ADHD on the basis of a single office visit, this approach routinely proves inadequate. The quality of a child's relationship with a specific caregiver is *both* a function of the child's direct experience of that caregiver *and* information she gleans about that caregiver from third parties (Thompson, 2000; Lieberman, Zeanah, & McIntosh, 2011; George, Isaacs, & Marvin, 2011; Bowlby & MacIntosh, 2011).[10] Thus, it is reasonable to expect that as Mom's drinking impairs her parenting, 14-month-old Sally will become less secure in that relationship. However, to observe that Sally has become less secure in her mother's care may have little to do with the objective quality of Mom's care. This is possible because Grandma's new arthritis medication has made her paranoid, prompting her to argue with Sally's mother and to demean Mom to and around baby Sally.[11] Grandma's negative and unwarranted words and actions can undermine Sally's otherwise secure relationship with her mother. In effect, Sally's internal model of her mother will incorporate Grandma's anxiety-inducing negative views. This is alienation at work (Garber, 2004a, 2012), the very dynamic that can both cause a child to need professional services and undermine the potential benefits of such services (Garber, 2004b). This is the essence of parental alienation: when one parent (or parent figure) undermines the child's relationship with the other parent (or parent figure).

Parental Alienation and Therapeutic Alienation

For the purpose of this chapter and consistent with the larger thrust of this book, parental alienation is defined as that dynamic which occurs when a child's IWM of Parent B is disproportionately[12] corrupted by her experience of Parent A's damning words and actions concerning Parent B. In the prior example, Grandma's rants about Sally's mother could be said to be alienating to the extent that they cause Sally to become less secure with her mother, despite the fact that Mom remains a sensitive and responsive caregiver. Child therapists must understand these dynamics, how they present, and how they commonly co-exist with other, related systemic dynamics (Friedlander & Walters, 2010). By extension, child therapists must be aware of the ways in which these same corrosive family dynamics can undermine the therapy relationship itself in the form of therapist alienation.

For example, Dr. Michelle Rouse was stumped, so she did what she always did when she was stumped: she talked the case through in her weekly case consultation group:

> Twelve-year-old boy; single mother; declining grades; apparent depression. I saw him about five times to work on positive self-statements. He was doing great. We had a good rapport, then *wham!* Something happened. Liam wouldn't make eye contact; barely grunted answers. He sat with his arms folded across his little chest. He wouldn't even look at the new Pokeman® cards I got!

Rouse's three colleagues brainstormed over coffee. They quizzed her about clinical methods and the words that she had used. They talked about diagnostic considerations (trauma? Asperger's?), medication possibilities (the newest selective serotonin-reuptake inhibitors), and transference and countertransference. They talked through the possibility that the child's apparent depression might have been the precursor of an emergent psychosis and whether something in the therapy had triggered a post-traumatic reaction.

This therapist's genuine caring, thoughtfulness, and routine consultation with peers[13] are laudable, but her failure to think outside the box that defines the therapeutic relationship is a problem. She is faced with a troubling impasse that is entirely common but can neither be understood nor resolved within the narrow confines of the therapist–client relationship. The problem could have been anticipated and could have been avoided (or at least minimized) and might still be resolved, but doing so will require that Dr. Rouse begins to see the child as part of a family system.

In fact, 12-year-old Liam spends alternate weekends with his father. What Dr. Rouse cannot know is that Liam mentioned his great new friend, Dr. R., during one of those recent weekends. Liam's father had not been aware of the therapy and, being mistrustful of the intentions of the child's mother ("the wench!"), he immediately assumed that Dr. R was just another tool with which his ex-wife was trying to pry father and son apart. This is precisely what he told his son because, after all, at 12 years old Liam deserved to know the truth. He explained that the formerly beloved therapist was working for the mother to tear the boy from his father. Liam was instructed not to say another word to Dr. Rouse.

Thus, unbeknownst to Dr. Rouse and far outside the therapy hour, the child–client's slowly emerging IWM of his new therapist as caring, sensitive, and responsive to his needs—the rapport that is critical to the success of any therapy—is being corrupted by extra-therapeutic dynamics. Like any attachment relationship, the quality of the therapy relationship is built upon *both* the child's direct experience of therapist *and* the child's experience of third-party information about the therapist. In the same way that Grandma's paranoid rants undermined Sally's relationship with her mother, this father is undermining Liam's relationship with his therapist.

Therapeutic (or therapist) alienation is the first cousin of parental alienation. It describes a rupture in the therapist–client relationship that is at least in part due to the disproportionate and deleterious impact of a third party's words or actions on the treatment rapport. Therapeutic alienation may be among the primary reasons why some child therapies fail, and a critical contributor to therapist compassion fatigue, actions that result in administrative board review and malpractice actions. Perhaps even worse, when child therapies are compromised by destructive extra-therapeutic dynamics, the child can be harmed.

In the broadest sense, therapist alienation is akin to the peer group's pressures on the addict not to comply with sobriety treatments or the abusive husband's efforts to keep his victimized wife from attending assertiveness training. At this level, it is a parent's effort to undermine a child's therapy relationship in a self-serving and ill-informed effort to preserve the status quo, no matter how dysfunctional.

Child therapies are at greatest risk for becoming triangulated into parents' conflicts when the child–client is herself triangulated into her parents' conflicts. This poses the critical question of how to protect the child–therapist relationship from the corrosive systemic influences that have caused the child to need psychotherapy in the first place.

Managed Mental Health Care

I offer this caveat in the interest of transparency and in anticipation of your concerns that some of the recommendations to follow may be impractical: It is sophistry to resist sound practices simply because managed health care prohibits them. To the extent that we allow managed care to dictate our practices, we risk compromising our ethics, the quality of our services, and our clients' well-being, not to mention our own mental health and incomes. You may find that some of the prophylaxes and remedies discussed in these pages are inconsistent with and even expressly prohibited under your existing managed care contracts. It is all about choices. I have never yet known a licensing board or malpractice court to excuse professional misconduct because the clinician was complying with managed care dictates, nor have I known a managed care company to stand up in court and take the blame for a contracted clinician's behavior.

I made the choice to leave managed care more than 12 years ago and have never looked back.[14] You can do the same and, in the process, better serve both your clients and yourself (Walfish, 2010).[15] Even if you do not take this (admittedly very scary) step, at the very least lobby those companies with whom you contract to allow you to serve your clients in the best way that you know how.

Forestalling Therapist Alienation: The First Phone Call

In the same way that therapists establish limits and boundaries and clarify roles so as to minimize the risks commonly associated with outpatient mental health practice (e.g., non-payment, no-shows, breaches of confidentiality), therapists must take similar precautions in the interest of minimizing the risk that alienation will corrupt child therapies. The investment of time and effort up front, even in anticipation of the first phone call, is always worthwhile. True, this time is uncompensated, but it pays off in the long run in terms of liability management and quality and efficiency of care (Coulter, 2007).

What happens when a mother calls seeking services for her son? In most settings, standard operating procedure calls for a minimally trained administrative person to collect 5 minutes' worth of demographics and to schedule an intake appointment. Ten days to three weeks later (Smith et al., 2010), the mother arrives at the appointed hour with her child in tow. A sheaf of paperwork (office policies, HIPAA acknowledgements, releases, payment agreements) are completed in a crowded waiting room, introductions are made, and the clinician proceeds to engage the parent and/or child in some combination. Sound familiar?

Not only does the pressure of this process usually preclude collecting a comprehensive history, it is a set-up for the accompanying parent to needlessly compound the child's exposure to potentially alienating messages under the guise of, "But the doctor asked me!" Critically relevant questions like, "Why are you divorced?" and "Is there any history of violence in the home?" should be discussed in an initial adult meeting, entirely separate from the child. But the most common trap may be less obvious. It occurs when the well-intended child therapist asks the accompanying parent simply, "Where is her other parent?"

A healthy caregiver will be polite and offer a neutral and benign excuse ("He's busy") and request to discuss the matter later, away from the child. But in far too many of these families the child would not need therapy if the parents were healthy. Instead, the accompanying parent is likely to take the question as a valid opportunity to recite her former partner's failings at great length, with both the inquiring therapist and the triangulated child held as captive audience. Indeed, the therapist needs to know about both parents, the child's relationship with each, whether there are court orders detailing their respective caregiving responsibilities, and how each sees the child's present strengths and weaknesses, but not in front of the child and well in advance of the first meeting with the child. This means that that first phone call must be longer than 5 minutes and may require more skills than are typically associated with front office staff.

The clinician must take the time in advance of the initial adult interview to determine whether the absent parent knows that his daughter is being enrolled in psychotherapy, whether the absent parent supports the proposed intervention, and whether the absent parent shares the accompanying parent's concerns and perspectives on the child's strengths and weaknesses.

As a legal matter, when co-parents share legal responsibility for a child (as when they are married or the court has assigned shared (or "joint") decision-making authority (or "legal custody") most states allow that one legal guardian's request for child services is sufficient to initiate services.[16] However, those same laws typically allow that either parent's objection to the service is sufficient to prohibit that service from occurring or continuing. Thus, to commence psychotherapy with a child exclusively at one parent's request may not be illegal or unethical, but may nonetheless be a set-up for failure, thereby creating for the child–client yet another breach in trust and needless and sudden loss (American Psychological Association, 2002; Younggren, Fisher, Foote, & Hjelt, 2011).

Returning to the case of Liam: if the father, upon learning that his son was in therapy, had said nothing to his son and later called Dr. Rouse to object to the therapy continuing, the therapist would likely have had to cancel the boy's appointments immediately. In this very undesirable situation the clinician would be well advised to write a very carefully worded letter to both parents: (1) requesting a joint parent meeting to try to resolve the conflict, (2) seeking their mutual consent to conduct a final meeting with Liam to at least say goodbye, and (3) providing referrals to other providers and recommendations for the child's continued therapy. That letter should probably be vetted by the clinician's peer consultation group and/or the practice's attorney (in part to assure that the clinician's frustration over the abrupt termination is not influencing the tone of the letter) and copied to the child's chart. Far better than facing this very difficult outcome is to lay a proper systemic foundation from the first phone call forward.

Ascertain Role and Status of Both Parents

"I appreciate your call and I'd be glad to do what I can to help Suzie, but we need to be sure that Suzie's dad is on board before we move forward" Only an adult with custodial rights can enroll a child in treatment. On occasion, this will include adults who are not the child's parents (as sometimes occurs when a child is in foster care or otherwise placed in the legal custody of child protection services pending an abuse or neglect investigation). In these relatively unusual conditions, the non-parent legal custodian can enroll the child in therapy, but it may still be clinically and ethically appropriate and necessary for the success of the intended child therapy to enlist the co-parents' support.[17]

Ascertain Legal Rights of Each Parent

"Do you share legal responsibility for Suzie with her dad?" As a good rule of thumb, in the absence of adequate legal documentation granting the calling parent exclusive decision-making authority ("legal custody") over the potential child–client, information about the therapy or the child cannot be kept from the other parent. This should be explained to the calling parent, and contact information for the other parent should be requested. In the absence of clear legal documentation, assume that the parents have shared or joint legal custody/decision-making authority.

Obtain Necessary Documents to Review

"Please get me a copy of the legal document giving you exclusive decision-making authority." If the calling parent does have (or at least believes she has) exclusive legal decision-making authority, she must provide this documentation at the time of the first contact and certainly before the first meeting with the child. For the clinician who does not happen to also have a law degree, it is advisable to have a family law attorney on retainer and available to review such documents. Note this consultation thoroughly.

Inquire About the Child's Relationship with the Other Parent

"Is your daughter in touch with her other parent?" Even when the calling parent has exclusive decision-making authority, the child may still have an active and (emotionally) significant relationship with her other parent. In this case, contact information about the absent parent should be requested with the understanding that the calling parent can refuse to provide it or, even if she provides this data, she can prevent you from communicating with the child's other parent.[18] Keep in mind that it is possible (and often wise) to decline the referral if such a prohibition is counter to the child's needs. While it may be unorthodox to decline the referral, it is far better to have an open hour than to naïvely compound a child's pain and suffering by allowing a child's therapy to needlessly become triangulated into her parents' conflict. The calling parent can be referred to a colleague familiar with the dynamics of divorce, co-parental conflict, and therapist alienation.

Try to Get a Sense of the Co-Parenting Relationship

"Does the child's other parent know that you're calling?" Asking this question will provide the therapist with some information about the working relationship between the two parents. An affirmative answer is a good sign, but should not be taken as a sure thing. A negative answer is a red flag. In either case, if the co-parents share decision-making authority, the calling parent should be informed that child therapy is most successful when both parents are aware and supportive and that the absent parent's contact information is required so that he can be invited to not only support the proposed therapy but participate as well. The calling parent can be advised that either parent can legally interrupt the therapy at any time.

Some calling parents will respond with a statement such as, "But I don't want him to know that my son is seeing you! He's _____!" (fill in the blank: "violent," "alcoholic," "a pedophile"). The calling parent may have excellent reason to preclude her former partner from being alerted to the proposed therapy and there may be excellent reason to take care that the two parents never come face to face, but none of this is reason for the child clinician to implicitly align with the calling parent to exclude the child's other parent, a set-up for therapist alienation at least, if not grounds for a formal complaint.

Try to Involve Both Parents

"Please let the other parent know about the plans that we've made and ask him to reach me as soon as possible." The therapist should request that the calling parent inform the other parent of the intent to enroll the child in therapy. It might seem easier for the therapist to make this call him- or herself but, in doing so, the therapist is placing himself between the parents in the same way that they are likely to have triangulated their child. By empowering the calling parent to take this step, the therapist is taking care not to set a precedent by becoming the adults' go-between, avoiding unnecessary ethical, legal, and procedural complications, and implicitly testing the co-parents' ability to communicate constructively in their child's best interests. The latter, in particular, is critical to understanding the child's well-being and is sometimes in and of itself reason to refer the adults to co-parenting therapy (Garber, 2004c) in addition to or instead of pursuing child therapy. At the very least, it is important to document the calling parent's assurance that, "I spoke with him and he said go ahead but he's too busy/far away/angry/stupid/narcissistic to care about his daughter's treatment." If this is the response, then the therapist may want to ask the calling parent to reach her co-parent via e-mail, with a copy to the therapist. In this way, not only does the therapist have documentation that the absent parent has been notified of the proposed intervention, but she also has the means of establishing mutual communication in the child's best interests. The absent parent can "reply to all" with his consent, questions, and/or to make scheduling arrangements

Decline to Treat if the Other Parent Objects

"I'm sorry. Your co-parent doesn't want your daughter in therapy. Let's talk about alternatives." If the parents share legal custody and the absent parent objects to the proposed child therapy, the child cannot be seen unless and until the calling parent obtains a court order. Even then, with a court order in hand and carefully reviewed by an attorney, the therapist may be on solid legal ground but the risk of therapeutic alienation remains extreme. Unlike Liam's father, who stumbled upon his son's therapy, this creates the situation in which the absent parent has actively fought against the proposed therapy and lost. His motivation for (not-so-) subtly undermining the therapy can be tremendous and his attention to trivia like the court's order that, "Neither party will diminish the therapist or the therapy to or around the child in the interest of preserving the child's potential benefit therein" will be fleeting.

Alternatively: (1) if the parents could agree to let the child do therapy with a different provider, the child should be referred out; (2) if the calling parent's concerns are amenable to child guidance, behavior modification, or related parenting assistance the therapist can consider enrolling that adult as a client (keeping in mind that this will serve as a conflict precluding later serving as the child's therapist); or (3) the therapist should communicate apologies that he cannot be of service and make sure that the parents understand that they can return at any time should they agree on how to proceed. No matter which path is pursued, the process must be documented thoroughly.

Document, Document, Document!

Document communications when a case was never opened and the child was never seen? Absolutely. The same conflicts that are hurting the child, which precluded your willingness to provide services and which might have threatened to undermine the child's therapy had it been begun, bring these parents back to court often. They are recidivist litigants, prone to ask the courts to settle everything from child support to his assertion that she never made the effort to enroll their child in psychotherapy and her counter-argument that he undermined her effort to do just that.

The Value of a Functional Website

If therapist alienation can be avoided when both parents are aware of and support their child's psychotherapy, then having a website can prove to be very helpful. It is not difficult, expensive, or a breach of relevant ethics to maintain a practice website (Bailey, 2011). Done correctly, there should be no problem. Please see http://www.healthyparent.com as one example. Assuring a web presence allows the absent parent who hears that the child is being seen in therapy to check out the therapist using a completely non-confrontational method at any time of the day or night. Presenting oneself in a professional manner, espousing a child-centered perspective, and making contact information easily accessible will help to nip potential therapeutic alienation in the bud. Further, a website that allows potential clients or their caregivers to download paperwork and questionnaires makes compliance easier and can save significant costs in paper and postage.

Forestalling Therapist Alienation

The Intake Interview(s)

The initial interview should be 90 minutes, with all co-parents present. No children are invited. Unless there are safety concerns (as when there is a history of domestic violence), the ideal initial interview includes the calling mother and her live-in boyfriend, the child's father and new wife. Many calling parents who hesitate when they hear this request (they may never have met or sat down together to consider the needs of the child for whom they share responsibility) will be reassured to hear that the clinician intends to gather relevant history and background, that the therapist will ensure that it is a safe environment, and that the discussion will remain focused on the child. It is important to explain in advance that if the conversation begins to get off track or ceases to be productive and child-centered, the meeting will be interrupted or ended immediately. Nine times out ten, establishing these structures during the initial phone call(s) and again at the start of the meeting is sufficient to reassure all participants and to make the process productive.

And for that inevitable tenth out of ten callers who still refuse to meet together, it is often desirable to schedule two parallel initial interviews One for Dad and his parenting partner(s) and the other for Mom and her parenting partner(s). Beware that although this process may be necessary it can also be a set-up for splitting between the parents. Each will say that the therapist said something different, to the extreme of claiming that the therapist endorsed his/her point of view and damned the other. Watching this happen can make a therapist question his own sanity and, more pointedly, is a terrific insight into the child's experience. In order to minimize this prospect, everyone must be advised in advance of the two meetings that the therapist will follow up with written impressions and recommendations only after both initial interviews are complete.

Perhaps the best reason for choreographing the initial adult interviews so carefully in advance is the frequency with which such meetings help the participant parents recognize that much of the (systemic) problem is theirs, not the child's. By highlighting the co-parents' obvious hostility, failed communications, and efforts to undermine the child's relationship with one another some (relatively healthy) parents have a revelation. As a result, the successful child therapist ironically sees as few children in psychotherapy as possible, preferring to help their caregivers to better meet their children's needs. Child therapy, after all, carries with it all the stresses and stigmas associated with the idea that the child has or is a problem.

When the initial joint co-parents' meeting yields evidence that that the child may benefit from both individual therapy and from the adults' efforts to improve their mutual communication and consistency, one of these two distinct services must be referred out. Trying to serve both functions poses innumerable practical, ethical, and legal pitfalls better avoided.

Systemically, two therapists collaborating in the best interests of a single child–client (one seeing the adults and the other seeing the child) should work like a super-parental unit. The therapists' mutual ability to communicate, cooperate, and problem-solve in the best interests of the child and her family becomes a (process) model for how the co-parents might better meet their child's needs. By occasionally meeting together with the parents and copying the parents on the co-therapists' communications, healthy compromise, affect management, child focus, and respect can be modeled in a manner that can be far more powerful than any more didactic method intended to achieve the same.

Mid-Course Communications

Keeping current with both parents throughout the course of the child's therapy is one important way to diminish the likelihood of therapeutic alienation and to increase the efficacy of the intervention. Feedback can be provided, homework can be assigned, and adults can be asked to provide relevant data. The non-custodial mother's opinion can be sought about a new behavior, for example, in a time-efficient and up-to-date manner so as to assure that the therapist is current and that the parent feels valued and involved in the process. Of course, this communication must be conducted carefully, defining the limitations of roles, confidentiality, and obtaining informed consent releases along the way. Even though the child may not be legally eligible to restrict or enable these communications, it may still be important to assure that the relatively mature child, super-sensitized to adult conflict, provides informed assent for the process (Alkhatib, Regan & Jackson, 2008).

Here again, e-mail can be quite useful. However, the immediacy and apparent informality of e-mail can create its own legal, ethical, and practical dangers (McMinn, Bearse, Heyne, Smithberger, & Erb, 2011). Used correctly, e-mail can serve the purpose of keeping both parents up to date about their child's progress in therapy, help to keep the therapist up to the minute on the child's well-being, and establish a precedent for the co-parents' mutual communications, especially while they feel like "big brother" is listening in (Garber, 2010). Consider these five pointers for the appropriate use of e-mail:

1. Separate written informed consents should be obtained from each parent at the start of the therapy relationship acknowledging that electronic communications are not necessarily secure and allowing that all the adults involved may nonetheless communicate about their child in this way.
2. Each parent's written consent should be obtained to release his or her e-mail address to the other(s) in the context of joint child-centered communications.[19]
3. A tagline after the signature line should be included that reminds readers about these limitations.[20]
4. The co-parents should be asked to copy the therapist on their mutual child-centered communications. Scanning these typically takes very little time and can be an invaluable asset in the process of better understanding the child's world.
5. Even with all of these precautions in force, the child clinician is still well advised not to use last names or refer to very sensitive information online. Better to take either parent's reference to such a subject as reason to request an adult meeting or to refer them to their co-parenting therapist.

Keeping the Therapy Out of the Middle

The quality of the therapist–client rapport is the single best predictor and single most important ingredient of any successful therapy (Connors, 2011; Ligiero

& Gelso, 2002). Thus, efforts to win co-parental support and thereby to foresee and forestall therapeutic alienation are likely to be at least as important as the particular modality of therapy provided. Still, in this day and age of concrete behavioral goals and evidence-based practices (Corcoran, 2010), it can be quite difficult to argue for (not to mention get paid to conduct) relationship-based interventions. This is, nonetheless, precisely what children who live in the midst of their parents' interminable wars need from a therapist: a "port in the storm" (Garber, 2008, 2010).

Allowing a child's therapy to become triangulated into her parents' conflict threatens to leave the child emotionally adrift. Thus, having successfully navigated the first call, having enlisted both parents (and their partners) in the process, and having completed the initial interview with all parties present, the child's therapy (should it still prove necessary and appropriate) must continue to be supported by all of the players lest it fall victim to alienation. It is important that the efforts to keep co-parents involved in and supportive of their child's therapy do not compromise the child's trust in the therapist or trespass upon whatever degree of confidentiality the minor is allotted under relevant laws.[21] Two practical methods are helpful in managing this balancing act:

First, as a practical matter, it is routinely useful to have parents alternately transport the child to therapy appointments. This provides the therapist not only the opportunity to see the child–parent dyads in action, however briefly, and to stay current with the accompanying parent, but it can provide clues to the child's possible chameleon-like functioning. That is, the therapist can ascertain how the child's functioning and demeanor vary depending upon which parent is in the waiting room.

Children who migrate between two (or more) disparate and conflicting environments are at risk of becoming emotional chameleons (Garber, 2010). Like alienation, this term does not describe a diagnosis but a dynamic that arises amidst the pressures of conflicted family systems. The chameleon child has learned to change her emotional colors to suit her very different caregiving environments in the interest of fitting in. Thus, she may eagerly confirm Mom's belief that Dad is a jerk and Dad's belief that Mom is loser. When Mom and Dad do not communicate, it is easy for the chameleon child's statements to be taken as certain confirmation that the other parent is evil, driving the wedge between the co-parents deeper, fueling litigation, and initiating or compounding whatever degree of alienation may be present, all very much to the child's detriment. A child who presents very differently on weeks when her mother delivers her than on the intervening weeks when her father delivers her, may be a chameleon. Her therapy must not only give her a port in the storm of her parents' conflict, but the opportunity to explore who she is and what she thinks and feels outside the pressures she experiences in each parent's care.

When parents can alternate delivering their child to therapy, it is often useful to check in with the accompanying adult at the start of the therapy hour[22] and ask about what is new in that adult's home and how he or she sees the child's recent successes and failures. In making this time available, it is important to take care to remind the adult that the therapist will not keep secrets from the other adults.

Second, the child clinician must assure that the child understands the limitations of confidentiality ("privacy") in the therapy from the first meeting forward, recognizing both the child's changing needs and rights as a function of age. The bottom line is that the clinician should reassure the child–client:

> I'm here for you. Not your parents. If I ever believe anyone is in danger, I have to report that to keep people safe. If Mom or Dad ask what we are talking about or what you said, I may have to give them the general idea like "Kevin is sad" or "Kevin is happy" but I will try not to tell them exactly what we have said unless I tell you first.[23]

True, this can prompt some children to keep some secrets, but better this than risk doing anything that the child later experiences as yet another adult betrayal.

When Therapeutic Alienation is at Work

A therapist's rapport with a child–client can rupture for many reasons (Safran & Muran, 1996). Sometimes the clinician pushed too hard on a sensitive subject.[24] Sometimes the client feels vulnerable after sharing a secret or is angry at some perceived slight. It could be as simple and as humiliating as a child encountering a friend in the therapist's waiting room, or as complex as transference-triggered retraumatization. Some of these relationship wounds will not heal, and the therapy will simply end with a couple of no-show appointments and unanswered voicemails. Other relationships are resilient enough to endure the breakdown, which can eventually be explored as grist for the mill. In the absence of the child's sullen admission (as happens with some frequency), determining that therapeutic alienation is at work (with or without these other causes) must be a process of elimination. One important clue to alienation in any context lies in identifying a discrepancy between the child's feelings and thinking.

For example, Sammy was a very immature 9-year-old who had been doing well in therapy. His parents had never married, had never even lived together, but were working at being co-parents nonetheless. Sammy's therapist had successfully enlisted both Dad and his same-sex partner and Mom and her boyfriend from the start of the intervention. Together, the four adults had taken turns bringing Sammy to his appointments and keeping the therapist and one another up to date via e-mail. Sammy loved to play Lego®, but understood that his job in therapy was to talk before he played. That worked great for a while. Sammy used the time to talk about school and his big sister and having two dads in one home, and about how he felt when his parents argued every Sunday when he transitioned between homes. Then Sammy simply stopped talking. Not even a brand new Star Wars Lego® set could entice a word out of him, but his eyes were locked on the attractive toy all the while. He and his therapist sat side by side on a large couch.

"Hmmm …" the therapist wondered aloud. "I guess we're not talking today, huh?" Sammy shook his head back and forth, still eying the new toys, hands deep in his pockets. "No talking. Okay. How 'bout singing?" No answer. "Whispering?" No answer. Thinking quickly, the therapist flipped his notepad to a new page and wrote in big block letters, "Can we write?" Sammy took the pad and pen and smiled while he wrote silently, "OK." "Why so quiet?" the clinician wondered in block letters. "I'm not supposed to. Mama told me that you're on Dad's side and I shouldn't talk to you anymore." There were tears in his eyes. "That's okay, Sammy. You should do what Mama says. Is it okay to play?" The look of gratitude on his face was tangible. Darth and Luke never fought as hard on the screen as they did in the office that day.

Later, the therapist called an emergency adult meeting, careful not to alert Sammy. Sitting between Sammy's warring parents was like sitting between Sammy's Darth and Luke characters. The therapist highlighted how important therapy was for Sammy and scratched his head, wondering aloud what had happened to the child's previous comfort in therapy, careful that confronting Mom with Sammy's admission might get the child in trouble. Dad thought maybe the sudden change had something to do with a custody hearing scheduled for the following week. The therapist reminded them that, as their son's therapist, he would not have any opinion about custody and would not participate in their litigation. With that, Mom seemed to deflate. The treatment contract was renewed out loud, reasserting that Sammy needed a safe place apart from each of them to sort through his strong feelings, and that he needed permission from both of them to say anything in therapy that he wished. If Mom intuited that the therapist somehow knew what she had done, it remained unspoken. When Sammy arrived for therapy the following week, he greeted the clinician effusively, asking about the Lego® characters.

Notes

1 All individuals named throughout this chapter are fictitious and introduced for illustrative purposes only. For ease of reference, the genders of individuals are randomly assigned and must not be construed as suggesting gender specificity. The words "client" and "patient" are used interchangeably. Psychotherapists are referred to as "therapists" without distinction for training or guild association.

2 This chapter must not be construed as providing legal advice. Consult with a family law attorney who knows the particulars of your practice and the relevant population and jurisdiction.

3 Learn more about the American Academy of Pediatrics' recommendations for the diagnosis and treatment of ADHD at http://www.aap.org/healthtopics/adhd.cfm. See *Pasquale* v. *Pasquale* (http://www.courts.state.nh.us/supreme/opinions/2001/pasqu130.htm) for a fascinating legal discussion of when and how a child can be medicated when divorced parents share legal decision-making authority.

4 See, for example, Garber (2001).

5 But beware that systemic dynamics cut both ways. In the same way that family conflict can cause distress that is easily mistaken for ADD/ADHD, a child's

genuine ADHD can contribute to family conflict: "Parents of youths diagnosed with ADHD in childhood … were more likely to divorce and had a shorter latency to divorce compared with parents of children without ADHD." (Wymbs et al., 2008, p. 735).

6 One caveat must be emphasized: our experience of interpersonal security and its derivative in the foundation of self is constantly evolving. Early experience can establish a trajectory, but is no guarantee of eventual outcomes.

7 This is perhaps nowhere more startlingly clear than in the research that demonstrates that late-term fetuses in utero can distinguish their mother's voice from the voices of other women (Kisilevsky & Haines, 2010).

8 See http://www.circleofsecurity.org/ to learn more about this very impressive program.

9 This point is particularly relevant to interventions intended to "reunify" a child and a rejected parent. Successful interventions must encourage change not only in that child and that parent, but in the larger system in which their relationship exists, and most particularly in the child's relationship with the aligned parent (Garber, 2011). Thus, rather than "reunification," the treatment goal must be to help the child enjoy a healthy relationship with both parents.

10 "The working models associated with secure or insecure attachments likely have their origins … not only in the child's direct representations of the sensitivity of parental care, but in the secondary representations of their experience mediated through parental discourse." (Thompson, 2000, p. 150).

11 Don't make the mistake of assuming that a 14-month-old with very limited expressive language capacity cannot understand or be affected by Grandma's damning words. Not only does language comprehension develop far in advance of language expression, children read their caregiver's autonomic cues (e.g., racing heart) and facial expressions from at least birth on!

12 In this context, "disproportionately" means that the words and actions which undermine the child's internal working model of Parent A risk corrupting the quality of the child's relationship with an objectively sensitive and responsive caregiver. When the child is exposed to the same words and actions and those words and actions are valid reflections of the targeted caregiver's objectively insensitive, unresponsive caregiving, the dynamic is known as estrangement. Estrangement is defensible to the extent that it serves the child's safety interests.

13 Participation in a peer consultation group is highly recommended. Above and beyond any relevant legal or ethical mandate, it is the single best way to prevent professional burn-out and to help clients/patients. But beware not to refer to the group as "supervision," which implies shared liability (Goodyear & Rodolfa, 2012).

14 See http://healthyparent.com/insurance.html.

15 Ironically, Crane & Payne (2011) find that under managed care, "Family therapy proved to be substantially more cost-effective than individual or 'mixed' psychotherapy."

16 In most states, decision-making authority or "legal custody" defines who can make non-emergency, major decisions in the child's life. "Joint" or "shared" legal custody grants the parents equal responsibility in these matters and requires their collaboration. By contrast, "physical custody" or "residential responsibility" defines which parent exercises care and day-to-day decision-making authority and when.

17 Beware that in these unusual circumstances you may need the legal custodian's informed consent in order to communicate with the child's parents. This is yet another reason to have a family law attorney on retainer.

18 On occasion, a parent will want to keep his e-mail address secret from the other. Don't agree to this. You are bound to fail. Instead, ask that parent to obtain a secondary free account (e.g., Yahoo, Gmail, Hotmail) exclusively for this purpose or that both parties subscribe to http://www.ourfamilywizard.com.

19 You would need the calling parent's written informed consent to speak with the other parent, just as you would to speak to the child's teacher or past therapist.
20 Mine says: "Unless otherwise specified, the contents of this message are not intended to be shared with minor children. Please do not assume that electronic communications including e-mail are either received or secure. Your participation in this electronic exchange signifies your consent allowing confidential and/or privileged information to be transmitted in this medium. This e-mail and any associated communications, attachment(s) and links are protected under the Electronic Communications Privacy Act 18 U.S.C 2510 et seq. and is confidential."
21 Many jurisdictions protect even young children's therapies from the prying eyes of litigating parents whose interest may be suspect. See, for example, *Berg* v. *Berg*, New Hampshire Supreme Court 2002, available at: http://www.courts.state.nh.us/supreme/opinions/2005/berg112.htm.
22 Many therapists check in with parents at the end of the hour, apparently to offer feedback from the preceding meeting with the child. I always find that this backfires: inevitably the parent has been holding information I needed during the hour just past and the parent has no incentive to be brief.
23 Federal law guarantees children privacy rights in certain matters from age 14 on, including information concerned with substance use, reproductive health and HIV/AIDS status (Behnke & Warner, 2002; McCurdy & Murray, 2003).
24 In this context, the therapist's faux pas which impedes the child's security in the therapy might be called therapist estrangement.

References

Ainsworth, M., Blehar, M., Waters, E., & Wall, S. (1978). *Patterns of attachment: A psychological study of the strange situation.* Hillsdale, NJ: Erlbaum.

Ainsworth, M., & Wittig, B. (1969). Attachment and exploratory behavior of one-year-olds in a strange situation. In B. Foss (Ed.), *Determinants of infant behavior IV* (pp. 111–136). London: Methuen.

Alkhatib, A., Regan, J., & Jackson, J. (2008). Informed assent and informed consent in the child and adolescent. *Psychiatric Annals, 38(5)*, 337–339.

American Psychological Association (2002). Ethical principles of psychologists and code of conduct. *American Psychologist, 57(12)*, 1060–1073.

Bailey, T. D. (2011). *Electronic representations of your professional image: Tips on creating a web presence.* Available at: http://www.apadivisions.org/division-31/publications/articles/individual/bailey.pdf [accessed Nov 23, 2011].

Behnke, S. H., & Warner, E. (2002). Confidentiality in the treatment of adolescents. *Monitor on Psychology, 33(3)*, 44.

Bowlby, J. (1969). *Attachment and loss. Vol. 1: Attachment.* New York: Basic Books.

Bowlby, J. (1973). *Attachment and loss. Vol. 2: Separation.* New York: Basic Books.

Bowlby, R., & McIntosh, J. (2011). John Bowlby's legacy and meanings for the family law field: In conversation with Sir Richard Bowlby. *Family Court Review, 49(3)*, 549–556.

Connors, M. E. (2011). Attachment theory: A "secure base" for psychotherapy integration. *Journal of Psychotherapy Integration, 21(3)*, 348–362.

Corcoran, J. (2010). *Mental health treatment for children and adolescents. Evidence-based practices.* New York: Oxford University Press.

Coulter, S. (2007). The impact of engagement processes on the first-appointment attendance rate at a regional outpatient psychological trauma service. *Child Care in Practice, 13(2)*, 117–123.

Crane, R. D., & Payne, S. H. (2011). Individual versus family psychotherapy in managed care: Comparing the costs of treatment by the mental health professions. *Journal of Marital and Family Therapy, 37(3)*, 273–289.

Cummings, E. M., & Davies, P. T. (2010). *Marital conflict and children: An emotional security perspective.* New York: Guilford Press.

Friedlander, S., & Walters, M. (2010). When a child rejects a parent: Tailoring the intervention to fit the problem. *Family Court Review, 48(1)*, 98–111.

Garber, B. D. (1994). Practical limitations in considering psychotherapy with children of separation and divorce. *Psychotherapy: Theory, Research, Practice, Training, 31(2)*, 254–261.

Garber, B. D. (2001). ADHD or not ADHD: Custody and visitation considerations. *New Hampshire Bar News*, New Hampshire Bar Association.

Garber, B. D. (2004a). Parental alienation in light of attachment theory: Consideration of the broader implications for child development, clinical practice and forensic process. *Journal of Child Custody, 1(4)*, 49–76.

Garber, B. D. (2004b). Therapist alienation: Foreseeing and forestalling dynamics undermining therapies with children. *Professional Psychology: Research and Practice, 35(4)* 357–363.

Garber, B. D. (2004c). Directed co-parenting intervention: Conducting child centered interventions in parallel with highly conflicted co-parents. *Professional Psychology: Research and Practice, 35(1)*, 55–64.

Garber, B. D. (2008). *Keeping kids out of the middle: Parenting effectively in the midst of adult conflict, separation and divorce.* Deerfield Beach, FL: Health Communications.

Garber, B. D. (2010). *Developmental psychology for family law professionals: Theory, application and the best interests of the child.* New York: Springer.

Garber, B. D. (2011). Parental alienation and the dynamics of the enmeshed dyad: Adultification, parentification and infantilization. *Family Court Review, 49(2)*, 322–335.

Garber, B. D. (2012). Security by association? Mapping attachment theory onto family law practice. *Family Court Review, 50(3)*, 467–470.

George, C., Isaacs, M., & Marvin, R. (2011). Incorporating attachment assessment into custody evaluations: The case of a 2-year-old and her parents. *Family Court Review, 49(3)*, 483–500).

Goodyear, R. K., & Rodolfa, E. (2012). Negotiating the complex ethical terrain of clinical supervision. In S. J. Knapp, M. C. Gottlieb, M. M. Handelsman, & L. D. VandeCreek (Eds.), *APA handbook of ethics in psychology. Vol 2: Practice, teaching, and research* (pp. 261–275). Washington, DC: American Psychological Association.

Hetherington, E. M., & Kelly, J. (2003). For better or for worse: Divorce reconsidered. *American Journal of Psychiatry, 160(3)*, 601–602.

Kisilevsky, B. S., & Haines, S. M. J. (2010). Exploring the relationship between fetal heart rate and cognition. *Infant and Child Development, 19(1)*, 60–75.

Lieberman, A., Zeanah, C., & McIntosh, J. (2011). Attachment perspectives on domestic violence and family law. *Family Court Review, 49(3)*, 529–538.

Ligiero, D., & Gelso, C. (2002). Countertransference, attachment and the working alliance: The therapist's contributions. *Psychotherapy: Theory, Research, Practice, Training, 39(1)*, 3–11.

McCurdy, K., & Murray, K. (2003). Confidentiality issues when minor children disclose family secrets in family counseling. *The Family Journal, 11(4)*, 393–398.

McMinn, M. R., Bearse, J., Heyne, L. K., Smithberger, A., & Erb, A. L. (2011). Technology and independent practice: Survey findings and implications. *Professional Psychology: Research and Practice, 42(2)*, 176–184.

Powell, B., Cooper, G., Hoffman, K., & Marvin, R. S. (2009). The circle of security. In C. H. Zeanah Jr. (Ed.), *Handbook of infant mental health* (3rd ed.) (pp. 450–467). New York: Guilford Press.

Safran, J., & Muran, J. (1996). The resolution of ruptures in the therapeutic alliance. *Journal of Consulting and Clinical Psychology, 64(3)*, 447–458.

Smith, T. E., Burgos, J., Dexter, V., Norcott, J., Pappas, S. V., & Shuman, E. (2010). Best practices for improving engagement of clients in clinic care. *Psychiatric Services, 61(4)*, 343–345.

Sroufe, L. A. (2005). Attachment and development: A prospective, longitudinal study from birth to adulthood, *Attachment and Human Development, 7(4)*, 349–367.

Sroufe, L. A., Egeland, B., Carlson, E., & Collins, W. A. (2005). *The development of the person: The Minnesota Study of Risk and Adaptation from Birth to Adulthood.* New York: Guilford Press.

Sroufe, A., & MacIntosh, J. (2011). Divorce and attachment relationships: The longitudinal journey. *Family Court Review, 49(3)*, 464–473.

Thompson, R. (2000). The legacy of early attachments. *Child Development, 71(1)*, 145–152.

Walfish, S. (2010). *Earning a living outside of managed care: 50 ways to expand your practice.* Washington, DC: American Psychological Association.

Wallerstein, J. S., & Lewis, J. (1998). The long-term impact of divorce on children. *Family Court Review, 36*, 368–383.

Wymbs, B. T., Pelham, W. E., Jr., Molina, B. S. G., Gnagy, E. M., Wilson, T. K., & Greenhouse, J. B. (2008). Rate and predictors of divorce among parents of youths with ADHD. *Journal of Consulting and Clinical Psychology, 76(5)*, 735–744.

Younggren, J. N., Fisher, M. A., Foote, W. E., & Hjelt, S. E. (2011). A legal and ethical review of patient responsibilities and psychotherapist duties. *Professional Psychology: Research and Practice, 42(2)*, 160–168.

10 Reunification and the One-Way Mirror

Jack Weitzman

Introduction

We are well past the time when the concept of parental alienation is in doubt and its presence in child custody cases is widely disputed. There is a growing body of books as well as hundreds of peer-reviewed articles written about parental alienation over the two decades since Dr. Richard Gardner originally proposed the idea in 1985. A recent summary of quantitative research now puts the magnitude of this problem at 1% of children living in the United States (Bernet, 2010), or approximately 700,000 cases. There are many single-case studies as well as anecdotal evidence among forensic clinicians who have written and provided expert testimony about it. The concept may continue to have its detractors, and its status as a medical syndrome is still at issue, but it is nonetheless a troublesome problem that appears to be here to stay. Despite ongoing dialogue about how the concept of alienation can be construed, used, and abused by professionals in the forensic community, it is widely accepted that parental alienation exists and stands at the center of many custody disputes. Twenty years of discussion and debate about parental alienation is a testament to its veracity. As testimony to how widely accepted it has become, it is now being seriously considered as a diagnostic category in the DSM-V (Bernet, Boch-Galhau, Baker, & Morrrison, 2010).

Alienation is now a much better understood phenomenon. We are long past simplistic, one-dimensional explanations of causality. Furthermore, it is now clear that either parent can be an alienator, not just pathological mothers. It is clear that not all cases of refusal to visit are due to programming and parental alienation. More complex, multidimensional models of how alienation occurs have emerged, as well as typologies and decision trees that better differentiate types of alienators, and alienators from abusers (Drozd & Olesen, 2004; Kelly & Johnston; 2001; Darnall 2008, 2010) In addition, years of research regarding the reliability of memory has added important knowledge about suggestibility in children, whose feelings and thoughts are vulnerable to distortion and influence by influential others, including a vindictive parent (Ceci & Hembrooke, 2002; Loftus, 2003a, 2003b). It has become clear that memories can be implanted and that children can be influenced to believe what never happened. That is not to say that all recalled memories are false or that all recovered memories are sheer fantasy (Terr, 1994; Van der Kolk, McFarlane, & Weisaeth, 1996). Memory is malleable, especially in small children. When researchers can so easily convince cohorts of children to recall events and experiences that never happened, as demonstrated in the work of Elizabeth Loftus (1997), how much more susceptible are they to the emotional storms, lies, manipulation, and pressures of an obsessed parent to whom they are attached? A vengeful parent can implant memories and engender anxiety, hatred, and real fear in a susceptible child.

An alienated child is frequently a frightened child. In cases where alienation is less severe, children may get caught up in the divorce crossfire, but are able to resist the influences of angry parents and do not refuse visitation. When alienation is severe, fear and anger engulf the child and visits stop. These children become defined by the extreme nature of their symptoms. When fear exists—even fear that has been falsely implanted by the favored parent—it is imperative to acknowledge its presence and design interventions that are sensitive for the scared child of any age, lest the reunification retraumatize him or her and minimize any genuine concerns about the targeted parent by everyone involved. Redress by the court is essential for the sake of the child-victims involved because relationships are ruined and the alienated children will villainize the targeted parent. Reversing the effects of alienation is not always possible. If, however, there is a chance that alienation can be reversed, specialized procedures such as the assignment of special masters, supervised visits, and other interventions such as the one-way mirror can play a pivotal role in the recovery and reunification process.

Impasses to Visitation

There are usually multiple factors that contribute to a child's refusal to visit, and obsessive programming by a parent is only one of them, an important distinction described in a multitude of articles (Darnall, 2010; Drozd & Olesen, 2004; Gardner, 2004) because it clarifies that alienation is not a singular construct, and that the phenomenon is multidetermined and often bilateral. Reasons for a child's refusal to visit range from being estranged and disconnected from a disengaged, mentally ill, or abusive parent to full-blown parental alienation syndrome (PAS), in which the child becomes completely engulfed by the alienating parent's hatred of the other parent.

In cases where alienation is present as a factor in visitation conflicts, there have been increasingly greater attempts to define levels and types of alienation. Gardner (1992) described the process of alienation as mild, moderate, or severe. Following Gardner, many clinicians have cited the need to differentiate cases based on how endemic alienation is in different custody situations (Kelly & Johnston, 2001; Garber, 2011). Darnall, for example, constructed a typology that describes naïve, active, and obsessed alienators (Darnall, 2008, 2010). In another approach, Baker (2007) differentiated three parental patterns of alienator: the narcissistic mother in divorced families; the narcissistic mother in intact families; and, the abusive, alienating parent of either gender. Warshak (2010) describes pathological alienation and differentiates that from less poisonous forms of alienation. Obviously, in cases where alienation is less severe, ordinary interventions such as counseling or even court orders prohibiting badmouthing and other forms of alienation may be sufficient to improve the case. When alienation is severe, more concerted and well-planned interventions such as the one-way mirror become essential to breaking the spell of severe alienation.

A Brief History of Reunification

Reunification interventions in child welfare cases have been around for decades, mostly used by social services agencies in dependency courts. It is a child welfare practice that was codified by the Adoption Assistance and Child Welfare Act of 1980, and extended in the Adoption and Safe Family Act of 1997 (Child Welfare League of America [CWLA], 2002; Gendell, 2001). It mandates that child welfare workers make reasonable efforts to reunify parents with their children who were placed in protective custody mainly owing to child abuse or neglect. The reunification plan generally requires treatment interventions for the offending parent(s), such as enrollment in drug and alcohol programs, domestic violence groups, individual and family therapy, and parenting classes. While the child is in placement, there are mandates for regular and continuous (usually supervised) contact between parent and child, and there are deadlines for the completion of the treatment plan that the parent must fulfill (Fahlberg, 1991), or lose their parental rights. Unlike many of the families who appear at family courts, generally these are families whose children are in protective custody, have been through an evaluation and assessment process, are involved in mandatory treatment programs, and have continuous contact with their parents. There is an established, codified reunification process in place throughout the nation's child welfare system.

Families who appear before family court, on the other hand, may have no involvement in the child welfare system despite serious issues of parental substance abuse, domestic violence, criminal behavior, or the severe emotional abuse that is typical of parental alienation. Reunification interventions are not codified or uniform in the family law system and are largely left up to individual family courts and their staff. Targeted parents and the children who have been alienated from them must depend on family courts to evaluate and rectify their situations; hence, the need for reunification protocols. Protecting these vulnerable children and their right to a healthy relationship with each parent should be a high priority as case facts are sorted out and decisions are rendered about custody and visitation.

Theoretical Foundation of the Mirror Approach

The use of the one-way mirror is not a new intervention. It has a long history in the field of family therapy and it has been used as a tool to train therapists and improve therapeutic efficacy (Haley, 1977; Hoffman, 1981). Using the mirror intervention in custody cases, however, is something relatively recent and can provide a safe, structured forum for rebuilding a damaged relationship between parent and child. In essence, the one-way mirror is a desensitization tool and an exposure process (Wolpe 1959, 1988; Suinn, 1990) designed to break the hypnotic spell of misinformation and brainwashing, implanted memories and lies that prevent a relationship from developing between the child and targeted parent.

The utmost concern of the mirror intervention is for the psychological and physical safety of the child, and to titrate exposure to the feared parent. After all, alienated children are usually anxiety riddled or even phobic about meeting the rejected parent. In a case involving a father who absconded to Mexico with his two small girls and told them that their mother wanted to murder them, it goes without saying that the girls were terrified of their mother. That was the fabricated reason he gave them for leaving the United States after he lost a custody decision. When they were returned to the United States, they refused to see her. Immediate and unconditional release of the children to her could have been a nightmare for them. Because of the fears and hatred instilled in them, alienated children can benefit from a graduated approach to reunification. Best practices in the anxiety disorders field recommends desensitization and exposure therapy as an effective way to treat phobic and avoidant behavior (White, 1999; Vidair & Rynn, 2010).

The mirror intervention is such a procedure. And yet, as simple and straightforward as it sounds, the procedure, when embedded in a forensic setting, can become complicated for a number of reasons. There are lawyers involved who advocate solely for their clients wishes, including fearful children, and are embedded in an adversarial system. There are parents whose pain about the divorce process inadvertently spills over onto their children, so-called cases of naïve alienation (Darnall, 2010), which must be differentiated from those who are obsessed, toxic, and vengeful and who intend to harm the other parent. There are issues about differentiating legitimate concerns of physical abuse, drugs, and psychopathology from false and damaging claims and distortions. There are developmental issues to consider about interventions with older children and adolescents, and whether or not children of any age should be allowed to decide issues of visitation and refuse an intervention, even if it is clear that they are engulfed by distortions and false memories—a *folie à deux*. Left to their own devices, it is conceivable that such children, especially young children, would never consent to a reunification process or would need years of mandated therapy before finally doing so, by which point even more damage and resentment may have been incurred. Still other issues include how to manage the custodial parent's reaction to the reunification process when there is serious resistance, whether a mirror system be installed in every facility, and should (or can) older adolescents be forced into a reunification process.

These issues are taken up in this chapter and an attempt is made to find solutions to these vexing problems in the reunification process. It is important to note that the remainder of the chapter describes the use of the one-way mirror for cases in which alienation is primarily or solely responsible for the breach in the parent–child relationship. The approach may also be appropriate for cases in which estrangement is the cause (i.e., the behavior of the rejected parent is the primary cause of the breach) but that is not the subject of this chapter.

The Person of the Therapist

Any therapist who chooses to conduct reunification in custody cases must be familiar with the literature on parental alienation. It is easy to be tripped up by PAS children or adults who are convincing when presenting their justifications of hatred for the targeted parent. Therapists who do not recognize the eight behavioral manifestations of PAS according to Gardner (1992) or the alienation behaviors that are indicators of PAS (Baker, 2007; Baker & Fine, this volume) can easily understate the severity of the problem. Alternately, they can also overstate the degree of alienation present in a case by failing to know about different typologies and intensities of alienation. Therapists can underestimate the fear that PAS children have toward the targeted parent and retraumatize them by moving too vigorously to reunite parent and child. Or, they can move too slowly and get bogged down in interminable therapy that allows the alienated child to control the pace of the treatment. Therapists can underestimate the alienating parent's capacity to sabotage the process and fail to have adequate monitoring resources. Some inexperienced therapists see only one parent and conclude (and collude) that alienation has occurred without ever seeing the other parent. These are just a few of the problems that can be created without adequate training and familiarity with the reunification and PAS literature and treatment process.

Reunification therapists must also be knowledgeable about the best practices in custody assessments and the scientific basis for psychological evaluations, so that their information about each case is as objective and verifiable as possible (Tippins & Wittmann, 2005). Finally, understanding developmental psychology and the construction of developmentally sensitive time-share arrangements is crucial to an appropriate reunification process, as well as an informed approach based on the principle of the best interests of the child.

A skilled reunification therapist must be willing to work collaboratively with other mental health and legal professionals. The reunification process is not a solo affair carried out in isolation by a single practitioner. It is largely transparent, subject to scrutiny, and requires close contact with the inner circle of professionals involved, including the parents' attorneys, *pro per* parents, the guardian *ad litem*, special masters, parenting coordinators, other therapists in the case, and family court staff. The reunification therapist must be willing to expose his/her own methodology to the other professionals and follow a protocol that everyone can feel comfortable with. Most fundamentally, the reunification process is an *in vivo* treatment and evaluation process. Other professionals in the case should be apprised of the treatment plan and issues that are to be targeted, as well as any obstacles to progress and stalemates, so that timely adjustments, reassessment, or other interventions can be carried out.

A therapist who is unable to be therapeutically confrontational cannot effectively address the powerful defenses of an alienating parent, nor the brainwashed, alienated child. It is common for the reunification therapist to have to take a position on various clinical issues, and to accept being in a position with parents and children of having to challenge their distortions and defenses at the same time that he or she remains therapeutic and professional. The reunification therapist has to be willing to be a strong authority figure and an expert in confrontational psychotherapy at the same time that he or she is able to maintain the integrity of the therapeutic process and be sensitive to the psychological circumstances of the human beings involved.

The Reunification Protocol

Laying the Foundation: Issues of Confidentiality and Collaboration

Custody disputes are embedded in an adversarial legal system. While the ostensible aim of the adversarial approach is to arrive at the truth, the adversarial court process usually exacerbates the conflicts of highly acrimonious parents and leads to endless allegations and cross-allegations, charges of contempt, investigations, and new motions; that is, until the money runs out. All too often these families end up much poorer or bankrupt as a result of litigation, and still have not resolved their differences. This is especially true with PAS cases where there is no motivation on the part of an alienating parent to reach a compromise. A judge may order reunification based on the evidence in a case, but objections to evaluations or new allegations that are raised during the reunification process can take months to be heard and create major setbacks to any progress toward resolution. In addition, traditional models of lawyer–client confidentiality and patient–client confidentiality (for mental health professionals) can create insurmountable obstacles to resolution as vital information is challenged, distorted, or suppressed.

Families arrive at reunification treatment by many paths. For example, some are sent by the court following a full trial or hearing, some stipulate to the intervention based on pressure from the judge or their attorneys, and others agree to reunification for a variety of motivations, including the hope or belief that it can be controlled and undermined. Because the alienating parent may be pressured into stipulating to reunification, and because of his or her mixed motivations, the process must be transparent and have serious limits on confidentiality.

Ideally, the therapist and attorneys will be comfortable with non-confidential intervention and be willing to share whatever pertinent information is necessary with the family and other professionals in order to address stalemates. It is helpful when the professionals are willing to accept this less private role and inform the parents and children involved of this imperative. That means being able to talk with parents and children about the limitations to confidentiality and that the goal of reunification therapy is to break relationship deadlocks, not to get stuck in confidentiality rules and adversarial contests that prevent addressing destructive and pathological behavior.

Parents should give informed consent for the reunification procedure that details the nature of the intervention, risks, benefits, and alternatives. Thoroughly reviewing the steps of the procedure with an anxious parent can alleviate many of the concerns that parents may have about their child's reaction to the process. Explanations of the use of the one-way mirror, the rationale for its use, reviewing the procedural rules and steps, and addressing any immediate resistance can lay a better foundation for the reunification process and set the stage for a successful outcome. Once the parents have given their consent, the children can be given the same orientation in a separate meeting. By signing consents, parents are also confirming their willingness to comply with the order for reunification.

As in many alternative dispute resolution programs, confidentiality should be quasi-protected and limited to the judge, attorneys, and professionals involved in the reunification intervention, a perspective that is evolving in problem-solving family courts (Adams & Chandler, 2002; Kaye, 2000). Exceptions should be included that prohibit special information such as psychiatric and medical records from being shared without a specific release. Parents who refuse to sign general consents and limited releases should be referred back to the case manager or judge.

Confidentiality may also be a concern for children and adolescents, who should be told that while every effort will be made to be sensitive to their needs and feelings, information about the process may be shared with other professionals involved in the reunification intervention. If this matter is presented with the goal in mind that a whole team of professionals are working together to support the child, whatever the outcome of the intervention, most children do not object to the sharing of information. Specific concerns by a child about retaliation from an angry parent can and should be addressed at this early juncture. For example, it is not uncommon for a child who shows interest in the targeted parent to fear punishment or retribution from the alienating parent. The reunification therapist can share these fears with the parent, address the parent's reaction, and, hopefully, have the alienating parent make a commitment to the child that he or she will not be punished. Obviously, careful monitoring of this situation is essential as the alienating parent can be manipulative. Arranging meetings with the child and his or her therapist immediately following the mirror intervention can help to reduce any negative side effects of the intervention. Obviously, if the professionals who monitor the child's progress determine that the alienating parent is undermining the process, a conference with the relevant parties to discuss the viability of the intervention is essential.

Even in the face of the alienating parent's resistance to treatment, the inner circle of professionals must agree that despite the entrenched nature of a parent's beliefs, the legal process and the therapeutic process must go forward so that more time is not lost in reunifying the child with the targeted parent, lest the entire process be torpedoed by adversarial contests. Even in those cases where it is not possible to determine the exact causes of the child's refusal to visit (because of difficulty with reconstructing the history of the divorce process, or distortions of memory and cross-allegations that are impossible to verify), the child's refusal to visit still requires redress, especially when he or she is fearful. A consensus must be reached by the attorneys involved, or an order issued by the presiding judge, before the mirror procedure is implemented, that the child has been grossly affected by the divorce process, especially when the child's fear of the targeted parent is unwarranted and not due to actual abuse (or other factor such as severe mental illness) by the targeted parent.

Step 1: Initial Meeting with the Parents

A diagnosis of moderate to severe (as opposed to mild) parental alienation is *ipso facto* a declaration that the perpetrating parent is seriously dysfunctional or personality disordered, and likely to be resistant to the intervention process. Many alienating parents are pathologically self-involved, more concerned about destroying the other parent and blind to the detrimental effect of their behavior on their children. In fact, they seek their child's alliance and concurrence with their distorted beliefs and allegations against the other parent. They cast their own shadow of past wounds, unconscious reactions, and conflicts onto their children and the targeted parent. Many actually believe their own allegations, however distorted, and make every attempt to convince all others, including their child, attorneys, and treatment providers, of the evils of the other parent. They feel victimized and have little self-awareness about how extreme their opinions and feelings about the other parents might be. And yet, the targeted parent is rarely an innocent victim in the situation. Some alienation cases do involve parents who make their own contributions to the conflict (Gardner, 2004). Many targeted parents fail to act in their own interest (or the interests of their children) and do not always recognize how their passivity only exacerbates their position.

The initial meeting should generally be held individually because reunification of a child with the targeted parent can give rise to powerful resistance in the alienating parent. Each step of the reunification process, including information about the court's investment in seeing children develop healthy relationships with both parents, should be addressed with each parent individually. The first task is to obtain informed consent, explain confidentiality, and obtain release forms from the parents. Every opportunity should be provided to help parents discuss their fears, resistances, and concerns about the child's emotional well-being and how he or she might be impacted by the reunification effort.

In this initial phase, the goals are to educate parents and children about the reunification process, reduce anxiety, and encourage cooperation, goals that can be difficult to achieve when parent-figures or children have serious emotional conflicts. The custodial parent can be highly suspicious of the motivations of the other parent and overly protective of the child. Parents have to be educated by the reunification therapist that the child cannot make decisions on his or her own about visits, most especially if the child is preadolescent and is caught up in the alienating parent's position and not emotionally disentangled or mature enough to do so. Usually this takes the form of a therapeutic session with the parent that focuses on adult responsibility for visitation decisions and the hazards of putting a child in the middle of visitation conflicts.

At the same time, the non-custodial parent can be anxious, if not overzealous, to reunite with the child. An overanxious non-custodial parent can attempt to rush the process and minimize the child's anxieties by demanding to see the child, and may not realize how fearful the child might be. These parents need education and help with becoming more sensitive to the child's fears and loyalty conflicts. Individual therapeutic sessions that are focused on the child's fears of reprisal by the alienating parent, and discussion of such issues as the child's divided loyalties, can help the targeted parent be more patient with the reunification process.

Parents can be also be educated about the desensitization approach represented by the one-way mirror, as well as the child's developmental needs for attachment, gender identity, and basic trust in caretaking figures by sharing with them ideas from developmental psychology and behaviorism. The mirror intervention can be explained to the parents as a method to facilitate a safe rapprochement (Mahler, Pine, & Bergman, 1975) and reconnection with the targeted parent, and as a slow, calibrated reintroduction that will minimize the child's anxiety. Parents can be told that by using the one-way mirror the child is able to make whatever contact is comfortable and retreat when necessary, which is usually reassuring to the anxious parent. A parent can be told that contact might take the form of communication exchanges over the speaker system while the child views the parent and asks questions, or it might mean simply viewing the parent without auditory contact, on videotape or photographs. The child can stop the process, leave the viewing room, and return when he or she is ready.

The most difficult clinical situations are those where, despite all the preliminary work to ensure cooperation, the custodial parent remains opposed to the reunification process and continues to actively interfere with the child's relationship with the other parent. This can take the form of refusing to bring the child to the sessions or making unwarranted and extremely inflammatory comments about the targeted parent to or in front of the child. When attempts to inform, educate, and treat such resistant parents fail to gain their compliance, it is essential to review with that parent the court's reasons and expectations for reunification, including the serious consequences of non-compliance. If this discussion fails to yield an agreement to proceed, then these obstructive parents should be referred back to the court for additional intervention. This might include mandated psychotherapy, re-evaluation, assignment of an attorney for the children, assignment of a special master to the case, or the recalcitrant parent might confront a change in their time sharing and custody of the child—in stages of increasing severity (Lowenstein, 2011).

These parents will often relent and soften their stance when they recognize the court's serious intent to ensure the best interests of all involved parties (but most especially the child). However, making overt concessions is not the same as a genuine change of heart, and further court action to significantly equalize time sharing or remove custody is sometimes necessary in order to free the child of a pathological parent's influence. The risks and benefits of such extreme interventions must be carefully weighed of course.

Highly resistant parents are often caught up in past marital issues with their ex-spouse that resonate with their own childhood trauma. Even in a reunification process, it is possible to bring these issues to the awareness of the resistant parent and develop a treatment plan that addresses them. For example, a parent who has a childhood history of sexual victimization can be helped to become aware of how such early trauma might be influencing his or her feelings about the targeted parent and be referred to another therapist for ongoing work on those issues. Alternatively, the alienating parent's reality-based concerns about the targeted parent's history of violence, drugs, or psychiatric problems can be taken seriously and can be addressed with a reunification plan that builds in recommendations for evaluation, supervision, follow-up care, and treatment.

In other words, there are some cases in which the alienating parent's allegations may have some substance, though that does not mitigate the need to address the alienating parent's underlying motivation to destroy the targeted parent. The targeted parent may have a substance abuse problem or there may be a history of minor domestic violence between them. However, these cases are distinguished by the fact that the targeted parent's behavior is not a serious factor in the child's refusal to visit, though some PAS children will insist that it is. For example, there are cases where the targeted parent may have a substance abuse issue with marijuana, or there can be isolated episodes of domestic violence such as pushing or grabbing between the parents that the children never witnessed. The alienating parent will seize on these episodes and exaggerate their magnitude as part of the alienating campaign. It is prudent to assess and address these allegations and get them off the table so that treatment can proceed. Helping parents to disclose their concerns in the first meetings and giving them sufficient reassurances that their fears can and will be seriously considered can often lead to a better outcome.

Step 2: Meeting with the Child(ren)

While many alienated adolescents may have developed enough personal strength to subdue their fears and anxieties about the targeted parent sufficient to forego the highly structured mirror intervention, they may still refuse visitation. Indeed, children of different developmental ages do require different interventions and adolescents usually desire a different reunification pathway than small children, who are more defenseless and require more protection. Still, where alienation has occurred, most children of any age are anxious about reunification. Thus, when first meeting the child or adolescent it usually works better to meet with the custodial parent and child together and have the parent explain the reunification process *provided that he or she is cooperative with the process.* A cooperative parent can have a powerful influence on the child's willingness to engage and can provide reassurance and psychological permission to do so. Talking to children in a general way about the goals of the intervention can help them accept the intentions of the court to see them develop a positive relationship with both parents.

When the custodial parent is not motivated and resists either overtly or covertly, the clinical situation is trickier. Having a resistant parent present during the preparation meeting can undermine the child's cooperation with the process. Meeting with the child alone can instead provide a rich opportunity to explore and grasp the child's fears and assess the depth of the alienation. Many children are forthcoming about their fears and worries, sometimes giving graphic detail of abuse by the feared parent, sharing memories of domestic violence or other traumatic events associated with the family's history. Where genuine alienation has occurred, children may share fantastic and fearful fantasies of the other parent or recall memories of events that were impossible for them to have known. For example, two 9-year-old girls who had not seen their mother since they were 3 years old "recalled" how their mother had tried to drown them as infants. Their father had abducted them to Mexico and was returned to the United States by law enforcement after 6 years. The girls were convinced that their devoted and loving mother was a killer. In these cases, working alone with the child about their unrealistic fears is more likely to ameliorate their distortions.

In some cases, resistant parents will refrain from being punitive toward the child once they see that the child is curious and the procedure is well orchestrated, carefully planned, and designed to protect the child's safety. However, negative side effects of the reunification process must be anticipated. Some parents can and will punish the child for disloyalty. Narcissistic or personality-disordered parents who intend to alienate their children from the other parent may react to their child's curiosity about the targeted parent with rejection and punishment. These cases must be handled with a good deal more clinical and legal intervention, as the child is vulnerable to retribution. A court-mandated therapist or case manager who can monitor the child's progress through the reunification process must closely track the child's welfare. The therapist or case manager and the child's attorney or guardian *ad litem* will need to collaborate on the case and provide close supervision.

Children who are genuinely frightened (even if the fear is a result of the concerted efforts on the part of the favored parent and are not based in reality) must be amply reassured that their safety comes first, that they will not be forced into face-to-face meetings with the feared parent before they are ready, and that they can take their time getting to know more about the parent before any direct contact is made. Many children express serious distortions about how the feared parent will look, dress, and behave, expecting the worst. Adolescents may decline the mirror intervention and be satisfied with photographs or video conferencing such as Skype. Younger children, though fearful, often express curiosity and even playfulness about the idea of spying on the feared parent from behind a one-way mirror.

Step 3: Orienting the Child to the Viewing Room

The next step in the protocol is to invite the child to explore the viewing room and to operate the speaker devices and one-way mirror. The feared parent is not present during this exploratory phase, and the child can be completely free to imagine how the whole procedure will go. Demonstrating through role play how the child can interview the feared parent from behind the one-way mirror can give the child a real sense of the procedure and alleviate anxiety and assuage the child's fears of being exposed, injured, or even abducted. The child can practice talking to his or her parent, control the interactive process, and stop the action. The child can see for him/herself how safe it is to be in the viewing room.

Having the child develop a list of written questions for use in interviewing the targeted parent, such as the parent's age, job, hobbies, and interests and other personal information, can enhance the intervention. The child can gain some real-world information about the parent that can modify the exaggerated fantasies about the parent's lifestyle, values, and interests. If photos of the parent are available, exposing the child at this juncture to a variety of pictures can also help the child compare the imagined parent with the real parent. A videotaped interview with the targeted parent, or old home movies, might also be used to desensitize the child to his or her fears. Pairing positive reinforcements such as popcorn or ice cream while viewing pictures or videotapes can also aid the deconditioning process, as the theory of systematic desensitization prescribes (Wolpe, 1988, 1959). The child should be free to ask whatever he or she wishes so that any emotionally loaded issues can be diffused. Helping the child compare facts and photos with his or her exaggerations and fears can effectively defuse cognitive distortions.

Step 4: Commencing the Use of the Mirror

In order to avoid an accidental meeting between child and targeted parent, a careful plan of arrival should be implemented. It is logistically simpler to have the targeted parent arrive first and wait in the treatment room that adjoins the viewing room. This avoids the problem of having the child anxiously wait for the feared parent to arrive or having to leave the child in order to attend to the non-custodial parent. The child can be scheduled to arrive some 15 minutes afterward, and have the full attention of the therapist, who can spend time reorienting the child about the procedure. As soon as possible, it is best to encourage the child to leave the custodial parent and enter the viewing room with the therapist. Most children easily separate from their parent when the preparation process has been successful. The custodial parent can either wait in the therapist's office or in the waiting room.

The non-custodial parent should be advised to keep the focus of the meeting as positive as possible. The therapist as director should make every effort to steer the interaction toward non-threatening and light issues that will not be upsetting to either the child or parent. The child should be encouraged to use a set of questions that avoids loaded, conflict-laden topics until a stronger and more positive rapport has been established. It would be counterproductive to allow the child to begin with questions about the parents' divorce or to repeat highly charged information about affairs, domestic violence, or financial matters. Rather, the focus should be on more benign information such as the parent's favorite color, what he or she does for work, where he or she lives, favorite vacations, favorite foods, and other non-threatening information. While the child may wish to bring up more emotionally loaded issues, in the early stages it is prudent to build a positive relationship that can weather more distressing topics.

When the child first views the parent from behind the mirror, there can be long silences or a flood of feelings and questions about the mismatch between the child's fantasies of the parent and the actual appearance. Frequently, the child experiences some cognitive dissonance over the image painted by others and the real figure in the room. Major inroads can be made at this point toward modifying frightening and menacing beliefs. Not a few children who were expecting giants and monsters are surprised at how mundane and ordinary the targeted parent appears. For example, one 9-year-old boy who believed his father was a 7-foot gangster momentarily dissociated when he saw the thin 5-foot figure in the treatment room.

Step 5: Interview the Estranged Parent in the Child's Presence

After the child has had sufficient time to observe the estranged parent as a physical being, the reconciliation counselor leaves the child and interviews the parent while the child watches from behind the mirror. The child's predeveloped questions are used for the interview, and the child is instructed to freely use the speakerphone to ask any additional information. Many children find this part of the process highly intriguing as they get an opportunity to hear the targeted parent's voice, to watch the parent interact with the therapist, and to gauge the parent's overall demeanor.

Sometimes the game Twenty Questions can be playfully used to soften the interaction between parent and child as the counselor acts as a go-between. Another idea is to have the targeted parent bring items of their shared past to the meeting that evoke positive memories. One father brought many family photos he had saved, as well as some of the child's loved toys, an old fire truck, and a pair of baby shoes. Even when a child is quiet and does not want to ask questions, the counselor can take the lead and interview the parent as the child watches. In most cases, children soon become demystified of the horror stories told by others and of his/her own fears or distorted projections. The resistance to a face-to-face encounter softens considerably.

Step 6: Repeat Interviews as Required from Behind the Mirror

While many children will not need more than one session of the one-way mirror to advance to a face-to-face meeting with the targeted parent, some will require more time. Rarely does it require more than two sessions before the child feels safe enough to willingly enter the treatment room. Having the treatment room stocked with age-appropriate toys and games can also make it more inviting for the child to engage in the process. Once the child decides that it is safe, many will spontaneously choose games, books, or blocks as a medium to engage the parent. This can be a very non-threatening way for parent and child to warm up to one another. Sometimes, children ask that the targeted parent be allowed to see them from behind the mirror, reversing the standard protocol. These children like the idea of having the targeted parent view them so that they can hear about the parent's reaction. This reverse-viewing process can give the parent a chance to see the child and prepare for the face-to-face encounter. However, it should only be used if the child is interested and willing. One highly anxious child was quite pleased that his parent liked his new cowboy shirt and was satisfied that a face-to-face visit would be productive. When the time arrives and the child indicates that he or she is ready for the face-to-face encounter, some children will want to go alone into the treatment room, while others will want the counselor to accompany them.

Many children will start the meeting by inviting the parent to play a board game or engage in a craft activity. Some children will play alone and interact with the parent from a distance. It is best to let the child determine his or her comfort level. Reminding the child that he or she can leave the treatment room as needed, or end the session at will, can give the child a sense of control required to ensure his or her own psychological and physical safety. As the process moves along and the child is comfortable, the reconciliation counselor can begin to address the child's more serious concerns, memories, and issues as they emerge in the re-engagement process. Once a friendly relationship is re-established, the family can move on to more traditional public or private family therapy.

Final Notes

Some reunification therapists may not have access to a one-way mirror. While the mirror intervention presents the best opportunity to provide a safe, structured approach to reunification with the targeted parent, a desensitization approach that uses other tools can work too. For instance, exposing the child to letters and photographs of the feared parent, followed in later sessions with videotapes, can be quite effective in reducing the child's anxiety. Ultimately, the child can meet the targeted parent using video conferencing such as Skype in sessions that are monitored by the reunification therapist, which can be a prelude to a face-to-face meeting.

A final issue is whether or not to force older adolescents into a reunification process. While it is quite possible that older adolescents can also be engulfed in the alienating parent's hostility toward the targeted parent, forcing a defiant and determined adolescent into reunification can backfire. Initial attempts to remediate the conflict are best achieved by trying to engage the adolescent in individual therapy until his or her positions softens—if it softens at all. One way to do this is to allow the adolescent sufficient time to talk about his or her feelings about the targeted parent and to share memories and stories about alleged abuse and mistreatment. Adolescents who are essentially brainwashed by the alienating parent usually have a very tough time coming up with concrete evidence of their complaints and some do relent in their hostility even as they remain reluctant to give up their positions. Some adolescents will vote with their feet about being forced into reunification and refuse to attend sessions. Adolescents who are angry, defiant, or even emotionally disturbed who refuse to engage can escalate their behavior if pressured to do so. It is clinically counterindicated to force such disturbed adolescents into reunification, as their behavior can escalate into aggressive or even suicidal acting out. The same can be said of emotionally disturbed younger children, and considerable caution and accurate psychological assessment is essential in order to safely and effectively manage these cases. Sometimes the alienation process is so complete and the adolescent is so defiant and disturbed that even well-intended therapeutic interventions are unable to undo the damage. These more extreme cases must be distinguished from those adolescents who are really tempests in a teapot, whose dramatized refusal to engage in reunification is a face-saving ploy that masks their deeper desire to reconnect with the targeted parent.

Restoring a Father–Son Relationship

From the time Edward, now 5 years old, was born there has been high conflict between the parents. Both parents were in the military at the time he was conceived, but the parents remained married for only 1 year due to serious conflicts over money, caretaking responsibilities, and the involvement of extended family. Mother is Hispanic and father is Caucasian. Both parents are in their 30s. They could neither agree on whether to call their newborn Edward or Edwardo, nor whether to speak to him in Spanish or English. His birth certificate says that his name is Edward. The father spoke no Spanish, but the mother was fluent in Spanish and English. During the time that they were still together as a family she began to speak to her son only in Spanish, despite the protests of her husband who said he could not understand what she was saying to him. They separated when the boy was 1 year old.

Neither parent sought a legal divorce or filed for custody at the point of their physical separation. The father agreed to the mother's terms regarding custody, visitation, and child support because he loved her and wanted her to come back. He did not want to risk losing her entirely by seeking a court action for custody. For the better part of the next 2 years he accepted her demands and avoided conflict, rarely challenging her about changes in the visitation schedule, missed visits, unavailability for phone calls, and refusal to share information about medical appointments or childcare arrangements. She would not tell him who the childcare provider was and refused to allow the father to take the child from daycare if he was free. She "gave" him time to see his son on a weekday and one day on the weekend as well as other random occasions when she was busy and had no childcare. The father was very invested in his son's welfare and took good care of him during their time together. There were conflicts at the exchanges, when the mother would send strangers to pick up Edward, mainly the mother's relatives whom the father had never met, or when Edward got upset because she refused to take the toys that the father had bought him.

When Edward was 3 years old his mother decided to move. She told the father that she had received orders to transfer to a military base in another state and that she intended to take Edward with her. He learned that there was another man in the mother's life who would be going with them. When he got the news, he realized that their relationship was doomed and he filed a motion to prevent her from taking Edward. His declaration stated that he was an involved parent who wanted 50/50 custody but could never get the mother to agree. He also detailed the multitude of conflicts and disagreements between them, but did not attack her parenting abilities or love for the child. The mother's declaration stated that the father was a poor caretaker and hardly involved, denigrated his extended family, reported that the mother-in-law was racist and that the child was not close to the father as evidenced by his difficulty with transitions at the exchanges and his refusal to talk on the phone when the father called. The mother could not produce documents from the military that ordered her to transfer and, along with all the other case facts, the court denied her motion for sole custody. During the period of the assessment, which took almost 3 months, conflict between the parents escalated, the mother insisted on a police stand-by at each exchange, and allegations that the father was causing conflict became rampant. The father denied that he was creating difficulties and recorded each exchange in a pocket voice recorder. The recordings proved his innocence.

The family court assessor gave each parent 50% custody because the military would not allow the mother to rescind her transfer, despite the fact that the transfer was not ordered but voluntarily requested by her. Each parent got custody of the child for three consecutive weeks. This was presumably a temporary arrangement until the child reached school age and could attend kindergarten and a more permanent arrangement could be decided.

When Edward was scheduled to be returned to his father after a 3-week stay with his mother he was difficult, unwilling to leave his mother at the airport, and had to be carried fitfully to the airplane, but not before the mother called a security guard to observe the boy's emotional reaction and complain that he should not have to go. The security officer read the father's custody order and let him take the child. The mother was talking to the boy in Spanish as the father carried him off. The father insisted that the mother was yelling to the boy that she was sorry that he had to go and that the father was mean for taking him away. Needless to say, the transition back to father's home was not easy but the father understood that, all other conflict notwithstanding, the boy might have difficulty with the exchange and visit because of his young age and the long period of separation. He was patient and tried not to overwhelm the child with demands for hugs and warmth, and after a few days he calmed down and was more cheerful. Yet Edward began to spontaneously make comments like, "My name is Edwardo, not Edward." He would call his father by his first name. When his father said to call him "Dad," Edward said, "You are Robert; my mother said so." He would spontaneously and mechanically say, "I don't love you" to his father, and he would tell him that he had another father now—the man who moved in with his mother.

The mother refused to allow the next visit and made a child abuse allegation because the boy had bruises on his legs. The father said they were ordinary bruises that happened when the child was jumping and playing. Her attorney filed a motion for supervised visits. The father's attorney got orders for phone calls and an evaluation for alienation. By the time it was all sorted out, 5 months had passed. Child protective services did not sustain the allegation of abuse, the mother became pregnant, and there was virtually no contact between the boy and his father. The mother continually interfered with phone calls or simply did not answer. At the next hearing, the mother insisted that the boy was frightened of the father and refused to see him; she could not get him to go. The parents stipulated to the reunification protocol, though only because the assessor in the case found that mother was undermining the boy's relationship with the father and determined that parental alienation was present. The mother was made to understand that she was in jeopardy of losing custody.

The boy was brought to the family court site for reunification. He spent the previous day at the maternal grandmother's home, and she brought him as agreed in the order. He was anxious but very curious about the one-way mirror intervention. When he viewed his father from behind the mirror, he asked, "Who is that man? I don't like him." He said, "He is a mean man." Initially, he refused to be in the same room with his father. Yet, as the intervention progressed, he became interested in all the toys and pictures that the father brought with him, and he was soon playing with his father. After a second session the boy's fears subsided and the inner circle of professionals who were managing the case decided that they would not alter the time share but require the mother to be in treatment with an expert in parental alienation, assign a guardian *ad litem* to the case, and have orders for phone calls, Skype, the father's access to the daycare provider, and clearly delineated consequences for any further evidence of alienation, including the possibility of losing custody. Mainly, they were concerned that changing custody was premature and might traumatize the boy, especially if the mother were given supervised visits. At this writing, the boy's relationship with his father has been restored, but continual monitoring is necessary and the prospect of a relapse is in the air as the pressure mounts over where the child will live when school starts next year.

Reuniting a Mother and her two Abducted Daughters

Maria and Esperanza, aged 5 and 7 years, were ordered to court with their father for an emergency screening. The children had been missing for 4 years. When their mother got word from a relative that the father and the girls were visiting a relative in Los Angeles, she hired a private detective and ultimately served him with a subpoena. He did not abscond with the children because he was out of money and decided to make a case that he had left with the girls because his wife was threatening to make false allegations against him of sexual abuse.

At the screening, the girls were interviewed together and appeared obviously frightened. They understood that they were at court because their mother wanted to see them. They insisted that they did not want to see her and that they thought she was dead and a murderer. Their father had told them that she wanted to murder them so he had fled the country to Mexico. They reported that their father had told them that their mother was crazy and that she was going to put him in jail "for no reason," that she was a wild woman who had many boyfriends and did not want to be their mother. They said their father saved them from a dangerous mother. Lucky for them, he told them, she had died in a car accident. At the beginning of the treatment they were told by the reunification counselor that their father was mistaken about the car accident and that the reason they had been taken away was that their parents did not get along and their father thought he was doing the best thing for them. They were told that their mother was not dangerous or crazy and that she missed them, but was not going to force them to see her because she did not want to scare them.

The girls were not reassured and refused the idea of meeting their mother. A conference with the attorneys was convened and everyone agreed to commence the reunification protocol. There were major issues to assess about abuse and alienation, the case history to assemble, and a plan to assign the children a guardian *ad litem*. There were sufficient grounds to temporarily remove the children from their father, but the girls could not be given to the mother. The father stipulated to supervised visits and arranged for the girls to stay with a neutral relative pending a decision by the District Attorney's office about possible kidnapping charges against him. A meeting to commence the reunification process was immediately arranged.

The girls came to the reunification facility with the paternal aunt. They were still quite confused, anxious, and fearful. They did not want to see their mother. One of the girls said that she was sure her mother would hurt them, that she was scary, and might try to run away with them. Their mother was waiting in the room adjoining the one-way mirror. She understood that the girls were frightened and that they were filled with distortions about her. The father was not present. The girls were told about the one-way mirror. Because they were so frightened they were told that they would not have to interact with their mother, talk to her or do anything forced. Like many children, they were quite curious about the viewing room and were comforted by the idea of a physical barrier between them and their mother. They were told that their mother was in the adjoining room and that the reunification counselor would talk with her while they watched, if they desired.

When they entered the room they stared in apprehension at their mother. She was quite attractive and slight figured and she sat on the couch reading a magazine. The girls talked between themselves. They talked about her dress, how pretty her shoes were, and how they did not remember her at all. They kept repeating, "Is that really our mother?" Their mother did not know that she was being observed by the girls. The girls were asked if they would like to see her talk and hear her voice. So long as they did not have to be with her, they agreed. The girls watched the counselor interview the mother from behind the mirror while they were supervised by another in-house therapist. The mother was asked benign and non-threatening questions about herself and what she had been doing for the past few years. She talked about everything from her favorite flavors of ice cream to her job, house, and favorite movies and foods. She was careful to follow instructions not to bring up any loaded issues about the abduction. After about 15 minutes the counselor returned to the girls to discuss their reactions. It was nothing short of fascination. They talked about her voice, how she sounded like she was nice, that they were curious about where she lived, her house, who she lived with. The girls refused to go into the same room as their mother, but they wanted to hear more about her.

The mother was prepared with photos and items from the girls' infancy and early childhood, and the girls wanted to see them through the mirror. The mother was delighted to talk all about the girls and her memories of taking care of them when they were babies. She cried, but talked lovingly of how she cared for them, made special meals for them, bathed them, and played with them. She held up photos of each child and described when they were taken and showed them toys and clothes she kept to keep the memory of them alive. The girls asked if they could hold the pictures to see if they could recognize themselves. They asked if they could have some of the items that their mother had brought, which their mother was happy to share with them. They still did not want to see her directly, but each girl said, "Maybe next time." The interview ended and another meeting was arranged.

The next meeting went well. The girls were hesitant but not frightened. They were eager to go to the viewing room. Their mother was there. The girls wanted to follow the same process, but were ready to meet their mother. They cautiously followed the counselor into the adjoining room and promptly sat on the couch across from their mother. When their mother greeted them she could not hold back her tears and softly cried as she tried to smile and reassure them. The 7-year-old spontaneously got off the couch and hugged her, and her sister immediately followed. That was the beginning of their healing.

The girls were ordered into treatment with their mother. They were enrolled in school. They lived with their aunt for a time while mother got increasingly more custodial time with the girls. The result of the evaluation process was that the father was found guilty of abducting the girls and that his allegations that their mother was threatening to make false allegations of sexual abuse were unfounded. He was not charged with kidnapping. He retained partial custody and was required to enroll in individual therapy and parenting classes. It was not long before the mother was granted substantial custody.

References

Adams, P., & Chandler, S. (2002). Building partnerships to protect children: A blended model of family group conferencing. *Family Court Review, 40(3)*, 503–517.

Baker, A. J. L. (2007). *Adult children of parent alienation syndrome: Breaking the ties that bind.* New York: W. W. Norton.

Bernet, W. (2010). *Parent alienation, DSM-5 and ICD-11.* Chicago: Charles Thomas.

Bernet, W., von Boch-Galhau, W., Baker, A. J. L., Morrison, S. (2010). Parental alienation, DSM-V, and ICD-11. *American Journal of Family Therapy, 38(2)*, 75–187.

Ceci, S., & Hembrooke, H. (2002). *Expert witness in child abuse cases: What can and should be said in court.* New York: American Psychological Association.

Child Welfare League of America (2002). Summary of Adoption and Safe Families Act of 1997. Available at: http://www.cwla.org/advocacy/asfapl105-89summary.htm [accessed May 28, 2004].

Darnall, D. (2008). *Divorce casualties: Understanding parent alienation.* Dallas, TX: Taylor Publishing.

Darnall, D. (2010). *Beyond divorce casualties: Reunifying the alienated family.* Lanham, MD: Taylor Trade Publishing.

Drozd, L., & Olesen, N. (2004). Is it abuse, alienation, and/or estrangement? A decision tree. *Journal of Child Custody, 1(3)*, 65–106.

Fahlberg, V. (1991). *A child's journey through placement.* Indianapolis, IN: Perspective Press.

Garber, B. (2011). Parental alienation and the dynamics of the enmeshed child-parent dyad: Adultification, parentification and infantialization. *Family Court Review, 49(2)*, 322–335.

Gardner, R. A. (1992). *The parental alienation syndrome.* Cresskill, NJ: Creative Therapeutics.

Gardner, R. A. (2004). Commentary on Kelly and Johnston's The alienated child: A reformulation of parent alienation syndrome. *Family Court Review, 42(4)*, 611–621.

Gendell, S. J. (2001). In search of permanency: A reflection on the first three years of the Adoption and Safe Families Act implementation. *Family Court Review, 39*, 25–36.

Haley, J. (1977). *Problem-solving therapy.* San Francisco: Jossey-Bass.

Hoffman, L. (1981). *Foundations of family therapy.* New York: Basic Books.

Kaye, H. (2000). Strategies and need for systems change: Improving court practice for the millennium. *Family Court Review, 38(2)*, 159–175.

Kelly, J., & Johnston, J. (2001). The alienated child: A reformulation of parental alienation syndrome. *Family Court Review, 39(3)*, 249–267.

Loftus, E. (1997). Creating false memories. *Scientific American, 277(3)*, 70–75.

Loftus, E. (2003a). Make-believe memories. *American Psychologist, 58(11)*, 867–873.

Loftus, E. (2003b). Our changeable memories: Legal and practical implications. *Nature Reviews: Neuroscience, 4(3)*, 231–233.

Lowenstein, L. (2011). What if the custodial parent refuses to cooperate with child contact decisions? *Journal of Divorce and Remarriage, 52(5)*, 322–325.

Mahler, M., Pine, F., & Bergman, A. (1975). *The psychological birth of the human infant.* New York: Basic Books.

Suinn, R. M. (1990). *Anxiety management training and behavior therapy.* New York: Plenum Press.

Terr, L. (1994). *Unchained memories: True stories of traumatic memories lost and found.* New York: Basic Books.

Tippins, T., & Wittman, J. (2005). Empirical and ethical problems with custody recommendations. *Family Court Review, 43(2),* 193–222.

Van der Kolk, B., McFarlane, A., & Weisaeth, L, (Eds.) (1996). *Traumatic stress: The effects of overwhelming experience on mind, body and society.* New York: Guilford Press.

Vidair, H., & Rynn, M. (2010). *Childhood anxiety disorders: Best treatment options and practice.* Cambridge, UK: Cambridge University Press.

Warshak, R. (2010). *Divorce poison: How to protect your family from bad-mouthing and brainwashing* (revised ed.). New York: HarperCollins.

White, J. (1999). *Overcoming generalized anxiety disorder.* Oakland, CA: New Harbinger.

Wolpe, J. (1959). *Psychotherapy by reciprocal inhibition.* Stanford, CA: Stanford University Press.

Wolpe, J. (1988). *Life without fear: Anxiety and its cure.* Oakland, CA: New Harbinger.

11 The Application of Structural Family Therapy to the Treatment of Parental Alienation Syndrome

Linda J. Gottlieb

Four Children Who "Hate" Their Father

The Attorney for the Child referred a family for reunification and therapy to a family therapist who practices using a structural family therapy modality (one school of family systems therapy). The therapy had been strongly advised by the judge. The attorney and the therapist had a long-standing collaborative relationship in addressing cases of alienation. The attorney had been educated by the therapist as to how to identify parental alienation syndrome (PAS) and also to implement his meaningful role in effecting a level playing field between the parents so that the therapist could be effective in reversing the PAS.

The parents had been separated for a year and were in the middle of a nasty divorce and custody battle. The attorney suspected parental alienation: there had been visit refusal for almost a year, and all four children, ranging in age from 6 to 17 years, arrived in his office and announced in unison, "We hate our father. We never want to see him again." When the attorney asked the children for an explanation, he received only vague, specious, and frivolous responses such as, "He's annoying." "He took us to too many movies." "That's not our definition of spending quality time." "He thinks he can buy us by taking us out to nice restaurants. You don't build a relationship over dinner." Another frivolous rationalization, offered even by the 6-year-old, was, "When he came to watch us at our games, he looked scary staring at us; we felt like he was stalking us." The 12-year-old boy exclaimed to the attorney, "He threw me away like I was a bill that he did not want to pay." And the 17-year-old expressed:

> I think he needs to understand that he is not yet divorced. He should not be going out on dates until the divorce proceedings

> are completely adjudicated. A mature, responsible person would have waited for the signed divorce decree in hand before he moved on.

The 12-year-old further expressed, “He is always taking us back to court for some ludicrous reason.” The attorney further conveyed to the therapist that he had observed the mother’s encouragement for the children’s dubious rationalizations when she commented to him:

> See. My children are quite expressive and know their own minds about their father. These are their thoughts, and I feel strongly that they are entitled to their opinions and that I should respect their wishes not to see him if they don’t want to.

When the attorney expressed his incredulity about the children’s justifications, the mother then exclaimed:

> There was always something suspicious about the way he gawked at my 17-year-old daughter. I could never put my finger on it, but I always felt he looked at her in a way that should have been reserved for me.

The girl then followed up her mother’s remarks:

> Yes. My mother is speaking the truth. That’s exactly how I felt. I always got a nervous feeling whenever my father gawked at me. I still can visualize a pair of underpants that I had as a child. When I think about those underpants now, it makes me want to vomit.

The attorney confirmed that no inappropriate touching between the father and any of the children had ever been alleged to Child Protective Services. Nor were any other reports filed alleging abuse and/or neglect by the father. The attorney expressed to the mother that he suspected alienation and that he would convey this to the judge if she did not cooperate with the therapy and with the rebuilding of the children’s relationships with their father.

A Father who is a Stranger to his Son

The attorney for a boy in his mid-teens referred him to a structural family therapist to facilitate a reunification with his father due to a year-long estrangement fostered by the boy's mother. The judge had forcefully conveyed to the mother that she will lose custody if she sabotages the therapy and the reunification process. The family had been in and out of court since the boy was 10 years old, the father having to request repeatedly that his parental rights and visitation be enforced. Recently, the mother arbitrarily refused to permit contact for extended periods, and the father sporadically reacted to these alienating maneuvers by withdrawing. Additionally, the mother failed to keep him apprised of his son's medical, educational, social, and extracurricular life and developments. When the father called or text-messaged his son, the boy rarely responded; but when he did, he deprecated his father by saying that he is not allowed to converse with strangers.

Introduction

A family systems model treats PAS using interventions that differ in two significant ways from the traditional, individual-oriented treatment models. Firstly, the family systems model intervenes to collaborate with the larger social systems which impact child custody and visitation decisions. According to Gottlieb (2012), when there is collaboration between the family therapist and the professionals in these systems, there is a higher probability that the alienation will be reversed (pp. xviii, xv–xvii, 257–259). This collaboration is essential because, in a family systems model, the conventionally accepted portrayal of the targeted parent as a helpless victim of a narcissistic alienating parent is rejected. Instead, it considers the victimization to result from the confluence of support for and empowerment of the alienating parent by the professionals in the traditional mental health, child protection, law enforcement, and judicial systems. All too frequently, these professionals are co-opted by the alienating parent and thereby embolden her/his alienation efforts (pp. xvi–xvii, 257–259).

The second significant difference between family systems therapy and individual-oriented therapy models relates to the assignment of the targeted parent as the deprogrammer of the alienated child. In the individual models, the deprogrammer is a professional who generally employs a cognitive intervention. In a systems model, according to Gottlieb (2012), the deprogrammer is the targeted parent, and the use of "the experience" is the predominant intervention (pp. 143–144, 151). Richard Gardner (2001) extolled the significance of "the experience" most poignantly when he stated, "If a picture is worth a thousand words then an experience is worth a million pictures" (p. 348). Family systems therapy, beginning with experiential family therapist Carl Whitaker (Whitaker, 1958, 1967, 1989; Napier & Whitaker, 1978; Whitaker & Bumberry, 1988), capitalizes on the wisdom of this axiom in treating the dysfunctional family. The family therapist fosters a process in which family members heal each other through their experiences with each other. According to Gottlieb (2012):

> It seems so marvelously simple to appreciate that we are most likely to change for someone whom we love and who loves us ... that no quantity or quality of words between an individual and the therapist—who is nonetheless a stranger—can possibly have as powerful and as meaningful an impact as when the therapist provides, instead, an environment in which emotions and experiences are released among family members. No therapist, however competent and well intentioned, can possibly recreate a relationship with the patient that rivals intimate family relationships—particularly the meaningful parent/child relationship. It seems so evident, then, that the crucial player to assume the deprogramming role is the formerly loved and loving alienated parent. (p.143)

The role then for the therapist is to serve as a catalyst who encourages and guides the creation of healthy, corrective transactions between the targeted parent and the child as well as among all the family members.

Overview of Family Systems Therapy

Family systems therapy emerged in the 1950s out of the observations by psychoanalytically trained psychiatrists who were treating schizophrenic populations on the hospital ward and children who had been placed in residential treatment facilities. These therapists, who became the first generation of family therapists: Ackerman (Ackerman, 1958, 1961, 1966; Ackerman & Franklin, 1965), Bowen (1971, 1978), Jackson and Weakland (1971), Bateson (1956, 1964), Haley (1963, 1971, 1973, 1977, 1990; Haley & Hoffman, 1968), and Minuchin (Minuchin, 1974; Minuchin, Baker, & Rosman, 1978; Minuchin & Fishman, 1981; Minuchin & Nichols, 1993; Minuchin, Lee, & Simon, 1996; Minuchin, Nichols, & Lee, 2007), to name a few, and whose observations and theories were subsequently validated by the second generation of family therapists: Hoffman (1981), Andolfi, Angelo, Menghi, and Nicolo-Corigliano (1983), Andolfi, Angelo, and De Nichilo (1989), Gottlieb (2012), Nichols (1992), and Nichols and Schwartz (2004), also to name just a few, began to observe a cross-generational coalition between one parent and the child–patient to the disempowerment and disengagement of the other parent. This interactional pattern placed the child in the double-bind/no-win situation of having to choose sides in a parental dispute, the consequence of such a choice being that the child risked losing the love and approval of the co-opting parent for failure to collude or must reject the other parent as the inevitable outcome of the collusion. Neither option afforded the child the ability to retain a connection to both parents. Haley (1977) labeled this transactional pattern "the perverse triangle," while Bowen (1978) referred to it as "the pathological triangle." The "triangle" is the characteristic interactional pattern of the PAS family, and because family systems therapy has a long history of working with these family dynamics, it has a wealth of knowledge and expertise to draw upon in its treatment of parental alienation. It is proposed here that family systems therapy offers a more effective approach to treatment of the PAS family than traditional individual treatment modalities for 11 reasons outlined here:

1. Family systems therapy (FST) recognizes that because PAS is created by the family "triangle," treatment should include all members of the triangle. Treatment with any subset may not be powerful enough to change the whole.
2. FST takes into account the reality of the situations in which people exist; namely that people live in intimate relationships and act upon and react to each other—what Minuchin and Fishman (1981) referred to as "complementarity." Treatment, therefore, should not focus on the individual in isolation. According to Minuchin and Fishman (1981), self-motivation is rarely enough for people to make the difficult behavioral changes necessary for symptom remedy; people usually need to be "kicked" into changing (p. 32), especially by people whom they love and who love them, because they have the leverage to demand changes.
3. FST capitalizes on the instinctive and deeply entrenched love that parents and children have for each other and which will likely surface in face-to-face experiential contact. Dyadic interaction between the therapist and the child in individual treatment models does not afford this opportunity.
4. FST does not blame the child for the family's problems, which is the inevitable interpretation the child makes when labeled as the identified patient. The individual model inadvertently normalizes the immoral, deceptive, and deceitful behaviors of the alienating parent because that parent is not in the therapy room.
5. FST nominates the denigrated targeted parent to the position of the deprogrammer and therefore elevates her/him to a respectable status in the family system, with recognition afforded to her/him by the therapist as an esteemed authority.
6. FST has developed expertise in rewriting specious and malevolent family myths, known as reframing (Haley, 1963, 1971; Haley & Hoffman, 1968; Minuchin, 1974; Minuchin & Fishman, 1981), which provides the child with an accurate family narrative in place of what is offered by the alienating parent.
7. FST avoids the trap of becoming co-opted by the alienating parent (which generally occurs in individual treatment modalities) because most individual therapists do not interview the targeted parent. These therapists obtain information from only the alienating parent, and the information is then corroborated by the brainwashed child.
8. FST avoids the trap of providing sympathy and validation to the child upon hearing the child's "heartbreaking" yet distorted, malicious stories about her/his relationship with the targeted parent.

9. FST obviates the need to assume the impossible task of becoming a "Ph.D. historian" of the family's experience, which the therapist can never know well enough to respond to all the curve balls that will inevitably be thrown at him or her by the alienated child in dyadic therapy, when the therapist assumes the role of the deprogrammer. Of course, the targeted parent has all this information at her/his fingertips.
10. FST relies upon objective observations of the family by the therapist rather than upon unreliable, subjective client/patient self-reporting, which is characteristic of individual treatment models.
11. FST, as demonstrated by Gottlieb (2012), is applicable to a variety of alienation situations, even when the alienating parent declines to participate (pp. 181–207).

Table 11.1 presents an overview of 14 key components of structural family therapy and explains how they can be applied to PAS cases.

Applying Structural Family Therapy to the Vignettes

These vignettes have been adapted from a book entitled, *Parental Alienation Syndrome: A Family Therapy and Collaborative Systems Approach to Amelioration*, by Gottlieb (2012).

Applying Structural Family Therapy to Vignette 1

Upon receiving the referral from the Attorney for the Child, the structural family therapist contacts the mother to schedule an individual session, the goals of which are to develop a collaborative relationship with her; to affirm her importance to the children but the father's as well (the first of many reframes to be offered by the therapist); to credit her for the role she has played in any positive developments which her children have attained (the joining); and to impress upon her the therapist's expectation for her unequivocal cooperation with the reunification process between her children and their father and for furtherance of those relationships (the challenge to achieve the restructuring). The therapist will further convey to the mother that her intention is not to support transfer of custody—a position that is contingent upon the mother relinquishing her alienating behaviors and facilitating the reunification (more joining and then another challenge). Because the therapist has developed collaborative relationships with several Attorneys for the Child and with inter-disciplinary professionals in the matrimonial system, she can further apprise the mother that she has no compunction about notifying the court should there be sabotage of the reunification process (unbalancing in furtherance of the restructuring). An important caveat, however, is in order here: the therapist is always pacing her challenges to the alienator's cooperation. That is, it is unnecessary to threaten judicial remedies should the alienator provide cooperation upon the conclusion of the joining process. In time, there will be substantial challenging during

Table 11.1 Overview of key concepts in family systems theory

Technique	*Explanation*	*Application to parental alienation syndrome (PAS)*
Joining	Connecting emotionally with each family member so that each feels understood and motivated to change. "Joining is the glue that holds the system together" (Minuchin & Fishman, 1981, p. 32).	Acknowledging and appreciating the contributions of the alienating parent (AP) to the children's strengths and positive developments, as well as that parent's motivations and fears. This affords the therapist the leverage to challenge the AP to engage in behaviors which will reverse the PAS. Joining with the targeted parent (TP) means understanding his/her anger resulting from the deprecations and rejections, which creates receptivity in that parent to coaching to develop sublimating measures to handle the anger and appropriate deprogramming techniques of the children. Joining with the children means that the therapist appreciates their double-bind situation of having to choose between two parents, of having to reject and deprecate a loving and nurturing parent, and of understanding that they have been manipulated to deny their own true feelings and do the AP's bidding. This empathy and understanding may, but not always, have the effect of supporting the children in confronting their AP. The more impactful change, however, is expected of the parents, particularly of the AP.
Spontaneity	Judicious self-disclosure in pursuit of attaining the therapeutic goals. To expect the family to take the risks of changing, the therapist must be willing to do likewise, creating an authentic emotional connection with each family member.	The therapist can share with the alienated child the painful feelings she has endured as a result of the same or similar experiences, commensurate with the child's age. Adolescents are particularly intrigued and engaged by therapist self-disclosure. If applicable, the therapist can share with the AP the negative outcome her experience with PAS or similar dynamics and her anger at the thoughtless and selfish behavior of the parent engaging in alienation. If applicable, the therapist can share with the TP how judiciously her own TP handled his/her anger due to the alienation, so that the TP does not transfer her/his anger to the children.
Enactment	Encouraging family members to talk with each other in order to observe and explore how the family has organized itself into coalitions and subgroups.	Enactment by the PAS family reveals the coalition between the AP and the co-opted child when the child takes that parent's side in a parental dispute; when the child becomes the puppet of the AP, mouthing that parent's words; and when the child deprecates the TP with spurious allegations. Indeed, the enactments that occur during the family interview provide the most confirming, empirical evidence of the PAS because all or most of the eight characteristic symptoms in the child, as identified by Gardner (1985, 1998, 2001), and most or all of the alienating behaviors of the AP, as identified by Baker (2007), can be observed by the therapist.

Table 11.1 Continued

Technique	*Explanation*	*Application to parental alienation syndrome (PAS)*
Mapping	An assessment of the family's organization, upon having observed their enactment, in order to identify coalitions, explain how power is distributed, and understand the boundaries that determine the current functioning and membership of the family's subsystems.	In the PAS family, the cross-generational alliance between the AP and the child to deprecate and reject the TP is typically manifest. The parental subsystem is diffuse; the TP/child subsystem is disengaged; and the AP/child subsystem is enmeshed. The alienated child demonstrates reflexive and dogmatic support for the AP's opprobrium for the TP.
Complementarity	An understanding of how the family members have co-created each other and are maintaining the homeostasis of the family system.	The AP and TP have co-created each other, live in intimate relationships with each other, and are known to each other in terms of what to expect from the other and whose behavior is predictable. The empowerment of the AP by the "rescuing" misguided professionals interferes with the family therapy process (Gottlieb, 2012, pp. xvi–xvii).
Reframing	The rewriting of the family's narrow, self-defeating, homeostasis-maintaining myths about itself which constrain the possibility for seeing options for problem resolution and change.	In the PAS family, rewriting the myths entails helping the members to see each parent realistically, including acceptance of the importance of the TP to the children; acknowledgement of the emotional and financial contributions of the TP to the family and to the children; recognition that input from two parents will likely produce healthier children; and appreciation for the AP's need to have a life outside of the children, which can be more readily attained when there is a partner in parenting.
Challenging	The therapist creates doubt about each member's way of thinking, about how each perceives reality and the presenting problem. The therapist intervenes to undermine each member's participation in maintaining the homeostasis of the family system.	The therapist creates doubt about each member's perfunctory methods of thinking and operating. It is akin to lifting the blinders that create tunnel vision.

Focus	Staying on the path upon which the therapist wants to lead the family and combating the family's pull to go off the path in order to maintain their homeostasis.	The coalition members in the PAS family are wedded to their drama and will resist the therapist's and TP's efforts at changing the script. The therapist must not relinquish her role as the producer and director.
Intensity	Allowing the family's full-blown conflicts to surface. Only by absorbing the family's complete drama will the therapist truly experience all the plots and subplots; the therapist then induces discomfort about the dysfunctional interactional patterns.	The intensity of the PAS family dynamic is most effectively revealed in the family session because it is so much more difficult to conceal one's passion when sitting face-to-face with one's "adversary." This gives the therapist much grist with which to work. And it is virtually impossible for the child to remain neutral in the face of parental conflict.
Unbalancing	Disruption of the family's dysfunctional interactional patterns (disturbing the homeostasis) by providing shifting support for each member in that member's efforts to achieve change.	In the PAS family, the therapist will side predominantly with the TP in order to level the playing field that has become lopsided as a result of the meddlesome intrusions of PAS-unaware professionals. Such unbalancing may include using authority to obtain judicial remedy and, ultimately, supporting the transfer of custody should the alienating behaviors continue.
Restructuring	Encouragement and support for the implementation of new, healthy, and corrective patterns of interaction.	Should the treatment of the PAS family progress as designed, the boundaries of the family's subsystems will be altered so that the enmeshment between the AP and the children will be weakened, and the boundaries between the TP and the children will be strengthened. The optimal result is the creation of a cooperative, shared, parental subsystem.
Strengths	Identifying and providing recognition for the positives in each member in order to support the member's efforts to maintain the restructuring.	Because the self-esteem of the TP and the children has been severely damaged by the PAS, therapy will need to facilitate the family members in conveying appreciation for the contributions of each member to the family. Attention will further need to be paid to the AP, who also has needs.
Collaboration	FST recognizes that the family is a system that exists in a world of much larger social systems which impact its functioning.	It is essential to work with any and all of the professionals in these systems in order to educate them about alienation, to gain their cooperation in guaranteeing to the family therapist a level playing field between the AP and TP, to work cooperatively to minimize the adversarial approach to child custody and visitation decisions, and to impress upon

Table 11.1 Continued

Technique	*Explanation*	*Application to parental alienation syndrome (PAS)*
		these professionals the child's need for a relationship with both parents. Gaining the cooperation of the individual family members to support restructuring (particularly the support of the AP) is paramount to a successful therapy outcome. Indeed, the most effective factor in reversing the PAS is the ceasing of the alienating behaviors by the AP.
Follow-up	Being available to the family should there be regression.	Being available to the members of the family regarding the presenting problem and/or to address additional issues should they arise.

See Minuchin and Fishman (1981) for an in-depth description of these techniques and Gottlieb (2012) for detailed application of the techniques to 16 PAS families.

the process of facilitating the restructuring, as there always is, even in less problematic families who present for treatment.

The therapist conveys to the mother that she appreciates that she is the expert on her children and that she will be essential for effectuating the reunification. This message acknowledges the mother's relevance to her children and that she, not the therapist, is the instrument of change. Having obtained from the children's attorney information regarding the children's educational, social, and emotional functioning, the therapist is in a position to comment to the mother that it is a reflection on her good parenting that all of her children are doing well: they behave in school, are on the honor roll, exhibit no behavioral problems, and actively participate in extracurricular and social activities. In response to the therapist's acknowledgements of her parenting abilities, the mother expresses her gratitude, asserting that her estranged husband failed to credit her parental accomplishments. At the same time, she acknowledges that it is very difficult being a single parent of four children: she is never off duty because they have very active lives.

The therapist listens to her story about how she felt controlled and unappreciated by her husband. But not wanting to reinforce her self-perception as a victim, the therapist empowers the mother by refocusing her on how she can achieve the goals to which she aspires (a reframing technique). Indeed, she had hoped to pursue her master's degree in education in order to become financially independent. The therapist also helps her to recognize the part she played in her marriage—for her to become victimized she must have permitted it in some way (punctuating complementarity). She concedes that she not only failed to be self-assertive about her needs, wishes, and opinions, but she simultaneously elevated her husband on a pedestal (when a person recognizes that s/he plays a part in how the situation unfolds, then s/he not only cannot be a victim but further has the power to produce remedy). The mother further expresses her fears about losing the affections of her children because her estranged husband controls the purse strings. She is grateful that the therapist is not judgmental of her nor blames her for the state of the relationships between her children and their father.

Although the therapist does recognize her participation in the children's unjustifiable rejection of their father, she conveys that her objective is to facilitate reconciliation (the family therapist is concerned with remedy, not blame; this is another intervention in support of restructuring). The therapist reassures the mother that the goal is to facilitate the rebuilding of the relationships between the children and their father and not to rob her of her children by supporting a transfer of custody or elevating the father into the role of sugar daddy. Such reassurance is crucial to facilitating the reversal of the PAS process as, very often, the fear of losing the children (if not physically, then emotionally) is a motivating factor for the alienating parent (but again, a reminder to the reader: this reassurance is contingent upon the alienator's cooperation in relinquishing alienating behaviors and cooperating with the reunification process).

The culmination of the joining process accomplishes the goal of the mother feeling understood and empathized with by the therapist. At that point the mother reveals that she has been a victim of PAS and is still suffering from its detrimental effects (it is quite common for PAS to be passed on inter-generationally). As the mother reveals her painful history she relives her childhood trauma, and she is determined that she will not subject her children to the same ordeal (collaboration with the alienating parent makes everything go so much more smoothly and expeditiously). The mother conveys her appreciation for the therapist's compassion in response to her painful story, and the therapist then reveals her own childhood victimization by PAS. As a result of the therapist's judicious self-disclosure (or, spontaneous use of self) there is an irreversible joining between her and the mother.

The therapist points out that two-thirds of children of divorce are vulnerable to severe emotional and behavioral disturbances. The single variable that accounts for the healthy adjustment of the remaining one-third is that the parents develop a cooperative, shared parenting relationship. The therapist further shares with the mother the statistics about children whose relationships with their fathers are severed (Pruett, 2000). These and other statistics are sobering for the mother. Having thus reached with the mother a level of intensity designed to motivate her for restructuring the family's dysfunctional interactional patterns, the therapist then addresses the changes that would be required of her to facilitate the reunification and rebuilding of the relationships between her children and their father. The mother commits to correcting the "perverse triangle" and to setting the relationships right. Specifically, she proposes explaining to the children that anger is inconsistent with their religious values, that anger is such a burden that it is like carrying around a 20-pound bowling ball on your back, and that she hopes that they will resolve their feelings for their father. She further volunteers that she will convey to her children that she knows that their father loves them. The mother and the therapist then schedule a session between her and the children, and the therapist is hopeful that the mother has accepted her role as the co-therapist (the family therapist always attempts to recruit a co-therapist from among the family members because this intervention is highly effective to achieving a successful therapy).

Although the therapist is pleased with the mother's initial response, she is aware that alienation is a deeply entrenched family interactional pattern and that translating words into corrective deeds may present many hurdles. The therapist must always have a backup plan. The therapist also hopes to determine with which child the mother is most enmeshed and who is, therefore, most likely to be the parentified child, because this coalition will have to be initially respected but later challenged through not too ego-dystonic unbalancing interventions. This child can be anticipated to maintain the family's homeostasis and will therefore be the most resistant to restructuring, even if the mother supports it. The therapist will further assess disunity among the siblings as to the intensity of each one's "enmity" for their father. Should the mother renege on her commitment to be a co-therapist, perhaps the sibling who feels closest to the father might accept that role. The therapist will attempt to unbalance the family's homeostasis through a number of interventions, which may include encouragement of her "co-therapist" to create cognitive dissonance about the family's myths—such as the father being perceived as the devil and the mother an angel. And, at some point in the therapy, another "co-therapist" in the person of a child may challenge the mother about her deprecations of the father.

The family arrives, and the therapist observes how the members seat themselves because this reveals information about the family's organization. Mother and her 17-year-old daughter sit virtually on top of each other, as if they were a couple, signaling that daughter is the parentified child (mapping). The children are encouraged to express their thoughts and feelings and, as the therapist has anticipated, they convey their fallacious deprecations of their father. The 12 and 17-year-old-children express the most hostility.

The therapist then encourages the mother to engage in a conversation with her children (the enactment) in the hopes that she will steer them towards corrective messages (reframing) about their father, as she and the therapist have prearranged. Much to the therapist's chagrin, she begins by validating their negative perceptions of their father. Her parentified 17-year-old daughter repeats these statements verbatim. As the enactment continues in this unfavorable direction, the therapist gently reminds (challenging) the mother of what has been discussed in their prior session, and the mother mercifully reverses course. She then dispels her children of their misperceptions about their father (restructuring) although without acknowledging that she has been responsible for implanting the misconceptions (in a structural family therapy model, the therapist is not interested in pointing the finger of blame at the alienating parent for her/his misdeeds; if the alienator is demonstrating corrective behaviors, that is sufficient). The mother persuasively expresses to her children, using the bowling ball metaphor, that they must relinquish their anger. She encourages them to work their issues through with their father because "You need him, and he loves all of you" (restructuring). Having observed this enactment, the therapist is in a position to assess the mother's powerful influence over her children: the three younger children's feelings predictably turn on a dime as soon as their mother conveys to them her desire that they rebuild their relationship with their father. The 17-year-old girl is less persuadable, however, and the therapist anticipates having to devise a strategy to counter the anticipated sabotage from her.

The individual work with the mother and the work with her together with her children will hopefully provide the foundation for a successful session between the children and their father. This face-to-face experience between the children and their father will capitalize on the innate love that parents and children have for each other, as well as upon the powerful effects that the "experience" affords (Gardner, 2001; Haley, 1971; Jackson & Weakland, 1971; Napier & Whitaker, 1978; Minuchin, 1974; Minuchin & Fishman, 1981; Whitaker & Bumberry, 1988).

When the therapist contacts the father to arrange a session between him and his children, she suggests that he brings videos and pictures that reflect his previous involvement with his children. As agreed, the father arrives early in order to discuss his version of the family's history. He disputes every issue of which he has been accused—principally that he was not involved in his children's lives prior to separating from their mother and that he has not been financially supporting them subsequent to the separation. The therapist advises him to bring to the next session documentation which disputes these assertions. He responds that the children's attorney has informed him that sharing such information will put the children in the middle of the parental battles.

Unfortunately, targeted parents frequently become inadvertently victimized by the actions of the professionals who impact child custody and visitation decisions because these professionals generally do not understand how to respond to PAS, if they are at all aware of its existence. It is just such a situation as this which justifies the need for the family therapist to educate these professionals as to how to address the malicious and specious deprecations of the alienated parent (collaboration.) Situations such as this create one of many double-binds to which targeted parents are subjected: when they attempt to clarify the misperceptions and malicious fabrications about them, they are accused of putting their children in the middle of parental disputes. But if targeted parents do not correct the misinformation then it remains alive in the minds of their children. It often seems to escape the logic of some attorneys for the children, judges, individual therapists, and child protective staff that it is the alienating parent who has initially put the children in the middle by revealing to them court proceedings and by fabricating malicious deprecations.

The therapist in this case vignette informs the father that it is imperative for him to correct any misperceptions about himself and that this can be accomplished without casting aspersions on the mother. That is, he can provide his children with accurate information without blaming or expressing anger for the source of the information.

The children arrive for the session with their father, and they all convey their thoughts and feelings through the 17-year-old girl, who functions as the chief complaint officer. Their major grievance is their father's alleged failure to support them. He responds (reframing) that he has regularly provided monthly support for all their needs and that he will produce the supporting canceled checks and other documents at the next session. The two younger children accept their father's denial of the allegation, but his 17-year-old daughter remains antagonistic, dismissive, and disbelieving. The 12-year-old boy is not forgiving either, although not as hostile as his older sister. The children then accuse their father of his lack of involvement with them while he was living at home and after he moved out. The father again clarifies (reframing) their misperceptions by reminding them of all their activities in which he had participated. He further expresses that he had been unable to attend every event that their mother had attended as he was the sole support of the family. He explains that his extended work schedule was a result of an agreement between him and their mother, and this arrangement has enabled her to be a full-time homemaker while he is the sole breadwinner. He expresses (reframing) that after he moved out he was either not provided with a schedule of their activities or else they had made it clear to him that he was *persona non grata*.

He begins to sob as he conveys (reframing) his undying love for them, that he would never turn his back on them, that he misses them terribly, and that the previous year has been the worst year of his life. He then removes from his briefcase an enormous album of family photographs and declares it to be his most valuable treasure. His sobbing intensifies as he thumbs through the pages of the album, exclaiming to his children how he spends hours each night perusing it as a vicarious replacement for his relationships with them (intensity). His two youngest children are soon sobbing with him, climbing upon his lap (restructuring). The 12-year-old boy maintains his distance but expresses to his father that he desires that he attend his next soccer game but, "must attend incognito until you can prove that you have been supporting us." The boy soon joins his two younger siblings in sobbing, although he is still unwilling to physically embrace his father (restructuring). These emotional interactions are incredibly powerful and intense and, accordingly, are an unrivaled antidote to the alienation. Other than the alienator relinquishing the alienating maneuvers, such interaction is the single most effective measure to counter the brainwashing. The 17-year-old girl, however, makes no movement during the entire session and insists to the very end, "I don't want a relationship with my father. I have no use for him" (efforts at homeostasis).

Immediately subsequent to the session between the children and their father, the therapist arranges with the mother for another individual session and requests that she obtain from her children prior to the meeting feedback about the session that has occurred between them and their father (joining again). Upon meeting, the mother reports to the therapist that the three younger children have expressed positive feelings about their father but her 17-year-old daughter remains livid with him. The therapist poses the possibility that the girl is worried that she will be betraying her mother if she allows her father to re-enter her life. The mother affirms for the therapist that she has encouraged her daughter to reconcile with her father and that she intends to keep reassuring her daughter of her fervent desire that she reconnects with him and recognizes that he is particularly important to her during this stage of her life. She further agrees to convey to her daughter that she need not fight her battles for her with her father, especially now that they will be resolving their differences in co-parent counseling (restructuring).

Another session is scheduled between the father and his children, at which time he provides the supporting evidence to reframe the myths about him. As he had pledged, he brings the canceled checks of support and other documentation that he has been providing for all of their needs (reframing). The children are impatient to review the documents, and they are all, including the 17-year-old girl, won over upon viewing the supporting evidence. The children breathe a sigh of relief, needing a moment to take it all in. One by one, the children begin to update their father about what is transpiring in their lives. They each provide him a list with their extracurricular activities, and they enthusiastically request his attendance (restructuring). The session is so remarkably positive that the father and the children, upon conferring by phone with the mother, arrange to spend the afternoon together. Subsequent to that outing, the father returns to the therapist's office to attend a co-parenting session with the mother. Upon returning, the father elatedly proclaims to the therapist, "I have my kids back!" (restructuring).

One must marvel at how the human psyche can hold simultaneously two diametrically opposed beliefs when the emotional life dictates that this occurs. In this situation, the children had to recognize on some level that their mother had been lying to them when she told them that their father has not been supporting them. Now, irrefutable evidence reveals the contrary. Yet the children continue to love and respect both of their parents. Neither do they question their mother about her overt and deliberate lying to them. So strong is the instinct and desire to have a relationship with a parent!

Additional sessions between the father and his children are unnecessary as he just did his "fatherly thing," and they respond positively to him. The parents and the therapist meet for eight co-parenting sessions, during which time they resolve their significant parental disagreements (restructuring). The parents work out a flexible and liberal schedule for visits; they mutually agree on extracurricular activities for the upcoming year; they develop a plan for mutual involvement in their daughter's college applications and interviews; and they arrange for the father to be kept apprised of and involved in the decision-making of all the children's activities and interests, and educational and medical developments etc. They arrive at a mutually acceptable agreement on most of the issues confronting the family and the children. They further accommodate each other's needs, realizing that they will be treated by the other in kind. For example, the father is supportive of the mother's wish to complete her master's degree by rescinding his insistence that she obtain employment in order to help with the finances. In return, the mother agrees to relinquish her sole custody petition in favor of joint legal custody. They mutually agree that the mother will retain residential custody with the father having liberal visits. They further agree to speak to the children together and convey to them that there is no devil or victim in the divorce decision but rather that they have mutually grown apart (it is important for parents to recognize that how they handle their feelings and what they convey to their children regarding the decision to divorce will impact how their children will cope with the divorce and will come to view male–female relationships).

The treatment of this family using a structural family therapy modality certainly reached a successful conclusion—the total reversal of the PAS and the further success of achieving a healthy co-parenting relationship—in less than three months! It is irrefutable that the systemic work with the mother was vital to the positive outcome. It is also irrefutable that the mother's fear of the authority of the children's lawyer played a significant role in effectuating this outcome as she did not wish to appear as an alienator to the court.

Applying Structural Family Therapy to Vignette 2

Upon receiving this referral from the Attorney for the Child, the structural family therapist schedules an appointment with the mother in keeping with her routine practice of meeting initially with the alienating parent for the purpose of joining and establishing collaboration. The therapist conveys to the mother that she is the expert on her son and that her guidance is essential to how the therapist proceeds with the therapy (joining). During the session, the mother conveys to the therapist that she questions her former husband's motivations to have a relationship with her son and that she does not trust his commitment to him, alleging that he waltzes in and out of the boy's life. The mother declares that she has been a single parent most of her son's life, doing alone all the hard work of child-rearing a youngster. She is exasperated that the father has chosen now to re-enter boy's life, presumably when the chaotic and difficult developmental stages of childhood have ended (the mother has conveniently wiped from her memory the father's diligent efforts throughout the years to enforce his parental and visitation rights, only to be rebuffed by her). Except for a brief period when he allowed her to triumph in her goal of alienating him, the father has been persistent in returning each time.

The therapist surmises that the mother is speaking in derivative form when she references the father's alleged abandonment of their son as she, herself, actually feels abandoned by him. The therapist further wonders if the mother fears that the father will become a more significant parental figure to her son than she is because her son is now in the adolescent stage. But the therapist withholds expressing her hypotheses at this time believing that she is not yet well joined with the mother. The therapist determines that she must continue to allow the mother to "free associate." Prefacing her next comment with, "I do not wish to deprecate my ex-husband or bias you against him," the mother alleges that the father has an "anger management issue." Because of this "issue," according to the mother, her son is silenced by him. The mother asserts that her son consequently fears his "controlling" father and that this fear will prevent him from openly and honestly expressing his feelings and opinions to him. The therapist responds by assuring the mother that facilitating healthy communication between her son and his father can certainly be one focus of the therapy (the therapist acknowledges the mother's concerns, another joining maneuver).

Recognizing the mother's hostility for her former husband and her ambivalence, if not contempt, for the reunification, the therapist embarks on a course to challenge her gently by employing the Socratic method. The therapist asks a series of questions that will hopefully lead the mother to the conclusion about the relevance of her son's father to him. The therapist begins by exploring with the mother her understanding of what fathers, as opposed to mothers, differently but importantly offer their children; whether she understands the detrimental effects on children if they feel rejected and unloved by a parent; whether it is possible that her son may have different feelings for and opinions of his father than she does, etc. These are challenges of the least confrontational nature. The mother perfunctorily mouths the proper answers.

The mother declines the therapist's suggestion to participate in co-parenting counseling, explaining that she has nothing to discuss with the father and that she exerts no influence over her son's attitudes towards his father. Although acknowledging that she still harbors considerable anger for the father, she pledges not to demean him to her son or sabotage the therapy between them. The therapist responds to the mother by combining a joining maneuver with a challenge for the required restructuring:

> I have heard all of your concerns for your son. I have further heard you state that you appreciate the detrimental affects to him if he feels caught between his parents. And I have noted that you are aware of the detrimental effects on children when a parent disappears from their lives. But I am holding you accountable to follow through on your word not to sabotage the reunification.

The therapist further reminds the mother about the admonition from the judge that she could lose residential custody if she engages in alienation. The therapist creates intensity by making the point that New York State case law declares:

> Indeed, a custodial parent's interference with the relationship between a child and a non-custodial parent has been said to be an act so inconsistent with the best interests of the child as to per se raise a strong probability that the offending party is unfit to act as a custodial parent. (*Young* v. *Young*)

The therapist further unbalances by cautioning the mother that she has no compunction about informing her son's attorney about any sabotage. The mother acknowledges the warning and reaffirms that she will not be an instrument of sabotage.

The therapist schedules a session with the father in order to develop the appropriate interventions with his son. Lacking the hoped-for collaboration with the alienating parent, the therapist must formulate a strategy with the targeted parent to counter his son's likely resistance to the reunification. The therapist explores with the father what he anticipates from his son and what his goals are for the first session. The father responds that he has no doubt that his son will accuse him of having abandoned him, stemming from a very brief period of time when he withdrew from his life due to the seemingly insurmountable barriers which had been erected by his former wife. The therapist suggests that the father considers a non-defensive response which acknowledges his own behaviors in that episode (joining, reframing, and a challenge). The therapist validates (joining) the father's belief that his son has likely become a puppet of his alienating mother. This development will require of the father that he not transfer his anger for his ex-wife onto his son (challenge). The father accepts the therapist's counsel to correct any misperceptions about himself without casting aspersions on the mother (reframing).

The boy enters the therapist's office and addresses his father by his first name (their enactment begins). The boy grants the recognition of "father" only when preceded by the word "absentee." He further labels his father with degrading epithets, such as "selfish," "opportunistic," and "untrustworthy." Tears well up in the father's eyes, and he expresses his pain upon hearing these demeaning comments (reframing, challenging, intensity). The boy is unmoved and unapologetic. He tenaciously holds firm that his father is worthless because he "abandoned" him; and, in puppet-like mode, the boy exclaims to his father that he does not have genuine motives for seeking a relationship with him. The father apologizes profusely for the brief period when he withdrew from his life, and the father further declares that he would do it very differently if he had it to do over (reframing, intensity). He clarifies for his son that, while he was responsible for some of their estrangement, he was not at fault the preponderance of the time, when he had fought tenaciously to have contact with him. The father begins to sob about the events in their lives that have brought them to the current sad state of affairs (reframing, intensity). The boy, again, is not at all gracious in response to his father's vulnerability and humility. He adamantly declines to accept his father's apology, regrets, or his efforts at rebuilding their relationship. Nevertheless, the therapist observes the boy holding back tears (restructuring) and then quickly masking his emotions with bravado by exclaiming that his mother has told him that his father will see him only if another obligation brings him to their neighborhood and that his father cannot be trusted to remain in his life.

The therapist's optimism that the mother will not sabotage the reunification is fading. It is further clear to her that the boy feels caught between his parents out of loyalty to his mother on the one hand and to the efforts being put forth by his father on the other: the boy's deprecations of his father were reminiscent of the mother's prior comments to the therapist that the father was insincere and manipulative. At the same time, the boy's unsuccessful attempts to repress his positive emotional reactions to his father are patently observable. The therapist determines to contact the mother again in an attempt to gain her collaboration. The mother refuses a face-to-face session but accepts an extended phone session. The therapist discusses with her the frightening statistics on the damage done to children due to a hostile parental relationship. The mother is more receptive to the therapist's input, and she listens to the statistics which the therapist quotes from the book, *Fatherneed* (Pruett, 2000) (reframing). She is sobered by the high rate of suicidal ideation, acting-out behaviors, and criminal activities of adolescent males when their father does not play a meaningful role in their lives (intensity). The therapist again reminds the mother of the admonition from the court about the expectation for her to support the reunification process (challenge, unbalancing). The mother commits to do a better job at masking from her son the negative feelings she holds for his father (restructuring).

On his part, the father does not give up, despite his son's anger, resistance, and challenge at almost every turn. He keeps showing up—to every degrading session; he shares his pain regarding the state of their relationship, at times sobbing about his fear of losing his son permanently; he expresses to his son that he is the most important person in his life and that he gets depressed at the thought that they may not overcome their estrangement; and, without casting aspersions on the boy's mother, he recounts all his legal efforts to enforce his parental rights and visitation (reframing). He is coached by the therapist to avoid transferring his anger for his former wife to his son when his son enacts the role of the puppet of his mother (challenge). The boy begins to soften in about 6 weeks, at which time the father asks him for suggestions as to how they can move forward (restructuring). The boy suggests meeting outside of the sessions for lunch, for short walks in the park, for a trip to the beach, etc. The mother sanctions these arrangements, which supplement the weekly therapeutic sessions (restructuring). The boy and his father report to the therapist that these more natural settings have facilitated an ease and comfort in their relationship. The limited outside activities are so successful that all-day visits begin after 2 months of the therapy's commencement, and weekend sleepovers commence after 3 months. And, yes, by the end of the second month, the boy began calling his father "Dad."

When the extended weekend visits are initiated the therapist suggests to the mother that being "off duty" had been well earned, and the therapist explores with her in what ways she might use the time to take care of herself (joining). The mother appreciates the therapist's concern for her well-being.

The therapy sessions transitioned from an environment which was merely a venting of deprecating comments by the boy that had to be combated by the father, to one that facilitated the deepening of the father–son bond (restructuring). The therapist coached (challenged) the father to relinquish his defensiveness when hearing his son's legitimate concerns, such as how he silences him by interrupting him, and at the spurious allegations, as well as to tolerate his son's difference of opinions. Shortly thereafter, the boy reported that he had informed his mother that he does not like it when she demeans his father to him or when she puts him in the middle of their parental disputes (terrific restructuring). Ten months into the therapy, the boy and father were spontaneously sharing their respective fears of being hurt, and had developed a metaphor for their respective pain: they each carry a "mask" behind which they can hide in self-protection (positive intensity). The father helped his son with his issue with trust by using self-disclosure about how he handled his own difficulties with peers when he was his son's age. The father encouraged his son to engage in peer activities, such as sports, as the boy was socially withdrawn. The therapist used self-disclosure (spontaneity) about her own traumatic childhood due to peer rejection, the purpose of this being to keep the father and son focused on the issue. Several times during the therapy they diverted from the subject to avoid the painful feelings associated with the material. By taking the risk of sharing her own painful experiences, the therapist pushed the father and the boy to delve into more emotionally charged material (focus). The father learned from the therapy to respect his son's differing opinions about life and to respect his right to his own feelings (restructuring). The therapist congratulated (working with strengths) the father and affirmed for him that this is how healthy self-esteem develops—as a result of how parents relate to and respect their children as well as how they interact with each other.

The boy eventually accomplished what the therapist had been unable to do: get his parents to communicate with each other on his behalf (restructuring).

He did so by failing several subjects. The mother initiated contact with the father, and the two of them met on their own to implement a plan to set limits on and consequences for their son and to put an end to his ability to manipulate them. The therapist was convinced that this development was facilitated by the father, who overcame any temptation to demean the mother to the boy and because he did not blame her for their son's problems. The parents collaborated, and gradually the boy's behavior was brought under control.

The therapy reached a pinnacle when the boy and the father shared with each other in session their respective poetry writings. This experience opened up the two to a deeper and more meaningful exchange of feelings. The boy's fear of relationships was revealed in his poems, and his father guided him through this process acknowledging that his role models had not been the best. The father then added that he and the boy's mother were working conscientiously together to model the corrective relationship which they would like him to eventually develop with a partner. The father read one of his poems about a boy and his father who had been estranged but who eventually found each other. The two of them, along with the therapist, became particularly maudlin at that moment (positive intensity and restructuring).

The therapy lasted for a year and a half, beginning with weekly sessions between the boy and his father and then decreasing to biweekly sessions. The therapist remained in periodic phone contact with the mother throughout. When the therapist summed up treatment, the boy and his father agreed that their relationship was meaningful and that the boy was maturing age-appropriately.[1]

Concluding Remarks

PAS is a devastating form of emotional child abuse, but it is preventable. PAS is a dysfunctional family interactional pattern which intensifies appreciably when the professionals in the larger social systems (the mental health community, Child Protective Services, law enforcement, and the judiciary) become co-opted by the alienating parent and empower her/him in response. Eradication of PAS therefore requires a systemic approach to intervention—intervention must be undertaken with the entire family system and with these larger social systems so that the therapist is afforded a level playing field upon which to treat the family. The professional in the mental health community is generally the first line of defense in prevention because therapy is frequently sought *prior* to the decision to divorce. At such time, the perverse triangle is likely in its nascent stages and is therefore most amenable to reversal. It is incumbent upon the mental health professional to involve both parents, when both are available, in order to obtain a full and accurate picture of what is happening in the family and to the child. This approach has the optimal possibility of producing healthy family functioning, even if divorce is later sought. Should therapy be initiated subsequent to the decision to divorce, the therapist must not become seduced by the alienating parent and by the child into maintaining the homeostasis of the family, which is all too often the outcome of an individual treatment approach.

Effective treatment of the PAS family requires knowledge of family dynamics and of effective intervention strategies for dealing with a highly rigid family organizational pattern. Treatment of only the alienated child, who is typically diagnosed with anxiety and post-traumatic stress disorder owing to the spurious allegations of child abuse, addresses only the symptoms. This approach fails to remedy the underlying dysfunctional family interactional patterns that are creating and maintaining the symptoms.

Regrettably, no treatment modality can claim to be a panacea for any particular emotional or behavioral issue. Indeed, research indicates that one-third of individual patients and one-third of families fail to return to treatment after the initial therapy session. The larger social systems are currently inundated with professional literature and widespread therapy practices that have documented and substantiated the existence of PAS and how to diagnose it. But very little has been documented about treatment. Gottlieb's (2012) treatment summaries are a good anecdotal beginning, but research on treatment is acutely needed. With PAS, time is of the essence: the earlier it is treated, the more likely is a reversal; the longer it persists, the more likely there will be a point of no return. The existence of PAS should no longer be disputed. It is therefore time to refocus energy on its prevention and treatment.

Note

1 Identical treatment interventions are offered when the alienator is the father. Appropriate literature on the importance of mothers to their children is offered in place of the information from *Fatherneed.*

References

Ackerman, N. W. (1958). *The psychodynamics of family life.* New York: Basic Books.

Ackerman, N. W. (1961). The emergence of family psychotherapy on the present scene. In M. I. Stein, (Ed.), *Contemporary psychotherapies.* Glencoe, IL: Free Press.

Ackerman, N. W. (1966). *Treating the troubled family.* New York: Basic Books.

Ackerman, N. W., & Franklin, P. (1965). Family dynamics and the reversibility of delusional formation: A case study in family therapy. In I. Boszormenyi-Nagy & J. Famo (Eds.), *Intensive family therapy.* New York: Harper and Row.

Andolfi, M., Angelo, C., Menghi, P., & Nicolo-Corigliano, A. (1983). *Behind the family mask: Therapeutic change in rigid family systems.* New York: Brunner/Mazel.

Andolfi, M., Angelo, C., & Nichilo, M. (1989). *The myth of atlas: Families and the therapeutic story.* New York: Brunner/Mazel.

Baker, A. J. L. (2007). *Adult children of parental alienation syndrome: Breaking the ties that bind.* New York: W. W Norton.

Bateson, G., Jackson, D., Haley, J., & Weakland, J. (1956). Toward a theory of schizophrenia. *Behavioral Sciences, 1,* 252–264.

Bateson, G., & Jackson, D. (1964). Some varieties of pathogenic organization. *Disorders of Communication, 42,* 270–283.

Bowen, M. (1971). The use of family theory in clinical practice. In J. Haley (Ed.), *Changing families: A family therapy reader* (pp. 159–192). New York: Grune & Stratton.

Bowen, M. (1978). *Family therapy in clinical practice.* New York: Jason Aronson.

Gardner, R. A. (1985). Recent trends in divorce and custody litigation. *Academy Forum* (a publication of the American Academy of Psychoanalysis), *29(2)*, 3–7.

Gardner, R. A. (1998). *The parental alienation syndrome* (2nd ed.). Cresskill, NJ: Creative Therapeutics.

Gardner, R. A. (2001). *Therapeutic interventions for children with parental alienation syndrome.* Cresskill, NJ: Creative Therapeutics.

Gottlieb, L. J. (2012). *The parental alienation syndrome: A family therapy and collaborative systems approach to amelioration.* Springfield, IL: Charles C. Thomas.

Haley, J. (1963). *Strategies of psychotherapy* (1st ed.) New York: Grune & Stratton.

Haley, J. (1971). *Changing families.* New York: Grune & Stratton.

Haley, J. (1973). *Uncommon therapy.* New York: W. W. Norton.

Haley, J. (1977). Toward a theory of pathological systems. In P. Watzlawick & J. Weakland (Eds.), *The interactional view* (pp. 37–44). New York: Basic Books.

Haley, J. (1990). *Strategies of psychotherapy*, Rockville, MD: Triangle Press.

Haley, J., & Hoffman, L. (Eds.). (1968). *Techniques of family therapy.* New York: Basic Books.

Hoffman, L. (1981). *Foundations of family therapy.* New York: Basic Books.

Jackson, D. D., & Weakland, J. (1971). Conjoint family therapy: Some considerations on theory, technique, and results. In J. Haley (Ed.), *Changing families* (pp. 13–35). New York: Grune & Stratton.

Minuchin, S. (1974). *Families and family therapy.* Cambridge, MA: Harvard University Press.

Minuchin, S., Baker, L., & Rosman, B. (1978). *Psychosomatic families: Anorexia nervosa in context.* Cambridge, MA: Harvard University Press.

Minuchin, S., & Fishman, C. (1981). *Family therapy techniques.* Cambridge, MA: Harvard University Press.

Minuchin, S., Lee, W., & Simon, G. (1996). *Mastering family therapy.* New York: John Wiley & Sons.

Minuchin, S., & Nichols, M. (1993). *Family healing.* New York: Free Press.

Minuchin, S., Nichols, M., & Lee, W. (2007). Assessing families and couples: From symptom to system. New York, NY: Pearson.

Napier, A. Y., & Whitaker, C. (1978). *The family crucible: The intense experience of family therapy.* New York: Harper Perennial.

Nichols, M. P. (1992). *The power of family therapy.* Lake Worth, FL: Gardner Press.

Nichols, M., & Schwartz, R. C. (2004). *Family therapy: Concepts and methods.* New York: Pearson.

Pruett, K. D. (2000). *FatherNeed: Why father care is as essential as mother care for your child.* New York: Free Press.

Whitaker, C. A. (1958). Psychotherapy with couples. *American Journal of Psychotherapy, 12(1)*, 18–23.

Whitaker, C.A. (1967). The growing edge. In J. Haley & L. Hoffman, (Eds.), *Techniques of family therapy.* New York: Basic Books.

Whitaker, C. A. (1989). *Midnight musings of a family therapist.* M. Ryan (Ed.) New York: W. W. Norton.

Whitaker, C. A., & Bumberry, W. (1988). *Dancing with the family: A symbolic-experiential approach.* New York: Brunner/Mazel.

Young v. *Young*, No. 94/09240. (Supreme Court, Nassau County, NY. 1994). *Young* v. *Young*, 212 A.D.2d 114; 628 N. Y. S.2d 957 (1995). Available at: http://www.jdbar.com/cases/young.html [accessed August 14, 2012].

12 Family Reunification in a Forensic Setting

Jane Albertson-Kelly and Barbara Burkhard

Introduction

Family reunification in a forensic setting refers to treatment services that are ordered by a court as part of ongoing litigation. The word "forensic" itself is defined as that which pertains to the court. Family reunification treatment (FRT), as developed under the auspices of the Foundation for Child and Family Inc., is one of several types of therapeutic visitation services specially designed for children experiencing difficulties with one or both parents, including children who are victims of maltreatment or abuse. FRT, the subject of this chapter, specifically targets children who refuse visitation with a parent. Most of these children meet the behavioral criteria for parental alienation syndrome (PAS) (Gardner, 1998). From a legal perspective, a court has failed to find a legal basis to warrant the children's continued estrangement from the parent and has turned to the mental health professional to assist in solving the problem. Thus, the treatment is not only initiated by the court, but is also an integration of court and clinical services.

Court orders for FRT typically arise out of the Family Court or Supreme (or Superior) Court where family disputes involving divorce and custodial issues are adjudicated. Consider as a typical example, the case of the Smith[1] family. Mr. Smith was seeking a change from joint custody to sole custody of his daughter. In his motion he alleged that his ex-wife had denied him contact with his daughter for 9 months, in violation of the terms of their divorce. In reviewing the case, the court heard from the mother that the child was refusing to see her father. She explained that Mr. Smith had always had a difficult relationship with the child, as he is short-tempered and expects too much from his daughter. Ms. Smith stated that she supported the child's wish not to see him. Mr. Smith maintained that prior to the divorce he had had a positive relationship with his daughter, enjoying family trips as well as sports and weekend activities. When interviewed by the judge in chambers, the child reported that she was fearful of her father because he was "always mean and threatening." She denied ever having had any positive experiences with him. When shown photographs of herself and her father, taken during the previous summer (provided by Mr. Smith), the child informed the judge that she was "just faking" the broad smiles evident in the pictures.

When a case such as the Smith's is heard in the family court, it may be ordered that the parents participate in some form of reunification treatment to resolve the problems and avoid further legal intervention, including a trial. When this occurs a court order is signed by the judge, directing the parents and the child to participate in the treatment at an agreed-upon facility.

The court order received by a forensic treatment facility typically provides only basic guidelines. In the case of the Smith family, the court order specified that: (1) the agency was to provide reunification treatment for the child and her father, (2) both parents and the child were to cooperate with all therapeutic procedures, (3) the parents were to share equally in the costs of the treatment, and (4) the court was to be provided with periodic status reports, with the treating psychologist responding to the court as the court's witness.

Over the past 8 years the Foundation for Child and Family has been working with court-referred children and their families in an attempt to meet the needs of these families. The treatment model developed and presented here is the result of this experience with the PAS population.

An Integrated Treatment Model

Initial experience with families referred by the court led to the observation that treatment without the court's involvement was not likely to be effective. The approach that evolved is a model of treatment that utilizes an integrated relationship between the mental health professionals and the court in order to bring about changes to mitigate both the legal and psychological problems associated with PAS.

The model assumes two theoretical principles. The first is that positive change in the family requires that *the parents re-establish their roles as the primary decision-makers for their children.* In working with PAS families, it has been observed that the children are frequently over-empowered to make decisions. This is most evident in (but not limited to) the child's freedom to choose to avoid all contact with the targeted parent. In many cases the "favored" or current residential parent has abdicated the decision-making to the child. In typical cases the child's empowered "decisions" to avoid or denigrate the targeted parent may not, in fact, be the child's true desire, but reflect the child acting on the favored parent's behalf. Nevertheless, from a functional perspective, the child behaves as if all of his decisions are of his own making and the favored parent defers to the child. The targeted parent, the one who is estranged from the child, has typically lost parenting authority altogether. That is, if he or she attempts to insist that the child follow rules, even those agreed upon by both parents, the child will, in all likelihood, disregard that parent's authority and find ways to work around compliance with that parent's requests or directives.

From a developmental perspective there is reason to be concerned about the over-empowerment of children that PAS may engender. It is not surprising that alienated children are often observed to generalize their rejection of the parents' authority to school personnel and other authority figures. Although data are only now being gathered, case examples strongly suggest significant antisocial sequelae in severe PAS cases. For example, a lovely young adolescent in a local forensic practice never reunified with her mother. The girl's denigrating and acting-out behaviors were successful in convincing a court that she should not have contact with her mother. However, once the case was decided in the father's favor her behaviors continued and expanded to school refusal, and she left the father's home to spend time with drug-involved friends. This once high-achieving adolescent eventually became a crack cocaine addict and high-school dropout.

Irrespective of the long-term developmental consequences, preliminary research indicates that children who are referred for FRT and who are overly empowered in terms of decision-making also tend to act out behaviorally with greater frequency and severity during treatment than children who are ordered to therapy for other reasons (Baker, Burkhard, & Albertson-Kelly, 2012). These children behave as if they have license to do as they wish. Their inappropriate behaviors may extend from the parent to the office and therapeutic staff as well. The first goal, then, is to assist the family in reallocating the power so that both parents have reasonable authority to set limits on the children's behaviors that are outside the boundaries of acceptability as per the beliefs and values of the parents.

The second principle underlying the model is that all family members need to *accept personal responsibility for their own thoughts and actions.* In the course of a high-conflict divorce it is not uncommon for parents to minimize their responsibility for problems while exaggerating claims of wrongdoing by the other parent. Children who are caught in the conflict and take up the cause of the favored parent may take on that parent's exaggerated recollections as their own. A child might report, for example, "My father broke my model airplane when I was seven. He is *always* mean and I never want to see him again." It is not uncommon for severely alienated children to deny that their targeted parents ever acted in a positive manner toward them. Many report that they cannot recall a single pleasant experience involving the targeted parent. When confronted with photographs memorializing them having fun with the targeted parent, alienated children have been known to accuse the targeted parent of altering the photographs. Perhaps even more enlightening are children's recollections of events that preceded their ability to have memory. For example, "My dad spanked me when I was only two" or "Before my parents got married, my mom told my dad that she didn't want to have any children."

As per the identified characteristics of alienated children (Gardner, 1998), it is not uncommon for a child to make exaggerated or unrealistic claims against the targeted parent, neglecting to acknowledge his or her own responsibility for his or her share of an incident. Failure to accept personal responsibility is apparent when a child directs unfiltered blame toward the targeted parent so as not only to denigrate the parent but also to avoid punishment for his/her own misdeeds. For example, in the early stages of treatment, a child was observed working on his homework during a reunification visit with his father. Quite early in the session, the child informed his father that he was ready to play a game because he had completed all of his assignments. In fact, the child had hidden additional worksheets in a separate folder in his book bag. When later confronted by the favored mother as to why his homework was not completed, the child alleged that the father refused to do his homework with him and forced him to play a game instead. The mother blamed the father for the incident. The responsibility for the unfinished homework was thus deflected to the conflict between the parents and the son received little, if any, consequence for lying and not doing his homework. This family dynamic is associated with a negative impact on children's moral development (Baker, 2007; Warshak, 2001).

In order for normal family functioning and a healthy trajectory for child development to be restored, all family members need to assume normal responsibility for errors or wrongs, apologizing for mistakes or incidents that have harmed another and describing how they will behave differently in the future. Parents, as well as children, must be permitted to seek forgiveness for human errors and to forgive others. One cannot be held forever accountable for perceived failures, some of which have not yet occurred (e.g., "He will *never* do anything right for me"). Healthy family development is established by applying the principles of rational thinking, truthful perception, and accountability in all familial interactions.

Treatment Components and Procedures

The treatment model is a multifaceted approach to intervention that can be deconstructed into its components. Although these parts are presented separately, it should be understood that they operate simultaneously. The components are presented from a conceptual point of view and are not meant to function as a session-by-session guide. The application of the components may vary from one case to another and skill is required of the treating professional to determine the most effective way to adapt the various components to each case.

Component 1: Integration of Clinic and the Court

An essential component of the treatment model is the use of the court system to assist in moving the parties toward the desired goals. As in the old joke, it only takes one psychologist to change a light bulb, but the light bulb *really* has to want to change. In the case of FRT, the desire for change in the children and the favored parent is often absent. Parental alienation characterizes a state of dysfunction that, at least in the short term, may appear to meet the needs of some family members. As a result, this state is often strongly maintained. The alienating parent is typically comfortable with the favored status and the children may feel some degree of relief at having established an entrenched camp on one side of the parental war. The only person who expresses a need for change is the targeted parent.

The work, to date, of the Foundation for Child and Family suggests that the balance between the clinic treatment and the court is an essential one.

When an effective and efficient working relationship between clinic and court is established, normal family functioning is more likely to be restored. As a result, legal cases can be resolved as well. For example, Michael, a 10-year-old boy, ran back and forth to the restroom, reportedly to "vomit," owing to extreme upset over meeting with his father. The child's presentation and arguments about the father were virtually identical to those of his mother, who also appeared emotionally distressed in the office. In-depth assessment of both mother and child suggested the possibility of a diagnosis of shared delusional disorder, highlighting the impact of the mother's histrionic behavior on the child. These concerns were discussed with the mother and a report was sent to the court reflecting these findings. In reviewing the report, the court indicated that unless immediate progress was made the court would consider removal of the child. The following week, not only did Michael stop "vomiting," he was able to leave the office and go out to dinner with his father. From that point, normal visitation was resumed and no further reunification services were required.

In a more difficult case, a targeted father reported at the outset of treatment that he did not expect his ex-wife to comply with the court order to bring his children to treatment, as this program was the third therapeutic service to be ordered by the court. Indeed, the mother maintained that the children had been "severely traumatized" by their father, although there were no protective services or judicial findings to support her claims. The day that the children were scheduled to come to meet the therapist for an orientation session (without the father being present) the mother called for assistance because she was unable to get the children into the car. She was advised that this was a parenting problem and she needed to do whatever she would normally do if her children did not want to do something important or necessary. Ultimately, the children did not appear for the appointment despite assurances that the father would not be present.

A letter was immediately sent to the court indicating that the mother had failed to meet the terms of the court's order and requesting the court's assistance. The response was an emergency hearing, after which the court ordered the mother to pay the full cost of any missed treatment sessions due to the children's failure to attend. This change in the court order resulted in this mother transporting the children to all scheduled appointments with no further difficulty.

This case illustrates a fundamental reality. That is, mental health professionals are limited with respect to their ability to gain the cooperation of clients who are not motivated to make changes in their behavior. In families afflicted with PAS the only means of eliciting cooperation from the alienating parent may be through the court, which has the power to demand compliance with treatment. In some cases, a warning from the court that there may be a change in custody may be sufficient to bring an end to seemingly pathological behaviors and problems. Other cases have necessitated the court enforcing the orders by providing legal or economic sanctions for non-compliance.

Component 2: Assessment and Orientation

At the beginning of treatment each of the parents and all of the children are interviewed individually in order to obtain basic background information and to assess each family member's perspective of the family dynamics. In the case of the parents, an individual intake appointment is also an opportunity to establish a relationship with each parent, providing emotional support for the difficult situation in which the parent finds himself or herself, and clarifying guidelines and boundaries. For example, it is frequently the case that each parent approaches the interview process as if it were a trial, with the expectation that the therapist will decide which side is right and which is wrong. It is important, then, to communicate at the outset that it is not the therapist's role to decide whether the child should visit with the targeted parent. Instead, the role of the therapist is to help develop and implement a plan to re-establish the parental relationship. It is important, therefore, to make clear that the therapist's agenda is to promote relationships between the children and both parents unless there are extenuating circumstances that would preclude such a relationship. In the latter case, a decision to interrupt a relationship between a parent and child would be made by a judge.

The individual intake/assessment session also sets the tone for gaining and giving important information. The therapist asks questions to determine reasons for the estrangement from the targeted parent and to detect ways in which the estrangement is manifested. For example, both parents are asked about the frequency of telephone and other contact, and the degree to which both parents are involved in the school and medical care. The parents are also asked about the child's activities with the extended families on both sides. Additionally, the assessment phase provides an opportunity to evaluate each parent's ability to view the family dynamics from the perspective of the other, an important factor in the success of the process. The intake session may be the first opportunity to assess the alienating parent's understanding of the negative longer-term results of the alienation process on the child's development. Specifically, the relationship between the child's sanctioned defiance of a parent and his or her healthy respect for authority figures in general can be explored at this time.

Finally, each parent is administered basic psychometric instruments that screen for child abuse potential (Milner, 1980) and for psychopathology and personality problems using the Minnesota Multiphasic Personality Inventory-2 Restructured Form (Ben Porath & Tellegen, 2008). The results of these instruments may be used to assist with treatment planning. The results can also be utilized in cases where there are allegations of physical child abuse or unsubstantiated mental illness levied against the targeted parent, or in cases in which there are suggestions that mental illness in a parent might pose challenges for parent–child contact (e.g., mood disorders resulting in unpredictable behavior changes).

The first meeting to assess the child is an orientation session in which the child is encouraged to acclimate to the treatment setting, specifically the room in which the visit is scheduled to take place. He or she is also given an opportunity to articulate the problems that are causing difficulties in the parent–child relationship. Often, the child is highly resistant to the idea of meeting with the parent. At the orientation session, the child is asked to supply a list of grievances that he/she has with the targeted parent, and discuss how these problems might be addressed in the first sessions to help the child feel safe. Generally, this is not an appropriate time to challenge past allegations. Rather, the goal of this orientation is to develop a plan for creating a sense of safety for the child when the child first encounters the targeted parent.

As with the adults, children are administered simple self-report instruments at the beginning of treatment. All children aged 6 years and older are administered a new instrument, the Baker Alienation Questionnaire, which has been demonstrated in a pilot study to discriminate between alienated and not-alienated children (Baker, Burkhard, & Albertson-Kelly, 2012). Additionally, measures of emotional and behavioral adjustment are administered depending on the nature of the case and the age of the children. These may include the Youth Self-Report (Achenbach, 1991), the Behavior Assessment System for Children—Child Self Report-2 (Reynolds & Kamphaus, 1991), or more targeted instruments such as the Child Depression Inventory (Kovacs, 1992). These instruments help to establish a baseline for the child's level of functioning prior to treatment and to determine whether or not challenges to treatment may be present (e.g., attention deficit hyperactivity disorder).

Component 3: Removal of the Child's Decision-Making with Regard to Visitation

As stated above, the child cannot begin the process of reuniting with the targeted parent if he continues to believe that he retains the power to decide whether to visit. It is critical that it is explained to the child that he is bound by a court order and thus does not have a choice about visiting. Furthermore, it is also important to clarify for the child that the decision to visit is not made by the therapist. Rather, it is the therapist's role to help the child make the visitation process go more smoothly. To make this point absolutely clear, the therapist may explain to the child that some children believe that if they act out in an extreme manner the therapist will come to the realization that the child should not visit with the targeted parent and will convey this information to the judge. The therapist explains that the judge already understands that the child does not want to see the targeted parent. It would be the therapist's job to suggest to the judge that the visits should stop only if the targeted parent behaved badly during treatment.

In order to emphasize the nature of the order and not single out the child, it is further explained that the order applies to everyone involved in the case. That is, the child is made aware that both parents are required to cooperate as per the order. Additionally, the therapist underscores to the child that the therapist is also bound by the court order to do her job in the way that the judge expects.

Component 4: Behavioral Management for the Children

In the initial orientation sessions with the therapist, children are also introduced to a second rule: that appropriate behavior is expected. Children who are alienated often act out in the office. Severely alienated children may scream, run out of the building, threaten the targeted parent or therapist, throw things, or present with a barrage of verbally abusive epithets. Experience has shown that it is often helpful in managing these behaviors to set the tone at the beginning of treatment that respectful behavior is required by all. This important rule is presented within the context of the office being a safe and secure place. Should behavioral acting out occur, prompts as to the established rule may bring a resumption of more appropriate behaviors.

In one extreme case of alienation a 10-year-old boy claimed that his father had been physically and verbally abusive to him "all" of his life. This child repeatedly taunted and provoked his father in rude and disrespectful ways. On one occasion he threw his backpack at his father, hitting his father in the chest. On another occasion he deliberately punched his father in the shoulder after learning that he was recovering from shoulder surgery. The father reacted to these behaviors in a reasonable fashion, directing his son to stop. The child's behaviors were brought under control by calmly reminding the child about the rule of respect that is required in the office. Furthermore, the child was reminded that as long as he was provocative and violent it would difficult for the therapist to detect the abusive nature of his father's behavior, something the child had alleged.

In some cases it may be necessary to ask for the favored parent's assistance in reining in the child's behaviors. In one such instance, severely alienated siblings eloped from the office and ran about the parking lot. As the favored parent could not reasonably endorse this behavior in her children, she was asked to intervene as the custodial parent and insist that the behavior cease as being unsafe and inappropriate. When the mother was held accountable for the behavior, it promptly stopped.

Component 5: Exposure in a Safe Place

Prior to the initiation of treatment, alienated children may have avoided all contact with the targeted parent. Because any past contact is likely to have been denigrating, parent and child need a place where more appropriate interactions can be established. In the safe office setting, the child and parent have the opportunity to re-establish some level of comfort in simply being together, playing, and talking.

Many alienated children report being afraid of the targeted parent. The integrated treatment model operates under the assumption that it is possible that the child is genuinely afraid of the rejected parent. This explanation for the child's avoidance of the parent must be explored and/or ruled out at the beginning. Anxiety is addressed in several ways. First, from a psycho-educational perspective, it is emphasized that the office is a safe and secure environment. It is especially helpful to provide information to the favored parent that children, even severely abused children, are able to determine that they will not be harmed in this safe setting. By establishing the expectation that the child will be able to perceive the office as a safe place, even severely alienated children can be distracted from false allegations of anxiety and trauma in the office setting.

Second, in preparation for the visits, parents and children are assisted in understanding the difference between feeling *uncomfortable* and feeling *afraid*. That is, feelings of discomfort or anxiety are likely to occur in situations that are associated with conflict. Therefore discomfort is likely to occur in treatment, at least initially. These feelings are managed through an *in vivo* desensitization process (Wolpe, 1958). The time that the child spends with the targeted parent is gradually increased. The level and intensity of therapist involvement and supervision is gradually decreased. The treatment approach utilizes techniques aimed at providing graduated exposure to the reported feared stimulus (e.g., the targeted parent). Depending on the child, and the degree of anxiety reported, this exposure may vary. For example, in the case of a child who reports terror at the thought of meeting with his/her parent, the therapist and child may develop a hierarchy consisting of gradually increasing steps toward exposure. For example, the child may begin by observing the parent via a one-way mirror while a second therapist engages the targeted parent in conversation. This would occur prior to more direct parent–child contact being initiated. Cognitive therapy together with relaxation techniques may be included as well. More commonly, the child is introduced to the targeted parent with the initial sessions designed to be very short and pleasant, perhaps recalling pleasurable experiences from the past. Subsequent sessions are of somewhat longer duration, and may involve "fading" of the therapist from the visitation room to the observation room. Comfort level is assessed based on direct observation and on the child's self-report using a simple questionnaire at the end of each session.

Children report fear and anxiety from multiple sources. In addition to that generated by the perception of wrongdoing by the targeted parent, many children express the belief that their targeted parent will be angry at their avoidance of him or her. Further, there is likely to be some anticipatory anxiety due to the fact that there has been a lapse in contact. It is assumed that for a child experiencing genuine anxiety, increased contact with the targeted parent in a physically and psychologically safe setting (e.g., with reassurances provided by the targeted parent) will result in a *decrease* in anxiety and a concomitant increase in comfort level with the targeted parent in this office setting. However, should the child or favored parent report *increased* anxiety and increased resistance to visiting in this setting, it is likely that the problems are not caused by actual anxiety or fear. Rather, it is more likely that these problems are the result of an effort on the part of the child and/or the favored parent to preserve the child's alienated status.

When the child or favored parent does report increased anxiety and resistance, the information is noted in the record, and may be provided to the court if requested. This observation may be a significant part of documentation that may lead to sanctions or other decisions made by the court in the event that FRT continues to be unsuccessful. Sometimes the information is presented to the favored parent in order to provide insight to this parent. That is, the favored parent is informed directly that increased anxiety symptoms in response to gradual exposure are *not* consistent with true anxiety. More importantly, he or she is informed that cessation of treatment is not indicated. Often, the favored parent's employment of this strategy to end contact with the targeted parent may then be abandoned.

Component 6: Developing Alternative Parenting Strategies

Targeted parents are often highly distressed individuals who feel an overwhelming desire to "set the record straight" with their children. It is not unusual for a targeted parent to believe that if he or she can just explain what *really* happened, or confront the child with the truth, the child will stop engaging in the alienated behaviors. Unfortunately, these solutions are not usually effective. PAS children simply reject offers of the truth and become more resistant.

In FRT, much of the work with the targeted parent is oriented toward avoiding confrontations over the truth and refraining from reacting to the abnormal disrespectful behaviors. Parents are coached as to how to respond when their children make accusations or behave provocatively (Baker & Fine, 2008). Typically, parents are taught ways to engage and respond to children so as to validate the children's reported feelings and show appreciation for them as valuable and loved children, while subtly setting limits on provocative and rude behaviors. Parents are specifically coached not to enter power struggles with their children and to refrain from attempts to make their children "wrong" when discussing the past. Although a basic principle of the program demands rationality, this applies primarily to the present and the future rather than the past, where "truth" is difficult to assess. The focus of treatment, particularly in the beginning, involves helping the parent and children find ways to work toward a resolution for the future without forcing the children to justify their past behaviors or beliefs.

Responding effectively is often extremely difficult for targeted parents. Targeted parents are often subjected to hurtful and disrespectful behaviors from their children, who perhaps only months before behaved in a loving manner. These parents are then asked by the therapist to abandon normal parenting practices aimed at correcting these rude and disrespectful behaviors. The parenting tactics employed in the treatment can be difficult for targeted parents to implement because they are at odds with normal parenting tendencies and are not consistent with a parent's natural inclination to correct a child's wildly rude and disrespectful behavior. Targeted parents require practice in learning these somewhat artificial ways of responding. They also require support and reassurance that their "real" children are alive and well under the façade of alienation. The most successful targeted parents are those who are able to see that their children are victims rather than perpetrators, and work hard to find those moments when they can give and, sometimes, receive some kindness and love. One father has been able to persevere even though his alienated children continue to be provocative during his visitation, call him names, refuse to eat his food, and make a mess in his home. He has noted that despite their destructive behaviors, his children have never harmed objects that represent their relationship with him from their earlier childhood, such as handmade Father's Day gifts and special toys he has given them.

Component 7: Problem-Solving and Contracting

In treatment sessions, children are offered an opportunity to work out difficulties, perceived or real, with the targeted parent. These issues generally reflect the child's perspective. The discussion facilitated by the therapist is aimed at helping the child identify what he or she believes to be the obstacles to a normal parent–child relationship. Efforts at overcoming the obstacles are then encouraged. In some cases it may be appropriate for the targeted parent to offer apologies for his or her part in the dissolution of the family or for being part of a process that caused the child conflict or upset. In many cases the child may demand apologies for transgressions that the targeted parent denies or that appear improbable. These demands create challenges in that the parent must respond to the child in a manner that validates the child's feelings. However, it is important to maintain the focus on the future by continuing to encourage the generation of solutions for potential problems, rather than defending or denying past behaviors.

Joseph B., a 10-year-old boy, insisted that his father had threatened to kill his mother's new husband, with whom Joseph had a very positive and perhaps competing relationship. Although his father, Mr. B., the targeted parent, was not happy with many aspects of the stepfather's relationship with his son, he described himself as a peace-loving individual who would never threaten to kill anyone. The "incident" was explored with Joseph but, as is typically the case, the only information forthcoming from the child was, "He said it; I am afraid of him; I never want to see him again."

This "memory" of wrongdoing was handled by having Mr. B validate Joseph's understandable fear, if he had in fact heard such a thing. That is, Mr. B. told Joseph that he could understand that if Joseph had heard him say such a thing, Mr. B. would understand that Joseph would be terrified. Mr. B. went on to say that he did not recall ever saying that, and he in fact did not wish the stepfather or anyone else in Joseph's family harm. Mr. B. explained that if he had said something that sounded like this, even as a way of speaking to someone else, and Joseph had heard him, he felt very badly. Mr. B. and the therapist then gave examples as to how this might have happened by mistake or through poor problem-solving. For example, Mr. B. might have said to someone else on the phone, "This is just killing me" or "This is enough frustration to make me want to kill him." Working with both father and child, the therapist asked

Joseph if there had been any indication that the father had ever tried to kill his stepfather. Joseph begrudgingly acknowledged that he had not, but quickly stated he could not trust his father. The therapist then asked Mr. B. if he could agree that he would (1) not harm the stepfather in the future and (2) be more careful about using the word "kill" in the future. Mr. B. agreed to this. The therapist asked Joseph if this agreement from his father would help him to feel better. Joseph, although non-committal, did not bring up this issue again during the treatment.

Contracting, as illustrated above, is used in conjunction with problem-solving and functions by encouraging the child and parent to come to an agreement as to how each will behave in the future. Contracting is a good way to allow children to "save face" in maintaining their allegations of wrongdoing, but enhances the process of reunification. That is, the child "contracts" to spend time with the targeted parent as long as he or she "contracts" not to engage in objectionable behaviors that allegedly occurred in the past. In the case of Joseph and his father, the father's agreement not to harm the stepfather and to be more careful using the word "kill" in the future resolved the issue for treatment purposes.

Component 8: Working with the Favored Parent

In cases involving parental alienation, treatment will not be fully effective as long as the alienation effort continues. In addition to explaining the process of FRT, it is essential to work with the favored parent to attempt to determine what may be generating and maintaining the alienation process. In some cases, the favored parent is not aware that his or her parenting is failing to foster a positive relationship with the targeted parent. In these cases, education may be sufficient to bring about a change.

In one case, a mother whose testing and presentation was consistent with a severe anxiety disorder acknowledged that it had been difficult for her to separate from her child. When it was time for the child to visit with the father, the mother described going to extra lengths to make sure that the child would be "comfortable" leaving her. As the visits continued the child began crying and clinging, displaying great difficulty leaving the mother. The mother, in turn, interpreted the child's responses as indicative of problems in the relationship with the father. This became the genesis of the full visitation refusal that ensued. In this case, work with the mother assisted in case resolution, as she was able to gain insight that her anxiety was inducing anxiety and visitation refusal in the child. When the mother was able to control her own behavior better during the transfer, and was able to act in a manner that was more supportive, the relationship between the child and the father was greatly enhanced.

In all cases it is important to make the best effort to work with the favored parent, even though this may be very difficult. It is critical that each parent becomes educated as to the needs of children to have a relationship with both parents and the negative impact of alienation. This is accomplished by eliciting the parent's ideas and also by offering psychoeducational information. The favored parent may be provided with research findings (e.g., Baker, 2007) as to how children may come to view this relationship loss later in life. In addition to informing the alienating parent as to the potential impact of the loss of parental relationships on children in general, the parent is encouraged to examine how such a loss may manifest itself in the development of his or her particular child. It is also critical for the favored parent to feel supported through the FRT process.

However, once a truly alienating parent understands that the therapist is not going to stop the visitation process, he or she may become very resistant. In severe cases of alienation, the favored parent may not be amenable to any intervention. Favored parents may act out, holding their quivering children in the waiting room, providing comfort before the children meet with the targeted parent. These parents may deliberately attempt to convey the message that there is much to be feared, thus undermining the treatment goal of creating a safe environment in which to proceed with reunification. In some cases, acting out by the favored parent is so extreme that the reunification process is better served by having someone other than the favored parent transport the child to and from treatment. In such cases, removal of the favored parent from the office often greatly improves the compliance and overall stability of the children. Should the favored parent be unwilling to cooperate with the therapist, the therapist may need to seek sanctions from the court. In cases in which the parent is removed from the process or is sanctioned by the judge, either monetarily or occasionally with a temporary change in child custody, the problems are often significantly ameliorated.

Component 9: Monitoring Check Out/Check In

As sessions in the office become more comfortable and the visitation becomes more routine, supervision may be gradually withdrawn by having the parent and children go out of the office for dinner or other activities. Children and parents "check out" with the therapist and then check back in to work on any difficulties that may have transpired during the outside visit. This procedure may be extended to visits that become in-home visits, overnights, and more extended stays with the targeted parent, until returning to the office for processing problems is no longer necessary. Many times, the "check-in" process becomes a burden to the children and they prefer to visit without therapeutic assistance.

Component 10: Co-Parenting

Because alienation occurs in the context of high-conflict parental relationships, the child–parent problems often develop as a direct result of disputes between the parents. In many FRT cases, the focus of treatment eventually shifts from a child–parent paradigm to a co-parenting model. Once children have re-established contact with the targeted parent on a normal schedule, or some approximation to a normal schedule, a co-parenting procedure can often be helpful in maintaining the gains and moving the case to healthier resolution for the entire family. Relatively insignificant problems can be discussed and worked out in a co-parenting session, rather than in sessions directly involving the child.

Often, in co-parenting sessions, the therapist is able to provide normative information regarding child behavior, which may correct a parent's misattribution about the other parent. For example, one co-parenting session was dominated by a young mother who believed that her toddler son's recent aggressive behavior toward his sister was the direct result of the child's father being punitive, which he denied. When the mother was given information about normal toddler behavior and appropriate strategies for managing the behavior, her view perceptibly changed.

Topics for Discussion

Is this therapy?

FRT is not traditional therapy in which a therapeutic alliance between the therapist and client is the primary means of facilitating change. The issue of an alliance between the mental health professional and the client is not the critical issue in FRT. That is, the focus of intervention in FRT is not the relationship between the mental health professional and the child, but rather the relationship between the child and his or her parents. To reiterate, the assumption underlying this treatment model is that the pathology observed in the child is the result of parental dysfunction, which empowers the child to make decisions and judgments that the child is ill equipped to make. The goal of the treatment is to alter this dynamic between child and parents. In this process it is not unusual for the child to express increasing dislike for the therapist who is working to significantly diminish his or her power. This should not be construed as meaning that the "therapy" is not working. Rather it is a likely indicator that treatment is beginning to be effective.

Coercion in Treatment

The question may be legitimately raised as to whether or not children, some of whom may be adolescent and capable of complex thought, should be forced to participate in treatment against their will. In FRT, children are often outspoken that they do not want to participate in or have anything to do with the treatment. Treatment within the context of parental alienation is likely to result in conflict for children. It is certainly understandable that a child would prefer to avoid the stress inherent in reunification with a parent rather than cope with the emotional discomfort associated with such meetings. Favored parents and their children often state that they would prefer to wait until the child is older, "is ready," or "wants to" see the targeted parent before proceeding with reunification. While in theory this may seem like a reasonable request, avoidance of a relationship is not likely to be an effective means of healing and may lead to a more deeply ingrained breach or the ultimate loss of an important relationship.

Consider a child taking an algebra course in high school. If ninth graders were presented with the option of taking algebra in school or waiting until they were "ready," say at the age of 25, some would undoubtedly choose the latter. Adults make this choice for ninth graders because it is adults who possess the insight regarding the long-term opportunities timely education in mathematics affords. A ninth grader opting out of algebra, because he or she does not like sitting through algebra class and doing all the homework, is like a child opting out of a parental relationship because he or he does not wish to experience the stress associated with the reunification process. In doing so, the opportunities for developing a meaningful relationship with the parent decrease. Further, the child learns that relationships are not really worth the effort it takes to work them through.

The very articulate 13-year-old daughter of two divorced parents who shared custody reported that she did not have any desire to see her mother ever again after they had had a particularly nasty verbal altercation. The girl stated that she intended to move in with her father full time and that she would no longer communicate with her mother, who caused her to be upset. This girl was asked what she would do if her mother and father lived in the same house and she was angry with her mother. Her answer was, "I guess I'd have to deal with it!" The essential social and emotional skill development derived from working out and resolving problems in primary relationships is significantly derailed in children who are empowered to walk away from, rather than work through, these interpersonal challenges. Sadly, many children in conflicted divorces are given the choice to opt out of resolving disputes with their parents because there is an easier "Plan B" (i.e., escape to the other parent).

Many children will report feelings of fear, anger, or resentment over being forced to participate in FRT. An adjunct question here is how the mental health profession should respond to the reports of these children. Do we, as a society, respond to children's reports of not wanting to study algebra or read *Great Expectations*, or go to school at all, by protecting them from the experiences that they seek to avoid? Or, are the children better served by supporting them through these experiences? Do we afford children the choice whether or not to be vaccinated against tetanus or do we listen to their concerns and support them through their fear so that they learn to cope with situations that are in the short term unpleasant, but in the long term essential or life enhancing?

Allegations of Abuse

Accusations against the targeted parent are part of the landscape in FRT. The favored parent is generally under the impression that claims of abuse against the other parent are likely to result in an immediate cessation of the targeted parent's contact with the child, which is typically the favored parent's desired outcome. FRT therapists are mandated reporters, and allegations of abuse not already addressed by the court or the local designated child protective agency are, of course, reported. However, vague, unreasonable, irrational accusations, or those that have been unfounded by the court or protective services, are not overly highlighted with unnecessary attention. To do so may reward a child's manipulative behavior. Rather, the allegations become an accepted aspect of the child's perception of his or her past. The emphasis remains to move past these perceived experiences with a focus on establishing a new rational outlook for the future.

Children who Play the Suicide "Trump Card"

When a teenager states that she will kill herself if she has to see her father, most judges and therapists respond quickly, but sometimes ineffectively, by stopping the FRT treatment completely. Certainly no judge or therapist wants to be in the position of under-reacting to a child who appears to be at risk. However, threats of self-harm are often utilized by children as a means of maximizing their power (functionally similar to a much younger child holding her breath to avoid having to take medicine). Of course, any child who presents with a serious threat of self-harm must be professionally assessed. If the assessment suggests that the child does not truly pose a significant threat to herself (due to severe psychopathology), this type of acting out can be managed within the context of FRT. As with many aspects of this treatment, support from the court is required. Cases that have been successfully resolved have involved: (1) psychiatric assessment and monitoring of the child and (2) a requirement that the parent in charge take the child to the hospital, immediately, in response to any subsequent suicidal threats or gestures.

The War of the Professionals

Alienated children are sometimes treated by a therapist selected by the favored parent with no affiliation or connection to the court-appointed FRT therapist. Typically, this therapist has only had contact with the favored parent. As a result, the family "story" reflects only the perspective of the favored parent and the child. Reunification can be severely compromised when the outside therapist has only this perspective, as the child and favored parent are at high risk for misrepresenting the events in FRT sessions to this individual.

It is natural for therapists to become advocates for their clients and their clients' points of view. For therapists not fully familiar with the dynamics of alienation, it is easy to become misled by the one-sided version of the family history related by the alienated child and favored parent. Some therapists, based on the child's report, will become convinced that the child is being mistreated by the targeted parent (or even the reunification therapist) during FRT. It is not uncommon for "outside" therapists to remain steadfast in this belief, even when informed by the FRT therapist that the child is not an accurate reporter of visits and that the visits with the targeted parent are actually going well. Some well-intentioned therapists have even written letters to the court recommending that the FRT cease immediately. Typically, alienated children are so persuasive that only actual observation of a visit session will change the opinion of the outside therapist.

The therapists in these cases are not inept or unprofessional. Rather, the problem is that children who are alienated can be quite believable to the inexperienced listener. Furthermore, professionals do not routinely suspect that a parent or a child would deliberately mislead a helping professional by providing an erroneous history of abuse or maltreatment. In some cases it is necessary to require that all outside therapy cease during FRT in order to accomplish the goals of the treatment.

When Treatment Fails

Family reunification cases, particularly those involving severe parental alienation, are often extremely difficult cases to manage. For many, the outcome is not successful reunification. Informal analysis of cases yields the following reasons for poor outcome:

Premature Withdrawal from Treatment

Mr. D. filed a motion in the family court for visitation with his children. He had had no contact with his three children based on allegations that he had abused alcohol during the marriage. Following the divorce, the children had been withheld from visiting with him by the mother, based on the assumption that he was an unfit parent because he had been arrested for driving while intoxicated during the third year of the marriage. Although Mr. D. maintained that he had completed alcohol treatment several years prior to the divorce, he had been unsuccessful in establishing contact with his children. Mr. D. maintained that his alcohol use had always been occasional and during the marriage had never interfered with what he described as a very positive relationship with his three children. FRT was ordered by the court. The children attended several visits and they appeared initially to have a very positive and even eager reaction to their father. However, the children's mother became increasingly critical, alleging a host of anxiety reactions in the children after each visit. The children's behavior deteriorated and they repeatedly told Mr. D. that they no longer wanted to have anything to do with him. Although Mr. D. was informed that the children's behaviors were to be expected, he became discouraged. He could not tolerate subjecting himself or his children to the conflict that continued treatment would cause. He decided to have a carefully orchestrated "farewell" session with them and stopped the treatment.

This case illustrates that some targeted parents choose not to engage in the struggle with their children and their ex-spouse to renew the relationship with their children. They usually terminate treatment after a few visitation sessions.

The treatment itself can take an emotional toll on the targeted parent. In some cases the problems are complicated by financial concerns. In many cases the court, believing that the problem is the responsibility of the targeted parent, places the financial burden of paying for the treatment solely on the targeted parent. In addition to becoming discouraged and disillusioned by the denigration and disrespect of their children, some parents simply can no longer afford to fight for a relationship with their children.

Targeted Parents who are or Become Abusive

Occasionally, the court may order FRT for cases in which one of the parents has significant problems meeting the children's needs and an estrangement has developed. The parent may claim to have been alienated and, in fact, may have been alienated by the other parent. However, upon working with the targeted parent, problems may emerge that would suggest difficulties in the parent–child relationship, independent of alienation, that are contributing to the estrangement. It may be observed in the treatment process that the parent refuses to make requested adjustments in his or her interaction with the children, or inadequately controls his or her anger. Sessions may be utilized to blame the children or the other parent for problems in the relationship. Occasionally, parents are observed in the treatment sessions to be verbally or otherwise inappropriate in their interactions with their children. In these cases, it is necessary for the treatment staff to communicate with the court in regard to these observations. Recommendations are provided as to how best to move forward, perhaps utilizing more intensive individualized parent psychotherapy or other therapeutic resources to alter the parent's behavior.

Favored Parents who Sabotage Treatment

FRT cases are markedly different from other treatment cases. This is often evident at the time of the first phone contact when resistance is first encountered. The office receptionist learns that the child's schedule is so cluttered with activities that it is, according to the favored parent, "impossible" to schedule an appointment for the child to visit with his other parent. Even play-dates take precedence over the child's relationship with his father!

Sabotage by an alienating favored parent can occur at any point throughout the process of treatment. Favored parents routinely schedule the child's activities or appointments to conflict with previously scheduled treatment appointments; and typical excuses for avoiding visitation sessions have included the alienating parent's illness, job requirements, or other appointments. More often it is observed that as the reunification process begins to yield results, and the visits between the targeted parent and child begin to be more congenial and normalized, the favored parent begins to report that the child's emotional state or school performance has deteriorated owing to the "stress" of the treatment.

Failure to Maintain Cooperation with the Court

Although, the interface with the court is a basic working principle of this treatment model, not all judges and legal representatives of the court understand the dynamics of PAS or understand the need for court involvement in treatment. Courts are not equally responsive to an integrated treatment model. In addition, there are other pressures on courts that compete with FRT needs. For example, there is pressure to resolve cases as soon as possible. When cases begin to improve with FRT, some courts may conclude that the case no longer needs court oversight and that the case will be resolved with treatment alone.

If cases are prematurely closed by the court, it generally means that treatment will be significantly compromised if not rendered totally useless. In such cases, when treatment begins to falter, the targeted parent is required to file a new motion with the court in order to reopen the case. This process is both costly and time-consuming and does not have the same impact as a more continuous process in which the court is receptive to consistent feedback from the therapist with no interruption.

In some jurisdictions, lawyers representing the children take the position that children have the right to decide for themselves if and when they will make contact with a parent. In these cases, courts may decide that FRT is no longer needed, is actually harming the child, and may decide that the child is better served by an alternative plan.

Does it Work?

Anecdotally, the large number of children who have received FRT have provided opportunities to observe multiple treatment outcomes. In many cases, when children are relieved of the responsibility of having to assume the role of fearful child, they embrace the opportunity to reconnect with the targeted parent. That is, when given "permission," either by the favored parent or even a judge, children readily engage with the other parent. Even severely alienated children, those who exhibited markedly fearful, disrespectful, and difficult behaviors, have been observed to rapidly shed these behaviors as if nothing had ever happened. These observations support the findings of other research that these children may have desired contact with the targeted parent all along (e.g., Baker, 2007). When "permission" is withheld, therapists report observing children in the waiting room joining the favored parent in a display of fear and trepidation in anticipation of seeing the targeted parent. Then, as soon as they are out of sight range of the favored parent, the same children run joyfully into the arms of the "feared parent." Sometimes the behavior change can be observed as a gradual transformation as the child walks down the hall from waiting room to treatment room.

In other cases, treatment is not as successful. For example, there are a number of complicating factors when treating adolescents. In these cases there has typically been more time in supportive therapy in which the child's role as victim may have been inadvertently reinforced by an outside therapist not experienced in the dynamics of PAS families. Furthermore, adolescents are more articulate, and the court may be less amenable to opposing the stated wishes of an older child.

At this point data are being analyzed on this treatment model based on 8 years of implementation. Preliminary outcome analyses are optimistic in supporting the effectiveness of the approach. Results to date suggest that the success rate ranges between 60% and 70%, depending on the definition of success. The vast majority of children treated exhibited normal non-alienated behaviors at the conclusion of treatment. The effectiveness of treatment appears to be related to the level of alienation exhibited by the child at the onset of treatment and the level of cooperation exhibited by the favored parent. Research aimed at better identifying factors that predict case outcome is underway. Outcome studies designed to target ways of enhancing treatment effectiveness are needed.

Note

1 All cases described in this chapter are hypothetical based on the cumulative experience of the authors. None of the examples present information that would identify any specific individuals.

References

Achenbach, T. (1991). *Manual for the child behavior checklist/4–18.* Burlington, VT: University of Vermont, Department of Psychiatry.

Baker, A. J. L. (2007). *Adult children of parental alienation syndrome: Breaking the ties that bind.* New York: W. W Norton.

Baker, A. J. L., Burkhard, B. & Albertson-Kelly, J. (2012). Differentiating alienated from not alienated children: A pilot study. *Journal of divorce and remarriage, 53(3),* 178–193.

Baker, A. J. L., & Fine, P. R. (2008). *Beyond the high road: Responding to 17 parental alienation strategies without compromising your morals or harming your child.* Available from: http://www.amyjlbaker.com.

Ben Porath, Y. S., & Tellegen, L. (2008). *Minnesota Multiphasic Personality Inventory-2 Restructured Form.* Minneapolis, MN: University of Minnesota Press.

Gardner, R. A. (1998). *The parental alienation syndrome: A guide for mental health and legal professionals.* Cresskill, NJ: Creative Therapeutics.

Kovacs, M. (1992). Child Depression Inventory. New York: Multi-Health System, Inc.

Milner, J. S. (1980). *The Child Abuse Potential Inventory.* Dekalb, IL: Psytec.

Reynolds, C. R., & Kamphaus, R. W. (1991). *Behavior Assessment System for Children* (2nd ed.). Circle Pines, MN: American Guidance System.

Warshak, R. (2001). *Divorce poison.* New York: Harper Collins.

Wolpe, J. (1958). *Psychotherapy by reciprocal inhibition.* Stanford, CA: Stanford University Press.

13 Working with Adult Children of Parental Alienation

Joe Rabiega and Amy J. L. Baker

The Adult Son who Struggles to be Free

A 20-year-old single male decides to make an appointment to see a therapist at his university student counseling center. The client is a junior studying psychology and is in a serious romantic relationship with a fellow student, which is not going very well (e.g., he reports feelings of distrust, abandonment, and extreme jealousy in the relationship). The client comes from a divorced family and has just started to live with his mother after almost 10 years apart owing to his father preventing him from seeing or having a relationship with his mother and the rest of his immediate family (e.g., his brother, sister, aunts, uncles, and cousins from his mother's side of the family). By conducting a thorough assessment, including collecting detailed information about the divorce and the child's relationship with both parents following the divorce, the therapist determines that the client has been the victim of many of the strategies used in parental alienation, such as negative attacks toward the targeted family members by the alienating parent, a refusal by the alienating parent to allow the client to experience personal autonomy, and subtle and overt threats of retaliation against the client or family members if he did not automatically and completely espouse the beliefs/demands of his father (Baker, 2007). As a result, the client has had a difficult time in his interpersonal relationships, which has led to depression, anxiety, anger, shame, guilt, employment/educational problems, and overall uncertainty about who he is as a person.

The client is aware that he has been the victim of alienation but is only in the beginning phase of understanding the impact this has had on his relationship with the targeted parent. Further complicating the client's reunification with his mother (the targeted parent) is the fact that his father (the alienating parent) is still active in his life and although he does not have the control he once did since the client is now an adult, he still attempts to manipulate the client and talk disparagingly of his mother. The client is desperately trying to "move away" physically and emotionally from his father but since the father's sense of well-being and livelihood is derived from living vicariously through the client, the father will not leave him alone. The son is torn between the guilt, anger, and obligation he feels about his father and the desire to know what it feels like to allow himself to love and be loved by his mother. Throughout the therapeutic journey, the clinician is mindful of the reparative implications of a healthy and respectful relationship with the client, the importance of exploring the client's unique alienation experience, and the possibilities for working through the alienation to build a more healthy and authentic future for the client.

Introduction

As a clinician working with adults who have experienced a parental alienation situation such as described in the case example, or a similar type of unhealthy childhood experience, it is important to make a key priority the need to build a positive and collaborative therapeutic relationship. Relationship building, both in the therapy room and in the client's interpersonal relationships, is something that a therapist will need to focus on from the beginning and throughout the process. Many clients who have been victims of parental alienation, witnessed a negative relationship between their parents, or had parents who were not healthy role models will probably have a difficult time understanding what constitutes positive, healthy interpersonal relationships with family, friends, coworkers, and romantic partners. Not only have they been exposed to unhelpful destructive role models with respect to healthy interpersonal relationships, but they also have been involved in an unhealthy relationship in which their own conflict resolution, problem-solving, perspective-taking, and critical thinking skills have been eroded and corrupted. They have been encouraged to be disrespectful to a parent, to walk away from conflict, and to subjugate their own thoughts, feelings, and perceptions to those of the favored parent. For these and other related reasons, adult children of parental alienation are at a significant disadvantage in forging and sustaining healthy adult relationships. It is likely that this—as opposed to an awareness of the alienation per se—is what brings a young adult into treatment. Thus, the client may not be aware that he[1] has been involved in an alienation family dynamic but will be aware of and troubled by intrapersonal and interpersonal difficulties such as anxiety, depression, co-dependency, failed or conflicted relationships, and fear of abandonment, to name just a few.

The main focus of this chapter is to discuss the strategies and techniques that are important in guiding adult children of parental alienation through the therapy process in a meaningful and positive way.[2] The first author is writing from the perspective of a mental health professional as well as that of a person who experienced significant alienation against one parent by the other. This chapter is written from both a personal and professional experience. For the purposes of full disclosure, the first author was also one of the 40 research subjects (with the pseudonym Jonah) who participated in the research that formed the basis of the book, *Adult Children of Parental Alienation Syndrome: Breaking the Ties That Bind* (Baker, 2007). The decision was made to acknowledge this personal connection to the topic in an effort to provide insights/struggles as someone who experienced parental alienation, and to highlight the fact that through successful therapy and education about the extremely powerful negative impact of parental alienation, individuals can learn how to love themselves, develop healthy and meaningful relationships, and be successful personally and professionally in life. Where appropriate, the chapter will include personal experience with alienation, as well as how it was dealt with, in order to demonstrate how adults who experienced alienation as children can work through the lingering and detrimental impact of this type of trauma on their sense of self and psychological well-being, and their ability to form meaningful interpersonal relationships.

Getting to Know the Client: Initial Therapeutic Issues

A therapist may come to the conclusion that a client is an "adult child of parental alienation" well before the client has come to that same understanding. From the client's perspective there is a parent with whom there is relationship (the favored parent) and a parent with whom there is little or no contact (the rejected parent), and this situation is a consequence of the behavior of each parent.[3] That is, the favored parent is viewed as loving, helpful, and protective while the rejected parent is deemed unsafe, unloving, and unavailable. Obviously, not all adult clients who have a relationship with only one parent are victims of alienation. Thus, the first task of the therapist is to pay attention to the way the client speaks about both parents in order to ascertain if the signs of alienation are present. As the clinician gets to know the client and formulates a hypothesis about whether alienation occurred, he can ask questions that may help bring clarity to the issue. An example is, "Can you tell me what was good and bad about each parent." Any black and white statements the client makes about the parents in which one is portrayed as all good and the other as all bad should be noted, along with indicators of enmeshment with one parent at the expense of the other (e.g., "Why didn't Daddy just leave us alone!"). Likewise, extreme reverence for one parent, who is described in idealized terms as the child's best friend, are potential red flags of alienation (e.g., "My father was my hero. Everything he did was perfect and I adored him."). With sufficient information, the clinician can make the differential diagnosis that alienation is a likely cause of the client's triangulated parental dynamics.

Depending upon previous therapy (if any) and the level of insight into the alienation, an adult child may not fully understand that his current psychological distress is a direct result of what happened with respect to alignment with one parent against the other. Therefore, it is the therapist's job, over time, to help the client understand how his current symptoms and problematic functioning are likely a result of the alienation. However, until the client is able to accept the link between the alienation and his current life situation, the therapist should not denigrate the favored parent because the client is likely to come to the defense of that parent and could end therapy prematurely as a result. If the therapist is too quick to criticize the favored parent this could be met with intense resistance, as the client is still invested in protecting that version of his childhood in which that parent was the victim/hero and the rejected parent was the villain. Ideally, the realization will come organically and authentically to the client through the therapeutic process rather than imposed upon the unwilling and resistant client by the determined clinician. Like all insights, understanding alienation in one's family of origin may be slow coming and hard won and should unfold according to the timing of the client rather than the expectations or needs of the therapist.

Thus, a significant challenge for a therapist, once it has been ascertained that a client has in fact experienced alienation from a parent, is to determine how to appropriately begin the dialogue of educating the client about how alienation impacts individuals and, more specifically, how the individual client himself has been impacted by his own personal experience with it. The clinician should bear in mind that, as Baker (2007) pointed out, realizing that one has experienced parental alienation may entail a significant shift in worldview for the client, one that entails several losses, including:

> The loss of the idealized version of the alienating parent, the loss of time with the targeted parent—once that parent's worth has been acknowledged—the loss of one's innocence as the client recognizes the role she played in the alienation, and the loss of the possibility of winning the love and approval of the alienating parent.
>
> (p. 219)

In other words, accepting one's experience with alienation can be quite painful for the client.

Because recognizing alienation will be a painful process, it is important for the clinician to have confidence that the client has the internal and external resources to handle it. Thus, the client's current functioning and social ecology needs to be thoroughly assessed before the topic is broached. Special attention should be paid to the following areas:

Status of Parents

The clinician needs to understand the current family structure and status of the parents, especially whether both parents are still alive and, if so, what is the current nature of the client's relationship with each parent. This is important information because it will allow the therapist to understand the potential for reconciliation with the rejected parent—a potential goal if the parent is still alive and the client has not yet reconciled with him or her. Obviously, if the rejected parent died prior to the client's ability to have a reconciliation, this will influence the course of the treatment and call for the development of creative methods such as role playing and letter writing for working through some of the guilt and loss of the relationship with that parent.

Likewise, knowing whether the favored parent is still alive and the extent of enmeshment between the client and that parent will allow the therapist to be aware of the potential for that parent to interfere in the client's life, control and manipulate the client, and act in vengeful, hurtful ways towards the client. The likelihood of these eventualities will need to be carefully explored with the client. While some adult children of alienation may overestimate the power and influence of the favored parent—a belief that has been fostered and nurtured by that parent because it helped maintain that parent's power and control over the child—it is worth exploring with the adult client whether and how the favored parent still has control over the client (i.e., does that parent financially support the client, does that parent have significant ties to important people or institutions in the client's life that could be jeopardized should the favored parent become angry with the client). In addition to material and objective control, the favored parent may have emotional control over the client such that the client feels compelled to please that parent and compulsively avoids incurring that parent's anger or disappointment. Exploring issues such as, "What would it feel like to have that parent be angry with you?" and "What is the worst thing that parent can do to you?" will be important prior to the client reconciling with the rejected parent.

First Author's Story

I was in my late teens when I started to move toward establishing a relationship with my mother again. A large part of the struggle related to the fact that early in my reunification I was still somewhat financially and emotionally bound to my father. My father's constant attempts to interfere with my relationship (reunification) with my mother negatively impacted my own sense of personal healing and caused fear for myself and my mother that my father would take revenge on us, since I now had a better relationship with her then I did with him.

Current Academic and Occupational Functioning

The clinician also needs to understand what is the adult child's current academic or occupational functioning. This is important in order to gauge the impact that the alienation is having on the client's adult life. Problems in these areas may need to be worked on prior to reunifying with the rejected parent. Academic and occupational functioning will likely be disrupted by the alienation because alienation can impair a child's ability to develop coping skills, a positive self-concept, and a realistic view of the motives of others and the world overall.

Academic and career difficulties can also be impaired by the client's low self-esteem and interpersonal insecurity, also common among individuals who experienced alienation (Baker, 2007). Since the adult child was forced to espouse and in many cases act out the thoughts, beliefs, and feelings of the alienating parent, his sense of self and ability to know and appreciate his own thoughts, beliefs, and feelings has become underdeveloped through lack of practice and encouragement, resulting in impaired autonomy and self-reliance. In order to develop a sense of agency, children need to experience admiration, celebration of accomplishments, and encouragement of progress from caregivers (Kohut, 1971). What alienated children experience, on the other hand, is psychological control—parental pressure to think and behave in certain ways to please the parent, regardless of the meaning or impact on the child (Buehler et al., 1998). This undermines autonomous development of the child by mitigating intrinsic motivation and constricting self-determining behavior (Joussemet, Landry, & Koestner, 2008).

It appears that some favored parents do not want their children—even adult children—to live fully functional self-sufficient separate lives. The desire for an unhealthy closeness and an inability to appreciate the separate personhood of their children is one psychological feature of alienating parents so it is not surprising to find that these children are discouraged from separating and individuating. Throughout their childhood, these parents may undermine the child's academic success in order to increase the likelihood that the child will remain enmeshed and dependent on them for a longer period of time. Thus, it would not be surprising if an adult child of alienation has difficulty functioning in the adult world. Baker (2007) found this to be the case in the qualitative interviews and has subsequently replicated this finding in an independent sample using objective measures (Baker & BenAmi, 2011).

First Author's Story

I had very low self-esteem throughout high school, the first part of my college life, and in my first jobs during and right after college. I had been so used to following my father's orders and not considering my own thoughts and feelings that once my father lost interest in controlling my every thought and action I felt unmoored. I wasn't used to thinking through problems, checking in with myself, or seeking advice and input from friends. Without my father to tell me what to do and think, I was adrift.

Current Interpersonal Relationships

A third area to explore with the client is how the adult child of alienation views and experiences his or her interpersonal relationships, including whether the client has close friends whom he trusts and intimate romantic relationships that can be sustained. This is extremely important in order to understand the impact the alienation has had on the client's ability to form and maintain relationships with peers, colleagues, relatives, and significant others, including romantic relationships. Most children learn about interpersonal relationships from their parents, and adult children of parental alienation are no exception. That is, early relational patterns create the blueprint for later styles of interpersonal interactions (Ainsworth, 1982; Shulman, Scharf, Lumer, & Maurer, 2001).

Therefore, when alienated children are convinced by one parent that the other parent is defective and should be discarded, their ability to accurately understand how to form and maintain and trust in interpersonal relationships is dramatically impaired. Exploring the status of the client's friendship and social circles will help the clinician gain a better picture of the emotional support network available to the client and the overall impact of the alienation on his interpersonal life. If the client has few intimate relationships and little or no social support network, the clinician should be cautious about threatening the client's defense mechanisms by discussing alienation because the client will have few people on whom he can rely to bolster his self-esteem and gain emotional strength during the difficult process of making sense of the alienation. One suggestion is to help the client join a support group for children with toxic parents or people with co-dependency issues (assuming that is relevant to the client). Ideally, there would be a social support network for adult children of parental alienation but that has not yet been formed as far as the authors are aware.

First Author's Story

From the beginning of my father's control over my existence I had a very difficult time establishing and maintaining friendships, which, looking back, was a direct result of the negative interpersonal experiences I was exposed to by my father. For example, my father showed little to no concern for the feelings of others and made it clear that his personal well-being and happiness were paramount. He would actively make fun of other people or treat them in a manner (belittlement is a word that comes strongly to mind) that devalued their opinions or importance as individuals. This way of "interacting" with others was consistent among family, friends, co-workers, strangers, etc. In the same way he used me, he treated people in a way that ensured his own happiness.

It is well-known that our personal and interpersonal development is shaped during our childhood through watching and learning from those most close to us, including parents, siblings, teachers, etc. Therefore, when I was exposed to the role modeling of my father, and I was forced to believe that one parent (my father) was omnipotent, my sense of self and others was dramatically and negatively skewed, which resulted in constant confusion about what friends are for and how to develop/maintain friendships. In my case, this led to very low self-esteem and I was bullied and picked on by other kids for most of my childhood/adolescence. I had very few meaningful relationships and any problems that arose did not get worked out because I had no one to turn to (e.g., my father) for advice or guidance since he was obviously not a good role model and would actually prefer that I not have positive outside relationships because they threatened my allegiance to him.

My problems with interpersonal relationships only intensified once I became an adult. I began college at 18, like most people that age, and began working on a more permanent basis once out of high school. To put it simply, I had tremendous difficulty understanding the intentions of co-workers or people in authority, such as supervisors and teachers. I took any constructive feedback very personally and would become extremely emotional, angry, and resentful. As I sit and write this I am startled as to why I never better understood my response to the feedback just described. It is clear to me now—I was either reacting to them out of rebelliousness because I was so tired of being controlled by others, since I pretty much was told how to think, feel, and act my entire life, or I was just reacting to them in the same manner I was taught to react to all other adults in my life, either directly or indirectly based on my observations of my father in his interpersonal relationships.

My low self-esteem and difficulty in relationships continued until I began intensive therapy in my early twenties. It has taken many years of therapy and support from those now close to me for me to overcome the damage inflicted by my father on my sense of self and well-being.

The difficulties I have described also were evident in intimate relationships. For the most part, I was not sure of what I wanted or needed out of these relationships until I progressed in therapy and met my wife, who changed my life in many ways. I will be married 10 years in June 2012 and now have two wonderful young children. My relationships before my wife were filled with strife and jealousy on my part and were a constant source of emotional pain for me. As I have said, my beliefs, emotions, and actions that led to my being jealous and over-reliant on the other person were directly related to the way in which my father controlled my life growing up.

Exposure to Other Forms of Maltreatment and Trauma

Clients may enter therapy for reasons apart from alienation, including problems dealing with other traumatic experiences that may or may not be related to the alienation. As Baker (2007) reported, a significant proportion of the adult children of parental alienation studied were also victims of physical and sexual abuse—perpetrated against them by the favored parent. Prior to exploring the alienation with a client, it is important to have a clear sense of the full extent of significant traumatic experiences, obtained through a comprehensive case history, in order to understand the context within which the client is functioning and in which the alienation occurred. To the extent that other forms of maltreatment were experienced by the client, the clinician can draw on the literature for working with these populations. For example, according to van der Kolk (1994), adult victims of childhood maltreatment are likely to be challenged in the areas of affect regulation, anger management, and interpersonal relationships, as well as be likely to experience symptoms of PTSD (dissociation, stress responses, intrusive thoughts, and so forth). That knowledge should be factored into the clinician's approach.

Herman (1992) warns clinicians working with abused populations to be mindful of traumatic transference, in which concerns about sensitivity to abuse of power are played out between client and clinician. This is particularly relevant for adult children of parental alienation, because they have been emotionally manipulated, lied to, tricked, and misled by the favored parent in order to satisfy that parent's needs and desires. The clinician therefore needs to be careful not to engage in any action that could be construed by the client as coercive or emotionally manipulative. Likewise, the clinician should be able to tolerate processing the client's feelings about these issues should they arise in the therapeutic relationship. The therapist might need to teach the client how to gauge and trust his own thoughts and feelings rather than assume that the client knows how to do that.

The trauma symptoms and cognitive and emotional suffering an adult child of parental alienation experiences may be subtle or reflect a full-blown disorder such as PTSD, major depression, and so forth. Regardless, it is essential that the therapist understands the symptoms of the client and uses these symptoms to create an individualistic treatment approach based on the client's history and current life circumstances not solely based on a diagnosis of a "disorder." The therapist needs to bear in mind that the symptoms do not define the individual and that the blame lies with the alienating parent.

First Author's Story

My father engaged in many abusive parental alienation strategies that led me to believe that I would not survive without him including: (1) while intoxicated, taking out his gun out and making me pledge my allegiance with the threat of his suicide should I refuse and (2) forcing me to act aggressively towards my other family members, which resulted in my father completely isolating me from them because they were unable to manage my assaultive behaviors. As a child, I believed my father was all powerful and if I did not feel, think, or act the way he wanted me to, something bad would happen to me or him. By the time I entered therapy I was experiencing a range of symptoms reflective of the type and extent of maltreatment I had experienced growing up.

Data also suggest that clients with a history of parental alienation may also have had alcoholic parents and this issue should be explored as well with the client. As Wotitz (1990) noted, adult children of alcoholics may feel shame and the need to maintain secrecy surrounding familial alcoholism. Therefore, a client with that history would not spontaneously elect to reveal that information directly. The clinician may need to raise the issue himself, drawing on the findings in Baker (2007) in order to help normalize the experience and lessen the sense of shame typically associated with admitting alcoholism in one's family of origin. If identified, it would be useful to explore presence of alcohol or other substance abuse issues in the client's own life, both past and present, in light of the intergenerational patterns known to exist (Chassin, Pitts, DeLucia, & Todd, 1999). If the client is at risk for currently using or abusing substances, the clinician should understand that exploring alienation may trigger the need to use substances as a means of modulating the intense pain and shame that the realization may cause (Khantzian, 1985).

Building a Successful Therapeutic Relationship/Environment

Adult children of parental alienation are victims of emotional and sometimes physical abuse by the alienating parent and have been stripped of any sense of self, as their main focus of life has been on merely surviving and following the strict rules and guidelines established by the alienating parent. Therefore, they have not been afforded the opportunity of a healthy and nurturing developmental and maturational process, which has negatively impacted their ability to develop a strong sense of self and positive interpersonal relationships (Baker,

2007). Thus, the rapport building and relational aspects of treatment are of the utmost importance.

There are specific therapeutic strategies that may not be new to a seasoned therapist but are particularly relevant for helping clients who are adult children of parental alienation feel safe, welcomed, and comfortable. It is important to remember that these clients likely have received many mixed messages about love, compassion, and trust. Therefore, it is essential that the therapist understands that an essential part of the process entails teaching and modeling the basics of what are healthy interpersonal relationships with family, friends, co-workers, and others. A non-directive, humanistic, Rogerian (Rogers, 1951) approach is ideal when therapy begins. At the same time, it is important to be mindful about the level of distress of the client and provide symptom relief as appropriate through cognitive behavioral techniques and possibly medication, depending on the severity of the client's emotional and psychological functioning. However, following the basics of Carl Rogers' approach, clients can be helped to begin a journey that will provide personal growth and open the window for important improvement in their self-concept and interpersonal relationships. Table 13.1 lists basic yet essential strategies to building a strong foundation for successful therapy and how they relate to working with adult children of parental alienation syndrome (Corsini & Wedding, 2000).

Table 13.1 Basic therapeutic techniques and their application to adult children of parental alienation syndrome (PAS)

Strategy	*Definition*	*Relevance for adult children of PAS*
Unconditional positive regard	The therapist maintains a neutral approach toward the client and provides support without judging the client, regardless of what the client says.	It is essential that the client is able to express himself without being judged or criticized since it is likely that he has experienced this for many years by the alienating parent. The adult child of parental alienation also likely feels a sense of shame and guilt for the things he has done to the targeted parent. Therapy may be the first time that the client can feel free to express thoughts/emotions that question the programming message of the alienating parent.
Genuineness or authenticity	The therapist presents himself in a congruent manner in which his thoughts and actions reflect a true concern for the client which is not impacted by the therapist's professional/personal views.	The client likely does not feel genuine or whole as a person so observing this in a therapist is very powerful and the therapist can serve as a model. The client is used to being in an exploitive relationship in which his needs were subjugated to the needs of the alienating parent. The client might be suspicious of the therapist and perceive an agenda or desire to control.

Table 13.1 Continued

Strategy	*Definition*	*Relevance for adult children of PAS*
Empathic listening/ reflection	The therapist listens attentively to what the client is saying and reflects back what the client says to ensure an accurate understanding of the client's problems.	This may be a very interesting and confusing experience for the client since the alienating parent generally does not respect the client's thoughts/emotions and any attempt by the client to express his own feelings may be looked at as a challenge to the parent's authority and a threat to the enmeshed, role-reversal relationship they have established in which the needs and feelings of the parent are more real and more important than those of the child.
Ensuring the client feels safe and understands that therapy is confidential (explain the limitations to this such as danger to self, others, etc.)	In general, clients who are new to therapy are unsure of the process and more specifically, for clients who experienced alienation, establishing an atmosphere where clients can be assured that they and their personal story of alienation will be kept private.	Take time at the beginning of therapy to describe the sacred nature of the therapist/client relationship and be sure to discuss the limits to confidentiality. When discussing the limits, ensure the client that if any of these exclusions happen that every attempt will be made to notify and talk with the client prior to breaking confidentiality. Clients, especially ones that have been the victims of alienation, need to know they can trust the therapist unconditionally.
Taking an individualized, client-centered approach to therapy	Treating each client as a unique individual who is capable of overcoming the trauma he faced. It is important to make the client feel empowered and focus on reinforcing his strengths and to "normalize" difficulties based on the parenting situation experienced.	Each client needs to be understood as a whole person and not just as a diagnosis or constellation of symptoms. Symptoms and diagnoses are important for helping the client and may be required for insurance purposes. However, understanding the client's strengths and other salient issues that may positively or negatively impact treatment is essential. For example, in addition to mental health concerns, it is important to take into consideration the client's physical health, cultural issues and environmental situation such as socioeconomic stressors.
Exercising humility	The clinician should not act as if he has all of the answers or knows and understands the client's lived experience better than the client.	Adult children of alienation have had their reality created for them by the alienating parent. In order to help the client develop a true and authentic reality, the clinician should not assume to truly understand what it is that the client went through, even if the clinician has also experienced alienation. Use self-disclosure judiciously and do not impose reality onto the client.

In many situations, building a positive and meaningful therapeutic relationship and implementing the Rogerian strategies described in Table 13.1 can bring about symptom relief, change, and a deeper understanding of the client's presenting problems. This has been demonstrated empirically (Cain & Seeman, 2001) and has been witnessed in the first author's work as a therapist and in personal therapeutic efforts to work through being an adult child of parental alienation. For clinicians trained in cognitive behavioral therapy who aim to alleviate symptoms through an examination of faulty thoughts and emotions, it may seem counterintuitive to propose that basic relationship building and interpersonal techniques can be so effective. Likewise, some clients may not want to focus on the past or may believe that doing so is irrelevant, a belief that is supported by some therapeutic approaches that espouse the belief that you "can't live in the past." While this is ultimately true, clients whose prior abuse/alienation is impacting their current functioning and well-being will need at some point in treatment to process the meaning of the past in order to be free from its influence in the future. Many clients may not want to immediately focus on the past and this may make sense. It is important to start with where the client is, which can be healing in itself if the client has had few relationships in which his needs were respected, honored, and valued.

Once a relationship of trust has begun, the clinician can begin to explore "themes" that come up and try to connect current situations/experiences with the past in an effort to both educate the client on how the past affects the present and to help the client to begin to "realign" his worldview regarding himself and his relationships. Once a strong therapeutic relationship is established and the client feels respected and can trust the therapist, the next stage or process of therapy can begin. The stages of therapy do not necessarily follow in any predetermined direction and the unfolding of therapy is likely to take on a life of its own based on the unique aspects of the clients' experience with alienation.

Understanding the Alienation Experience

Not all alienated children have had the same alienation experience. There are different familial patterns of alienation, different permutations, and different outcomes. While having a label with which to describe one's experience can be helpful, in and of itself it is not enough information for the clinician and client to understand and work through the experience. Some key aspects of alienation that vary on a case-by-case basis are discussed here and should be explored with the client.

Understanding the Personality Disorder of the Favored Parent

Favored parents appear prone to having personality disorders, especially the type II dramatic types of narcissism, borderline, and sociopathy. This has been explained by Baker (2007), who wrote that these disorders make it difficult for the parent to tolerate rejection, dissent, and separation from others, characteristics that create the kind of atmosphere in which alienation can flourish. However, this does not mean that knowing that a client was alienated tells the client and clinician whether and which personality disorder the favored parent had. That kind of information can only be gleaned from hearing about the parent and his or her parenting style in discussion with the client. Once the clinician and client have a clear picture of the personality style/disorder of the favored parent, they can begin to work on understanding the ways in which the relationship became warped and unhealthy.

Understanding the personality characteristics/traits of the favored parent can be very empowering for the client. As a therapist, it is extremely important to educate the client on the diagnostic criteria of personality disorders, which include a pervasive and unwavering style of behaving, thinking, and interacting with others that leads to significant dysfunction in personal and/or interpersonal functioning. Personality disorders generally are very difficult to treat owing to the fact that clients typically have little insight and the characteristics/traits part of the disorder has served a meaningful, although not necessarily healthy, role in their lives. By providing clients with this overview, the therapist can help the client understand that there was little he could have done to change the alienation. This is important since these clients grow up to feel shame and guilt about why they listened to or acted upon the demands of the favored parent. Caution must be used when describing the type of personality disorder/traits a parent may have had, especially if the description is extremely negative and if the client is in the beginning stages of therapy or still involved with the favored parent. Remember, these clients have been forced to believe in the favored parent to varying degrees for significant periods of time, so they may have a hard time believing that the parent was anything less than perfect. The most important thing for a therapist to do initially is described above: build a safe, confidential, and caring environment and develop a strong therapeutic relationship where trust is essential. Then, further exploration, definition, and therapeutic techniques can be used to understand and treat the client's symptoms/problems.

Understanding Which Parental Alienation Strategies were Used

According to Baker and Fine (2008, this volume) favored parents make use of an idiosyncratic mix of parental alienation strategies. Each alienated child is exposed to a different combination of behaviors at different frequencies, durations, and intensities. In that sense, each parental alienation story is unique and the only way to understand the client's specific alienation experience is to explore it with the client. Educating the client about the primary alienation strategies may help the client gain insight into how it was possible for one parent to manipulate him to reject the other parent. As discussed elsewhere in this book, there are at least 17 alienation strategies, including badmouthing the other parent, not allowing the child to see the other parent, and convincing the child that he is the only parent who cares about him and without whom the child would not be able to survive. When the clinician is educated about the client's exposure to these different behaviors, the therapeutic process can be tailored to the unique experience of the client.

Exploring the Metaphor of the "Cult of Parenthood"

Exploring with the client the ways in which the alienation was comparable to being in a cult may be a useful exercise. The clinician and client can read and discuss books and informational materials about cults. Many people are familiar with the concept of cults and understand how unsuspecting people can be led to align with a dangerous and manipulative leader who does not have the cult member's best interest at heart. Most people accept that individuals who join cults have been manipulated into their devotion and commitment. Thus, the client can apply the cult analogy to explain to himself and others what he experienced as a child and why he did what he did. The cult framework can also be useful for the client and clinician for understanding recovery from alienation. For example, a truism in the cult recovery movement is that leaving a cult is just the beginning point for recovery (Ryan, 1993). Former cult members have a lot of self-work to do to process and move beyond the cult experience and the same is true of adult children of parental alienation.

Understanding what Hooked the Child

As Gardner (1998) noted when he first observed and wrote about parent alienation, while the denigration of the targeted parent begins in the mind and heart of the favored parent, it is eventually taken on and owned, at least in part, by the child as well. Alienation involves the participation of the child, who joins the favored parent in an active campaign against the rejected parent. This is partly why the alienation is so painful, because the child is acting as if he believes that the rejected parent really is no good and is worthy of discarding.

Because the premise of alienation is that the rejected parent did not deserve the level of hatred and rejection (otherwise it would be referred to as estrangement and not alienation), there must be something that compelled the child to buy into the alienation dynamic. This is worth exploring, not to assign blame to the child but to allow the client and the clinician to gain a deeper understanding of the client's experience. Thus, the clinician can gently explore with the client whether there was some emotional hook that the favored parent used to keep the child actively involved in the alienation. In some cases it is fear that the favored parent will fall apart or kill himself if the child loves the other parent. In other cases the hook is self-interest on the part of the child, who has been convinced that his life will be substantially happier (materially or otherwise) if he aligns with the favored parent. Other alienated children have become convinced that the rejected parent doesn't really love them and that the only parent who really cares is the favored parent. Some alienated children are afraid of the wrath and disapproval of the favored parent and will do whatever it takes to avoid that experience. Understanding the psychological context of the alienation from the child's perspective is critical for the client to move past the shame and guilt and ultimately towards self-forgiveness.

Working Through the Alienation

Mourning the "Lost Years"

Most alienated children are deprived of the opportunity to love and be loved by both parents. To one degree or another, the alienated child and rejected parent lost time together and lost the opportunity to share significant events. For some this is an extreme cut-off with no contact for months or years. For other alienated children the loss may be more episodic. Nonetheless, all alienated children and targeted parents lose some aspect of their relationship.

How much time they spent together, how close and loving they could be with each other, and how they experienced each other was filtered through the lens and under the control of the alienating parent. The loss experienced by children who have been alienated from a parent should not be underestimated and should be acknowledged in all its specific ramifications for the client. The "lost years" need to be explored and grieved just like any other loss an individual experiences in life, such as the death of a loved one, the break-up of a serious romantic relationship, or any other experience that has a dramatic impact on an individual's emotional, psychological, or physical health. That is not to say that the grief of losing a loved one is synonymous with the grief experienced by someone who experienced alienation, but it is important to recognize that in many ways the alienated child has "lost" the rejected parent for many years and, typically, these years are ones that are essential in the development of the child/adolescent's sense of self, understanding healthy interpersonal relationships between a mother and father, and feeling loved and nurtured.

Exactly what was lost should be fully explored and grieved by the client and clinician together. For example, was the rejected parent absent from birthdays, important school events, and milestones (e.g., graduation, sweet 16, birth of child). The sad truth that these missed opportunities cannot be made up is part of the reality for the alienated child (and parent). It does not mean that the child is forever damaged and can never move past the loss. In fact, to acknowledge the loss is to diminish its negative impact while to deny it is to let it fester and continue to undermine the quality of life for the client. The client and clinician can work together to identify ways to symbolically make up for the lost years by perhaps writing or depicting the events and time missed and sharing that with the rejected parent (if reconciliation has occurred) or with the clinician.

Moving from Shame and Guilt to Forgiveness of Oneself

Shame and guilt are frequently felt by the adult child who participated in the emotional (and perhaps physical) abuse toward the rejected parent at the behest of the favored parent. Once the realization has occurred, the adult client may have substantial regret for his actions towards a parent who did not deserve such pain and suffering. The shame and guilt results from an awareness that the rejected parent was not the evil and unloving person that the favored parent made her out to be. Resolving this shame and guilt is essential for repairing and rebuilding the relationship with the rejected parent. The therapist needs to encourage an open and honest dialogue between the affected individuals that will open the door for growth and reparation of the relationship. This is true in many other situations, including couples therapy, family conflict, etc. Perhaps the client can invite the rejected parent to enter therapy with him since there are many different issues that need to be worked on, which in many cases can be best done with a trained professional. For example, putting the shame and guilt into perspective by outlining how it came to be (e.g., at the hands of the favored parent) is important so that the client and targeted parent can feel less blame and understand that they were both manipulated and harmed by the favored parent.

There may be some resistance to this prospect because, after many years of living the lives that many clients and targeted parents do, they typically do not want to relive the past and desperately want to just reconnect with each other and move forward. The therapist needs to acknowledge this and take a multi-perspective approach that is based on both the needs of the clients and the most effective therapeutic techniques that are warranted, which may include focusing at least partially on the prior alienation experience in order to explore whatever ways that experience is still impinging on the well-being of the client and on the parent–child relationship.

It is important for a therapist to be sensitive to the fact that as a child the client was not consciously aware of the damaging impact of his actions on the rejected parent and that despite being an agent of the alienation, ultimately the favored parent is the responsible party. Perhaps looking at a picture of the client when he was the age when the alienation began can bring home the point that really the client could not have made the alienation happen without the effort of the favored parent (Donaldson-Pressman & Pressman, 1994). Nonetheless, perhaps having the client write an apology to the rejected parent would be a healing exercise. If that parent is no longer alive, the therapist can engage in a role-play or guided imagery exercise to allow the client to experience acknowledging and expressing regret for his part in the alienation. If the rejected parent is not alive, there may be other persons (friends, relatives, colleagues of the targeted parent) with whom the client could share the apology, which could be healing for the client. Throughout this process, it is important that the clinician help the client balance regret with a realistic assessment of his role.

As Baker (2007) points out, if the client is suffering from guilt and shame, forgiveness has not yet been fully achieved. Because guilt and shame underlie depression, substance use, anxiety, eating disorders, and a host of other negative outcomes, it is important that they be worked through so that the client can have a chance at a healthy future.

Learning to Trust

In many cases, when a child is a victim of parental alienation his sense of security, safety, and respect for himself has been shattered due to the behaviors of the favored parent. This leads to mistrust and can have a negative impact on the individual's ability to have emotional and psychological stability within himself and in interpersonal relationships. As a child, the client only knew one way of being, thinking, feeling, and surviving: the way that was shaped and forced upon him by the favored parent. Therefore, when that child becomes an adult and begins to form close interpersonal relationships, especially romantic ones, he may experience jealousy, fear of losing the other person, and difficulties trusting or respecting other people. This can lead the client to push others away and resist forming meaningful and healthy relationships with colleagues, fellow college students, or romantic interests.

Thus, an important task of therapeutic work with an adult child of parental alienation is helping that person learn to trust himself as well as others. It is essential that an individual learns to trust or understand and believe in himself prior to being able to effectively trust others. The same is true for love, respect, and many other important aspects of one's personality and worldview that are essential for healthy and meaningful interpersonal relationships. By helping a client learn how to trust himself and others, love and respect will be easier to achieve because without trust nothing else will work. Unfortunately, many adult children realize that the trust and respect they had for the favored parent was based on manipulation and hatred toward the targeted parent. As discussed previously, children learn and develop their core values and beliefs from those close to them (i.e., parents); therefore, when they discover the favored parent's lies and manipulating behaviors, they feel like a victim and their ability to trust is shattered. A therapist can best help a client by helping him to understand that he was victim and that he has a right to trust, love, and respect himself and to receive these in return from others. This takes time and practice but can be done.

Resisting Replicating Alienation

Repeating the pattern with one's own children is something that may be a fear for adult children of parental alienation. Like many other patterns of behavior that are transmitted from one generation to another, repeating alienation is something that can occur if the client does not fully understand or has not successfully worked through the damage that was done by the favored parent and the loss of the rejected parent. Fear in this situation can be used as a catalyst for the client not to repeat what was experienced. Through therapy, the client's level of self-awareness will hopefully be heightened, which should help him identify warning signs or signals that he is in the process of or at risk of replicating behaviors that he learned from the favored parent. It is essential that the adult child have an open and honest discussion with his significant other about what he experienced as a child and the impact that it has had on his development, as well as the ongoing effects it may have on their relationship.

Therapists should help clients understand the themes and triggers that will help them identify if they may be engaging in strategies of alienation. Since parental alienation behaviors are typically engrained in the minds of the alienated child, it may be important for significant others to be part of the therapy process so they can better understand what the adult child has gone through as well as what to look for if their partner starts to engage in these behaviors. Couples in which one or both of the members have experienced alienation are not unlike other couples who have their own negative experiences from the past and benefit from therapy to "unload their baggage" or understand how to not repeat the past in their current relationship.

Reunification and Therapy with the Targeted Parent and Adult Client

Preparing the client for reunification with the targeted parent, or working with the client and rejected parent together if they have already reconciled, will likely be an important part of therapy with an adult child of parental alienation. If reconciliation has not yet occurred, the client and clinician can explore the client's goals in reaching out to that parent, and what are his fantasies and fears about that. It is vital that the reconciliation approach be well thought out and that the client is prepared for whatever response he receives. It could be crushing to the client to have his advances rebuffed or frustrated in some way and the clinician needs to help the client develop a strategy that is careful and allows for maximum protection of the client's well-being.

If the client and rejected parent have already reconciled, the clinician can discuss with the client the potential benefits (and drawbacks) of involving that parent in part of the client's therapy. If the client is amenable, some aspects of the healing can be productively engaged in with joint sessions (such as apologizing to the rejected parent and receiving that parent's forgiveness).

First Author's Story

I reunited with my mother around the age of 18 after being "formally" turned against her since the age of 12. I say formally, because the alienating strategies or "grooming" used by my father were evident from an early age. I was fortunate to have over 10 years with my mother after reunification until she passed away at a young age. My mother was truly an amazing person and never blamed me or criticized me for the way I treated her as instructed by my father. She was completely non-judgmental, showed compassion and unconditional positive regard for my well-being and success as an adult. Looking

> back, I think her positive approach was the reason we were able to come back together after so many years apart. However, I also think that she made it too easy, which resulted in me not taking a deep enough look at how I continued to view and treat her. If we had had the opportunity to explore the alienation in therapy, that could have helped us develop a more balanced and healthy relationship.

Confronting the Favored Parent

At some point in therapy the client may express interest in confronting the favored parent about the experience of parental alienation. Again, this should be discussed thoroughly with the client prior to him taking any actual steps in that direction. If the favored parent has a personality disorder it is not likely that the parent will be amenable to a discussion about how he interfered with or undermined the client's relationship with the other parent. Self-examination, flexibility of thought, and perspective taking are not strengths of people with personality disorders (Kernberg, 1975). Therefore, the confrontation is not likely to be productive if the client is seeking validation of the alienation and/or an apology for the pain and suffering caused to the client. Nonetheless, it may be worthwhile for the client and clinician to explore the fantasy/wish of such an experience and what, if anything, could be gained from trying to explain to the favored parent the client's perspective on alienation in his childhood. For example, sometimes it feels empowering to speak the truth, even if the person does not receive the message in a meaningful way. It is probably advisable for the client to write a letter or practice the confrontation in a role-playing session with the clinician in order to bring to light the client's readiness to take this step.

Conclusion

Working with an adult who experienced alienation or similar negative parenting during a time when he should have been developing his own identity and learning about effective and healthy interpersonal relationships and the meaning of family is extremely sensitive and difficult owing to the nature of the individual's suffering. Such a client could be experiencing depression, anxiety or other forms of psychological distress typically found in trauma victims or those who have experienced social deprivation. Assuming a non-judgmental and individualized approach to understanding the extent and type of alienation experienced by the client is an essential first step in effective therapy. It is important to approach clients from a humanistic standpoint prior to directly trying to implement cognitive behavioral techniques. It is vital that the clinician and the client truly understand the suffering and shattered sense of self, family, and "lost years" experienced through parental alienation. Only then can the client be adequately understood and hence fully benefit from therapy. The basics of what constitute a healthy self-concept, psychological stability, and meaningful and productive interpersonal relationships may not be well understood by the client. Through a respectful and honest humanistic therapeutic stance, the clinician can slowly build up and repair the client's sense of self, which is essential for a happier and healthier life.

Notes

1 The male pronoun will be used for clarity of writing but all information pertains to both genders.
2 The word child/children will be used to denote all minors, including adolescents.
3 In this chapter the terms "favored" parent and "rejected" parent will be used rather than "alienating" and "targeted" in order to capture the experience from the perspective of the client.

References

Ainsworth, M. D. (1982). Attachment: Retrospect and prospect. In J. Stevenson-Hinde & C. M. Parks (Eds.). *The place of attachment in human behavior.* New York: Basic Books.

Baker, A. J. L. (2007). *Adult children of parental alienation syndrome: Breaking the ties that bind.* New York: W. W. Norton.

Baker, A. J. L., & BenAmi, N. (2001). To turn a child against a parent is to turn a child against himself. *Journal of Divorce and Remarriage, 54(2),* 203–219.

Baker, A. J. L., & Fine, P. (2008). *Beyond the high road: Responding to 17 parental alienation strategies without compromising your morals or harming your child.* Available at: www.amyjlbaker.com.

Buehler, C., Krishnakumer, A., Stone, G., Anthony, C., Pemberton, S., Gerard, J., & Barber, K. (1998). Interparental conflict styles and youth problem behaviors: A two-sample replication study. *Journal of Marriage and the Family, 60(1),* 119–132.

Cain, D. J. & Seeman, J. (2001). *Humanistic psychotherapies: Handbook of research and practice.* Washington, DC: American Psychological Association.

Chassin, L., Pitts, S. C., DeLucia, C., & Todd, M. (1999). A longitudinal study of children of alcoholics: Predicting young adult substance use disorders, anxiety, and depression. *Journal of Abnormal Psychology, 108(1),* 106–119.

Corsini, R. J., & Wedding, D. (2000). *Current psychotherapies.* Itasca, IL: F. E. Peacock.

Donaldson-Pressman, S., & Pressman, R. (1994). *The narcissistic family: Diagnosis and treatment.* New York: Lexington Books.

Gardner, R. A., (1998). *The parental alienation syndrome: A guide for mental health and legal professionals.* Cresskill, NJ: Creative Therapeutics.

Herman, J. (1992). *Trauma and recovery.* New York: Basic Books.

Joussemet, M., Landry, R., & Koestner, R. (2008). A self-determination theory perspective on parenting. *Canadian Psychology, 49(3),* 194–200.

Kernberg, O. (1975). *Borderline conditions and psychological narcissism.* Northvale, NJ: Jason Aronson Press.

Khantzian, E. J. (1985). The self-medication hypothesis of addictive disorders: Focus on heroin and cocaine dependence. *American Journal of Psychiatry, 142,* 1259–1264.

Kohut, H. (1971). *The analysis of the self.* New York: International University Press.

Rogers, C. (1951). *Client centered therapy.* Boston: Houghton Mifflin.

Ryan, P. L. (1993). Eastern meditation group. In M. Langone (Ed.), *Recovery from cults* (pp.129–47). New York: W. W. Norton.

Shulman, S., Scharf, M., Lumer, D., & Maurer, O. (2001). Parental divorce and young adult children's romantic relationships: Resolution of the divorce experience. *Journal of Orthopsychiatry, 71(4),* 473–478.

van der Kolk, B.A. (1994). The body keeps scores: Memory and the emerging psychobiology of post traumatic stress. *Harvard Review of Psychiatry, 1(5),* 253–265.

Wotitz, J. (1990). *Adult children of alcoholics.* Deerfield Beach, FL: Health Communications.

Index